Other titles available from Broccoli Books

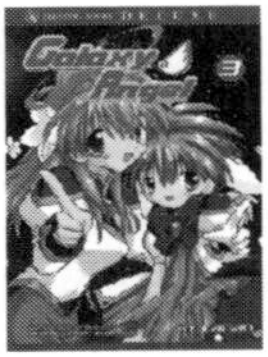

Galaxy Angel

The Angel Troupe has one mission; they must protect Prince Shiva, the sole survivor of the royal family decimated by a coup d'état. Milfeulle, Ranpha, Mint, Forte, and Vanilla each possess special gifts, making them ideal for the job at hand. Takuto finds himself leading the mission, getting caught between the five unique Angels and...space whales!?

Story & Art by Kanan
Suggested Retail Price: $9.99

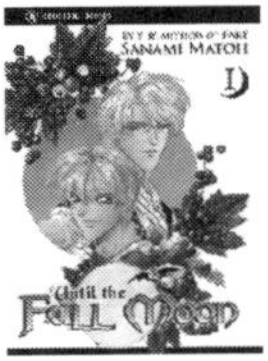
SANAMI MATOH
Until the
FULL MOON

Until the Full Moon

Marlo is half vampire, half werewolf with a problem. On nights when the full moon shines, Marlo undergoes a mysterious transformation... he turns into a girl.

Story & Art by Sanami Matoh
Suggested Retail Price: $9.99
Volume 2 coming in February 2004!

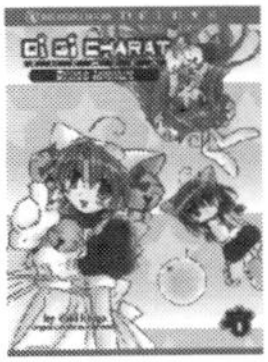

Di Gi Charat Theater – Dejiko's Adventure

Dejiko has destroyed the Gamers retail store! Now it's up to her and the rest of the gang as they search for the secret treasure that will save Gamers.

Story & Art by Yuki Kiriga
Suggested Retail Price: $9.99
Volumes 2-3 Coming Soon!

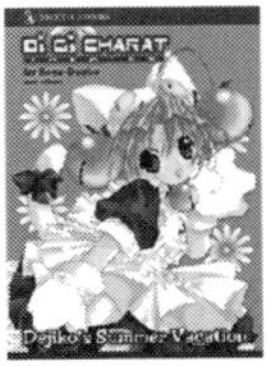
Dejiko's Summer Vacation

Di Gi Charat Theater – Dejiko's Summer Vacation & Piyoko is Number One!

Join Dejiko and the gang as they hit the beach, switch bodies, blow up the Black Gema Gema Gang, and discover the secret of Hokke Mirin and her cat corp! And watch out Dejiko! Piyoko and her gang attempt to steal the show with their very own book!

Story & Art by Koge-Donbo and others
Suggested Retail Price: $9.99 each

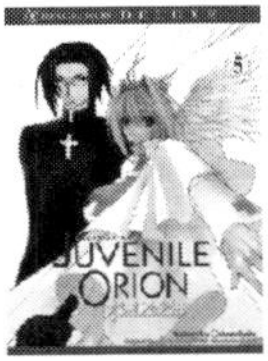
JUVENILE
ORION

Aquarian Age – Juvenile Orion

Sixteen-year-old Mana returns to her hometown and reunites with her childhood friend Kaname after 7 years. But he seems to have changed during their years apart. They soon discover that they are part of the Aquarian Age—a secret war raging for thousands of years—and Mana just might hold the key to end it!

Story & Art by Sakurako Gokurakuin
Suggested Retail Price: $9.99

For more information about Broccoli Books titles,
check out **bro-usa.com!**

by Hina.
Original Concept by BROCCOLI

brought to you by
BROCCOLI BOOKS
A DIVISION OF BROCCOLI INTERNATIONAL USA

Di Gi Charat Theater™ - Leave it to Piyoko Volume 1

English Adaptation Staff
Translation: Chinatsu Gallegos
English Adaptation: John Ghanotakis
Touch-Up & Lettering: Dennis Portugal
Cover & Graphic Supervision: Chris McDougall

Editor: Satsuki Yamashita
Associate Editor: Dietrich Seto
Sales Manager: Ardith D. Santiago
Managing Editor: Shizuki Yamashita
Publisher: Hideki Uchino

Email: editor@broccolibooks.com
Website: www.bro-usa.com

All illustrations by Hina.

A BROCCOLI BOOKS Manga
Broccoli Books is a division of Broccoli International USA, Inc.
12211 W. Washington Blvd, Suite 110, Los Angeles CA 90066

First published in 2002 by Media Works Inc.,Tokyo,Japan.
English translation rights arranged with Media Works Inc. through BROCCOLI Co., Ltd.

ISBN: 1-932480-17-X

Published by Broccoli International USA, Inc.
First printing, November 2004

ANIME GAMERS

BROCCOLI INTERNATIONAL USA
www.bro-usa.com

10 9 8 7 6 5 4 3 2 1
Printed in the United States

TABLE OF CONTENTS

Leave it to Piyoko!

OOooooooHH!

clap clap clap clap clap clap clap clap clap clap

THE STORY BEGINS PYO!

SYNOPSIS

The Black Gema Gema Gang are from Planet Analogue, and due to their poor resources they have been trying to conquer Planet Di Gi Charat for years. Finding out that the princess of Planet Di Gi Charat, Dejiko, went to Earth, they quickly follow suit to kidnap her and hold her for ransom to support their home planet. Piyoko is the leader of the Black Gema Gema Gang, and Rik, Ky, and Coo work under her loyally and lovingly. However, Piyoko's plans always seem to backfire, and the goal of a prosperous planet is far away…

ABOUT DI GI CHARAT

Dejiko was created in 1998 as the official mascot character for the popular anime/game store Gamers in Japan. When Gamers decided to create a commercial featuring Dejiko and her friends, a television network producer saw it and suggested that they make an anime. And thus, the TV anime series *Di Gi Charat* was born. Di Gi Charat was already featured on CDs and other merchandise, but it is the television series where she gained popularity nationwide, and eventually worldwide.

CHARACTERS

Pyocola Analogue III (Piyoko)

Piyoko is the head of the evil organization known as the Black Gema Gema Gang. She came after Dejiko to kidnap and hold her ransom to raise money for Planet Analogue. But her gullible personality allows Dejiko to trick her one way or the other, and she never succeeds in capturing Dejiko. Her dialect back at home makes her end her sentences with a "pyo."

Coo Erhard

Coo is the Major of the Black Gema Gema Gang. He is part of the Pyocola Keeping Operations, also known as PKO. He knows Piyoko from childhood, and thinks of her like a little sister. Thus, he is closest to Piyoko among the PKO. He treasures a stuffed panda. He is Piyoko's personal doctor.

Ky Schweitzer

Ky is the Lieutenant General of the Black Gema Gema Gang, and also part of PKO. He has a strong sense of responsibility. He is Piyoko's personal dentist, and is in charge of checking Piyoko's dental hygiene everyday.

Rik Heisenberg

Rik is the General of the Black Gema Gema Gang, and also part of PKO. He is calm and blunt; he easily comes up with cruel things to say. He is a veterinarian, and thus loves animals of all kinds.

CHARACTERS

Nazo Gema
Mysterious flying object that doesn't talk, but its actions speak volumes.

Black Gema Gema Gang Members
It's hard to tell them apart. They say "geba" at the end of their sentences.

Di Gi Charat (Dejiko)
Dejiko is the princess of Planet Di Gi Charat, and comes to Earth to study and become a star. Contrary to her cute appearance, she is self-centered and evil, and often plots against Rabi~en~Rose and Piyoko. Her dialect back at home makes her sentences end with a "nyo."

Rabi~en~Rose (Usada)
Rabi~en~Rose is a human being, and has been working for Gamers before Dejiko joined. She often competes with Dejiko for the number one clerk position. Her real name is Hikaru Usada, but hates it when people refer to her as Usada.

Petit Charat (Puchiko)
Puchiko has been with Dejiko ever since Dejiko saved her when she was stuck down a hole. Although she is quiet for most of the time, when she speaks she is really sharp-tongued. She ends her sentences with a "nyu."

Gema
Gema is Dejiko's unidentified flying caretaker. His duty is to stop Dejiko's reckless behavior, but for a lack of any special moves, he gets beaten up in return. He has a habit of adding "gema" to the end of his sentences.

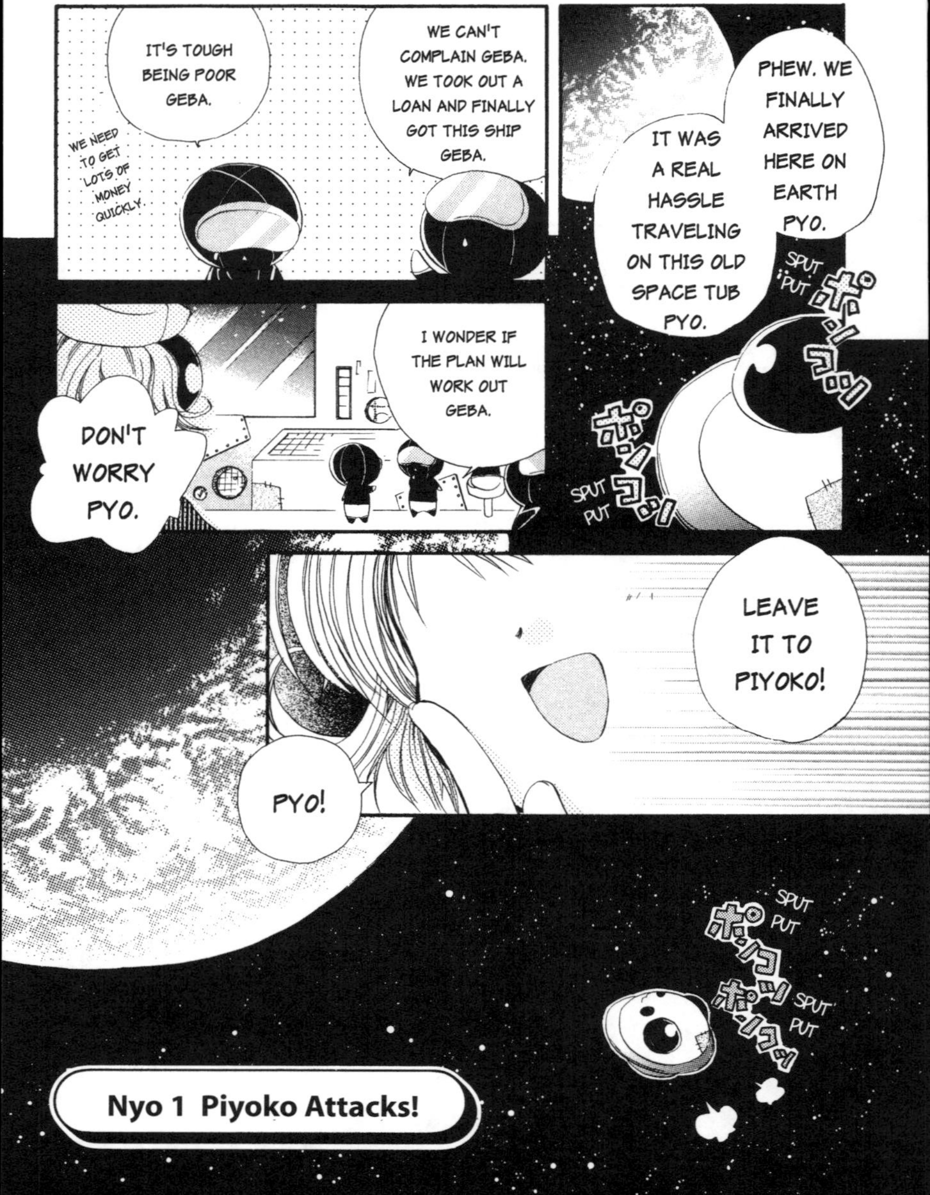
PHEW. WE FINALLY ARRIVED HERE ON EARTH PYO.
IT WAS A REAL HASSLE TRAVELING ON THIS OLD SPACE TUB PYO.
SPUT PUT
SPUT PUT
WE CAN'T COMPLAIN GEBA. WE TOOK OUT A LOAN AND FINALLY GOT THIS SHIP GEBA.
IT'S TOUGH BEING POOR GEBA.
WE NEED TO GET LOTS OF MONEY QUICKLY.
I WONDER IF THE PLAN WILL WORK OUT GEBA.
DON'T WORRY PYO.
LEAVE IT TO PIYOKO!
PYO!
SPUT PUT
SPUT PUT

Nyo 1 Piyoko Attacks!

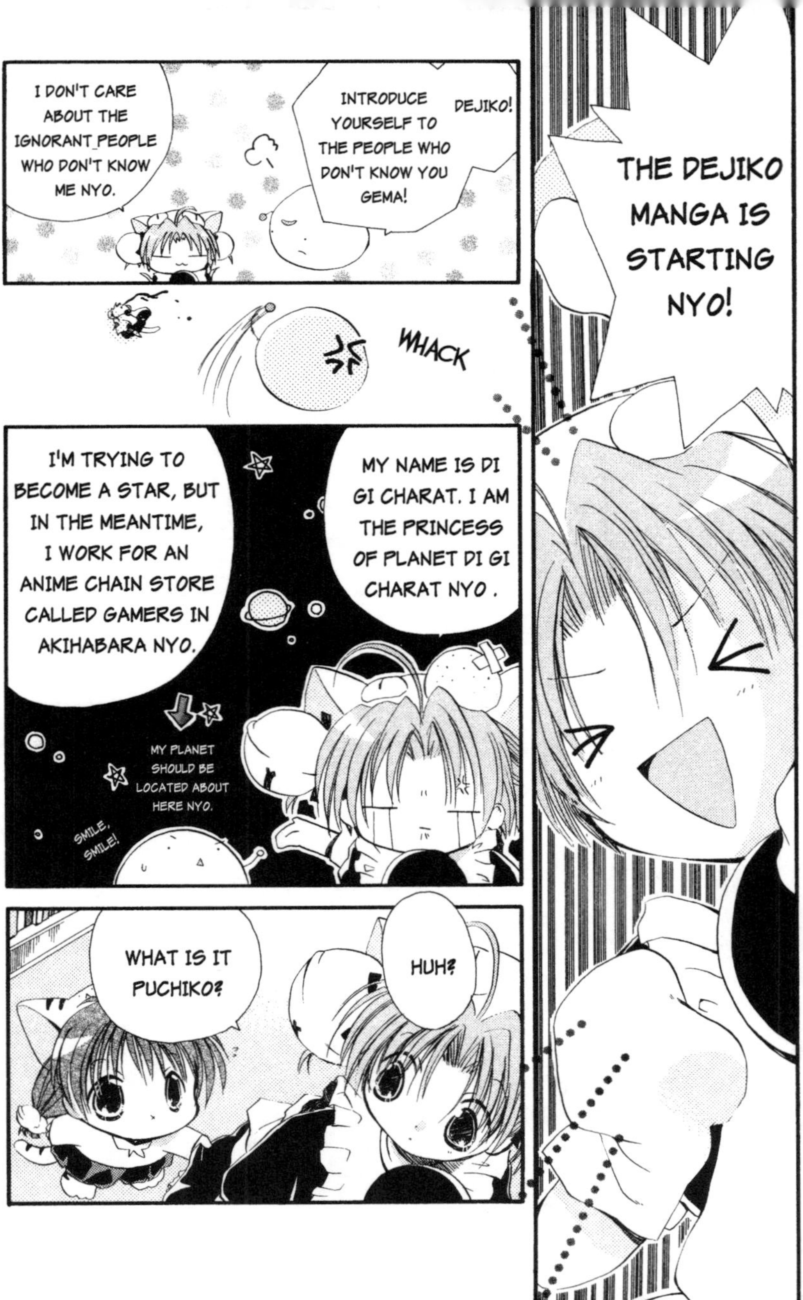
THE DEJIKO MANGA IS STARTING NYO!
DEJIKO!
INTRODUCE YOURSELF TO THE PEOPLE WHO DON'T KNOW YOU GEMA!
I DON'T CARE ABOUT THE IGNORANT PEOPLE WHO DON'T KNOW ME NYO.
WHACK
MY NAME IS DI GI CHARAT. I AM THE PRINCESS OF PLANET DI GI CHARAT NYO .
I'M TRYING TO BECOME A STAR, BUT IN THE MEANTIME, I WORK FOR AN ANIME CHAIN STORE CALLED GAMERS IN AKIHABARA NYO.
MY PLANET SHOULD BE LOCATED ABOUT HERE NYO.
SMILE, SMILE!
HUH?
WHAT IS IT PUCHIKO?

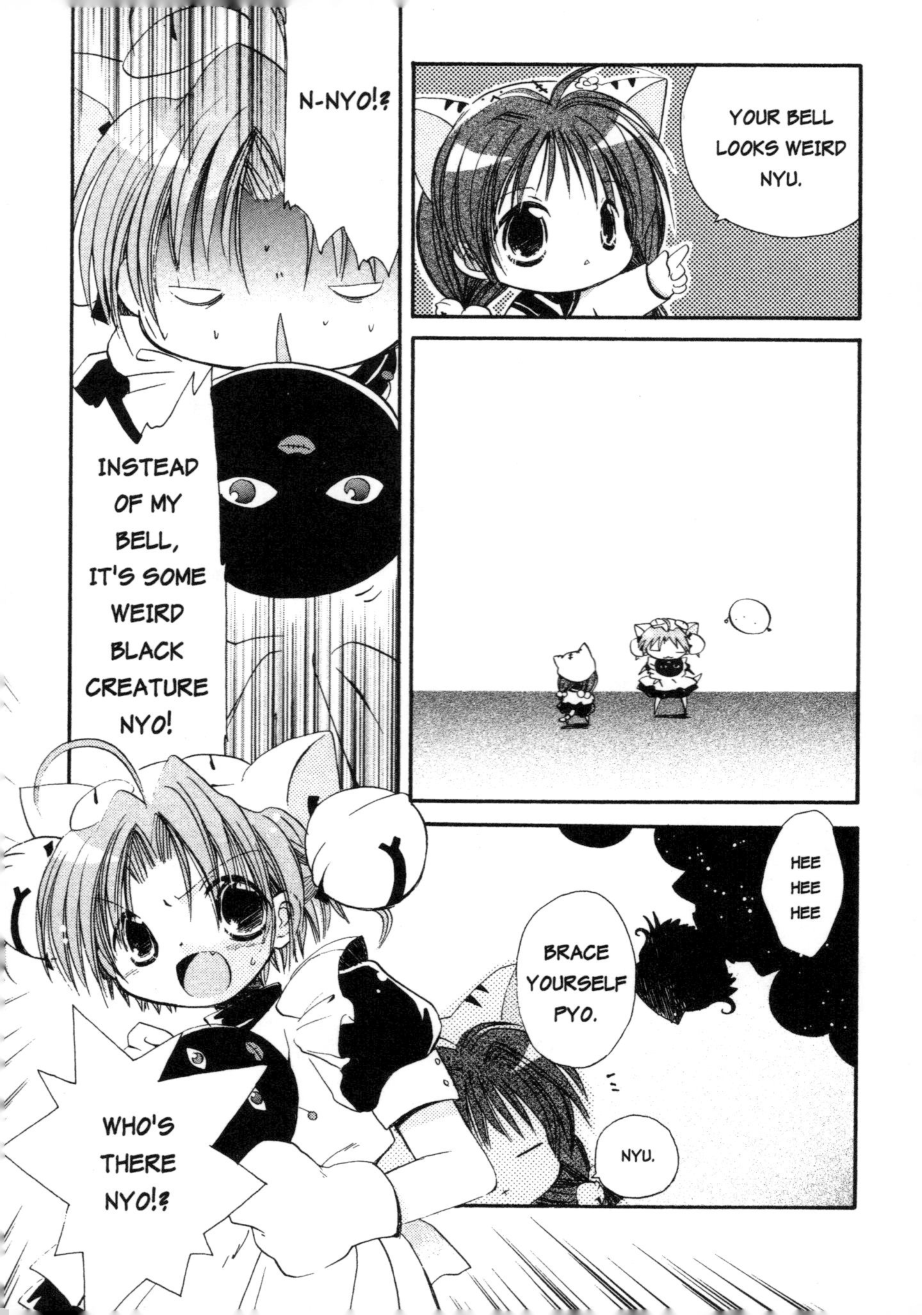
YOUR BELL LOOKS WEIRD NYU.
N-NYO!?
INSTEAD OF MY BELL, IT'S SOME WEIRD BLACK CREATURE NYO!
HEE HEE HEE
BRACE YOURSELF PYO.
NYU.
WHO'S THERE NYO!?

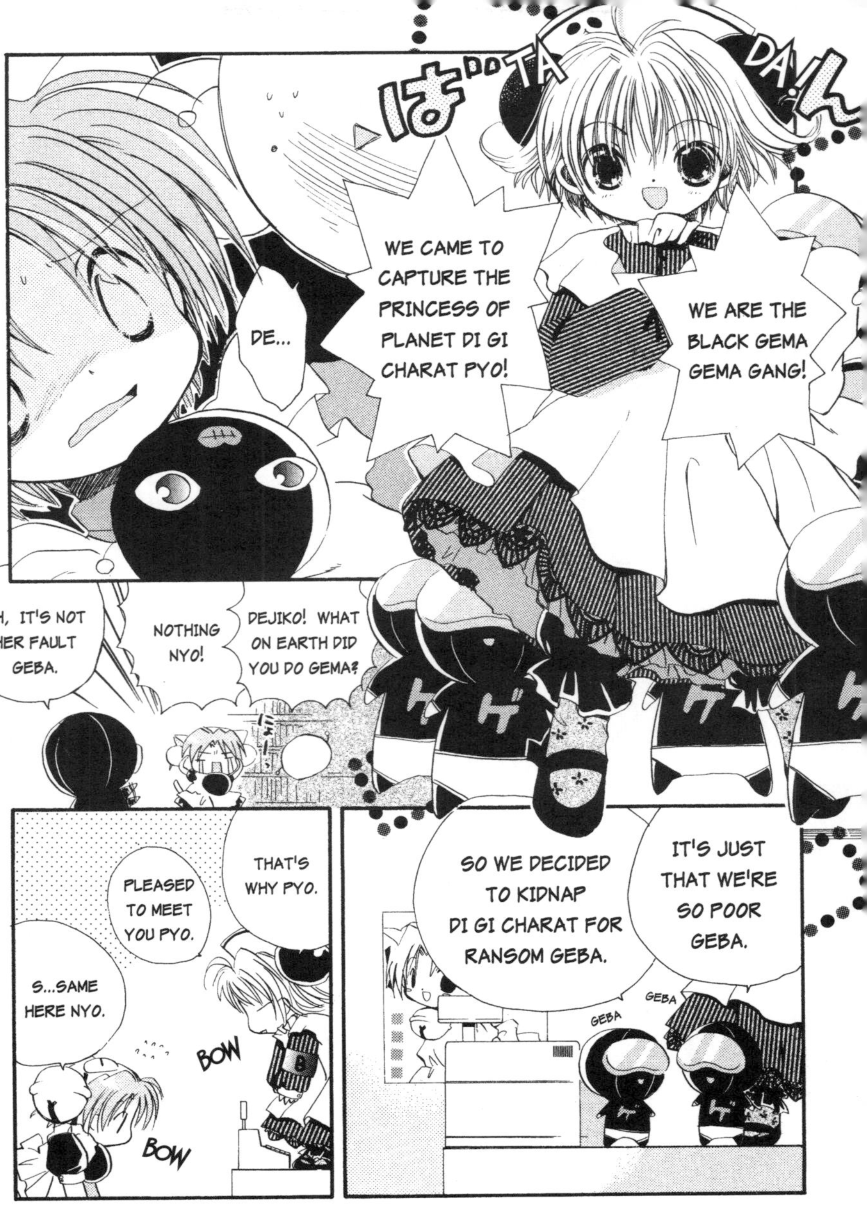
TA DA!
WE ARE THE BLACK GEMA GEMA GANG!
WE CAME TO CAPTURE THE PRINCESS OF PLANET DI GI CHARAT PYO!
DE...
DEJIKO! WHAT ON EARTH DID YOU DO GEMA?
NOTHING NYO!
OH, IT'S NOT HER FAULT GEBA.
IT'S JUST THAT WE'RE SO POOR GEBA.
SO WE DECIDED TO KIDNAP DI GI CHARAT FOR RANSOM GEBA.
GEBA
GEBA
THAT'S WHY PYO.
PLEASED TO MEET YOU PYO.
S...SAME HERE NYO.
BOW
BOW

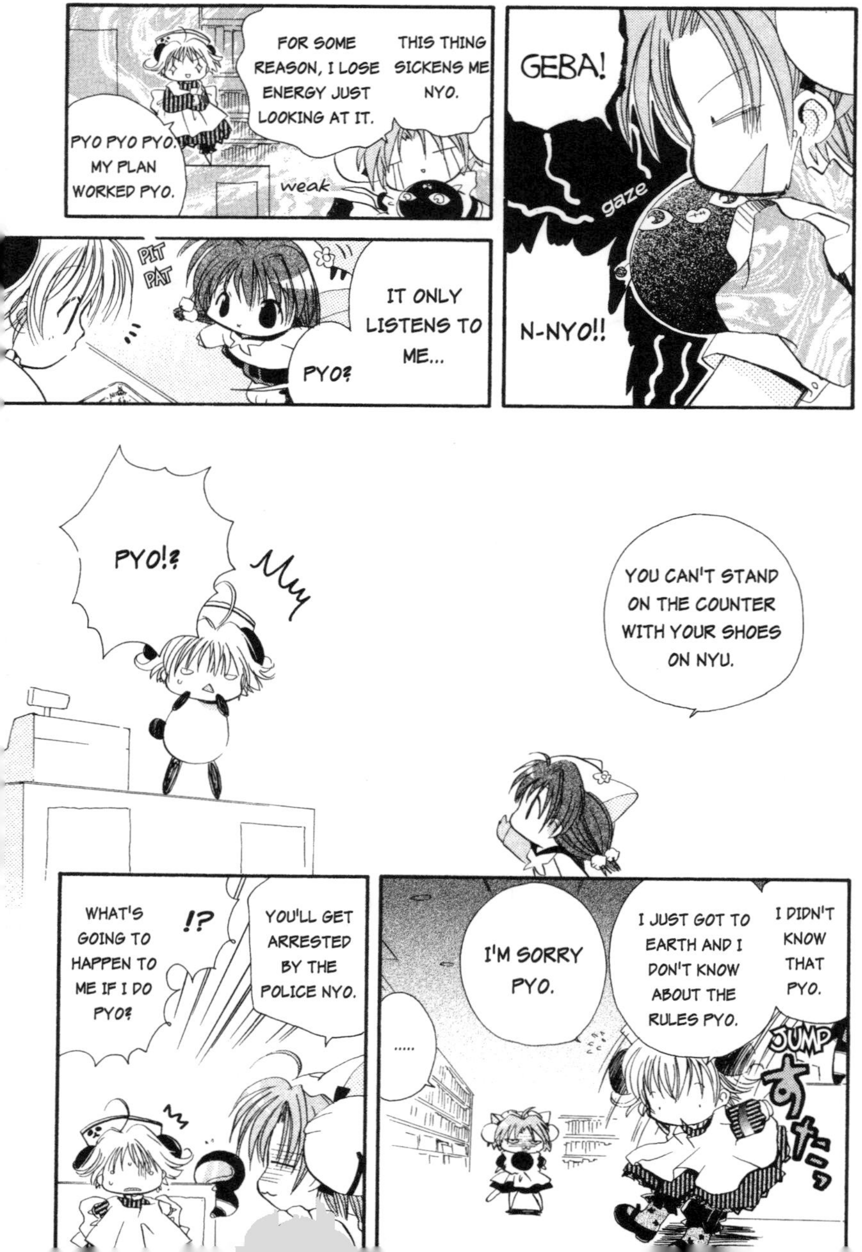
GEBA!
gaze
N-NYO!!
THIS THING SICKENS ME NYO.
FOR SOME REASON, I LOSE ENERGY JUST LOOKING AT IT.
weak
PYO PYO PYO. MY PLAN WORKED PYO.
IT ONLY LISTENS TO ME...
PYO?
PIT PAT
YOU CAN'T STAND ON THE COUNTER WITH YOUR SHOES ON NYU.
PYO!?
I DIDN'T KNOW THAT PYO.
JUMP
I JUST GOT TO EARTH AND I DON'T KNOW ABOUT THE RULES PYO.
I'M SORRY PYO.
.....
YOU'LL GET ARRESTED BY THE POLICE NYO.
!?
WHAT'S GOING TO HAPPEN TO ME IF I DO PYO?

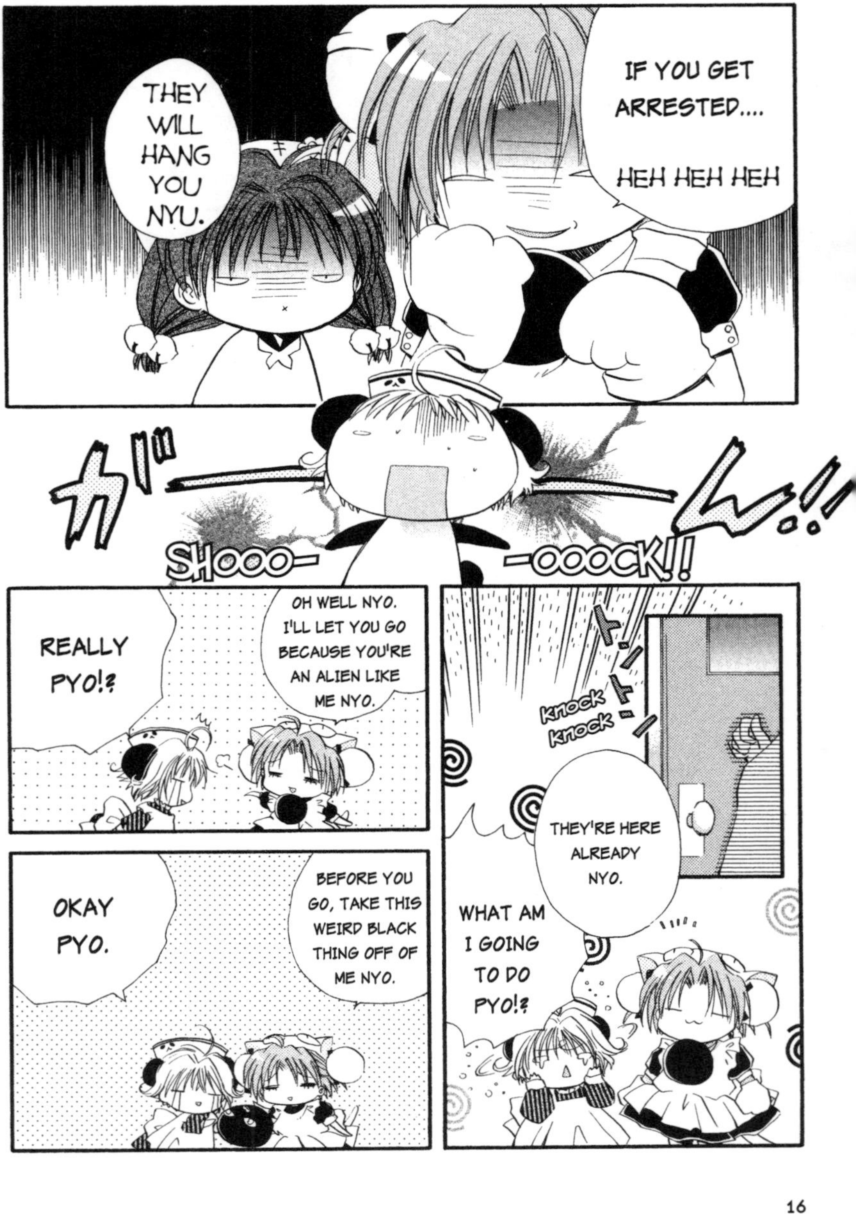

IF YOU GET ARRESTED.... HEH HEH HEH
THEY WILL HANG YOU NYU.
ガーーーん!!
SHOOO- -OOOCK!!
knock knock
THEY'RE HERE ALREADY NYO.
WHAT AM I GOING TO DO PYO!?
OH WELL NYO. I'LL LET YOU GO BECAUSE YOU'RE AN ALIEN LIKE ME NYO.
REALLY PYO!?
BEFORE YOU GO, TAKE THIS WEIRD BLACK THING OFF OF ME NYO.
OKAY PYO.

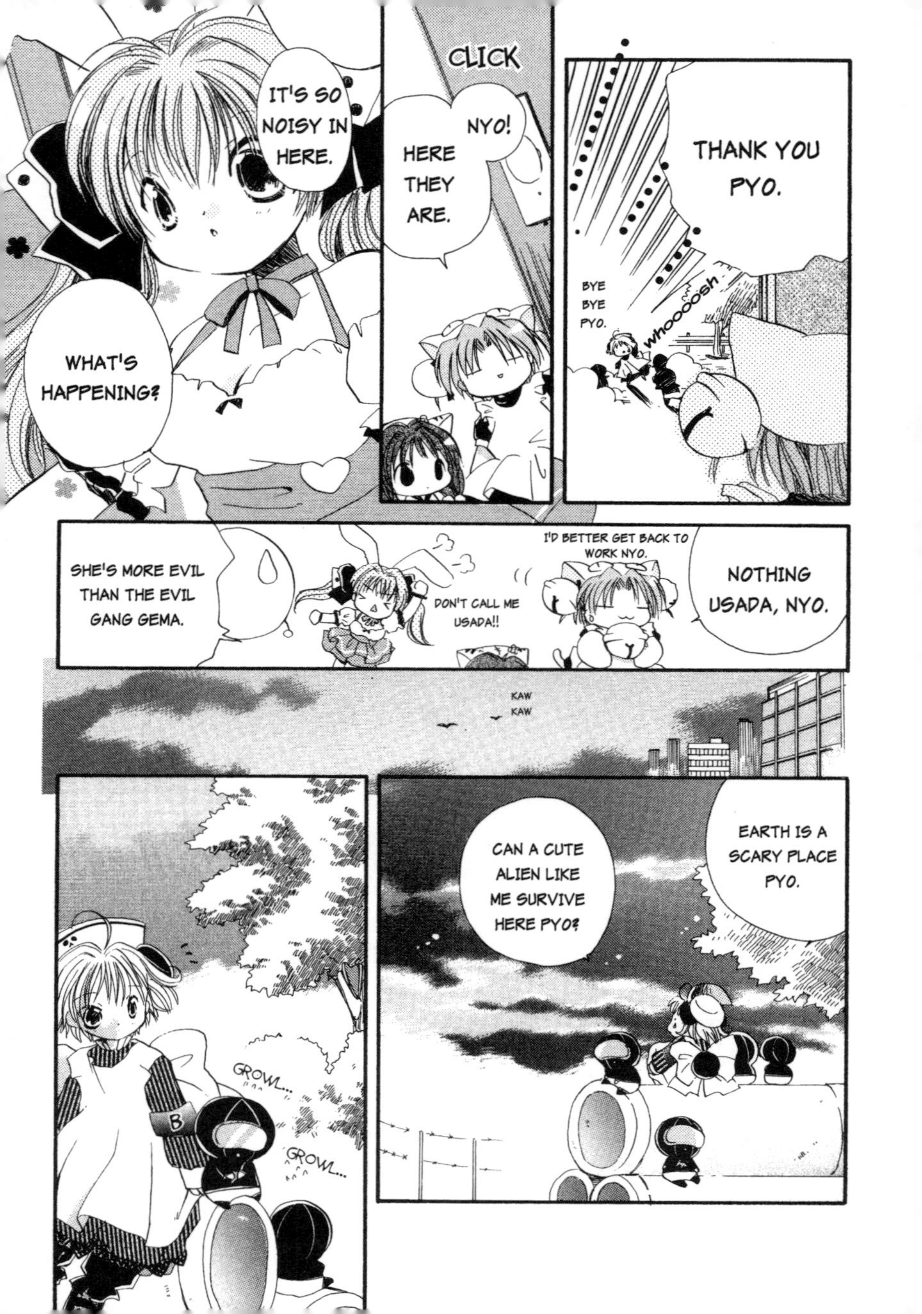
THANK YOU PYO.
BYE BYE PYO.
whoooosh
CLICK
NYO! HERE THEY ARE.
IT'S SO NOISY IN HERE.
WHAT'S HAPPENING?
NOTHING USADA, NYO.
I'D BETTER GET BACK TO WORK NYO.
DON'T CALL ME USADA!!
SHE'S MORE EVIL THAN THE EVIL GANG GEMA.
KAW KAW
EARTH IS A SCARY PLACE PYO.
CAN A CUTE ALIEN LIKE ME SURVIVE HERE PYO?
GROWL...
GROWL...

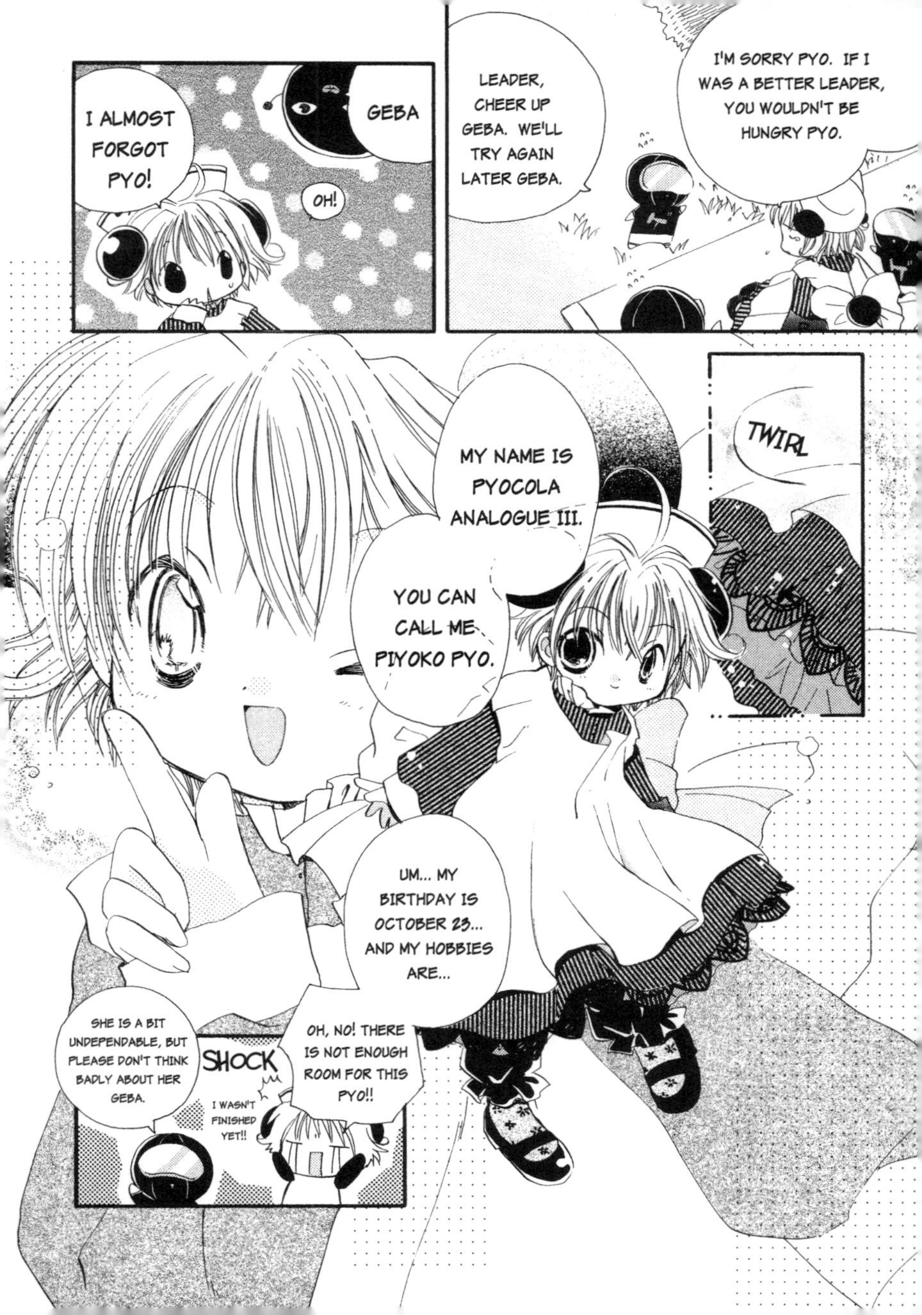
I'M SORRY PYO. IF I WAS A BETTER LEADER, YOU WOULDN'T BE HUNGRY PYO.
LEADER, CHEER UP GEBA. WE'LL TRY AGAIN LATER GEBA.
GEBA
I ALMOST FORGOT PYO!
OH!
TWIRL
MY NAME IS PYOCOLA ANALOGUE III.
YOU CAN CALL ME PIYOKO PYO.
UM... MY BIRTHDAY IS OCTOBER 23... AND MY HOBBIES ARE...
OH, NO! THERE IS NOT ENOUGH ROOM FOR THIS PYO!!
SHOCK
I WASN'T FINISHED YET!!
SHE IS A BIT UNDEPENDABLE, BUT PLEASE DON'T THINK BADLY ABOUT HER GEBA.

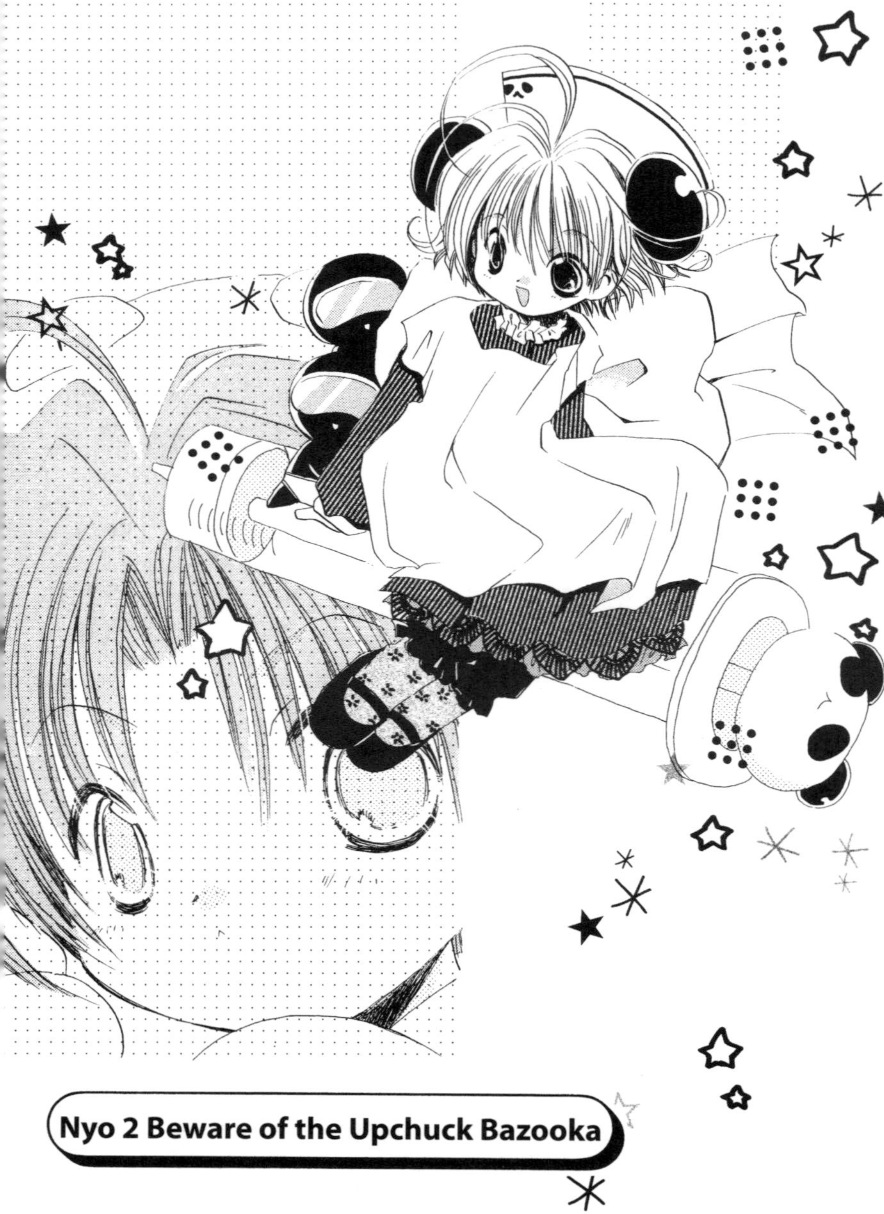

Nyo 2 Beware of the Upchuck Bazooka

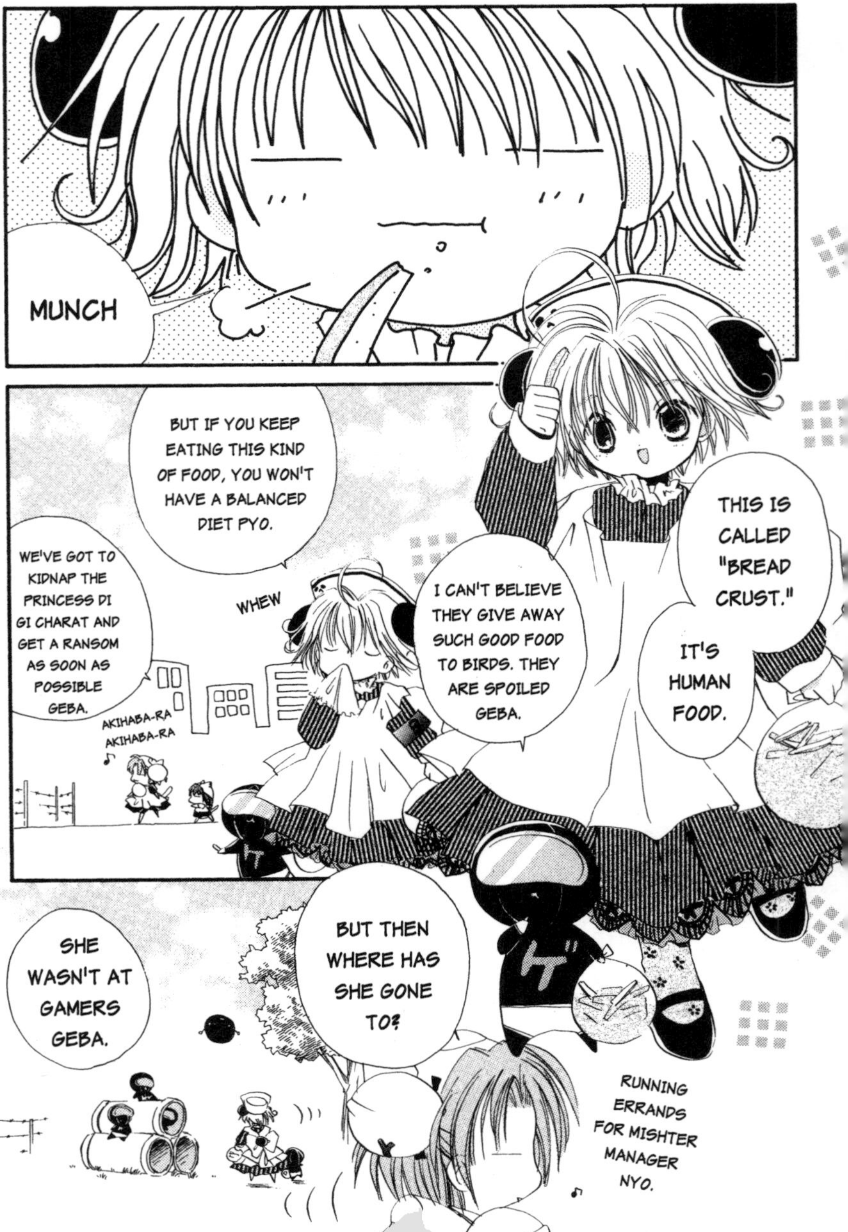
MUNCH
THIS IS CALLED "BREAD CRUST."
IT'S HUMAN FOOD.
I CAN'T BELIEVE THEY GIVE AWAY SUCH GOOD FOOD TO BIRDS. THEY ARE SPOILED GEBA.
WHEW
BUT IF YOU KEEP EATING THIS KIND OF FOOD, YOU WON'T HAVE A BALANCED DIET PYO.
WE'VE GOT TO KIDNAP THE PRINCESS DI GI CHARAT AND GET A RANSOM AS SOON AS POSSIBLE GEBA.
AKIHABA-RA AKIHABA-RA
BUT THEN WHERE HAS SHE GONE TO?
SHE WASN'T AT GAMERS GEBA.
RUNNING ERRANDS FOR MISHTER MANAGER NYO.

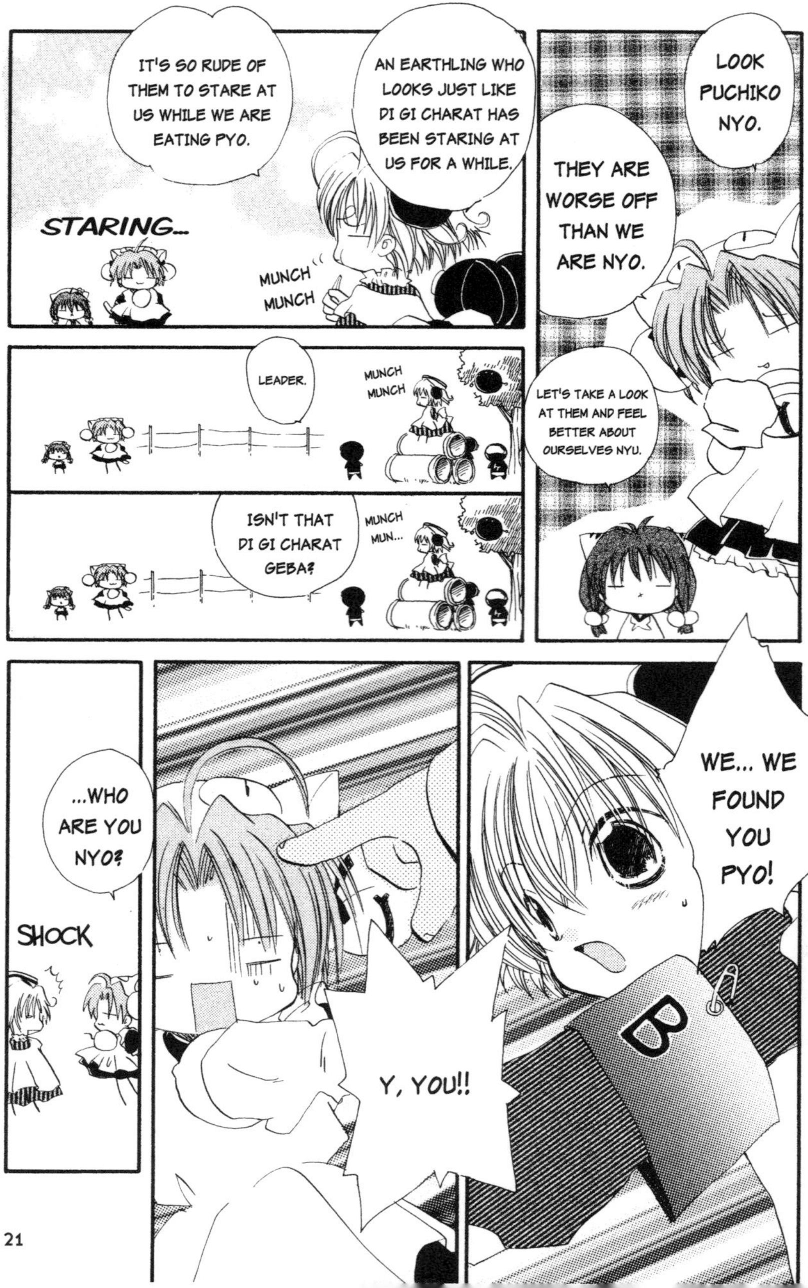
LOOK PUCHIKO NYO.
THEY ARE WORSE OFF THAN WE ARE NYO.
LET'S TAKE A LOOK AT THEM AND FEEL BETTER ABOUT OURSELVES NYU.
AN EARTHLING WHO LOOKS JUST LIKE DI GI CHARAT HAS BEEN STARING AT US FOR A WHILE.
IT'S SO RUDE OF THEM TO STARE AT US WHILE WE ARE EATING PYO.
MUNCH MUNCH
STARING...
MUNCH MUNCH
LEADER.
MUNCH MUN...
ISN'T THAT DI GI CHARAT GEBA?
WE... WE FOUND YOU PYO!
Y, YOU!!
...WHO ARE YOU NYO?
SHOCK

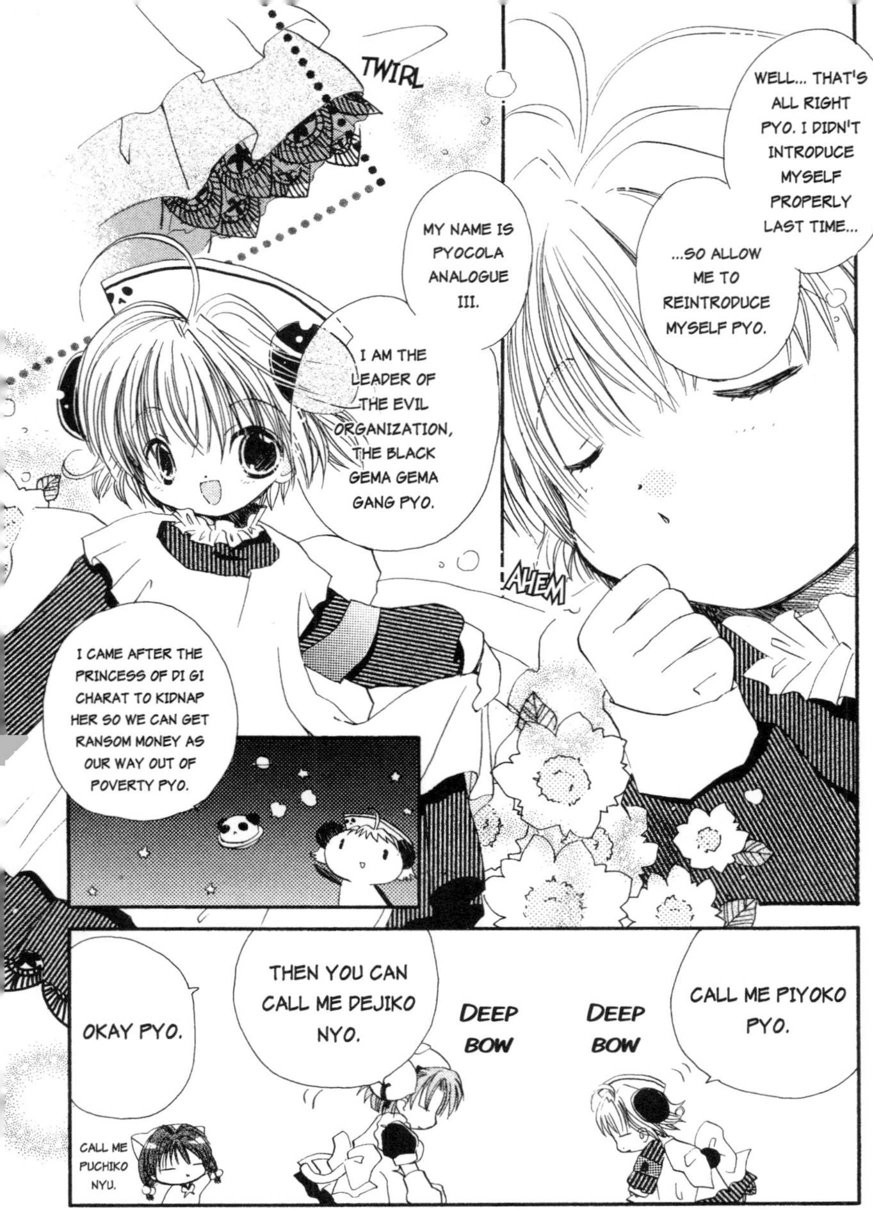
WELL... THAT'S ALL RIGHT PYO. I DIDN'T INTRODUCE MYSELF PROPERLY LAST TIME...
...SO ALLOW ME TO REINTRODUCE MYSELF PYO.
AHEM
TWIRL
MY NAME IS PYOCOLA ANALOGUE III.
I AM THE LEADER OF THE EVIL ORGANIZATION, THE BLACK GEMA GEMA GANG PYO.
I CAME AFTER THE PRINCESS OF DI GI CHARAT TO KIDNAP HER SO WE CAN GET RANSOM MONEY AS OUR WAY OUT OF POVERTY PYO.
CALL ME PIYOKO PYO.
DEEP BOW
DEEP BOW
THEN YOU CAN CALL ME DEJIKO NYO.
OKAY PYO.
CALL ME PUCHIKO NYU.

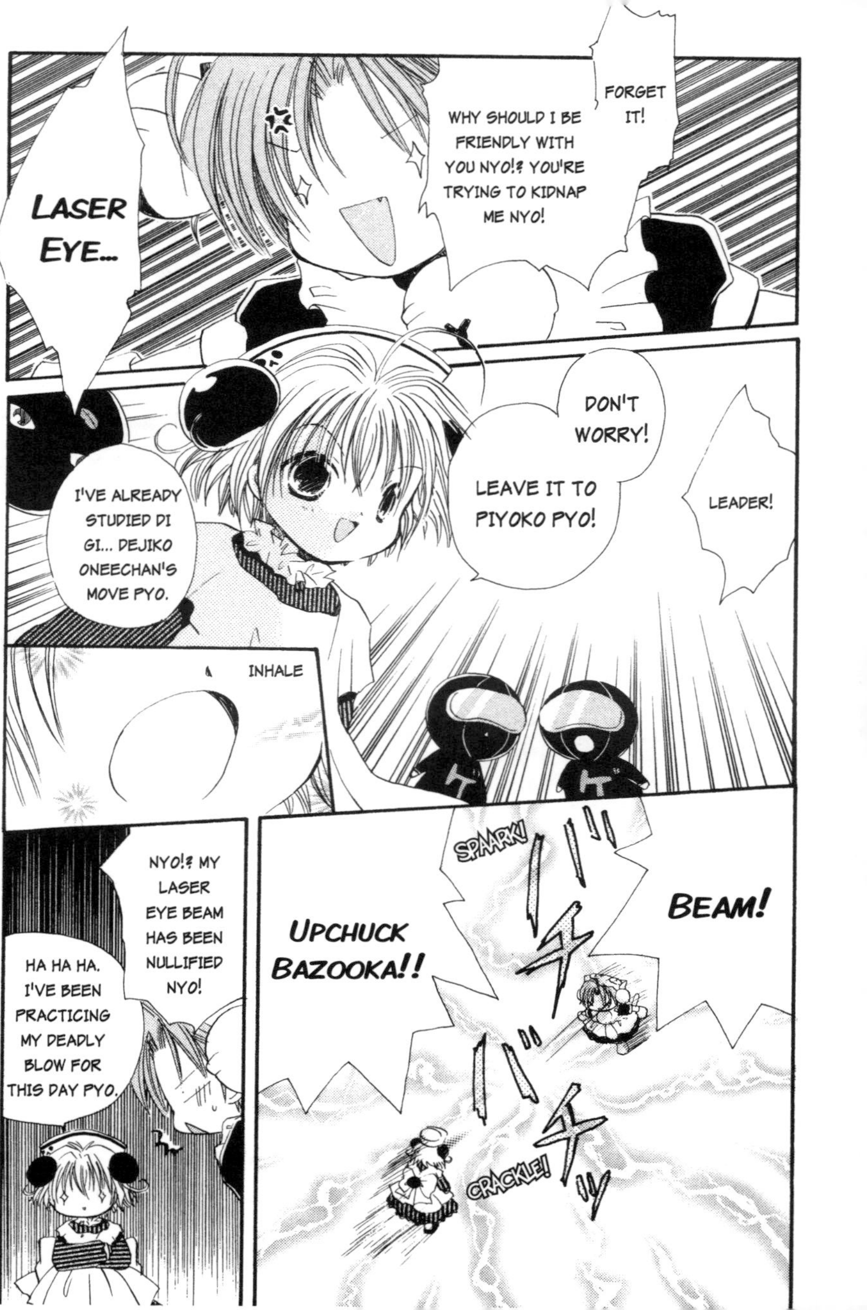
FORGET IT!
WHY SHOULD I BE FRIENDLY WITH YOU NYO!? YOU'RE TRYING TO KIDNAP ME NYO!
LASER EYE...
LEADER!
DON'T WORRY!
LEAVE IT TO PIYOKO PYO!
I'VE ALREADY STUDIED DI GI... DEJIKO ONEECHAN'S MOVE PYO.
INHALE
SPAARK!
BEAM!
UPCHUCK BAZOOKA!!
CRACKLE!
NYO!? MY LASER EYE BEAM HAS BEEN NULLIFIED NYO!
HA HA HA. I'VE BEEN PRACTICING MY DEADLY BLOW FOR THIS DAY PYO.

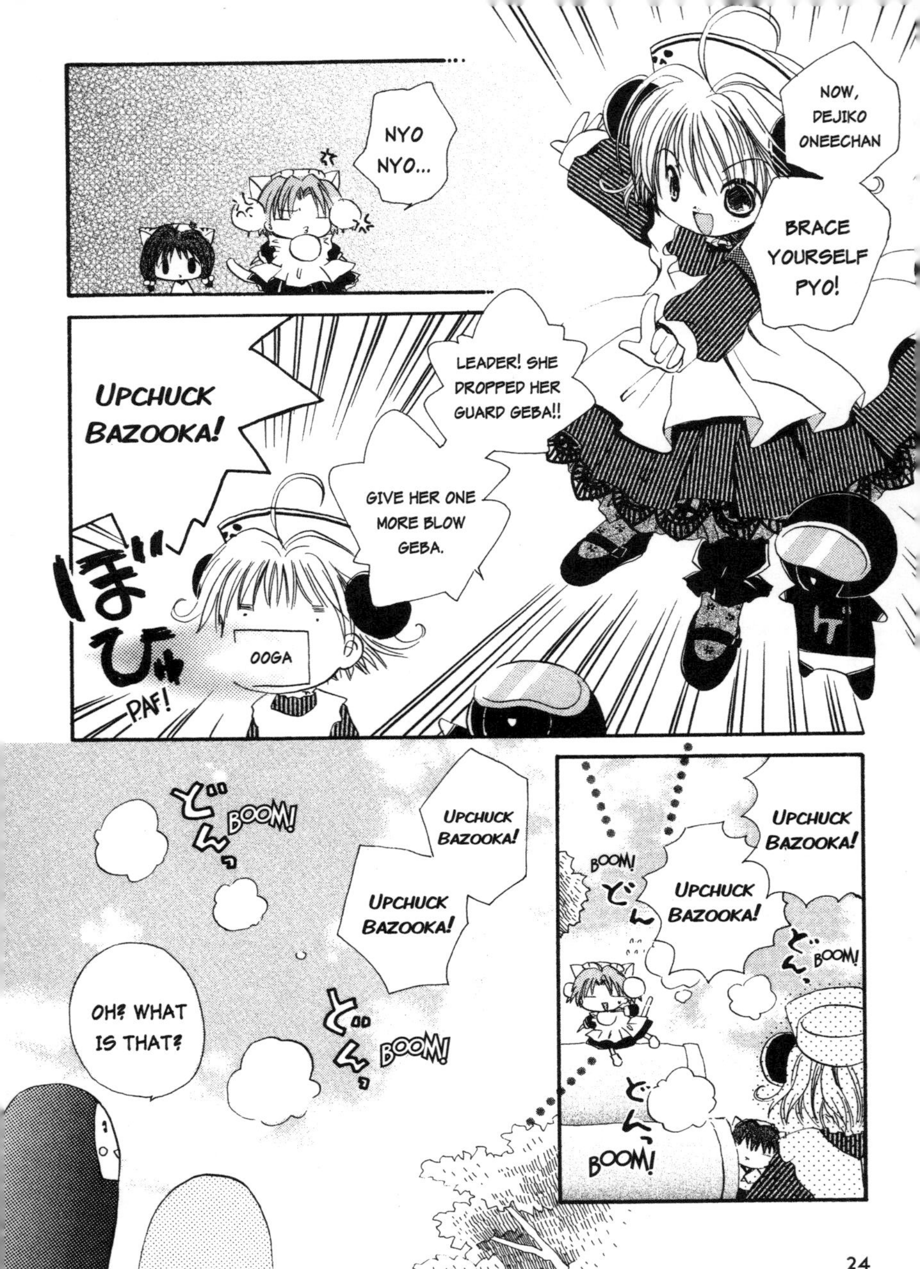
NOW, DEJIKO ONEECHAN
BRACE YOURSELF PYO!
NYO NYO...
LEADER! SHE DROPPED HER GUARD GEBA!!
GIVE HER ONE MORE BLOW GEBA.
UPCHUCK BAZOOKA!
ぼひゅ
PAF!
OOGA
UPCHUCK BAZOOKA!
UPCHUCK BAZOOKA!
BOOM!
どん
どん
BOOM!
どん
BOOM!
UPCHUCK BAZOOKA!
UPCHUCK BAZOOKA!
どん
BOOM!
どん
BOOM!
OH? WHAT IS THAT?

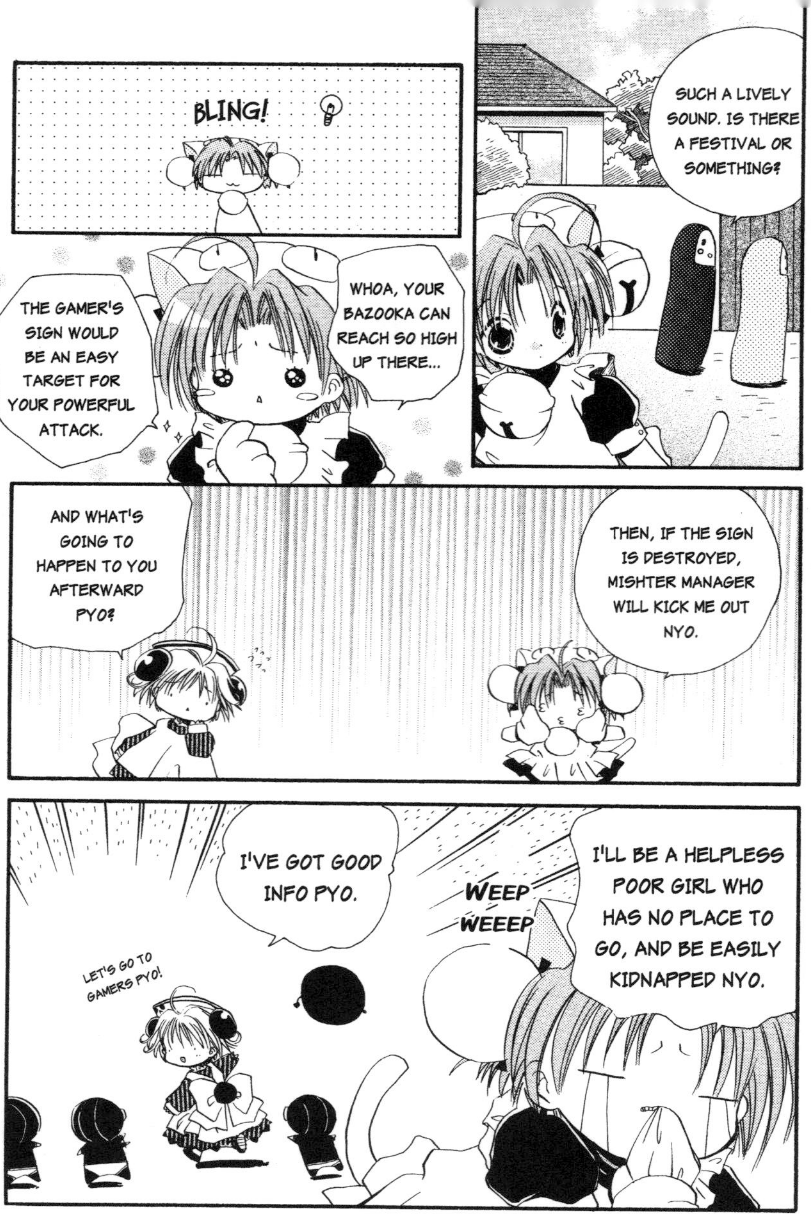
SUCH A LIVELY SOUND. IS THERE A FESTIVAL OR SOMETHING?
BLING!
WHOA, YOUR BAZOOKA CAN REACH SO HIGH UP THERE...
THE GAMER'S SIGN WOULD BE AN EASY TARGET FOR YOUR POWERFUL ATTACK.
THEN, IF THE SIGN IS DESTROYED, MISHTER MANAGER WILL KICK ME OUT NYO.
AND WHAT'S GOING TO HAPPEN TO YOU AFTERWARD PYO?
I'LL BE A HELPLESS POOR GIRL WHO HAS NO PLACE TO GO, AND BE EASILY KIDNAPPED NYO.
WEEP WEEEP
I'VE GOT GOOD INFO PYO.
LET'S GO TO GAMERS PYO!

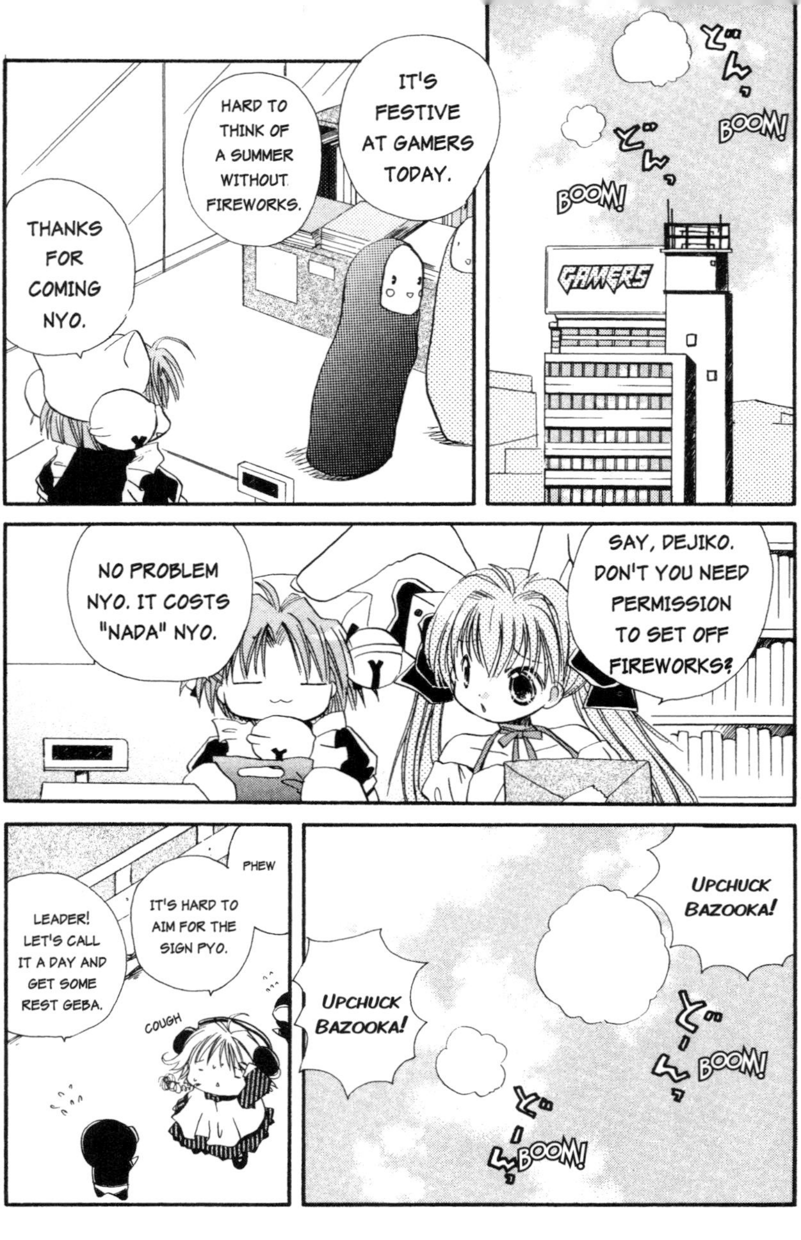
BOOM!
BOOM!
GAMERS
IT'S FESTIVE AT GAMERS TODAY.
HARD TO THINK OF A SUMMER WITHOUT FIREWORKS.
THANKS FOR COMING NYO.
SAY, DEJIKO. DON'T YOU NEED PERMISSION TO SET OFF FIREWORKS?
NO PROBLEM NYO. IT COSTS "NADA" NYO.
Upchuck Bazooka!
Upchuck Bazooka!
BOOM!
BOOM!
PHEW
IT'S HARD TO AIM FOR THE SIGN PYO.
LEADER! LET'S CALL IT A DAY AND GET SOME REST GEBA.
COUGH

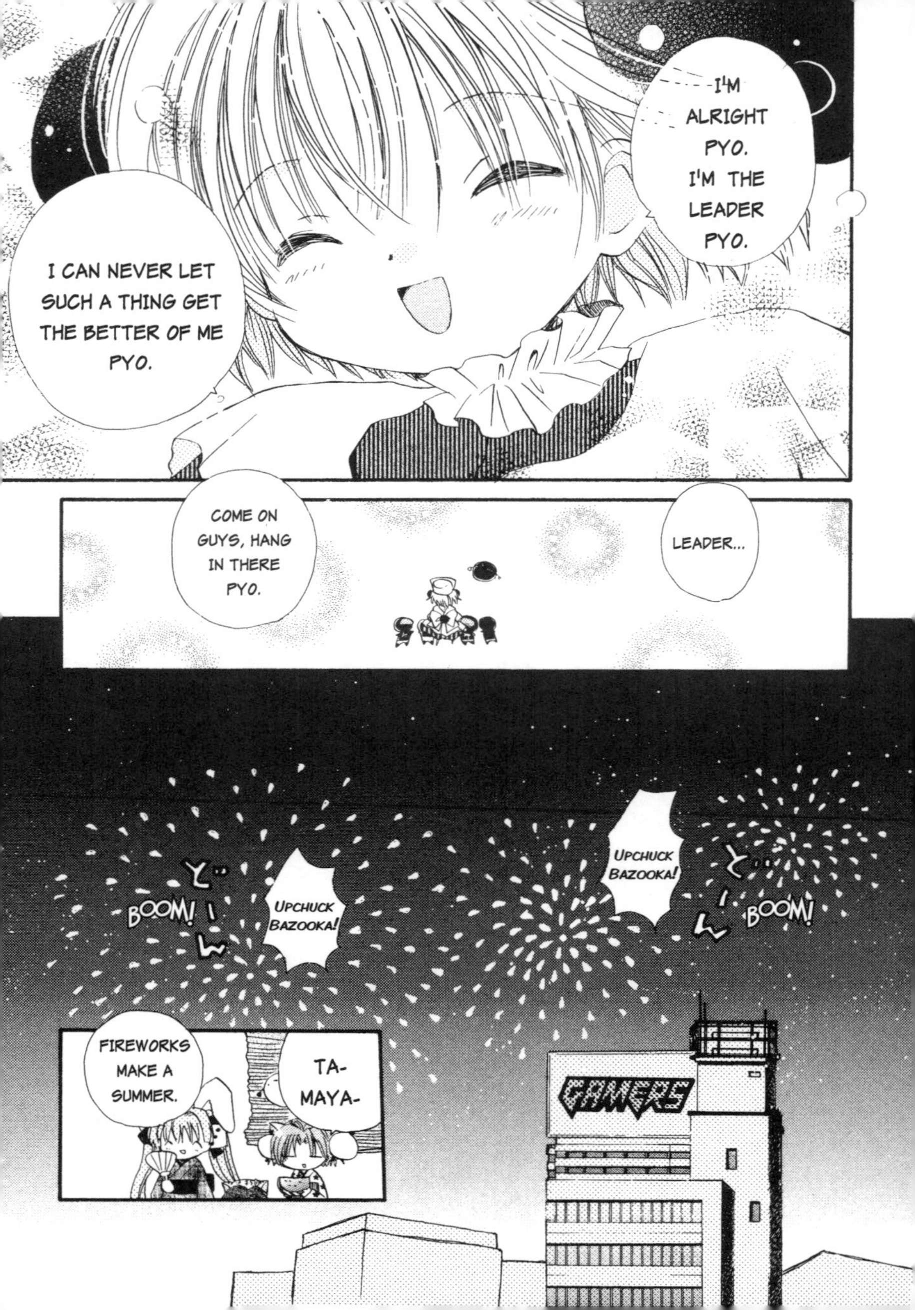
I'M ALRIGHT PYO. I'M THE LEADER PYO.
I CAN NEVER LET SUCH A THING GET THE BETTER OF ME PYO.
LEADER...
COME ON GUYS, HANG IN THERE PYO.
Upchuck Bazooka!
BOOM!
Upchuck Bazooka!
BOOM!
GAMERS
TA-MAYA-
FIREWORKS MAKE A SUMMER.

A Day in the Life of the Black Gema Gema Gang
8:00 AM Piyoko wakes up

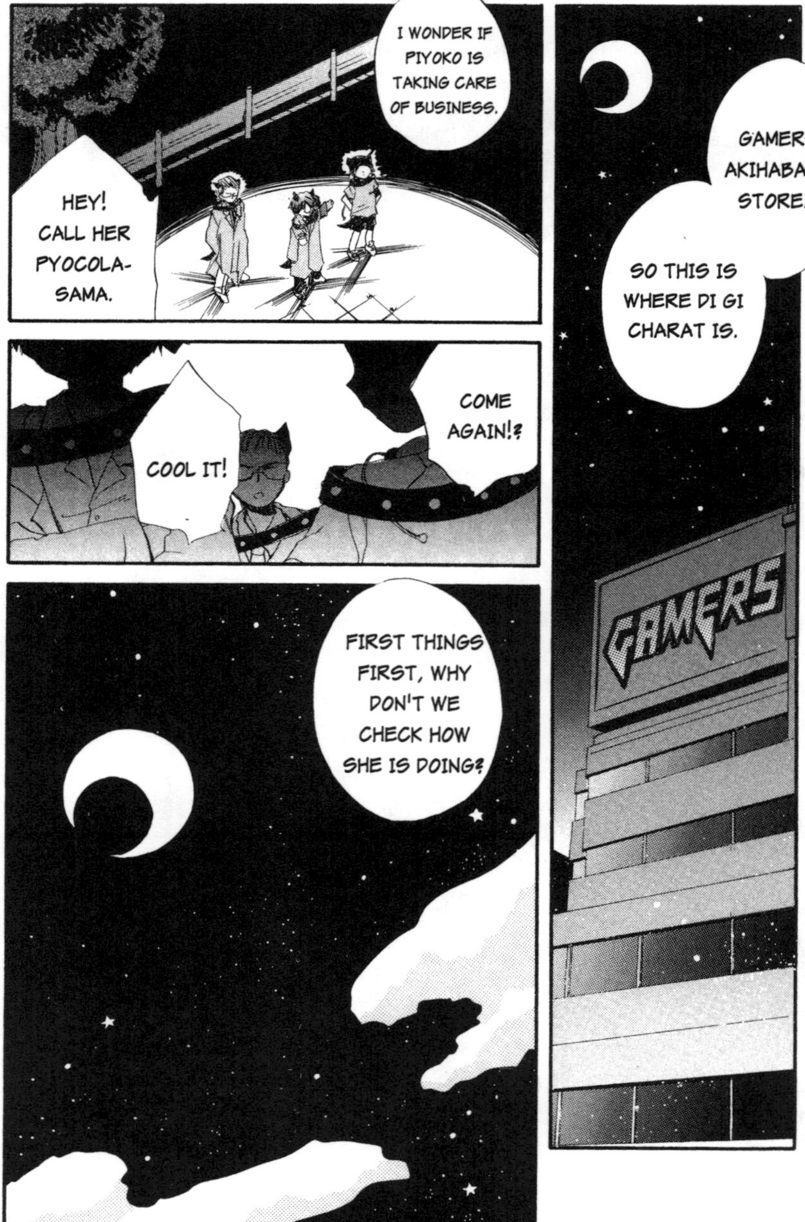
GAMERS AKIHABARA STORE...
SO THIS IS WHERE DI GI CHARAT IS.
GAMERS
I WONDER IF PIYOKO IS TAKING CARE OF BUSINESS.
HEY! CALL HER PYOCOLA-SAMA.
COME AGAIN!?
COOL IT!
FIRST THINGS FIRST, WHY DON'T WE CHECK HOW SHE IS DOING?

Nyo 3 Mysterious Reservoir Dogs!? Part

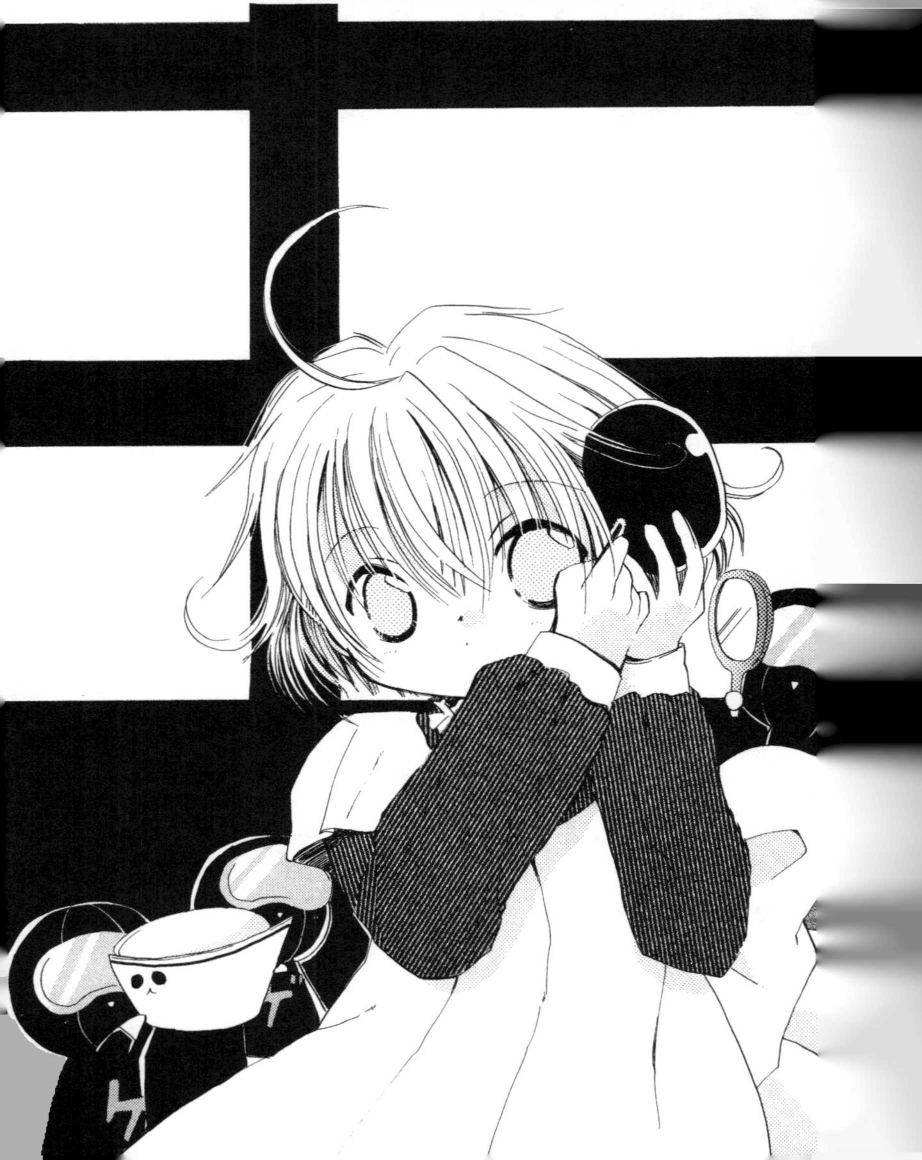

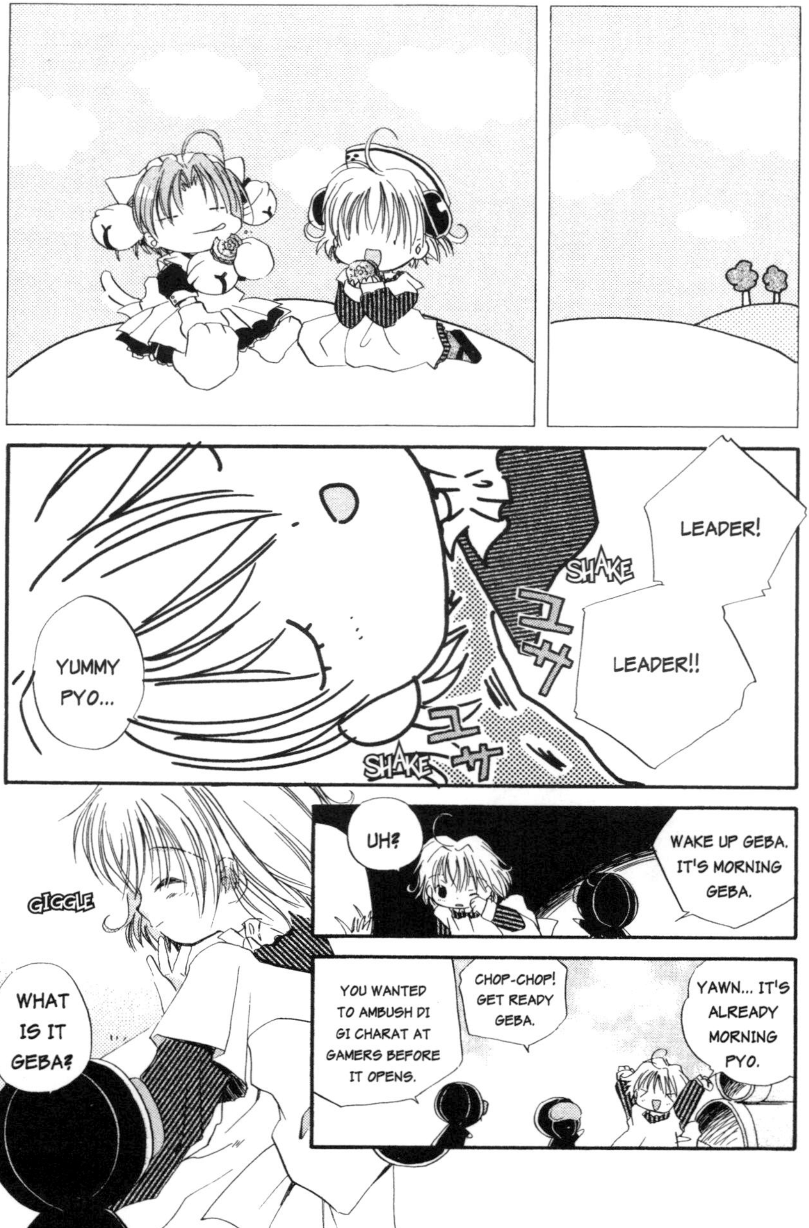
LEADER!
SHAKE
LEADER!!
ユサ
ユサ
SHAKE
YUMMY PYO...
WAKE UP GEBA. IT'S MORNING GEBA.
UH?
YAWN... IT'S ALREADY MORNING PYO.
CHOP-CHOP! GET READY GEBA.
YOU WANTED TO AMBUSH DI GI CHARAT AT GAMERS BEFORE IT OPENS.
GIGGLE
WHAT IS IT GEBA?

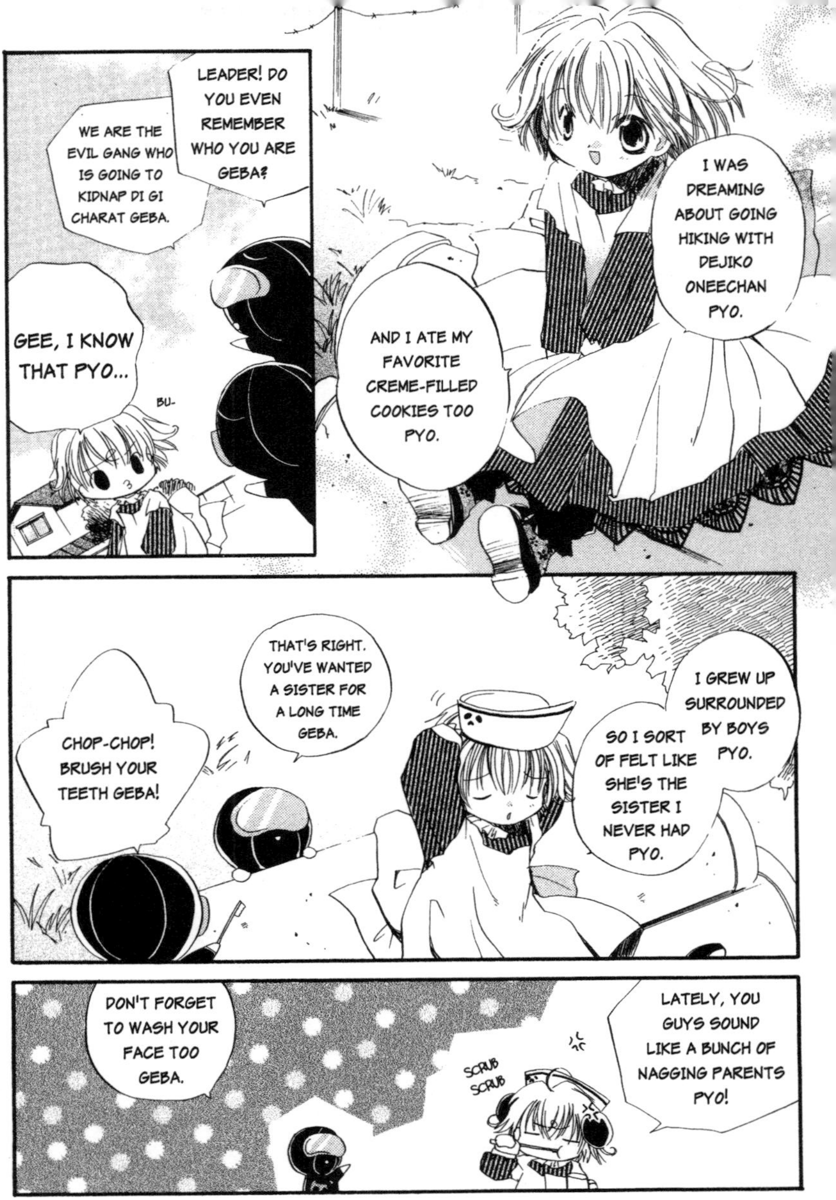
I WAS DREAMING ABOUT GOING HIKING WITH DEJIKO ONEECHAN PYO.
AND I ATE MY FAVORITE CREME-FILLED COOKIES TOO PYO.
LEADER! DO YOU EVEN REMEMBER WHO YOU ARE GEBA?
WE ARE THE EVIL GANG WHO IS GOING TO KIDNAP DI GI CHARAT GEBA.
GEE, I KNOW THAT PYO...
BU-
I GREW UP SURROUNDED BY BOYS PYO.
SO I SORT OF FELT LIKE SHE'S THE SISTER I NEVER HAD PYO.
THAT'S RIGHT. YOU'VE WANTED A SISTER FOR A LONG TIME GEBA.
CHOP-CHOP! BRUSH YOUR TEETH GEBA!
LATELY, YOU GUYS SOUND LIKE A BUNCH OF NAGGING PARENTS PYO!
SCRUB SCRUB
DON'T FORGET TO WASH YOUR FACE TOO GEBA.

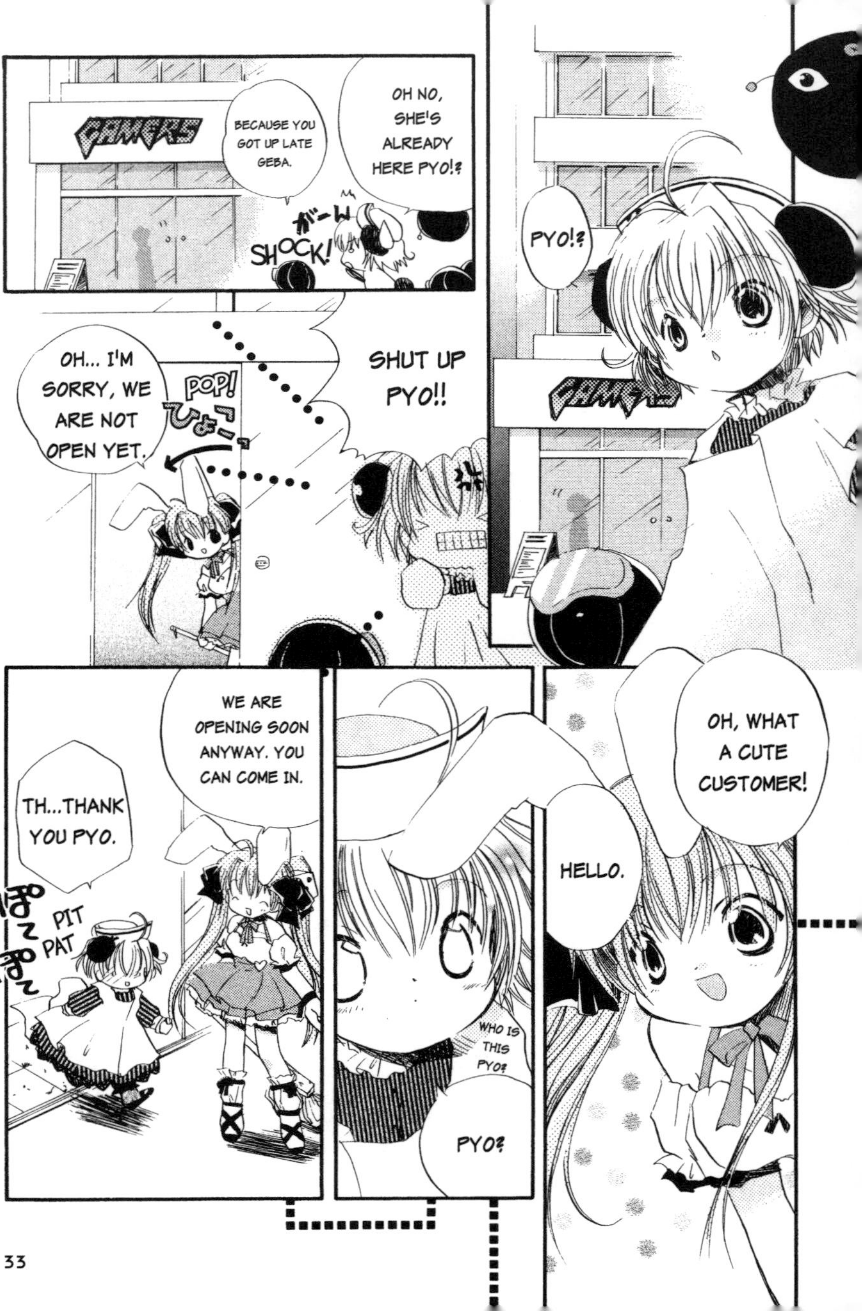
PYO!?
GAMERS
OH NO, SHE'S ALREADY HERE PYO!?
BECAUSE YOU GOT UP LATE GEBA.
ガーん
SHOCK!
SHUT UP PYO!!
POP!
ひょこっ
OH... I'M SORRY, WE ARE NOT OPEN YET.
OH, WHAT A CUTE CUSTOMER!
HELLO.
WHO IS THIS PYO?
PYO?
WE ARE OPENING SOON ANYWAY. YOU CAN COME IN.
TH...THANK YOU PYO.
ぽてぽて
PIT PAT

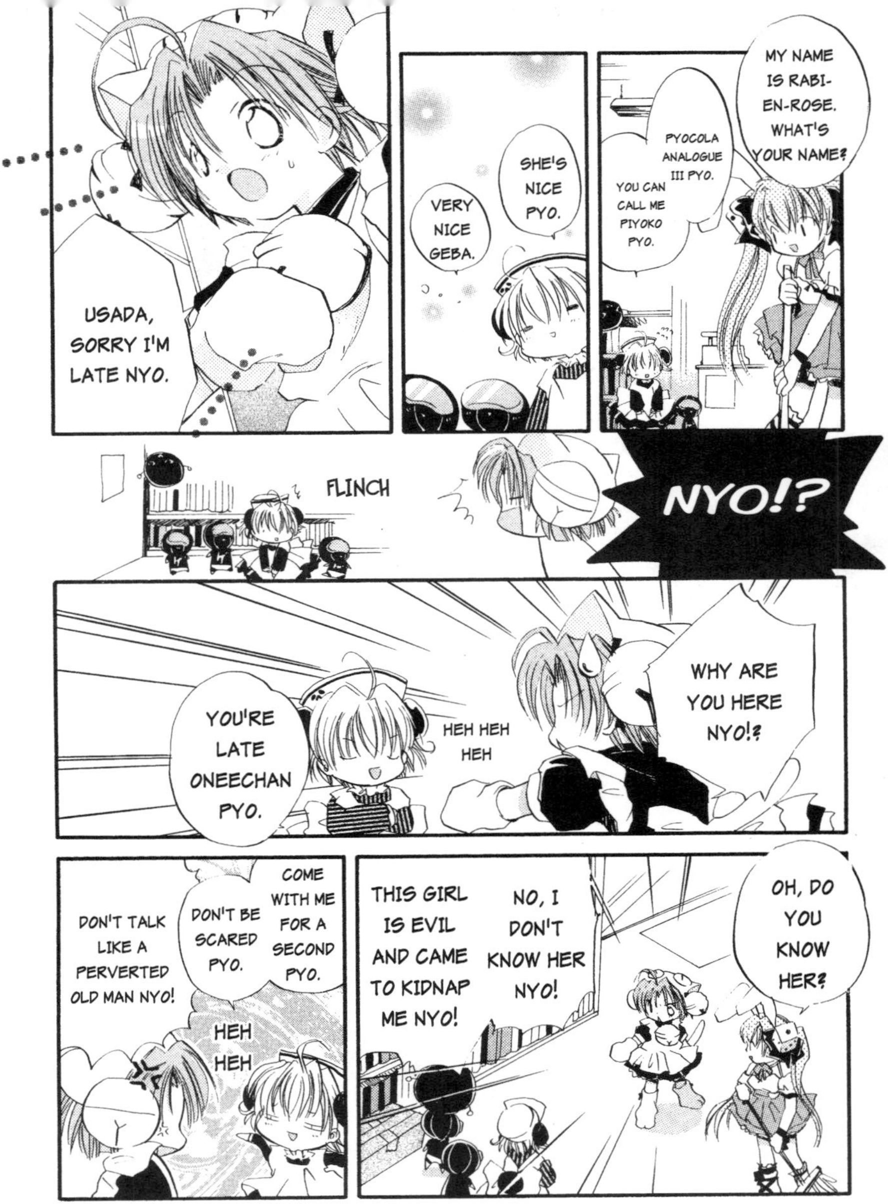
MY NAME IS RABI-EN-ROSE. WHAT'S YOUR NAME?
PYOCOLA ANALOGUE III PYO.
YOU CAN CALL ME PIYOKO PYO.
SHE'S NICE PYO.
VERY NICE GEBA.
USADA, SORRY I'M LATE NYO.
NYO!?
FLINCH
WHY ARE YOU HERE NYO!?
HEH HEH HEH
YOU'RE LATE ONEECHAN PYO.
OH, DO YOU KNOW HER?
NO, I DON'T KNOW HER NYO!
THIS GIRL IS EVIL AND CAME TO KIDNAP ME NYO!
COME WITH ME FOR A SECOND PYO.
DON'T BE SCARED PYO.
HEH HEH
DON'T TALK LIKE A PERVERTED OLD MAN NYO!

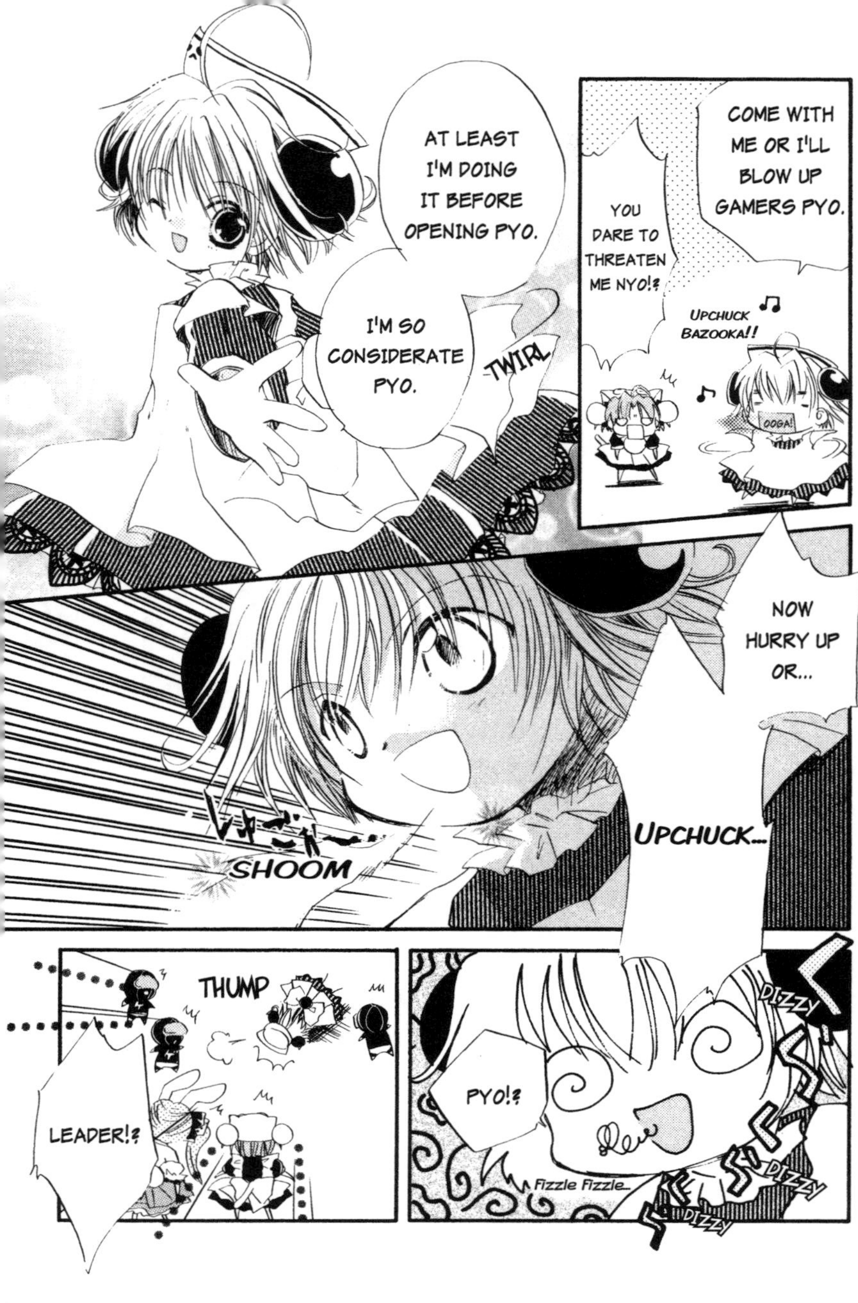

COME WITH ME OR I'LL BLOW UP GAMERS PYO.
YOU DARE TO THREATEN ME NYO!?
Upchuck Bazooka!!
OOGA!
AT LEAST I'M DOING IT BEFORE OPENING PYO.
I'M SO CONSIDERATE PYO.
TWIRL
NOW HURRY UP OR...
UPCHUCK...
SHOOM
PYO!?
DIZZY
DIZZY
DIZZY
Fizzle Fizzle...
THUMP
LEADER!?

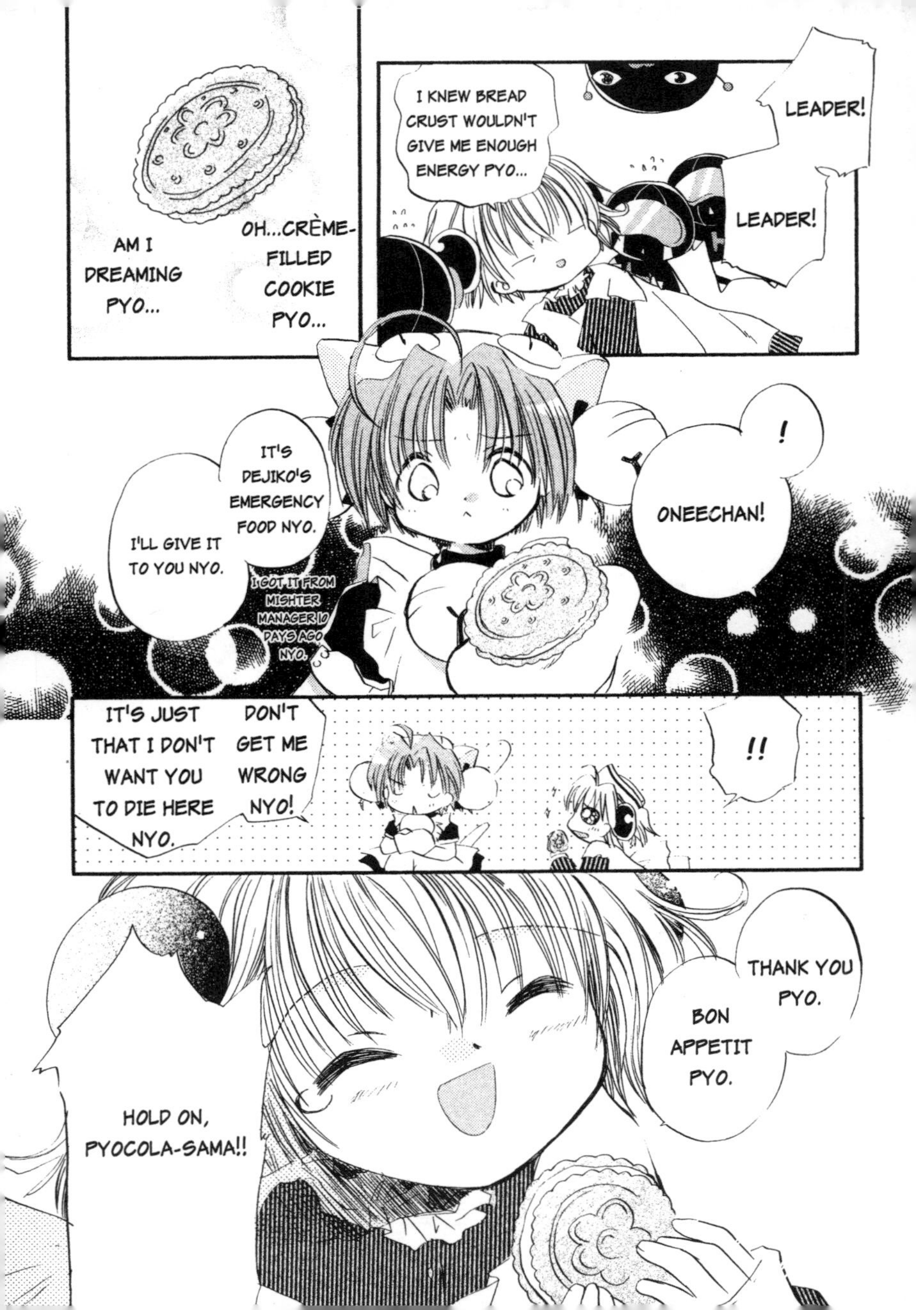
LEADER!
LEADER!
I KNEW BREAD CRUST WOULDN'T GIVE ME ENOUGH ENERGY PYO...
OH...CRÈME-FILLED COOKIE PYO...
AM I DREAMING PYO...
!
ONEECHAN!
IT'S DEJIKO'S EMERGENCY FOOD NYO.
I'LL GIVE IT TO YOU NYO.
I GOT IT FROM MISHTER MANAGER 10 DAYS AGO NYO.
!!
DON'T GET ME WRONG NYO!
IT'S JUST THAT I DON'T WANT YOU TO DIE HERE NYO.
THANK YOU PYO.
BON APPETIT PYO.
HOLD ON, PYOCOLA-SAMA!!

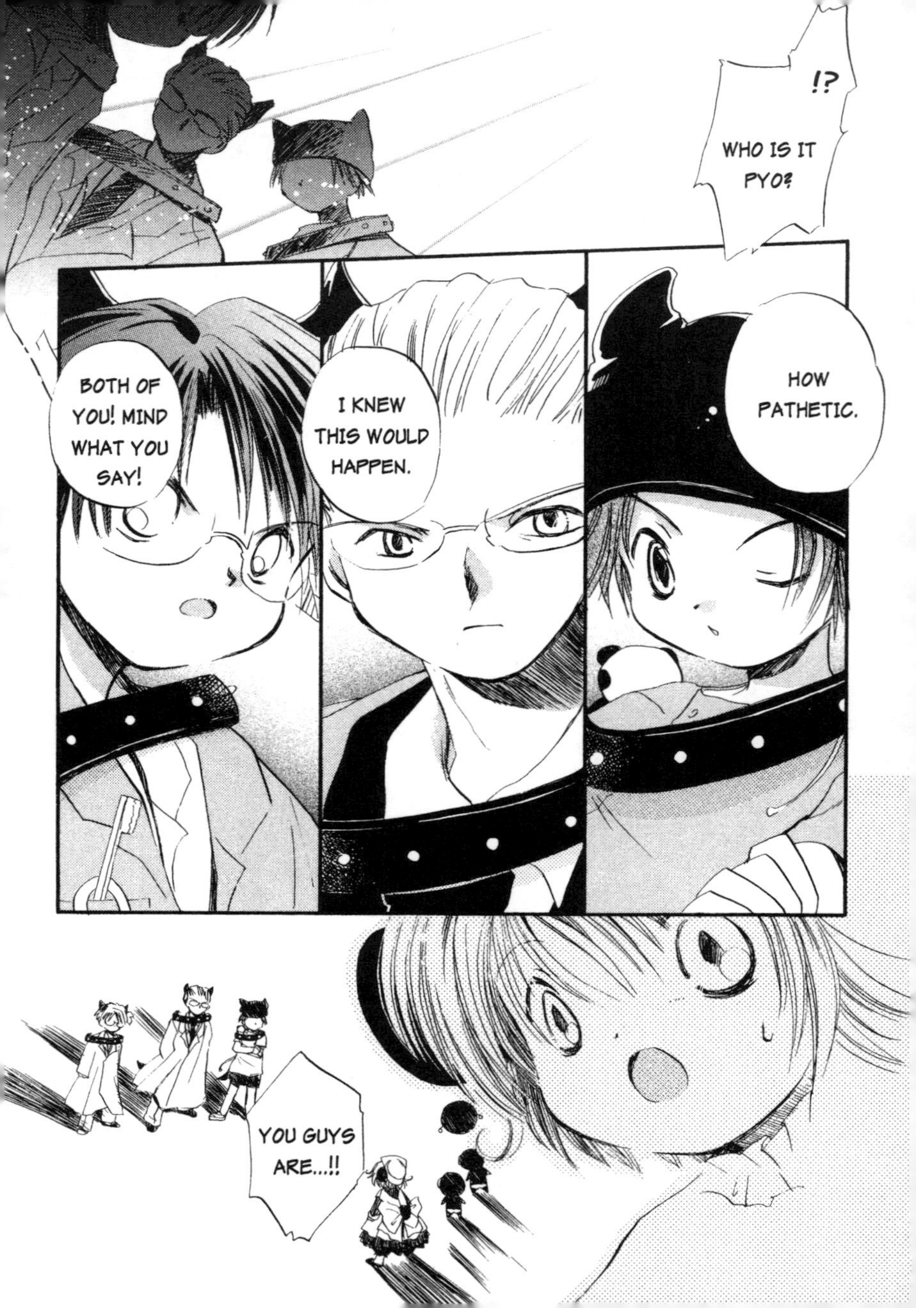
!? WHO IS IT PYO?
HOW PATHETIC.
I KNEW THIS WOULD HAPPEN.
BOTH OF YOU! MIND WHAT YOU SAY!
YOU GUYS ARE...!!

Nyo 4 Mysterious Reservoir Dogs!? Part 2

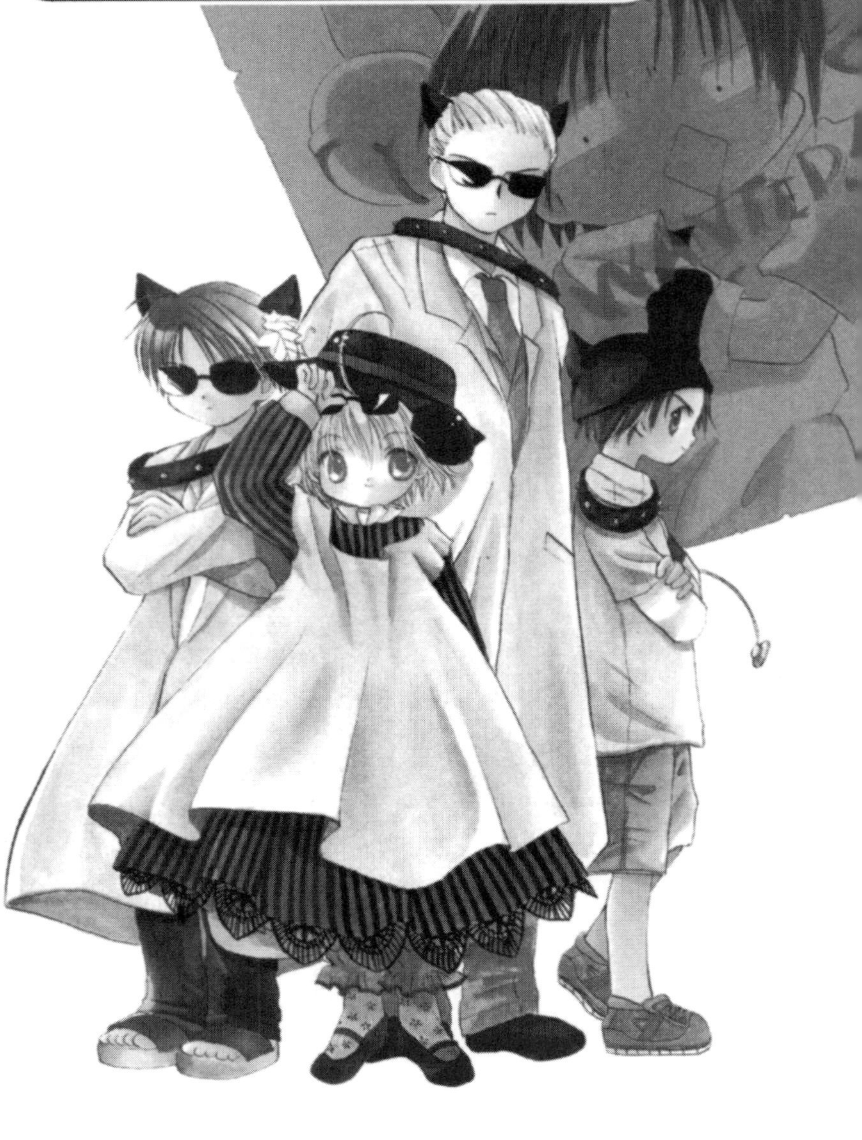

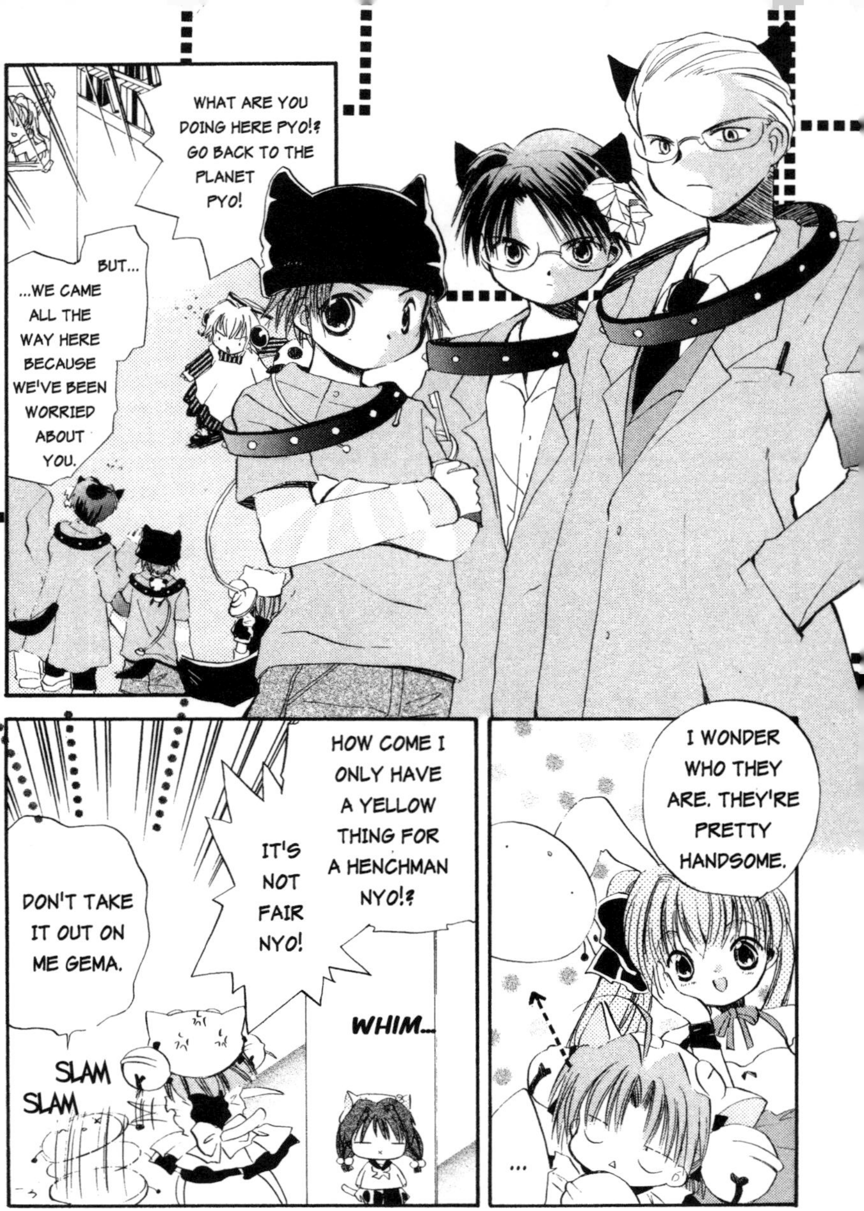
WHAT ARE YOU DOING HERE PYO!? GO BACK TO THE PLANET PYO!
BUT...
...WE CAME ALL THE WAY HERE BECAUSE WE'VE BEEN WORRIED ABOUT YOU.
I WONDER WHO THEY ARE. THEY'RE PRETTY HANDSOME.
...
HOW COME I ONLY HAVE A YELLOW THING FOR A HENCHMAN NYO!?
WHIM...
IT'S NOT FAIR NYO!
DON'T TAKE IT OUT ON ME GEMA.
SLAM
SLAM

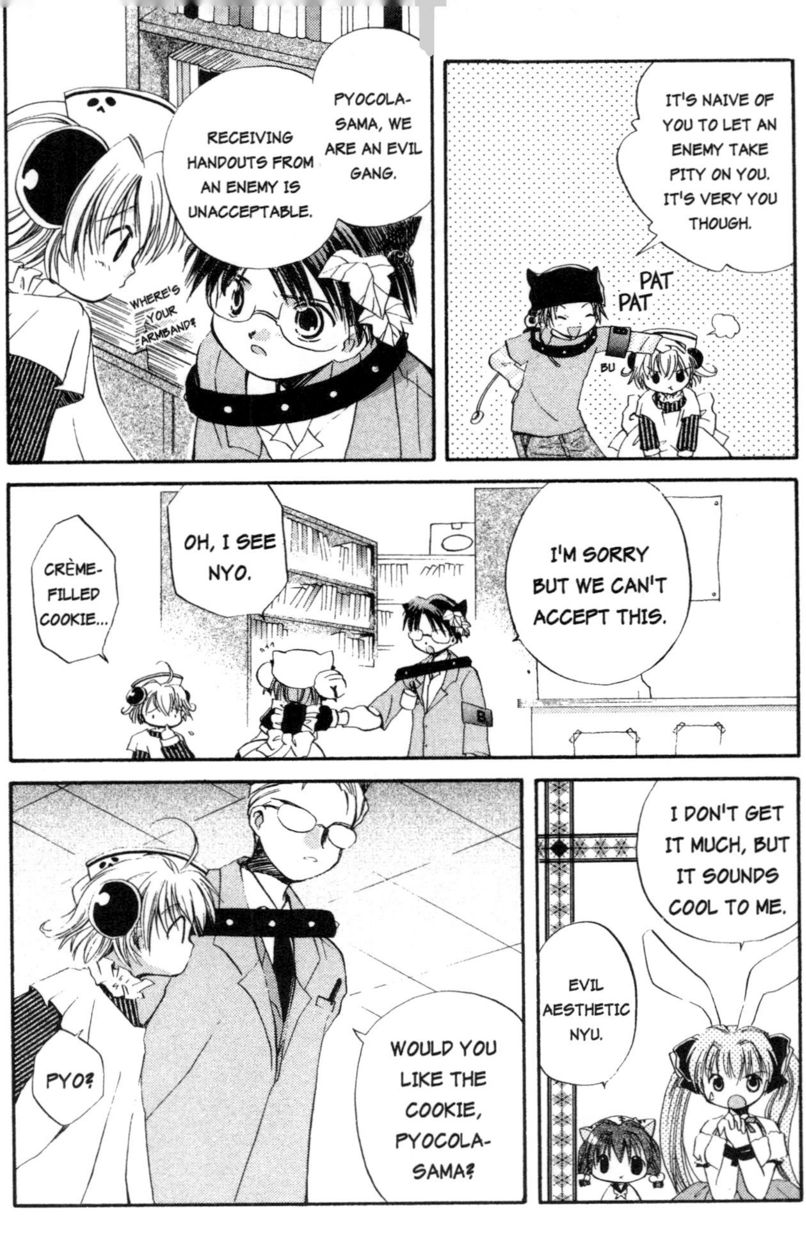
IT'S NAIVE OF YOU TO LET AN ENEMY TAKE PITY ON YOU. IT'S VERY YOU THOUGH.
PAT PAT
BU
PYOCOLA-SAMA, WE ARE AN EVIL GANG.
RECEIVING HANDOUTS FROM AN ENEMY IS UNACCEPTABLE.
WHERE'S YOUR ARMBAND?
I'M SORRY BUT WE CAN'T ACCEPT THIS.
OH, I SEE NYO.
CRÈME-FILLED COOKIE...
I DON'T GET IT MUCH, BUT IT SOUNDS COOL TO ME.
EVIL AESTHETIC NYU.
WOULD YOU LIKE THE COOKIE, PYOCOLA-SAMA?
PYO?

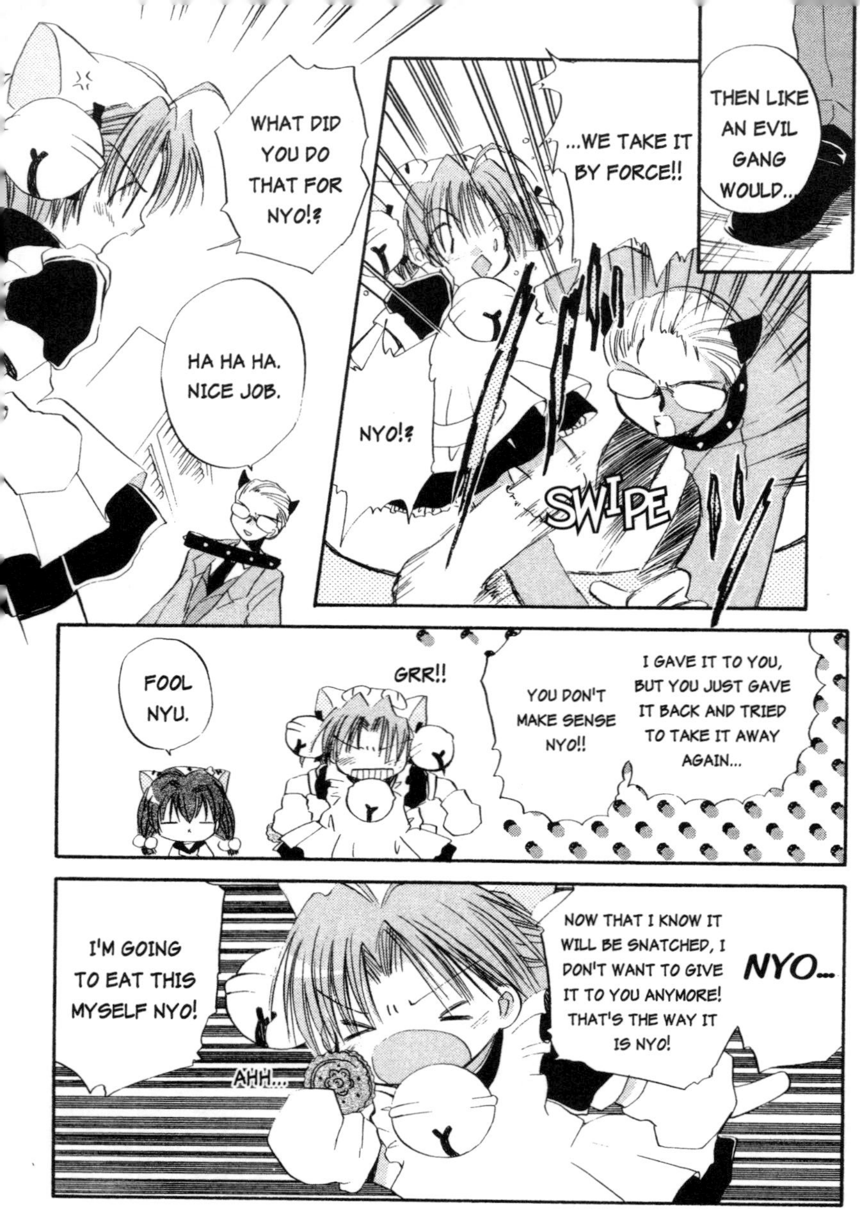
THEN LIKE AN EVIL GANG WOULD...
...WE TAKE IT BY FORCE!!
NYO!?
SWIPE
WHAT DID YOU DO THAT FOR NYO!?
HA HA HA. NICE JOB.
I GAVE IT TO YOU, BUT YOU JUST GAVE IT BACK AND TRIED TO TAKE IT AWAY AGAIN...
YOU DON'T MAKE SENSE NYO!!
GRR!!
FOOL NYU.
NYO...
NOW THAT I KNOW IT WILL BE SNATCHED, I DON'T WANT TO GIVE IT TO YOU ANYMORE! THAT'S THE WAY IT IS NYO!
I'M GOING TO EAT THIS MYSELF NYO!
AHH...

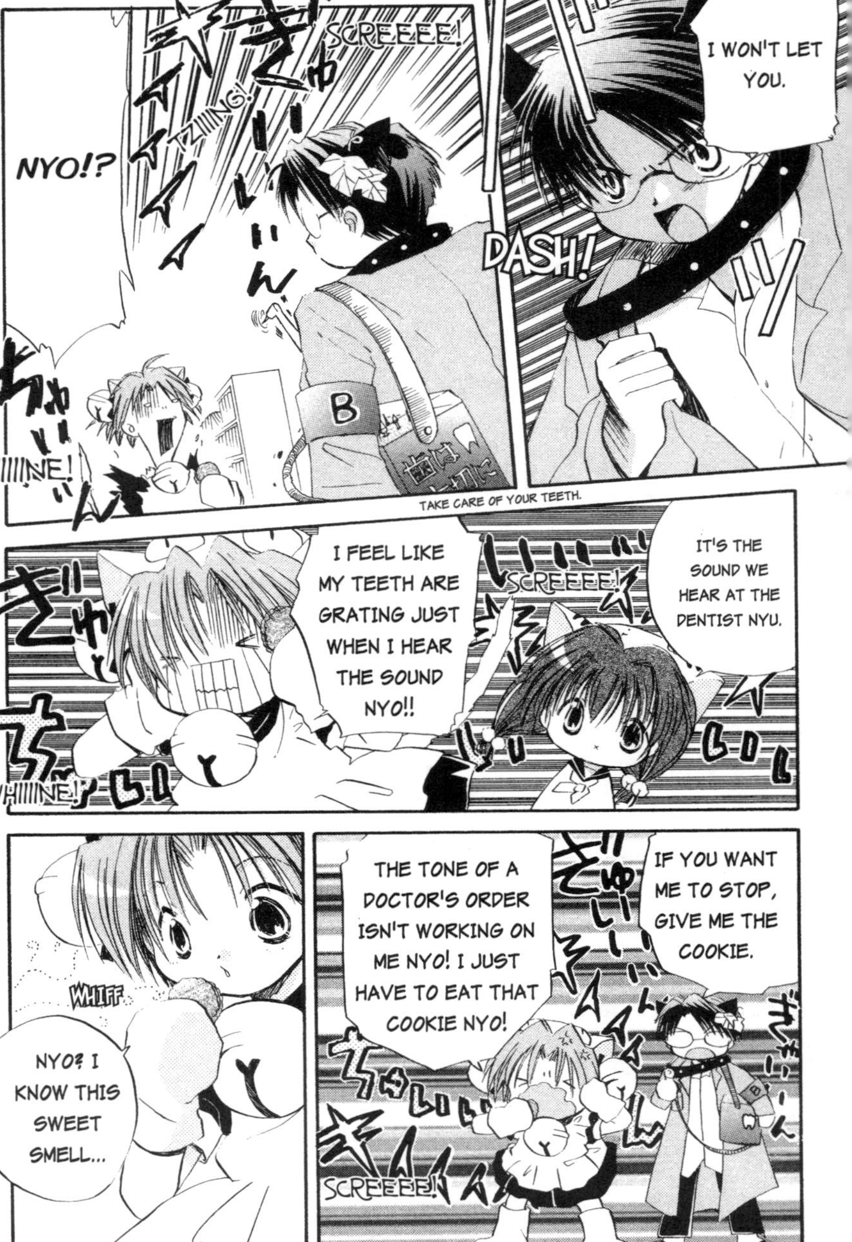
I WON'T LET YOU.
DASH!
SCREEEE!
ZZIING!
NYO!?
WHIIIINE!
TAKE CARE OF YOUR TEETH.
IT'S THE SOUND WE HEAR AT THE DENTIST NYU.
SCREEEEE!
I FEEL LIKE MY TEETH ARE GRATING JUST WHEN I HEAR THE SOUND NYO!!
WHIIINE!
IF YOU WANT ME TO STOP, GIVE ME THE COOKIE.
THE TONE OF A DOCTOR'S ORDER ISN'T WORKING ON ME NYO! I JUST HAVE TO EAT THAT COOKIE NYO!
SCREEEE!
WHIFF
NYO? I KNOW THIS SWEET SMELL...

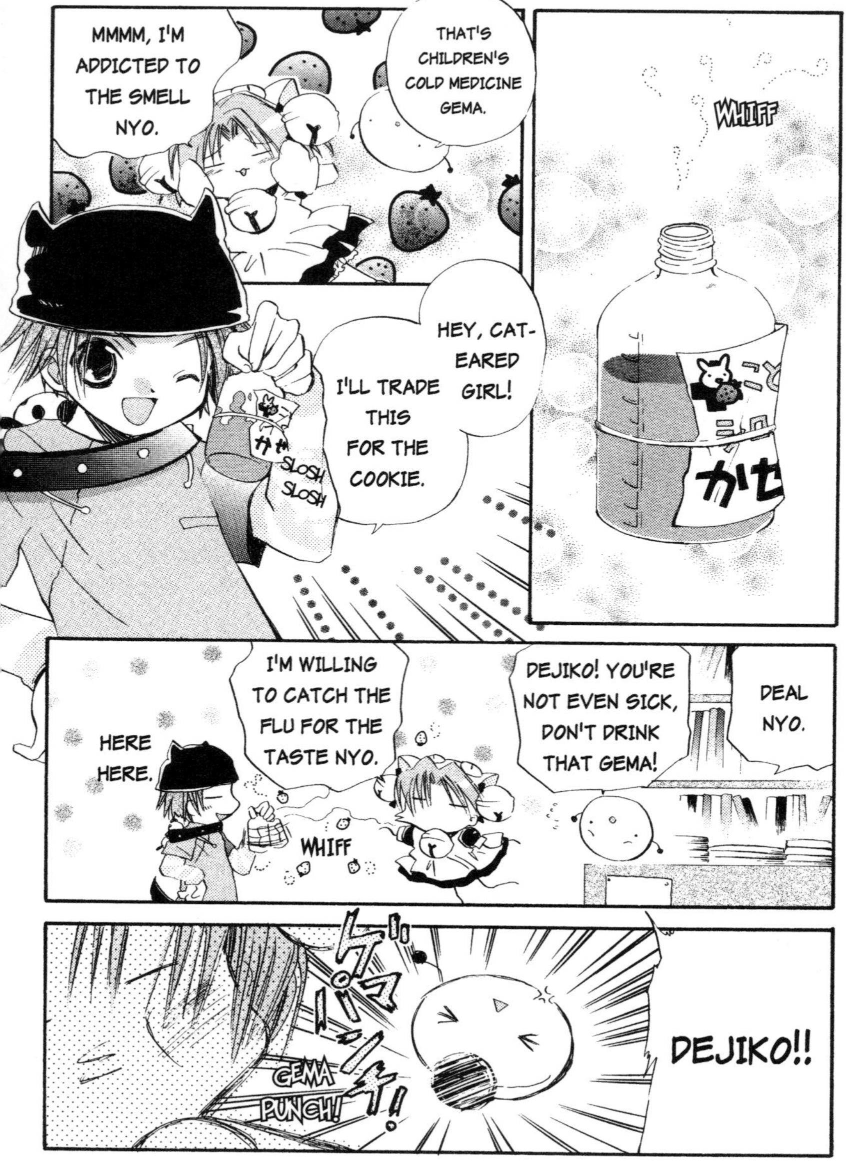
WHIFF
THAT'S CHILDREN'S COLD MEDICINE GEMA.
MMMM, I'M ADDICTED TO THE SMELL NYO.
HEY, CAT-EARED GIRL!
I'LL TRADE THIS FOR THE COOKIE.
SLOSH SLOSH
DEAL NYO.
DEJIKO! YOU'RE NOT EVEN SICK, DON'T DRINK THAT GEMA!
I'M WILLING TO CATCH THE FLU FOR THE TASTE NYO.
HERE HERE.
WHIFF
DEJIKO!!
GEMA PUNCH!

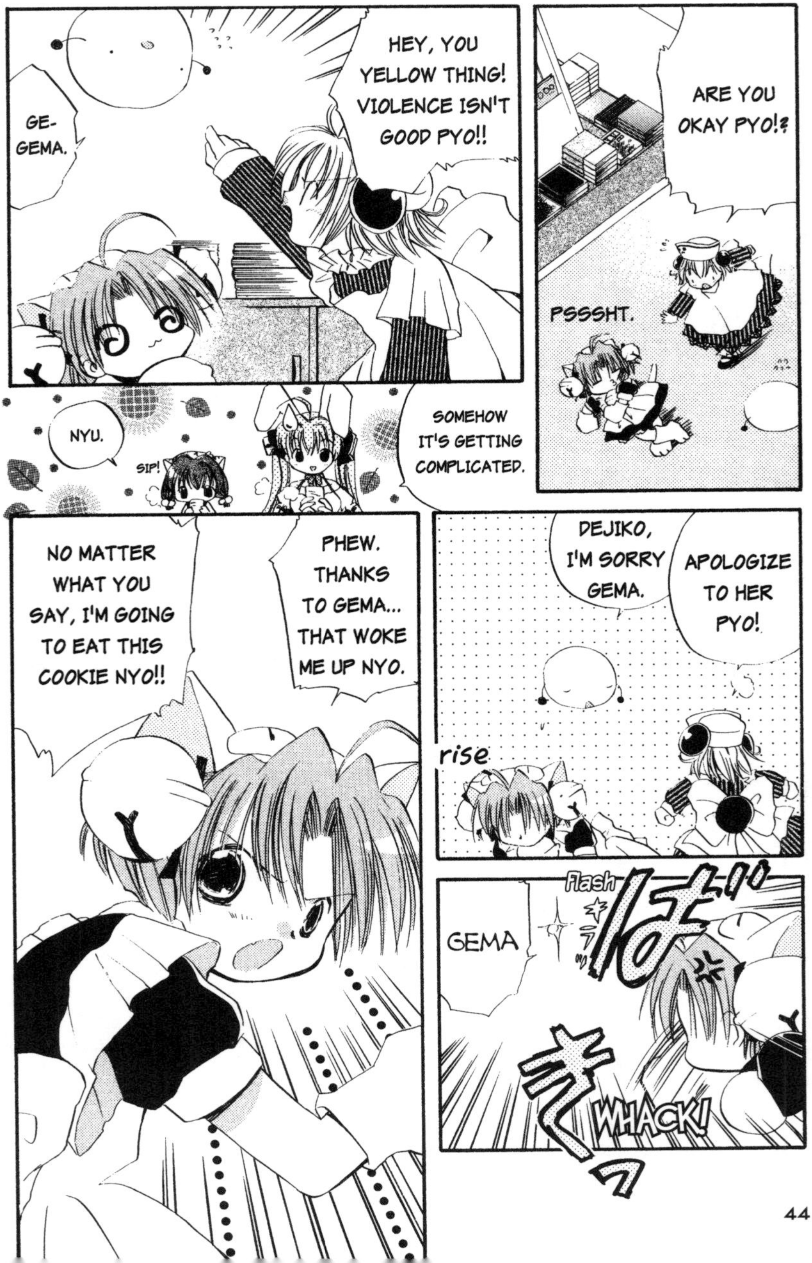
ARE YOU OKAY PYO!?
PSSSHT.
HEY, YOU YELLOW THING! VIOLENCE ISN'T GOOD PYO!!
GE-GEMA.
SOMEHOW IT'S GETTING COMPLICATED.
SIP!
NYU.
APOLOGIZE TO HER PYO!
DEJIKO, I'M SORRY GEMA.
rise
Flash
GEMA
WHACK!
PHEW. THANKS TO GEMA... THAT WOKE ME UP NYO.
NO MATTER WHAT YOU SAY, I'M GOING TO EAT THIS COOKIE NYO!!

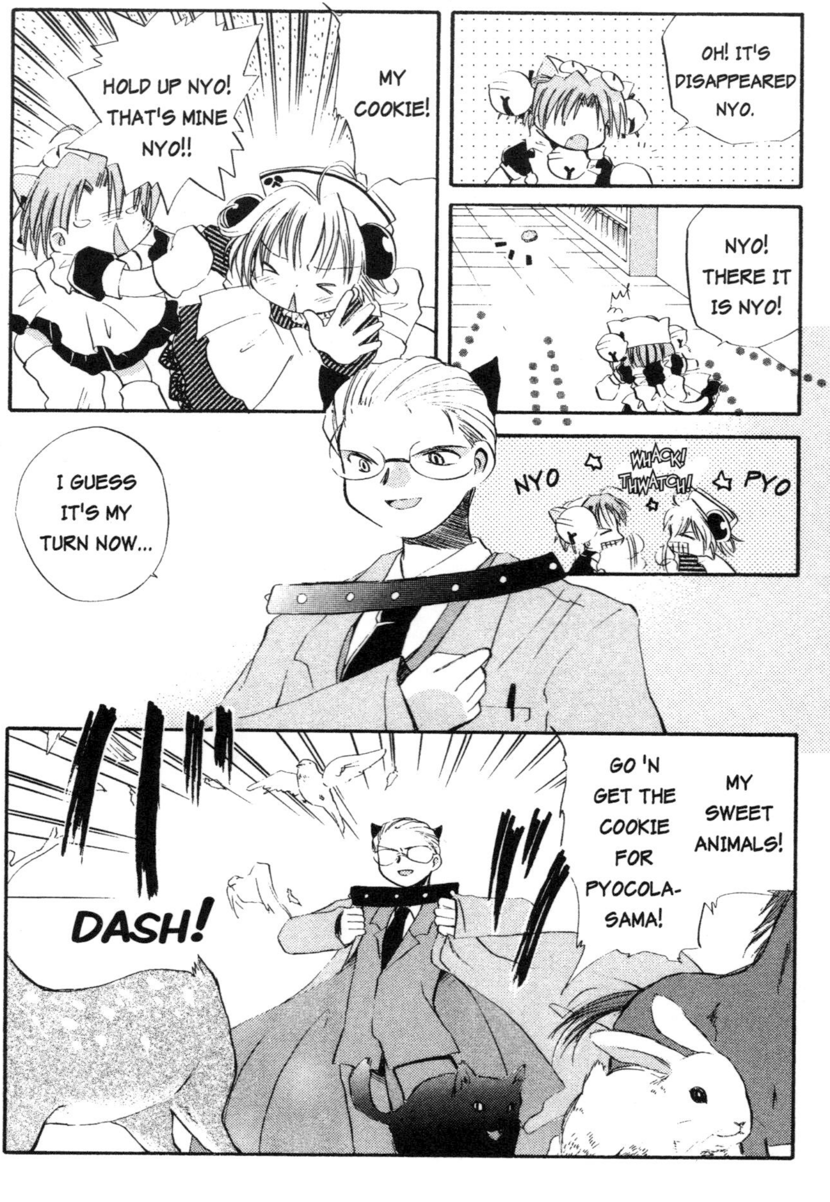
OH! IT'S DISAPPEARED NYO.
NYO! THERE IT IS NYO!
MY COOKIE!
HOLD UP NYO! THAT'S MINE NYO!!
PYO
WHACK! THWATCH!
NYO
I GUESS IT'S MY TURN NOW...
MY SWEET ANIMALS!
GO 'N GET THE COOKIE FOR PYOCOLA-SAMA!
DASH!

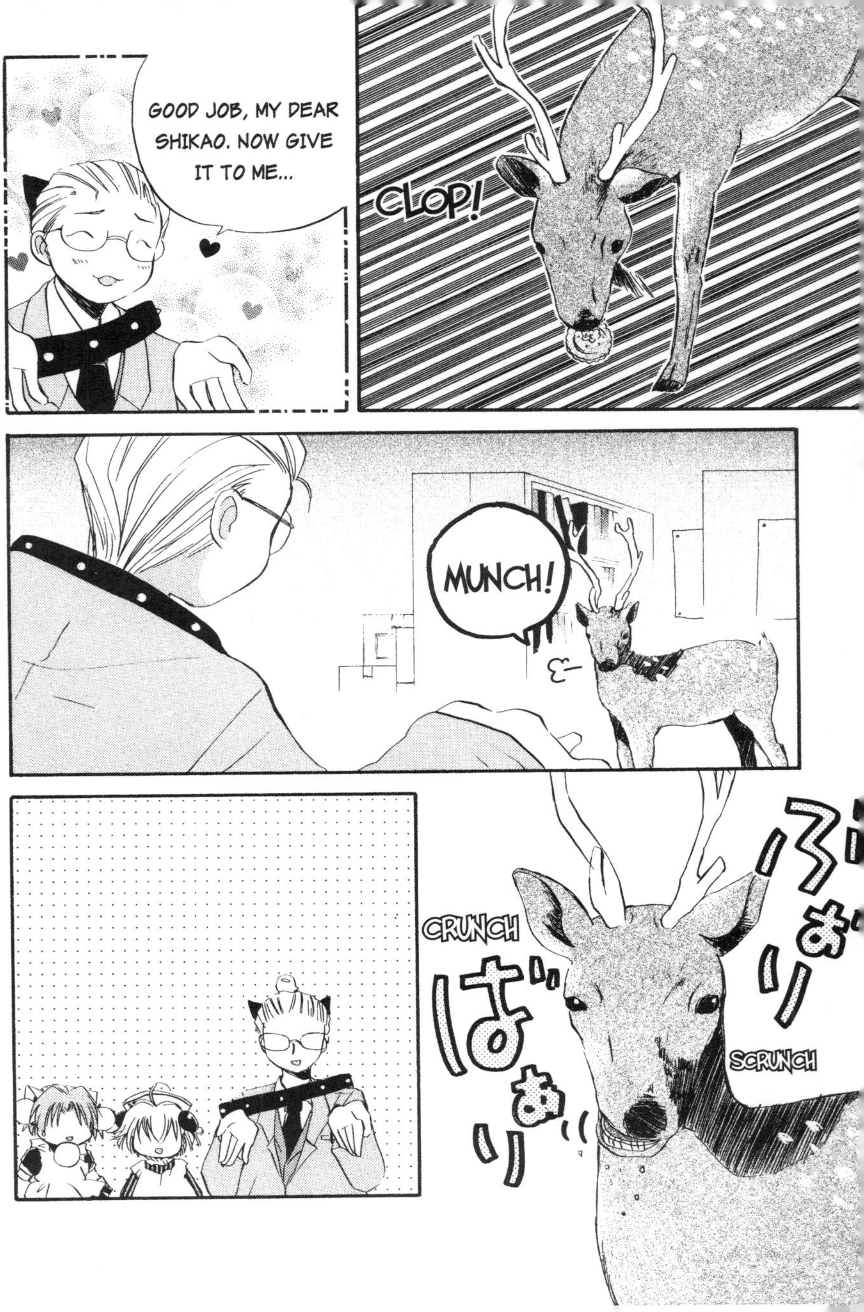
CLOP!
GOOD JOB, MY DEAR SHIKAO. NOW GIVE IT TO ME...
MUNCH!
SCRUNCH
CRUNCH

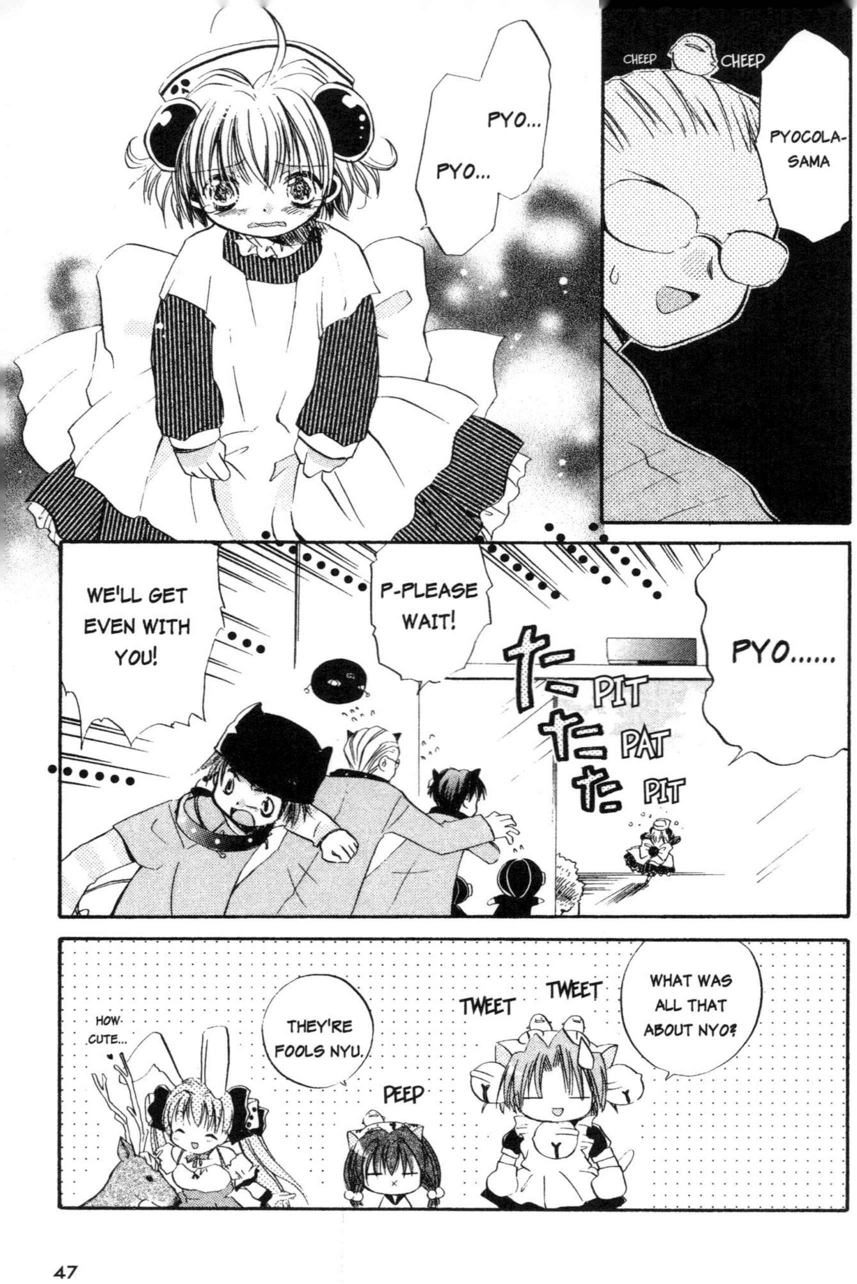
CHEEP CHEEP
PYOCOLA-SAMA
PYO... PYO...
PYO......
PIT PAT PIT
P-PLEASE WAIT!
WE'LL GET EVEN WITH YOU!
WHAT WAS ALL THAT ABOUT NYO?
TWEET TWEET
PEEP
THEY'RE FOOLS NYU.
HOW CUTE...

**A Day in the Life of
the Black Gema Gema Gang
9:00AM  Morning meeting**

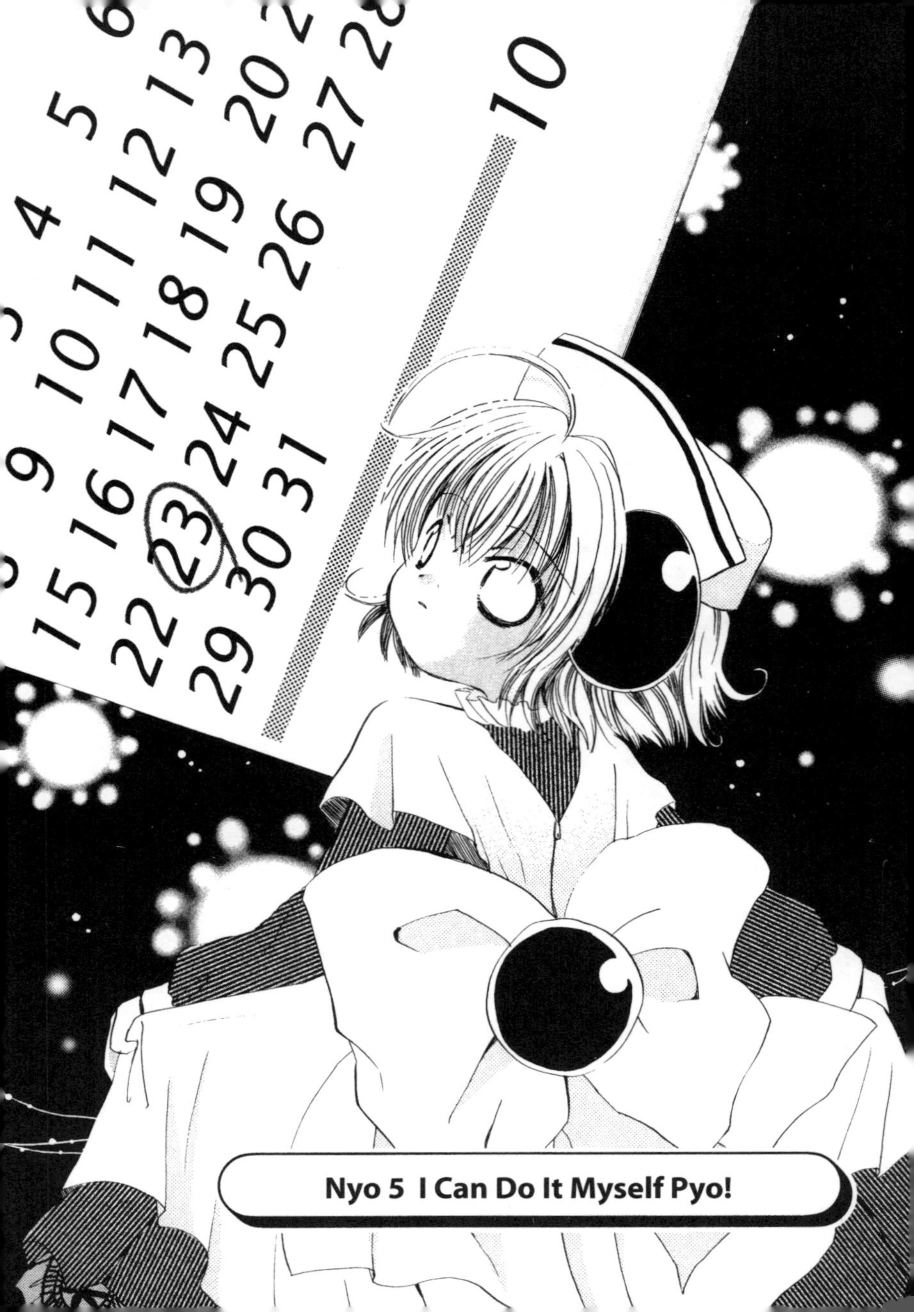

Nyo 5 I Can Do It Myself Pyo!

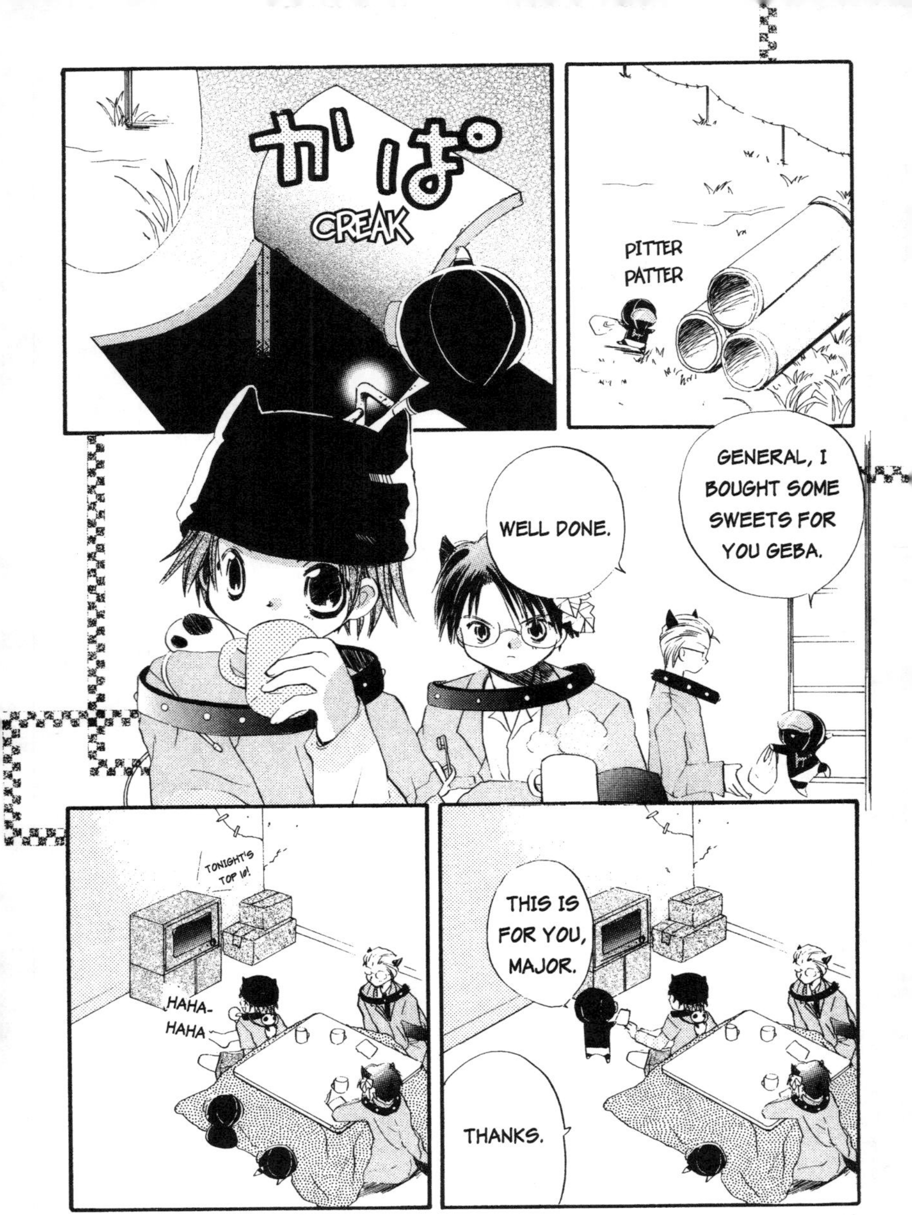
PITTER
PATTER
かぽ
CREAK
GENERAL, I BOUGHT SOME SWEETS FOR YOU GEBA.
WELL DONE.
THIS IS FOR YOU, MAJOR.
THANKS.
TONIGHT'S TOP 10!
HAHA-
HAHA

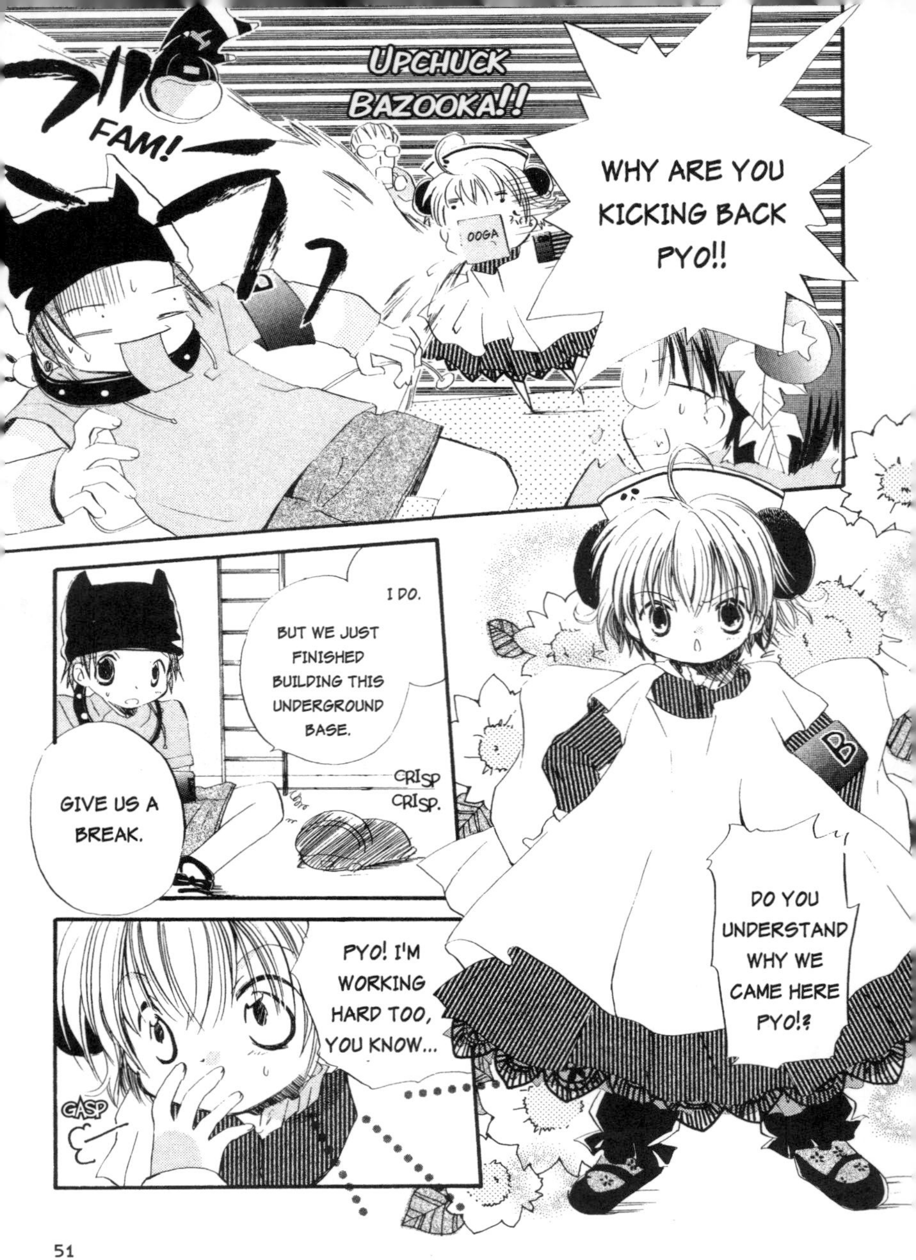
WHY ARE YOU KICKING BACK PYO!!
UPCHUCK BAZOOKA!!
FAM!
OOGA
DO YOU UNDERSTAND WHY WE CAME HERE PYO!?
I DO.
BUT WE JUST FINISHED BUILDING THIS UNDERGROUND BASE.
CRISP CRISP.
GIVE US A BREAK.
PYO! I'M WORKING HARD TOO, YOU KNOW...
GASP

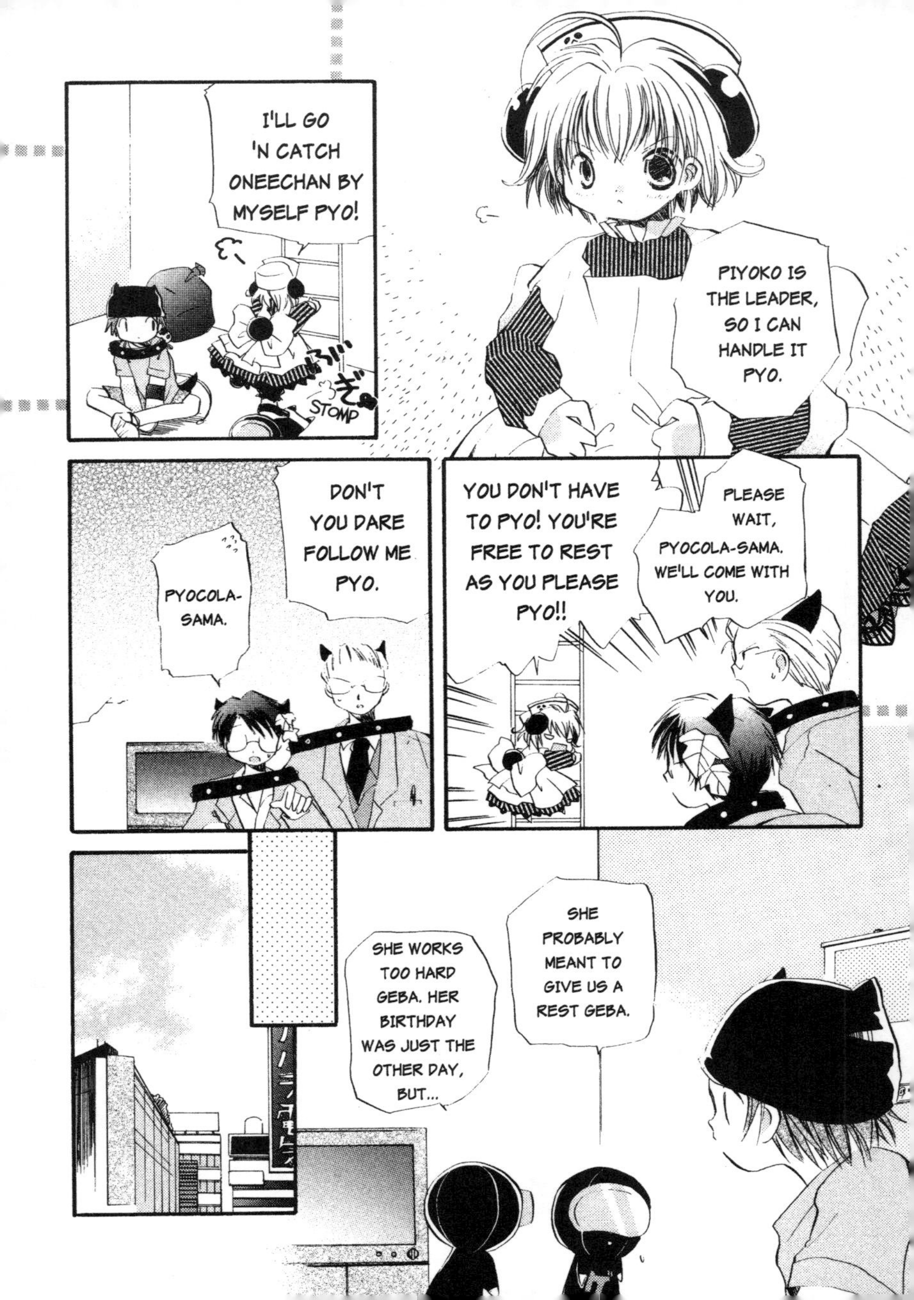
PIYOKO IS THE LEADER, SO I CAN HANDLE IT PYO.
I'LL GO 'N CATCH ONEECHAN BY MYSELF PYO!
STOMP
PLEASE WAIT, PYOCOLA-SAMA. WE'LL COME WITH YOU.
YOU DON'T HAVE TO PYO! YOU'RE FREE TO REST AS YOU PLEASE PYO!!
DON'T YOU DARE FOLLOW ME PYO.
PYOCOLA-SAMA.
SHE PROBABLY MEANT TO GIVE US A REST GEBA.
SHE WORKS TOO HARD GEBA. HER BIRTHDAY WAS JUST THE OTHER DAY, BUT...

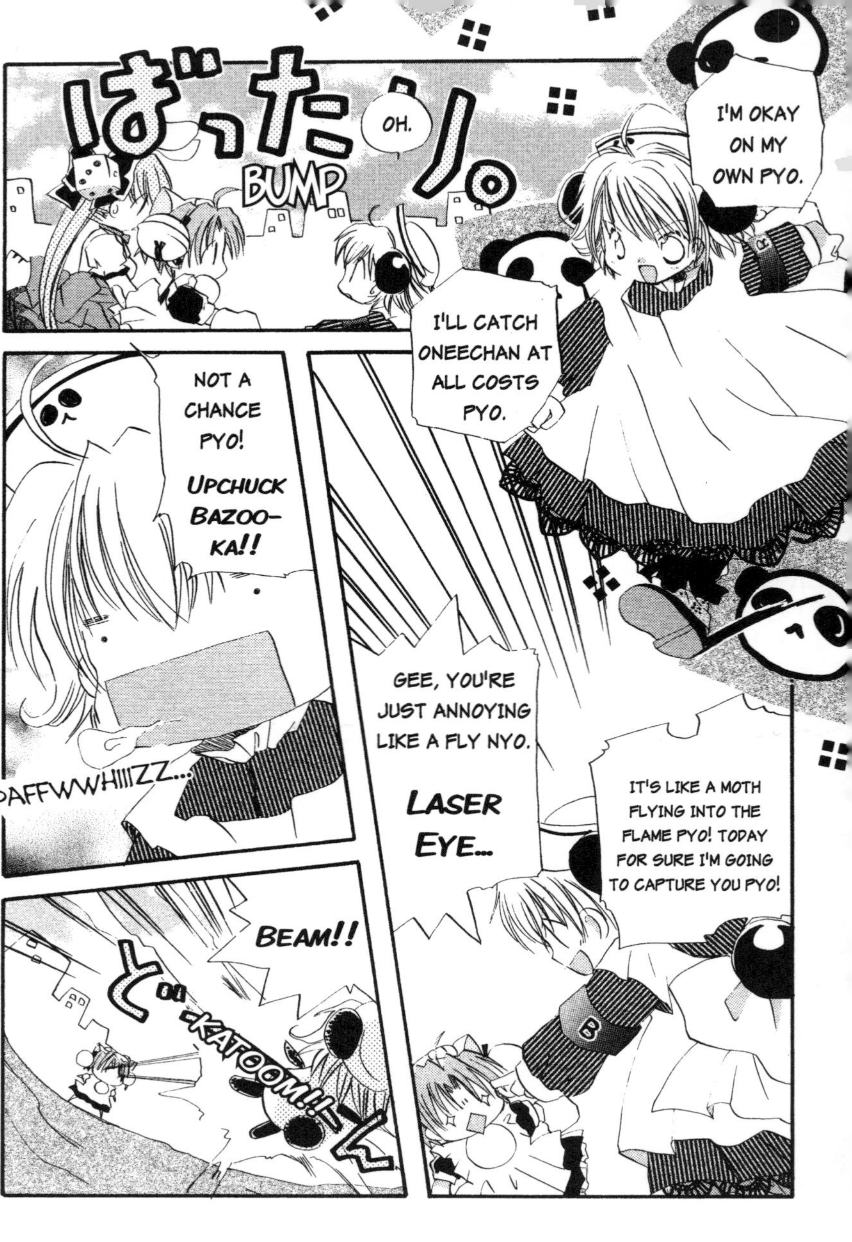
ばったり。
BUMP
OH.
I'M OKAY ON MY OWN PYO.
I'LL CATCH ONEECHAN AT ALL COSTS PYO.
IT'S LIKE A MOTH FLYING INTO THE FLAME PYO! TODAY FOR SURE I'M GOING TO CAPTURE YOU PYO!
GEE, YOU'RE JUST ANNOYING LIKE A FLY NYO.
LASER EYE...
NOT A CHANCE PYO!
UPCHUCK BAZOO-KA!!
PAFFWWHIIIZZ...
BEAM!!
KATOOM!!

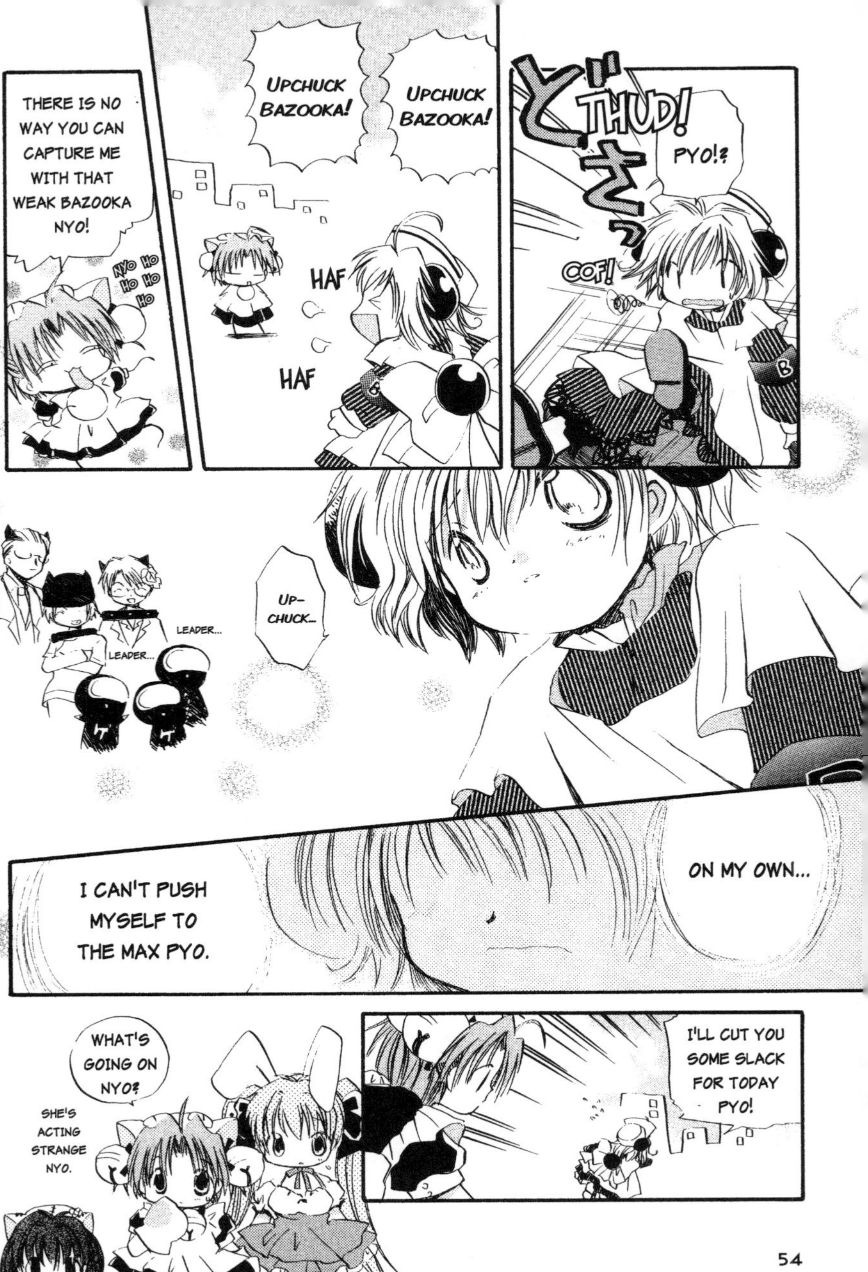

どさっ
THUD!
PYO!?
COF!
UPCHUCK BAZOOKA!
UPCHUCK BAZOOKA!
HAF
HAF
THERE IS NO WAY YOU CAN CAPTURE ME WITH THAT WEAK BAZOOKA NYO!
NYO HO HO HO HO
UP-CHUCK...
LEADER...
LEADER...
ON MY OWN...
I CAN'T PUSH MYSELF TO THE MAX PYO.
I'LL CUT YOU SOME SLACK FOR TODAY PYO!
WHAT'S GOING ON NYO?
SHE'S ACTING STRANGE NYO.

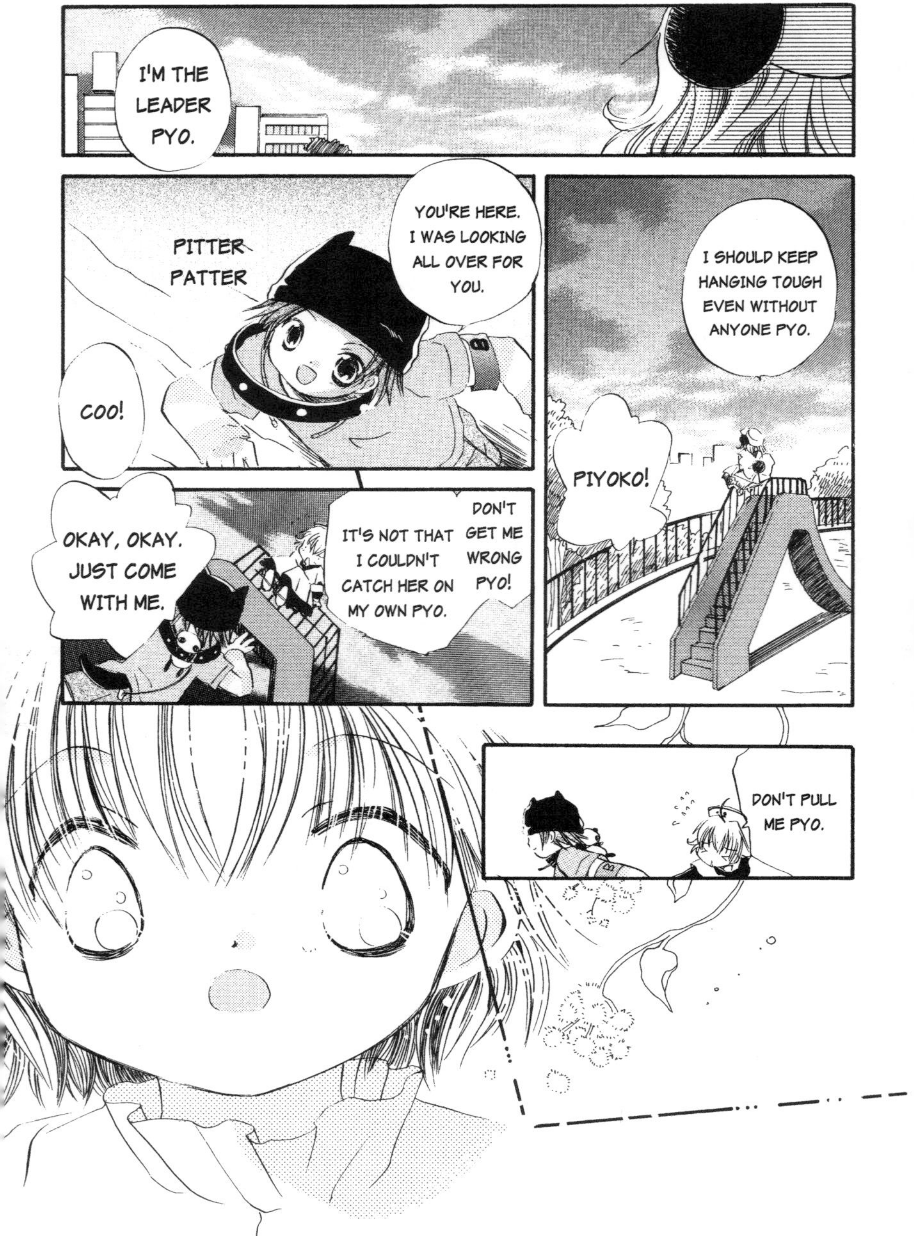
I'M THE LEADER PYO.
I SHOULD KEEP HANGING TOUGH EVEN WITHOUT ANYONE PYO.
PIYOKO!
YOU'RE HERE. I WAS LOOKING ALL OVER FOR YOU.
PITTER PATTER
COO!
DON'T GET ME WRONG PYO!
IT'S NOT THAT I COULDN'T CATCH HER ON MY OWN PYO.
OKAY, OKAY. JUST COME WITH ME.
DON'T PULL ME PYO.

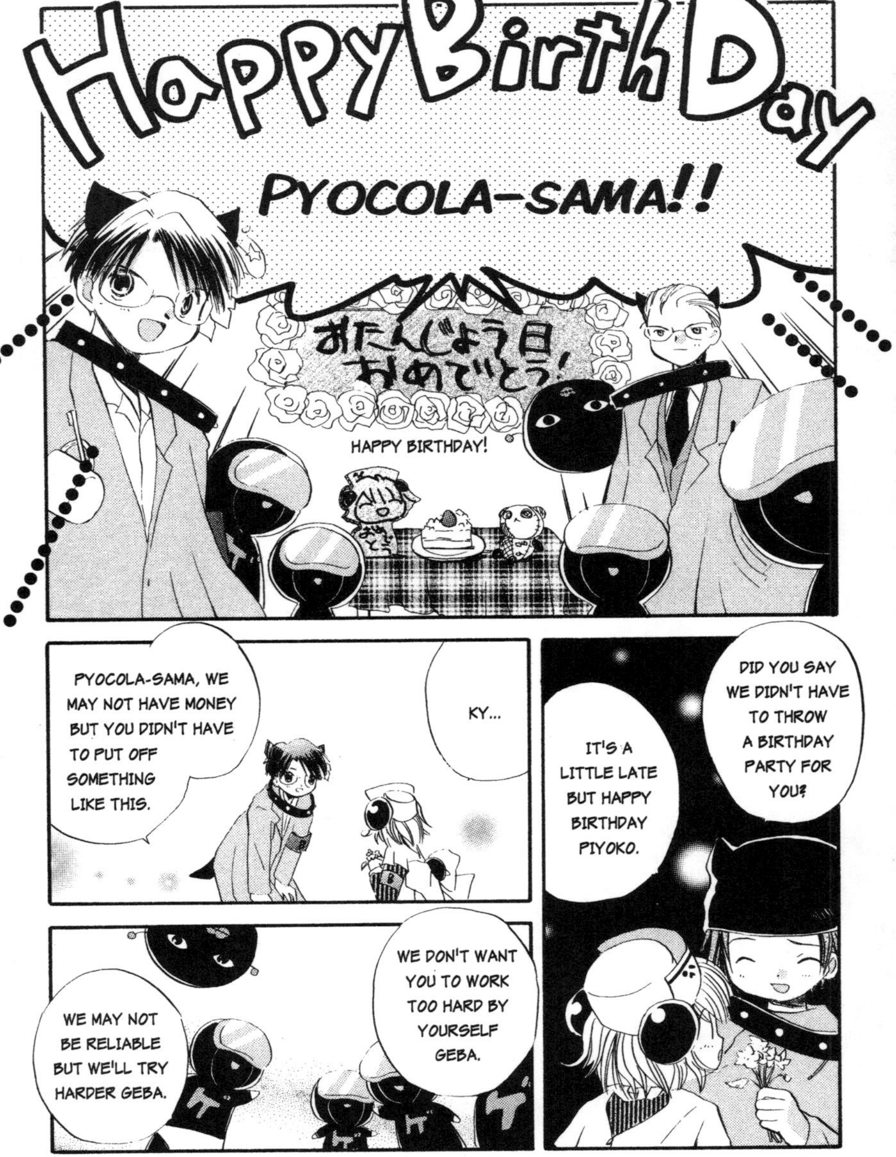
HAPPY BIRTHDAY
PYOCOLA-SAMA!!
おたんじょう日 おめでとう!
HAPPY BIRTHDAY!
DID YOU SAY WE DIDN'T HAVE TO THROW A BIRTHDAY PARTY FOR YOU?
IT'S A LITTLE LATE BUT HAPPY BIRTHDAY PIYOKO.
KY...
PYOCOLA-SAMA, WE MAY NOT HAVE MONEY BUT YOU DIDN'T HAVE TO PUT OFF SOMETHING LIKE THIS.
WE DON'T WANT YOU TO WORK TOO HARD BY YOURSELF GEBA.
WE MAY NOT BE RELIABLE BUT WE'LL TRY HARDER GEBA.

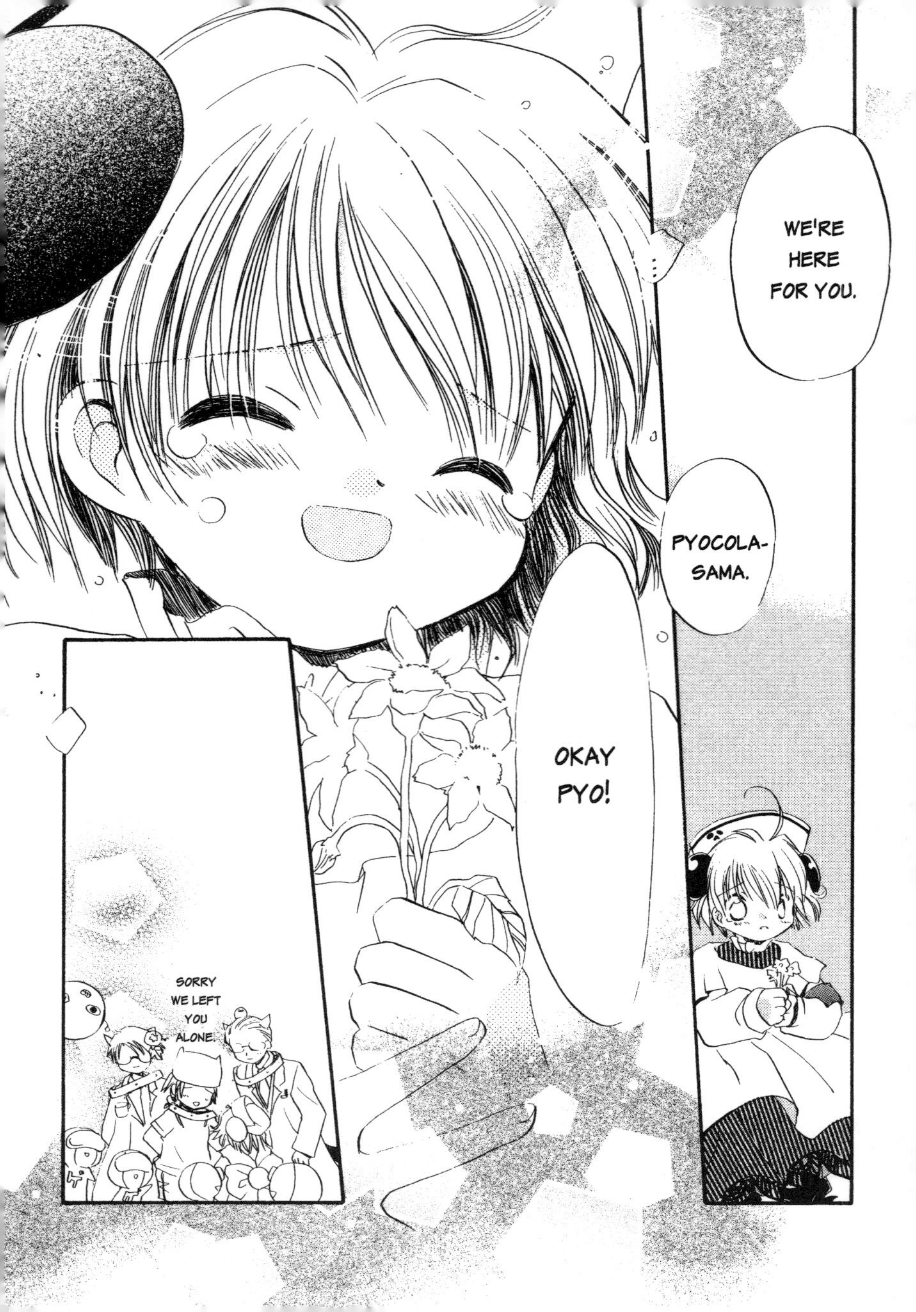
WE'RE HERE FOR YOU.
PYOCOLA-SAMA.
OKAY PYO!
SORRY WE LEFT YOU ALONE.

**A Day in the Life of
the Black Gema Gema Gang**
10:00 AM 🐾 Spy on Gamers

Nyo 6 Piyoko's Secret Recipe

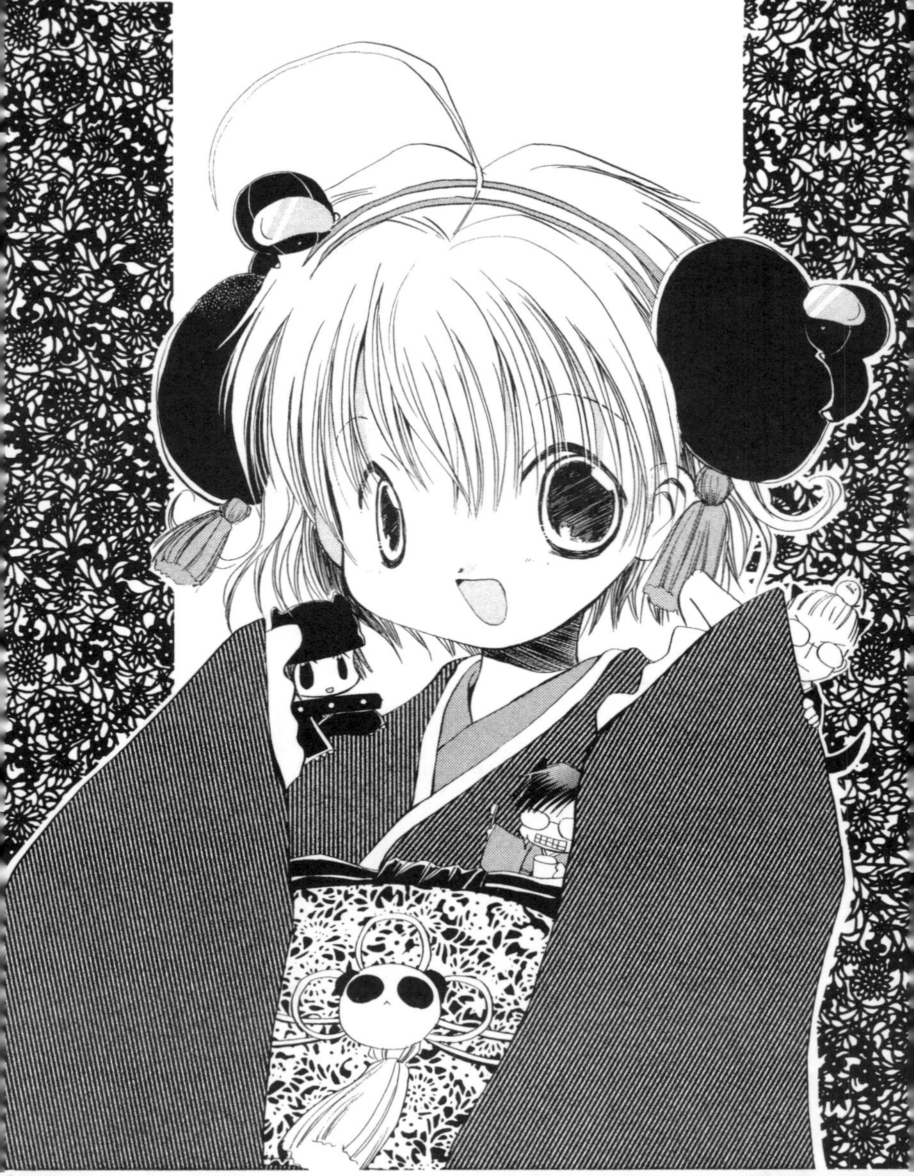

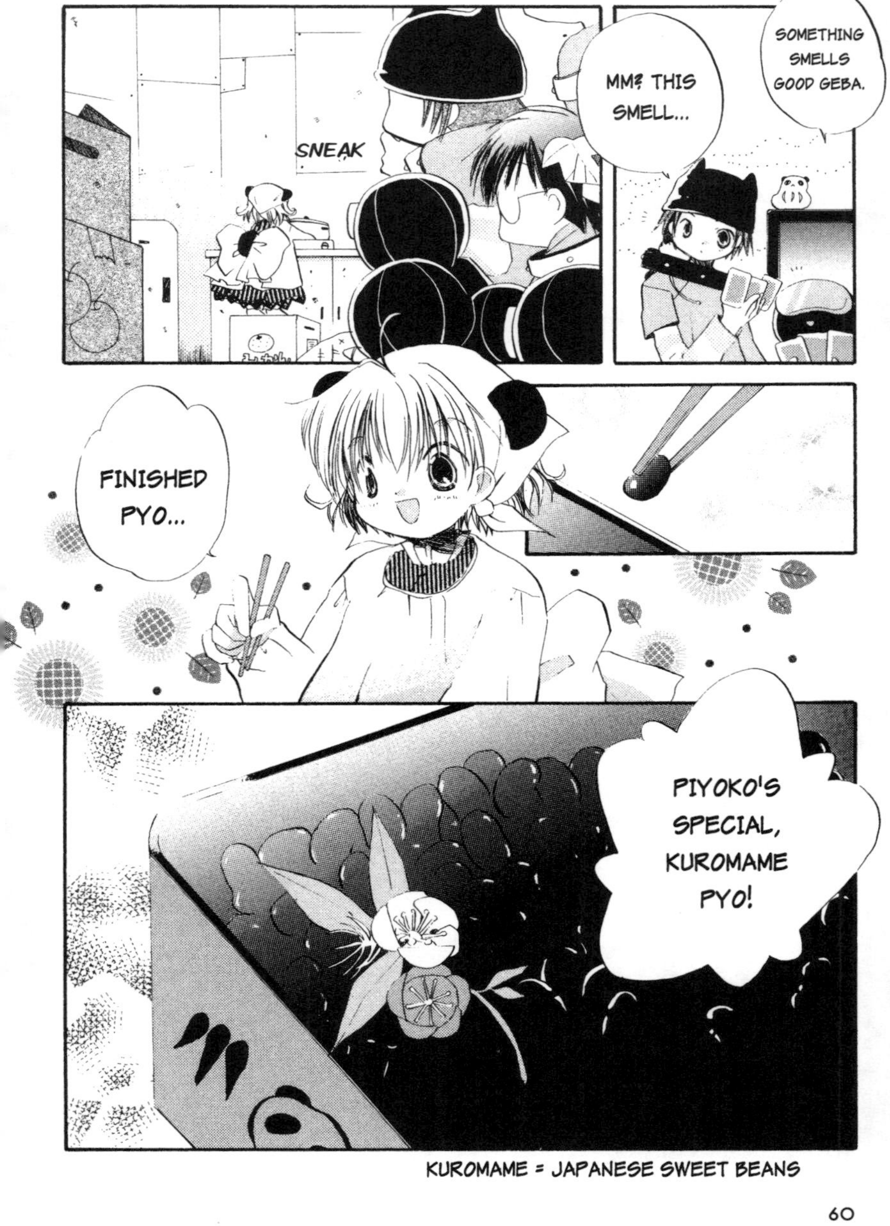
SOMETHING SMELLS GOOD GEBA.
MM? THIS SMELL...
SNEAK
FINISHED PYO...
PIYOKO'S SPECIAL, KUROMAME PYO!

KUROMAME = JAPANESE SWEET BEANS

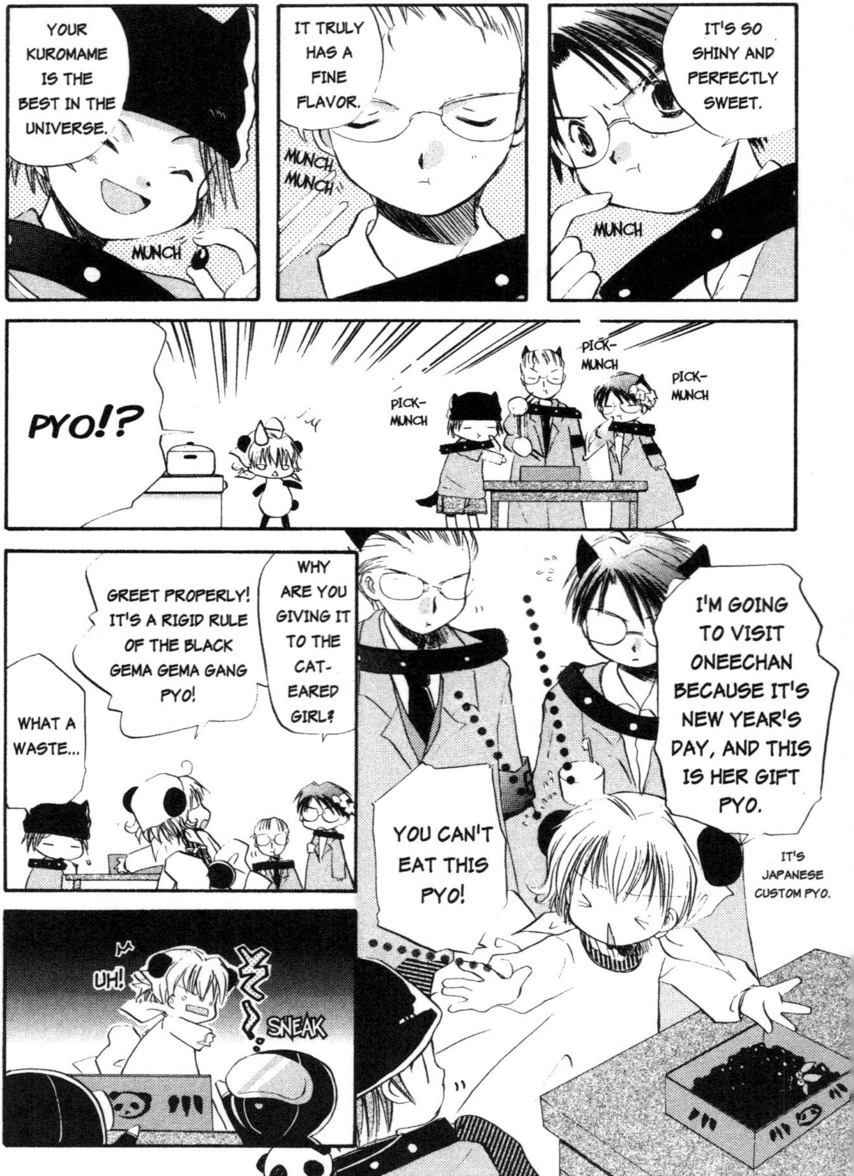
IT'S SO SHINY AND PERFECTLY SWEET.
MUNCH
IT TRULY HAS A FINE FLAVOR.
MUNCH MUNCH
YOUR KUROMAME IS THE BEST IN THE UNIVERSE.
MUNCH
PICK-MUNCH
PICK-MUNCH
PICK-MUNCH
PYO!?
I'M GOING TO VISIT ONEECHAN BECAUSE IT'S NEW YEAR'S DAY, AND THIS IS HER GIFT PYO.
IT'S JAPANESE CUSTOM PYO.
YOU CAN'T EAT THIS PYO!
WHY ARE YOU GIVING IT TO THE CAT-EARED GIRL?
GREET PROPERLY! IT'S A RIGID RULE OF THE BLACK GEMA GEMA GANG PYO!
WHAT A WASTE...
SNEAK
UH!

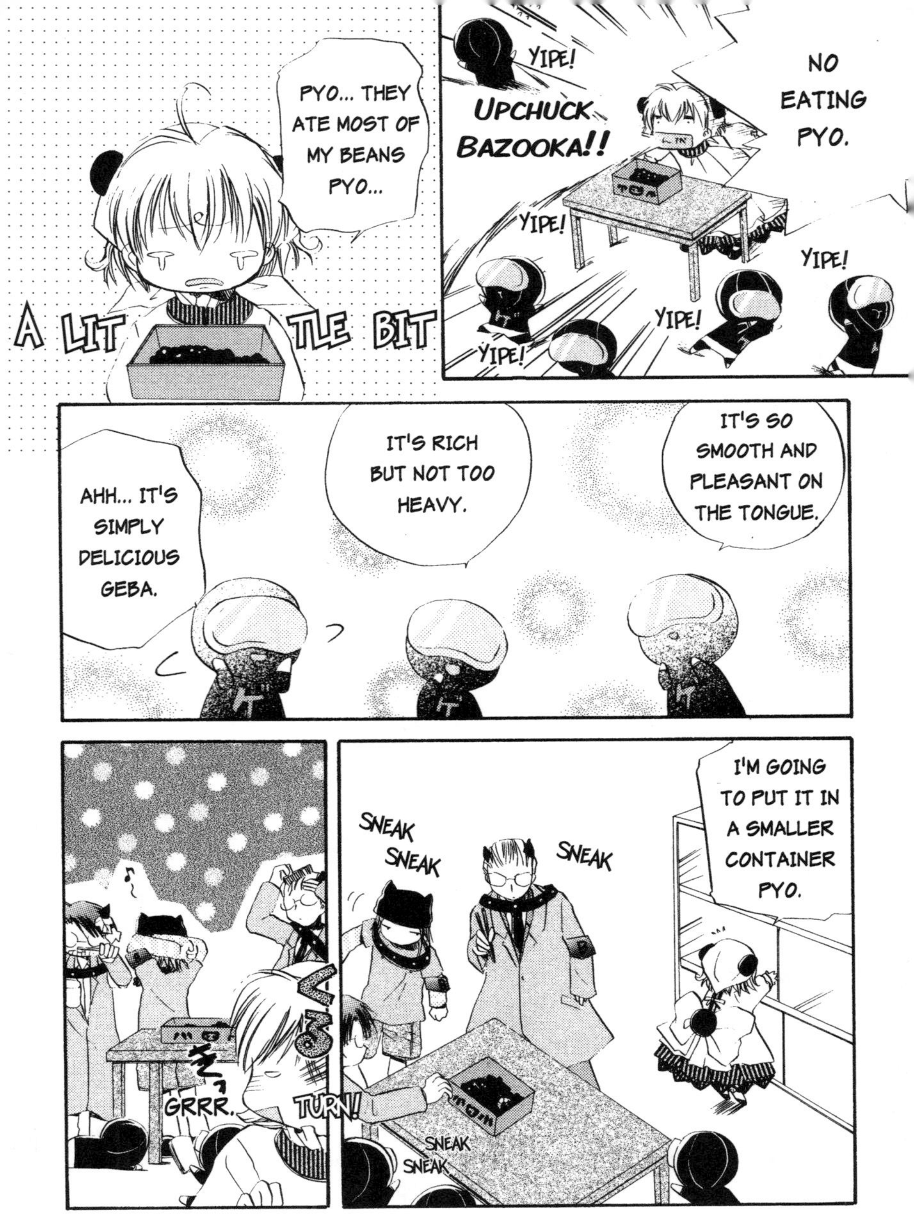
NO EATING PYO.
YIPE!
UPCHUCK BAZOOKA!!
YIPE!
YIPE!
YIPE!
YIPE!
YIPE!
PYO... THEY ATE MOST OF MY BEANS PYO...
A LITTLE BIT
IT'S SO SMOOTH AND PLEASANT ON THE TONGUE.
IT'S RICH BUT NOT TOO HEAVY.
AHH... IT'S SIMPLY DELICIOUS GEBA.
I'M GOING TO PUT IT IN A SMALLER CONTAINER PYO.
SNEAK
SNEAK SNEAK
SNEAK SNEAK
TURN!
GRRR.

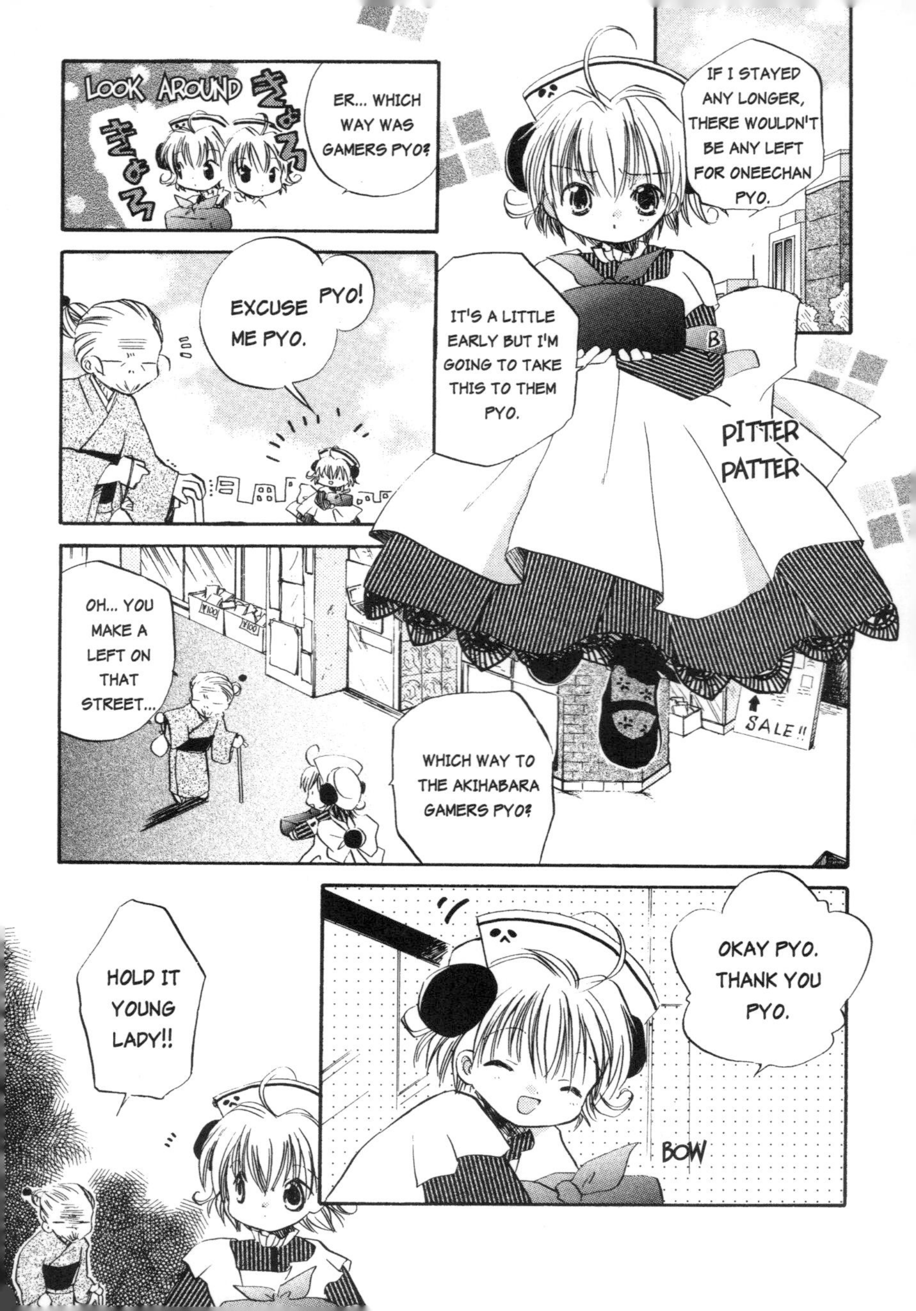
IF I STAYED ANY LONGER, THERE WOULDN'T BE ANY LEFT FOR ONEECHAN PYO.
IT'S A LITTLE EARLY BUT I'M GOING TO TAKE THIS TO THEM PYO.
B
PITTER PATTER
LOOK AROUND
きょろ
きょろ
ER... WHICH WAY WAS GAMERS PYO?
EXCUSE ME PYO.
PYO!
WHICH WAY TO THE AKIHABARA GAMERS PYO?
SALE!!
OH... YOU MAKE A LEFT ON THAT STREET...
OKAY PYO. THANK YOU PYO.
BOW
HOLD IT YOUNG LADY!!

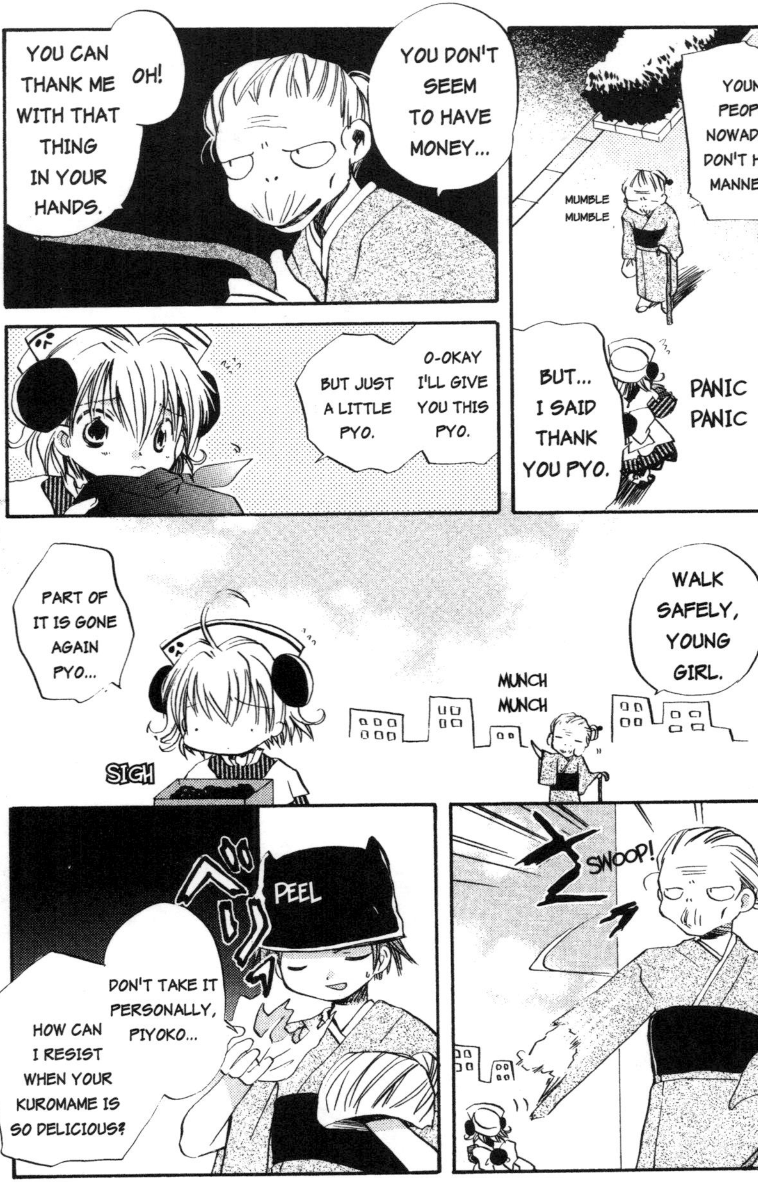
YOUNG PEOPLE NOWADAYS DON'T HAVE MANNERS.
MUMBLE MUMBLE
YOU DON'T SEEM TO HAVE MONEY...
OH!
YOU CAN THANK ME WITH THAT THING IN YOUR HANDS.
BUT... I SAID THANK YOU PYO.
PANIC PANIC
O-OKAY I'LL GIVE YOU THIS PYO.
BUT JUST A LITTLE PYO.
WALK SAFELY, YOUNG GIRL.
MUNCH MUNCH
PART OF IT IS GONE AGAIN PYO...
SIGH
SWOOP!
PEEL
DON'T TAKE IT PERSONALLY, PIYOKO...
HOW CAN I RESIST WHEN YOUR KUROMAME IS SO DELICIOUS?

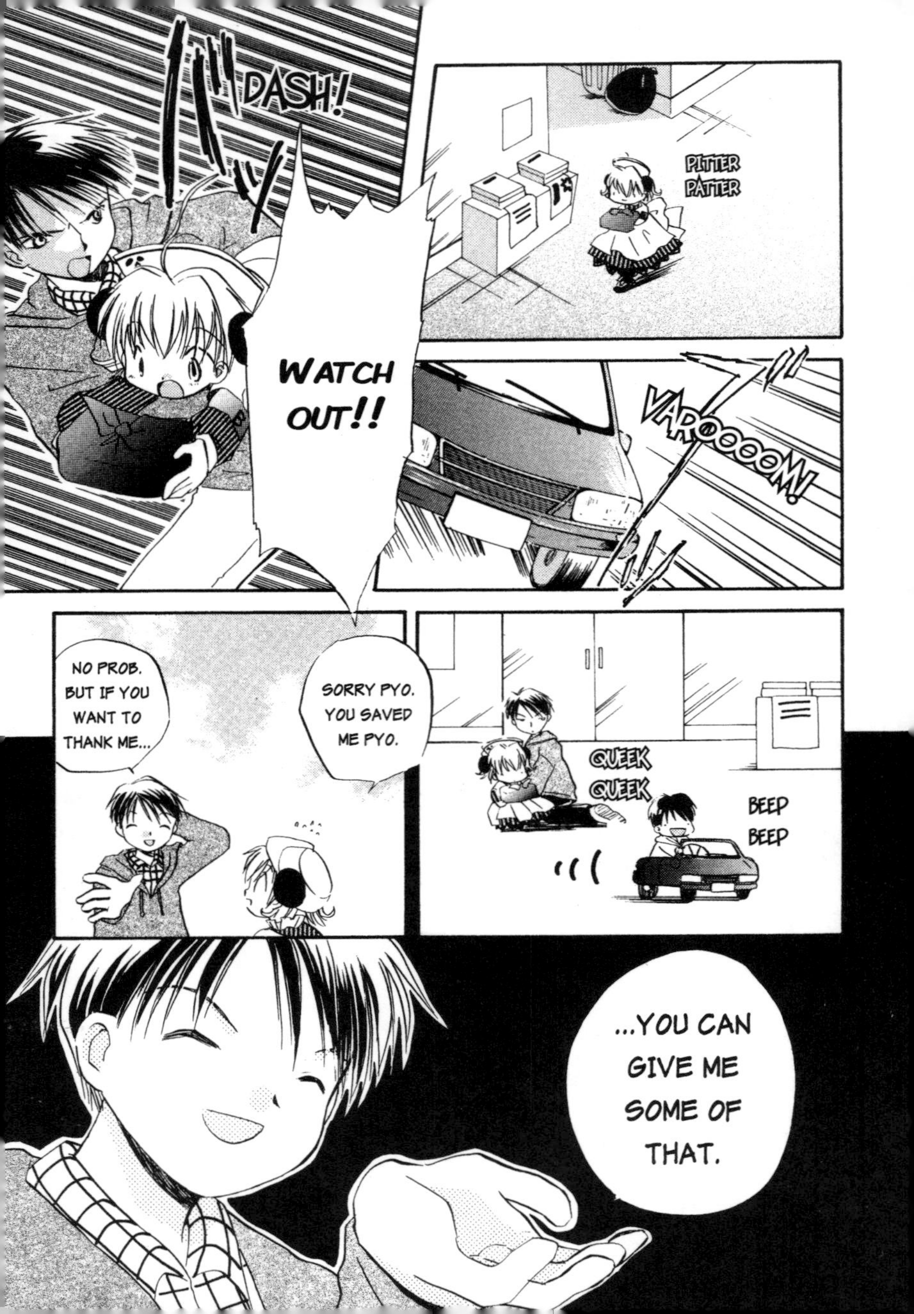
PITTER PATTER
VAROOOOOM!
DASH!
WATCH OUT!!
QUEEK QUEEK
BEEP BEEP
SORRY PYO. YOU SAVED ME PYO.
NO PROB. BUT IF YOU WANT TO THANK ME...
...YOU CAN GIVE ME SOME OF THAT.

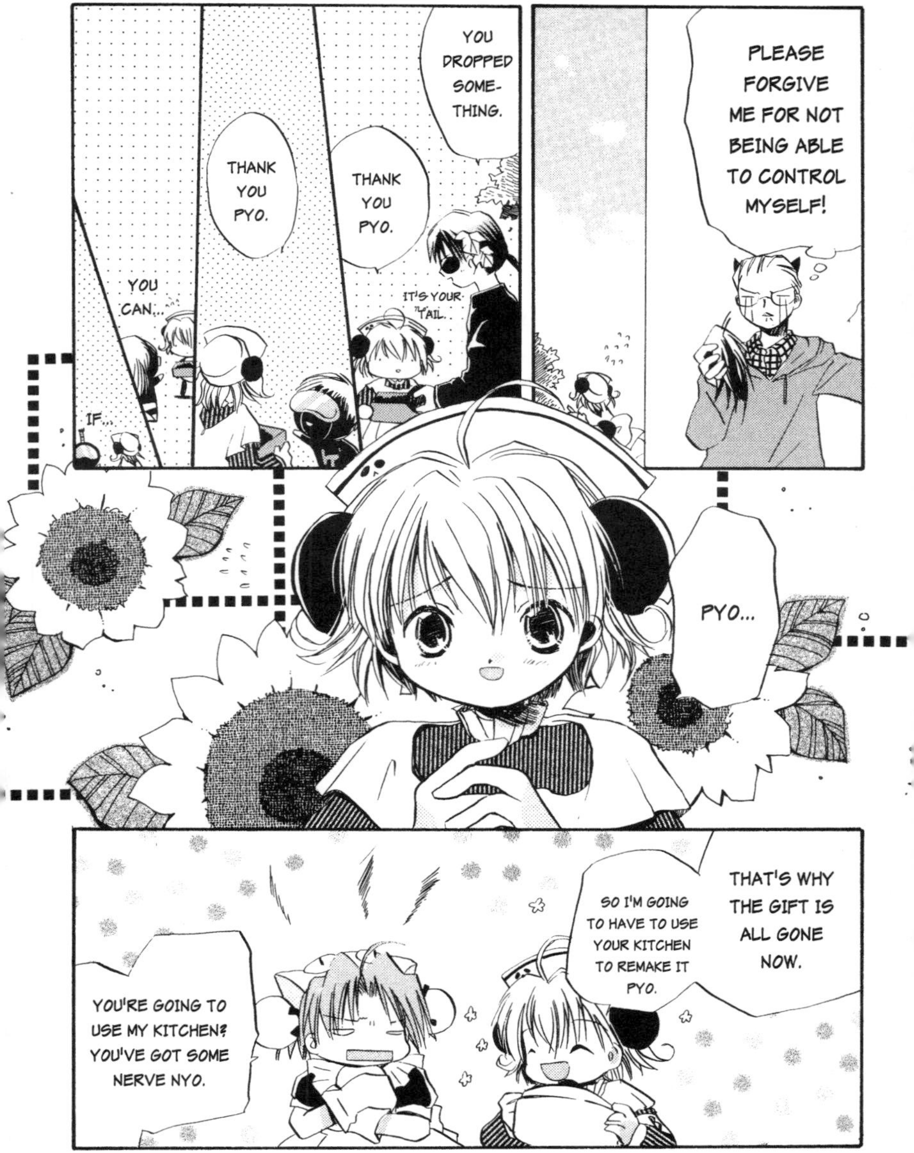
PLEASE FORGIVE ME FOR NOT BEING ABLE TO CONTROL MYSELF!
YOU DROPPED SOME-THING.
IT'S YOUR TAIL.
THANK YOU PYO.
THANK YOU PYO.
YOU CAN...
IF...
PYO...
THAT'S WHY THE GIFT IS ALL GONE NOW.
SO I'M GOING TO HAVE TO USE YOUR KITCHEN TO REMAKE IT PYO.
YOU'RE GOING TO USE MY KITCHEN? YOU'VE GOT SOME NERVE NYO.

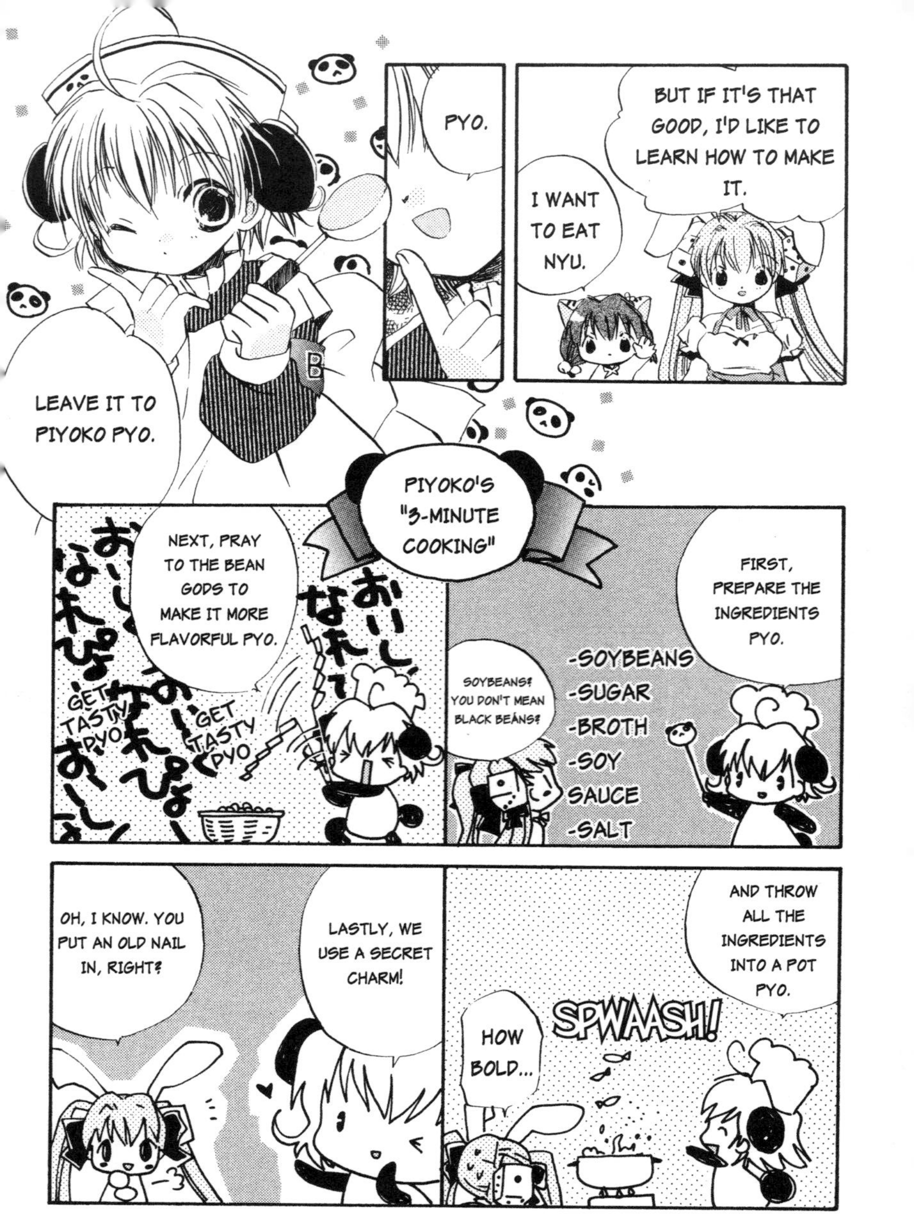
BUT IF IT'S THAT GOOD, I'D LIKE TO LEARN HOW TO MAKE IT.
I WANT TO EAT NYU.
PYO.
LEAVE IT TO PIYOKO PYO.
PIYOKO'S "3-MINUTE COOKING"
FIRST, PREPARE THE INGREDIENTS PYO.
-SOYBEANS
-SUGAR
-BROTH
-SOY SAUCE
-SALT
SOYBEANS? YOU DON'T MEAN BLACK BEANS?
NEXT, PRAY TO THE BEAN GODS TO MAKE IT MORE FLAVORFUL PYO.
GET TASTY PYO
GET TASTY PYO
AND THROW ALL THE INGREDIENTS INTO A POT PYO.
SPWAASH!
HOW BOLD...
LASTLY, WE USE A SECRET CHARM!
OH, I KNOW. YOU PUT AN OLD NAIL IN, RIGHT?

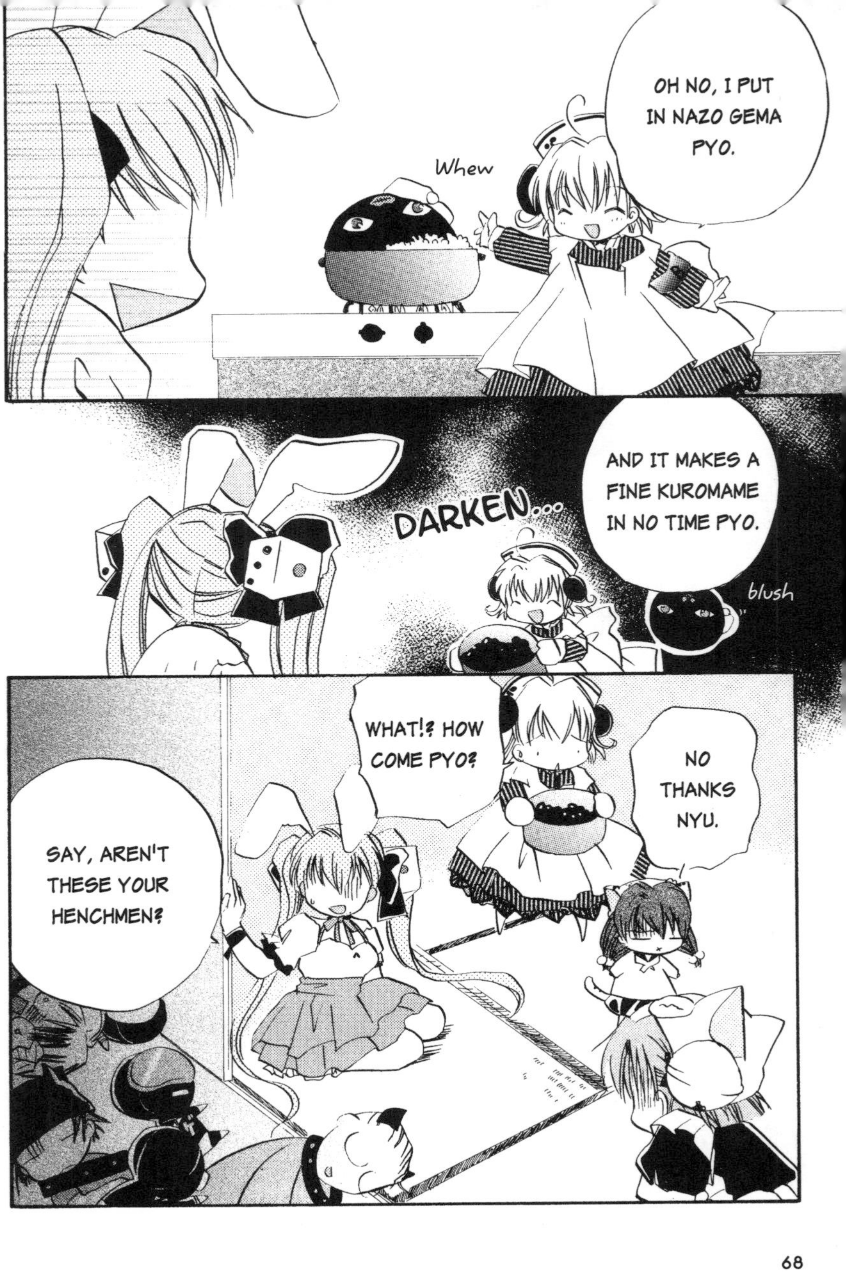
OH NO, I PUT IN NAZO GEMA PYO.
Whew
AND IT MAKES A FINE KUROMAME IN NO TIME PYO.
DARKEN...
blush
NO THANKS NYU.
WHAT!? HOW COME PYO?
SAY, AREN'T THESE YOUR HENCHMEN?

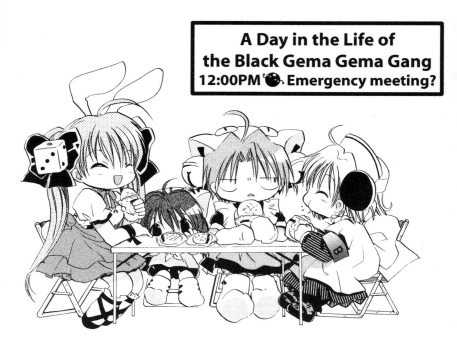

**A Day in the Life of
the Black Gema Gema Gang**
12:00PM Emergency meeting?

Nyo 7 A Midnight Gamers' Dream

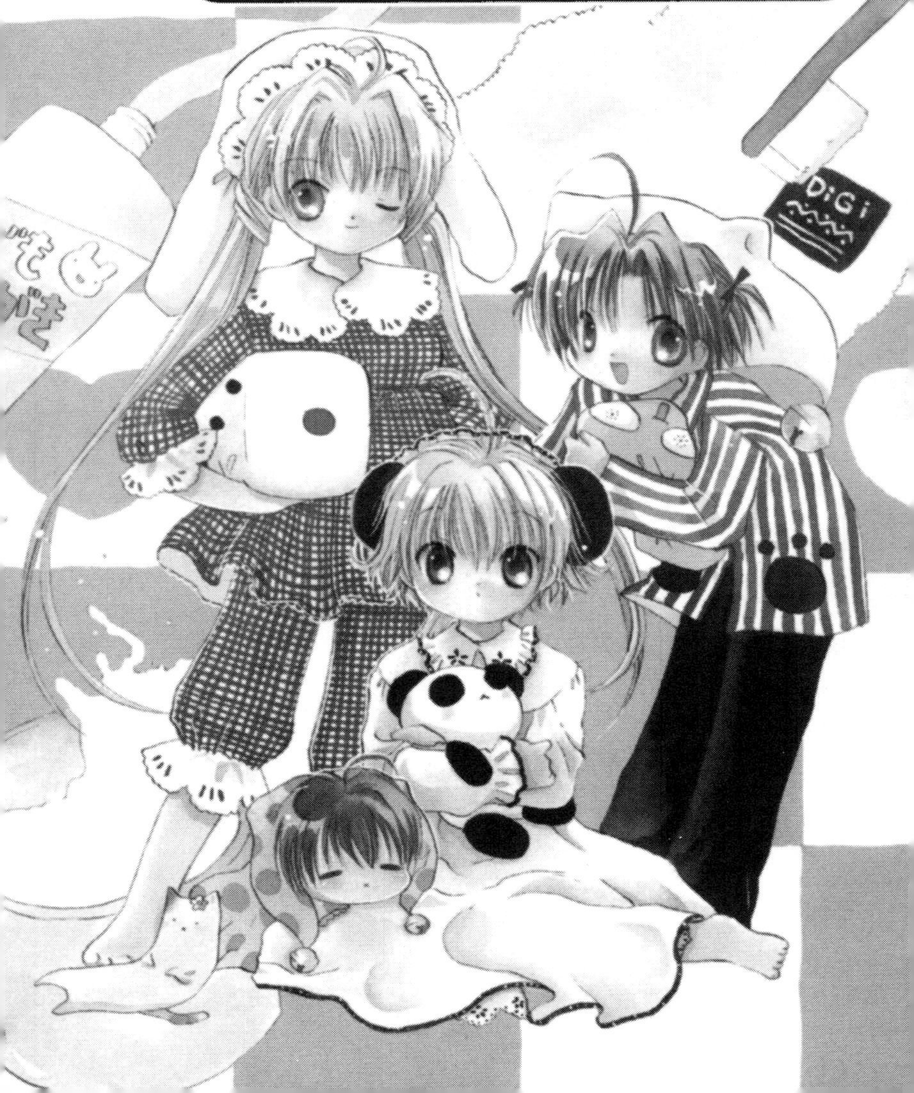
DiGi

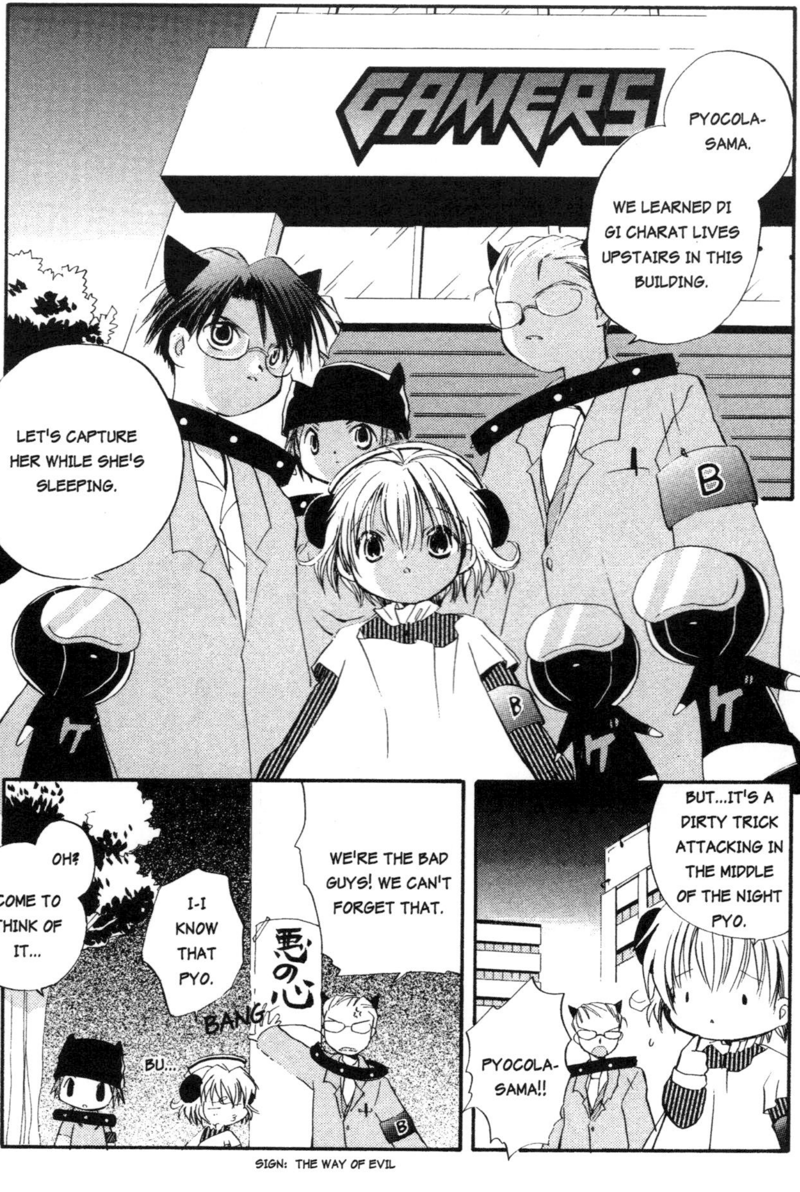
GAMERS
PYOCOLA-SAMA.
WE LEARNED DI GI CHARAT LIVES UPSTAIRS IN THIS BUILDING.
LET'S CAPTURE HER WHILE SHE'S SLEEPING.
BUT...IT'S A DIRTY TRICK ATTACKING IN THE MIDDLE OF THE NIGHT PYO.
PYOCOLA-SAMA!!
WE'RE THE BAD GUYS! WE CAN'T FORGET THAT.
悪の心
BANG
I-I KNOW THAT PYO.
OH?
COME TO THINK OF IT...
BU...

SIGN: THE WAY OF EVIL

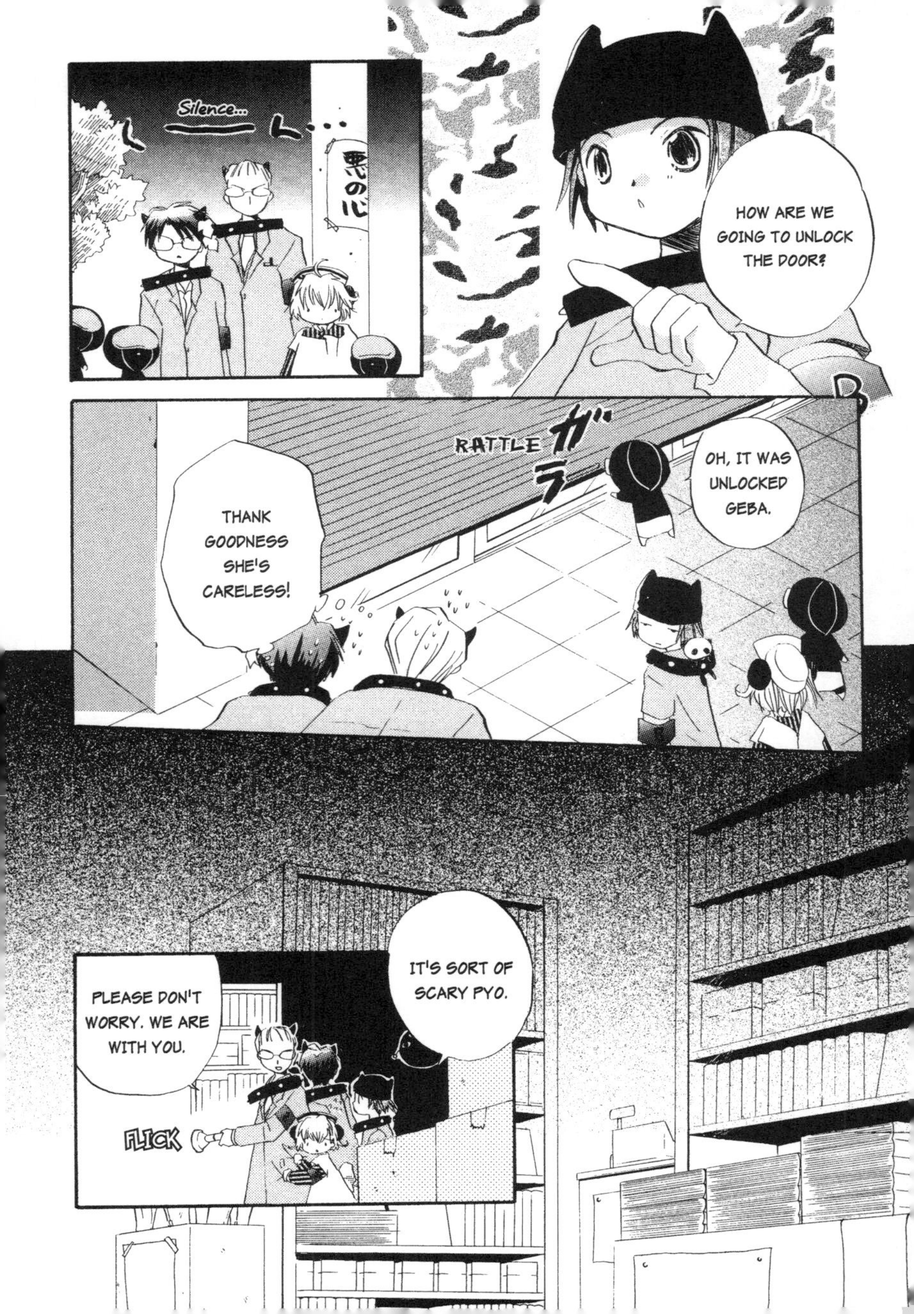
HOW ARE WE GOING TO UNLOCK THE DOOR?
Silence...
悪の心
RATTLE ガラ
OH, IT WAS UNLOCKED GEBA.
THANK GOODNESS SHE'S CARELESS!
IT'S SORT OF SCARY PYO.
PLEASE DON'T WORRY. WE ARE WITH YOU.
FLICK

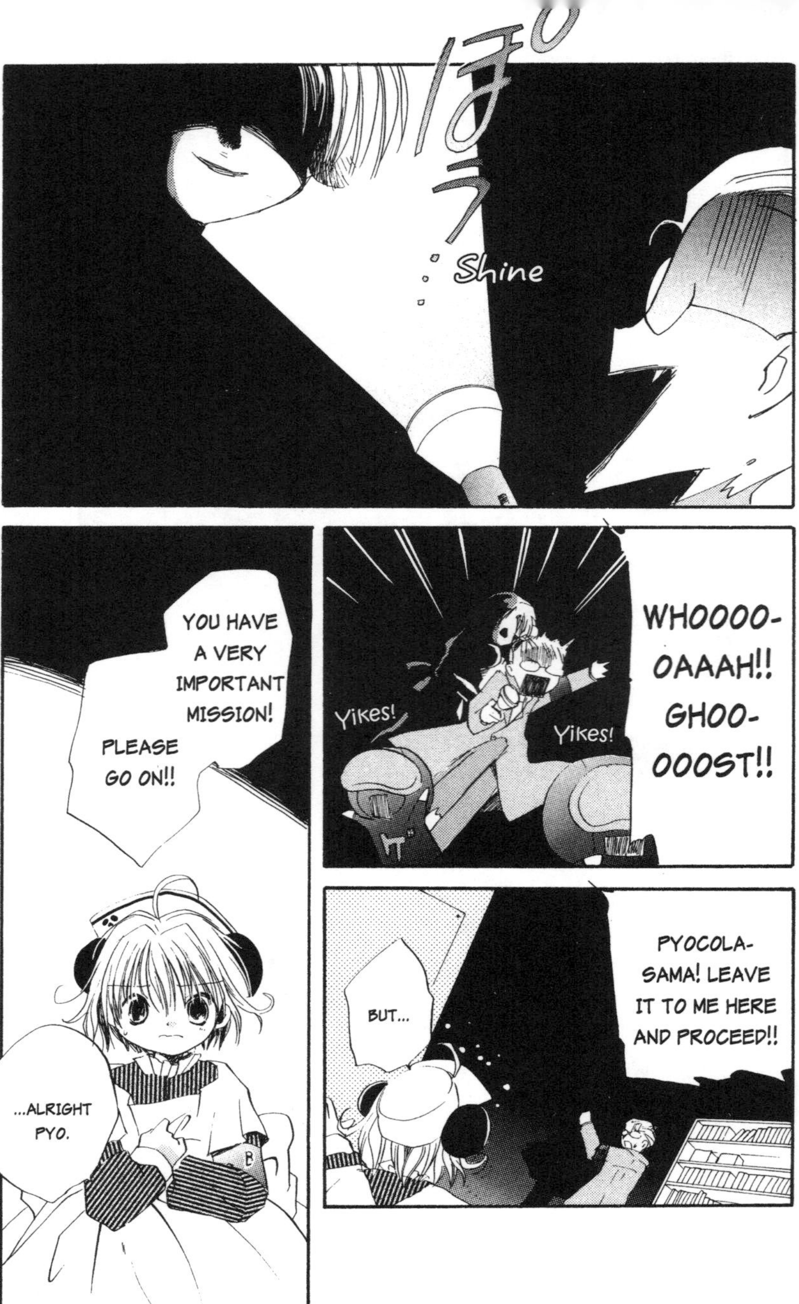

ぽう
Shine
WHOOOO-OAAAH!! GHOO-OOOST!!
Yikes!
Yikes!
PYOCOLA-SAMA! LEAVE IT TO ME HERE AND PROCEED!!
BUT...
YOU HAVE A VERY IMPORTANT MISSION!
PLEASE GO ON!!
...ALRIGHT PYO.

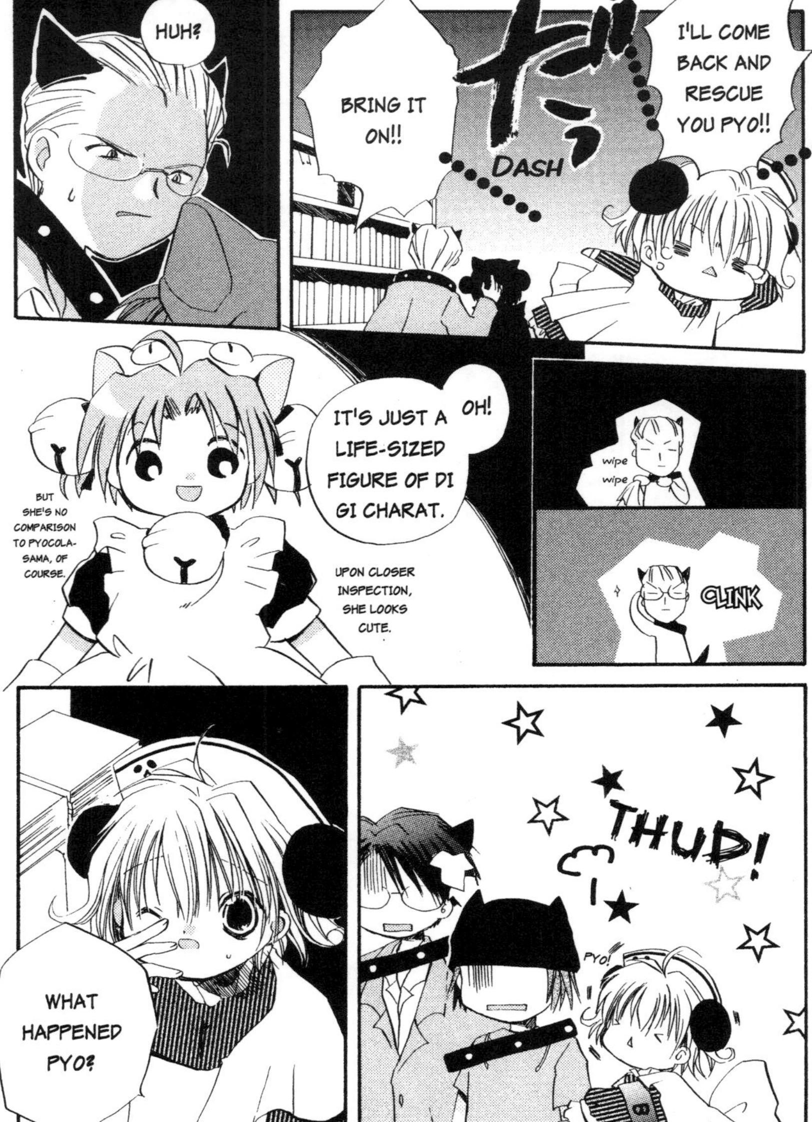
I'LL COME BACK AND RESCUE YOU PYO!!
ダッ
DASH
BRING IT ON!!
HUH?
wipe wipe
CLINK
OH!
IT'S JUST A LIFE-SIZED FIGURE OF DI GI CHARAT.
UPON CLOSER INSPECTION, SHE LOOKS CUTE.
BUT SHE'S NO COMPARISON TO PYOCOLA-SAMA, OF COURSE.
THUD!
PYO!
WHAT HAPPENED PYO?

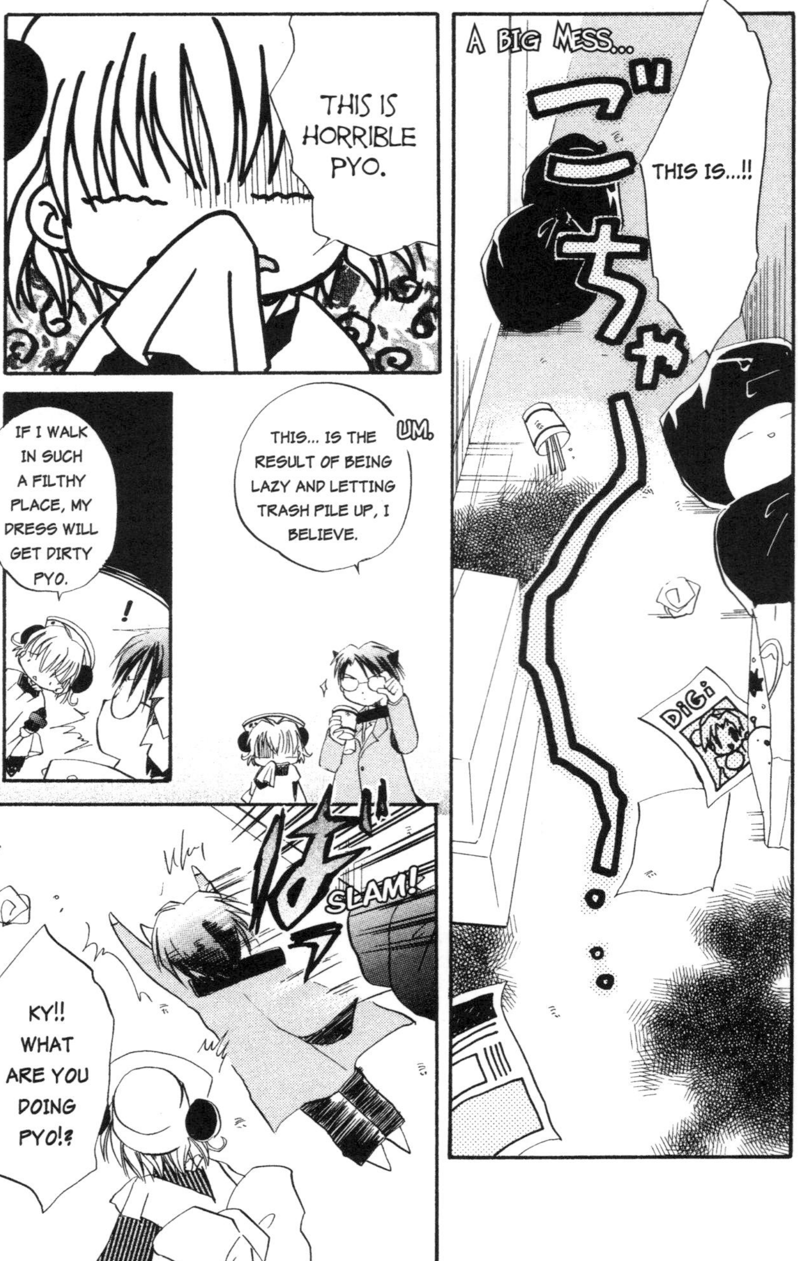
A BIG MESS...
THIS IS...!!
THIS IS HORRIBLE PYO.
UM.
THIS... IS THE RESULT OF BEING LAZY AND LETTING TRASH PILE UP, I BELIEVE.
IF I WALK IN SUCH A FILTHY PLACE, MY DRESS WILL GET DIRTY PYO.
!
SLAM!
KY!! WHAT ARE YOU DOING PYO!?

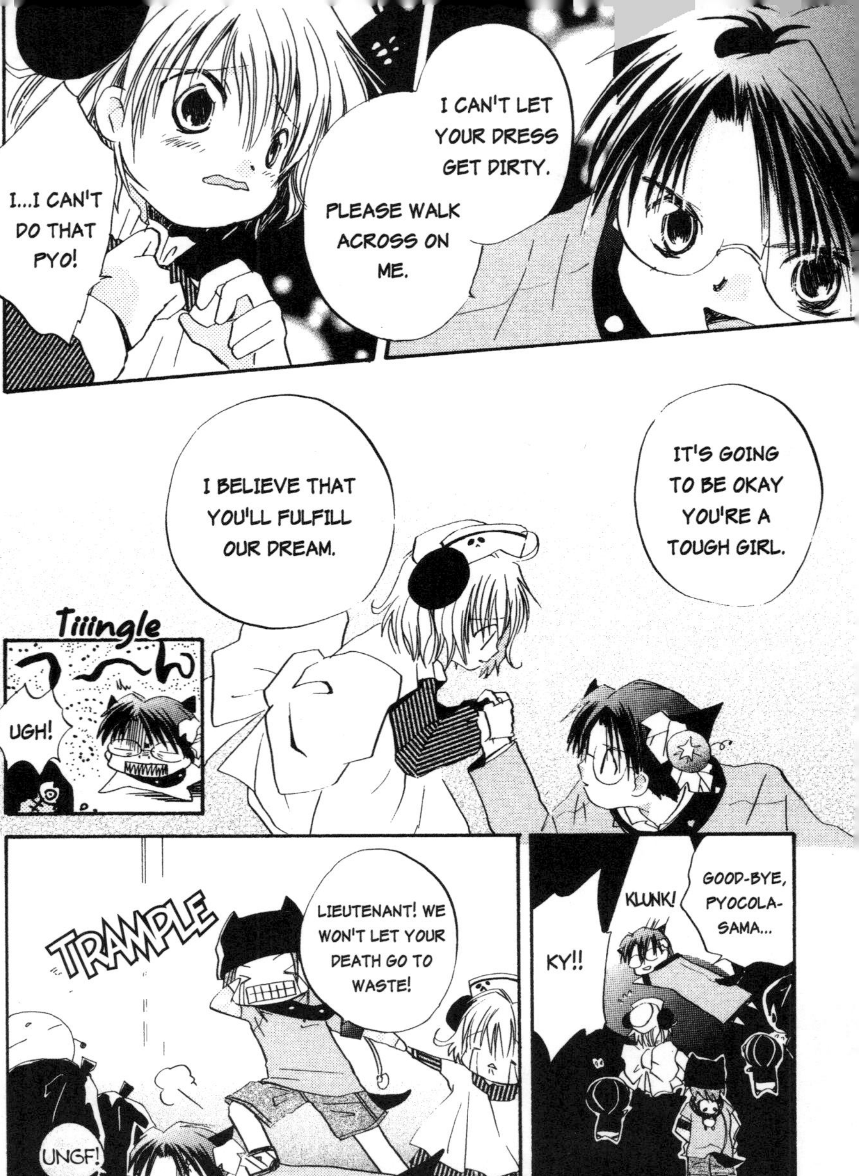
I CAN'T LET YOUR DRESS GET DIRTY.
PLEASE WALK ACROSS ON ME.
I...I CAN'T DO THAT PYO!
IT'S GOING TO BE OKAY YOU'RE A TOUGH GIRL.
I BELIEVE THAT YOU'LL FULFILL OUR DREAM.
Tiiingle
つ〜ん
UGH!
GOOD-BYE, PYOCOLA-SAMA...
KLUNK!
KY!!
TRAMPLE
LIEUTENANT! WE WON'T LET YOUR DEATH GO TO WASTE!
UNGF!

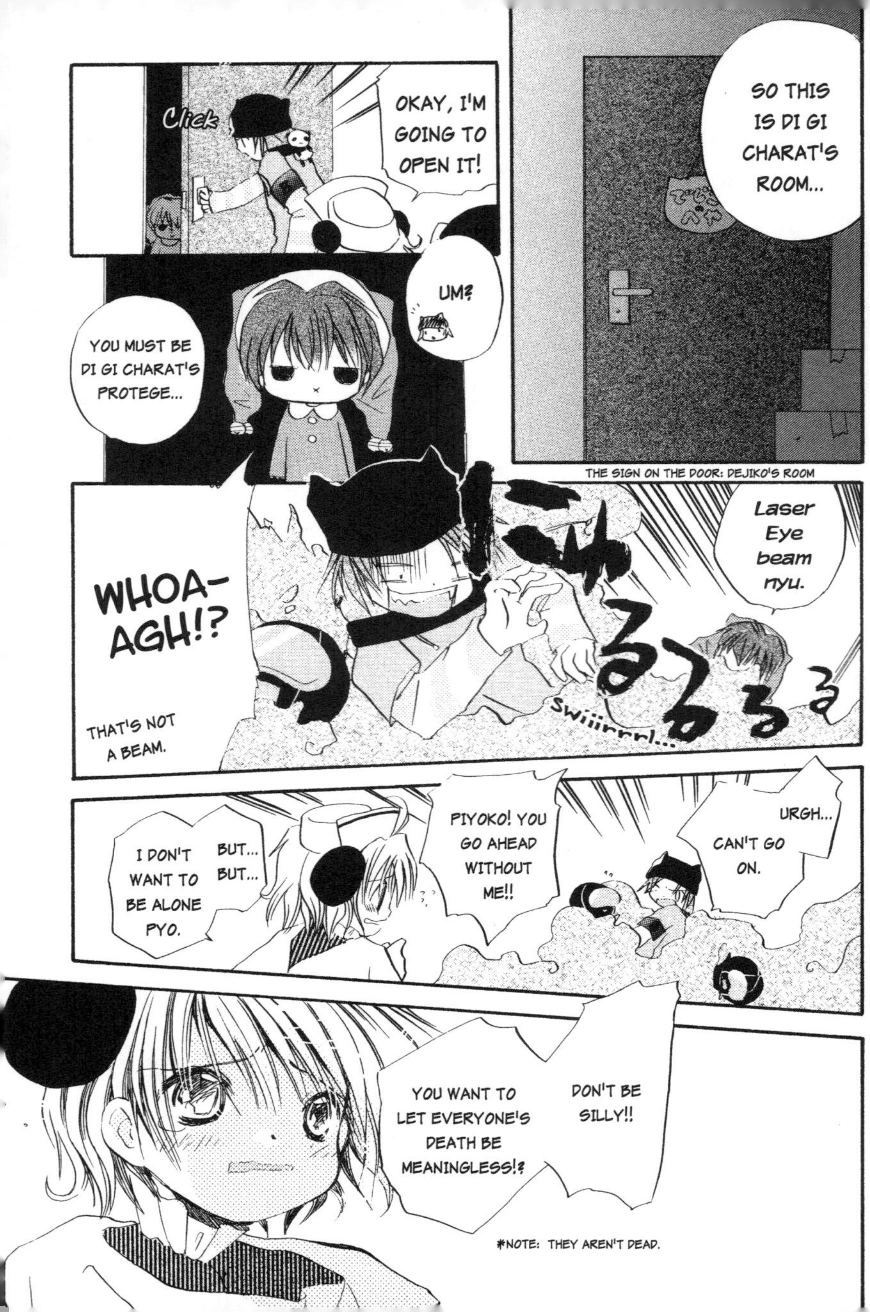
SO THIS IS DI GI CHARAT'S ROOM...
THE SIGN ON THE DOOR: DEJIKO'S ROOM
OKAY, I'M GOING TO OPEN IT!
Click
UM?
YOU MUST BE DI GI CHARAT'S PROTEGE...
Laser Eye beam nyu.
WHOA-AGH!?
Swiiirrrl...
THAT'S NOT A BEAM.
URGH... CAN'T GO ON.
PIYOKO! YOU GO AHEAD WITHOUT ME!!
BUT... BUT...
I DON'T WANT TO BE ALONE PYO.
DON'T BE SILLY!!
YOU WANT TO LET EVERYONE'S DEATH BE MEANINGLESS!?
*NOTE: THEY AREN'T DEAD.

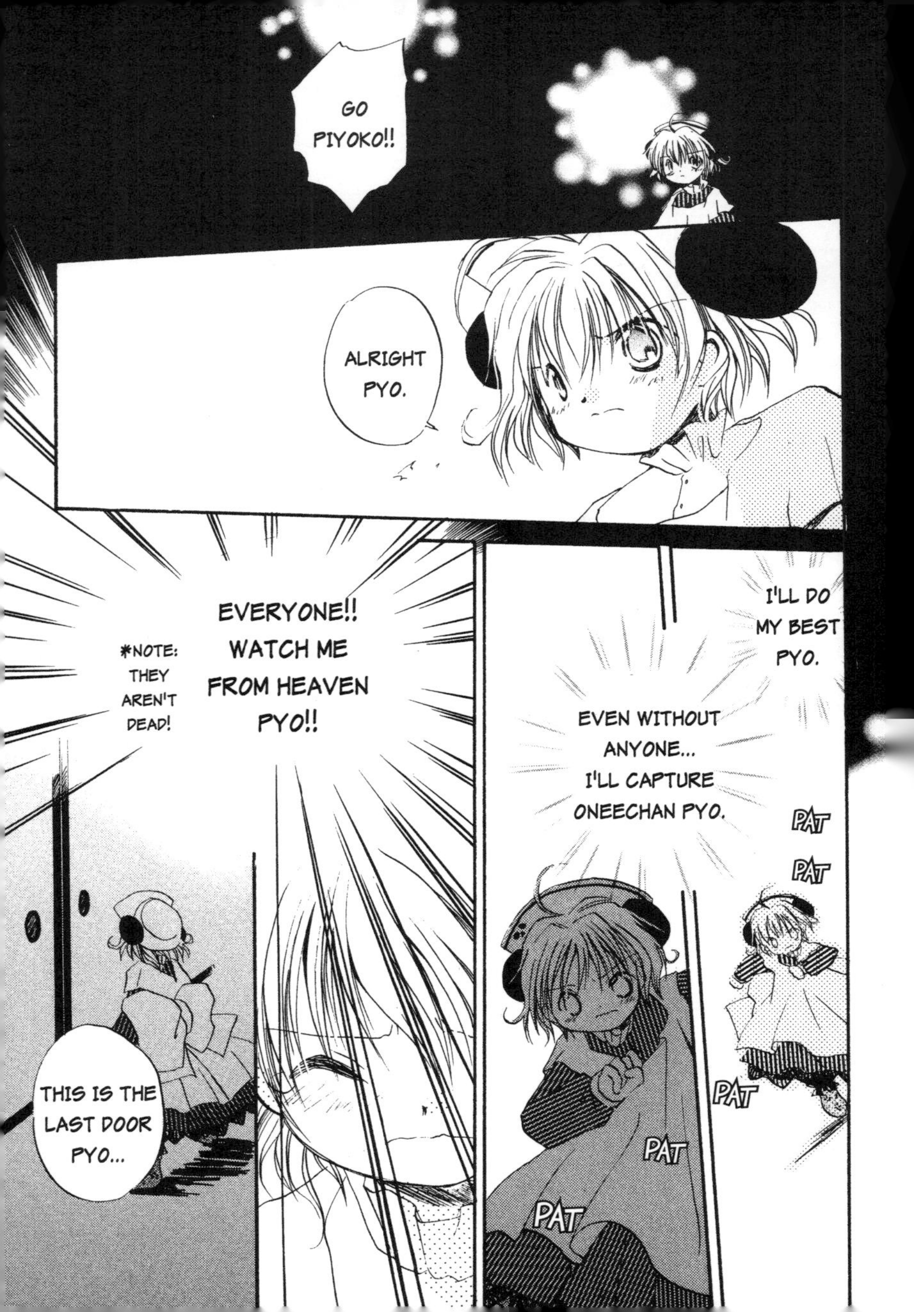
GO PIYOKO!!
ALRIGHT PYO.
I'LL DO MY BEST PYO.
EVEN WITHOUT ANYONE... I'LL CAPTURE ONEECHAN PYO.
PAT
PAT
PAT
PAT
PAT
EVERYONE!! WATCH ME FROM HEAVEN PYO!!
*NOTE: THEY AREN'T DEAD!
THIS IS THE LAST DOOR PYO...

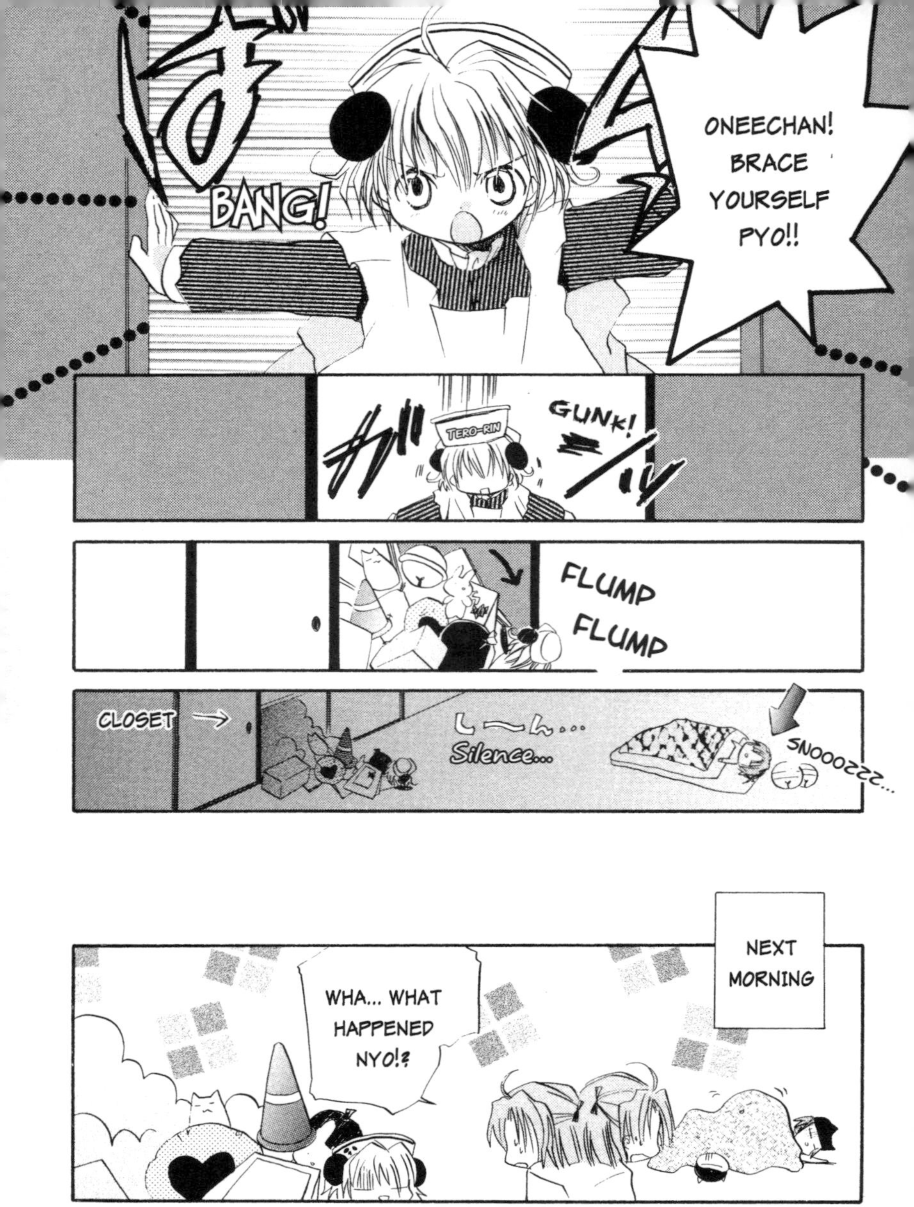
ONEECHAN! BRACE YOURSELF PYO!!
BANG!
GUNK!
TERO-RIN
FLUMP
FLUMP
SNOOOZZZZ...
しーん...
Silence...
CLOSET
NEXT MORNING
WHA... WHAT HAPPENED NYO!?

A Day in the Life of
the Black Gema Gema Gang
2:30 PM Work

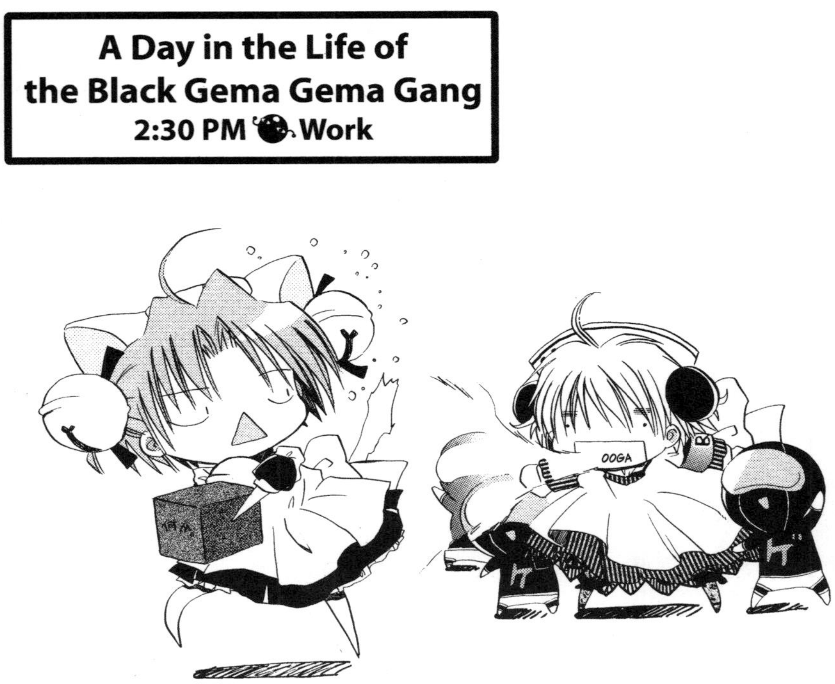
OOGA

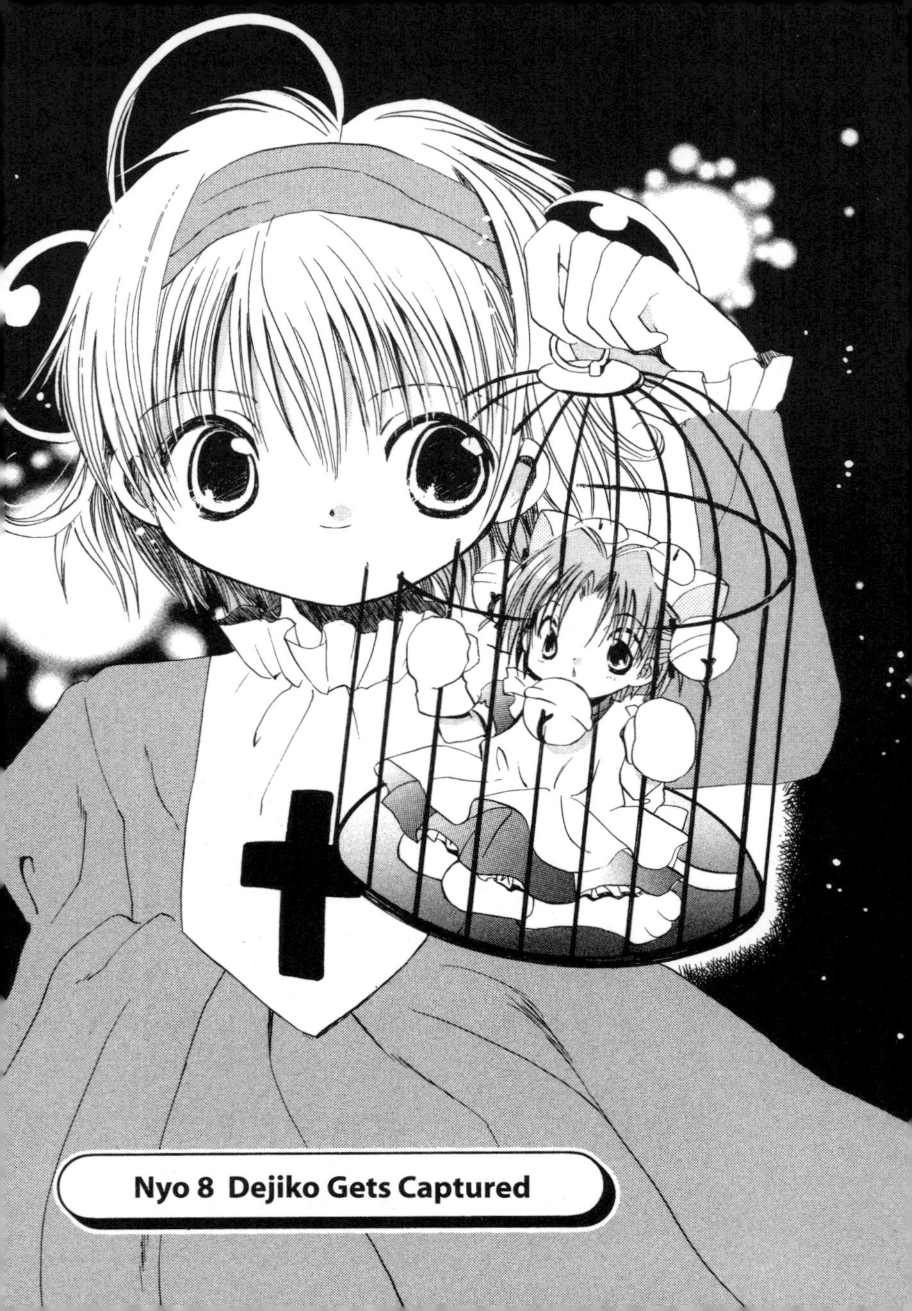

Nyo 8 Dejiko Gets Captured

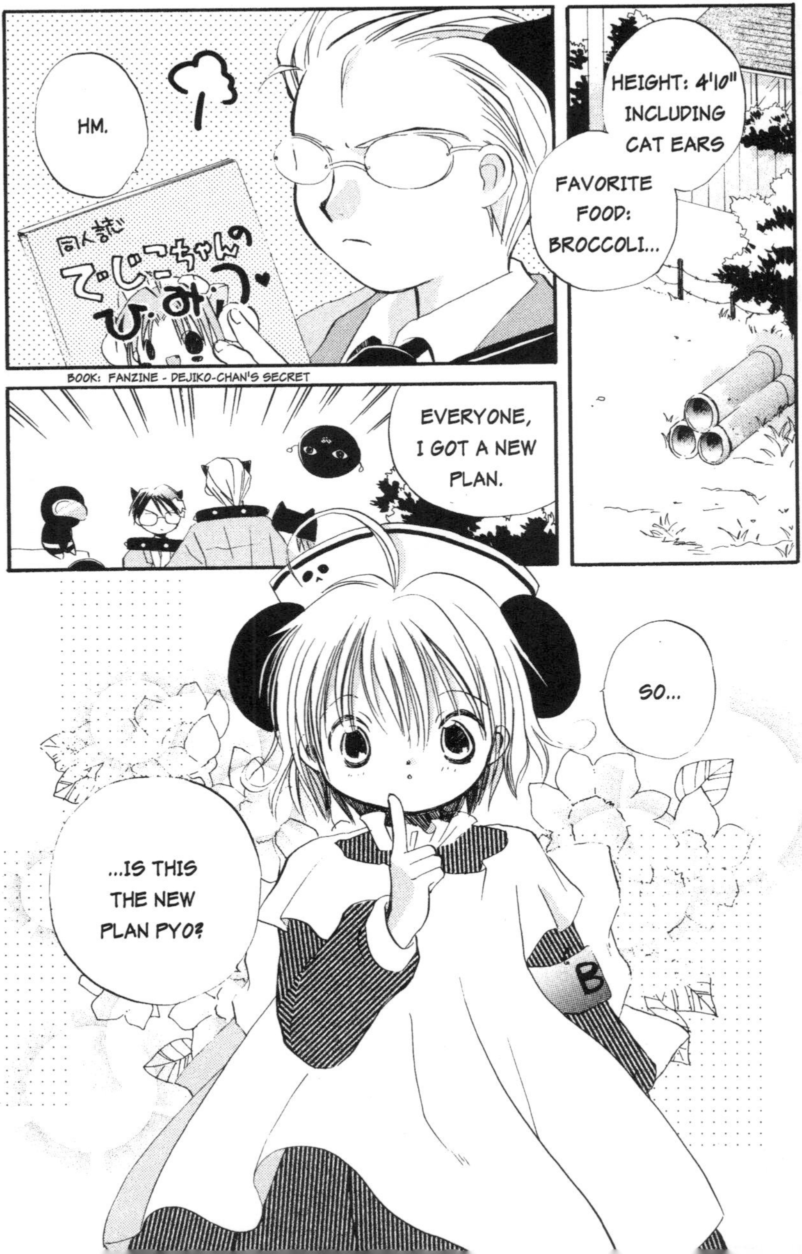
HEIGHT: 4'10" INCLUDING CAT EARS
FAVORITE FOOD: BROCCOLI...
HM.
同人誌
でじこちゃんのひみつ
BOOK: FANZINE - DEJIKO-CHAN'S SECRET
EVERYONE, I GOT A NEW PLAN.
SO...
...IS THIS THE NEW PLAN PYO?
B

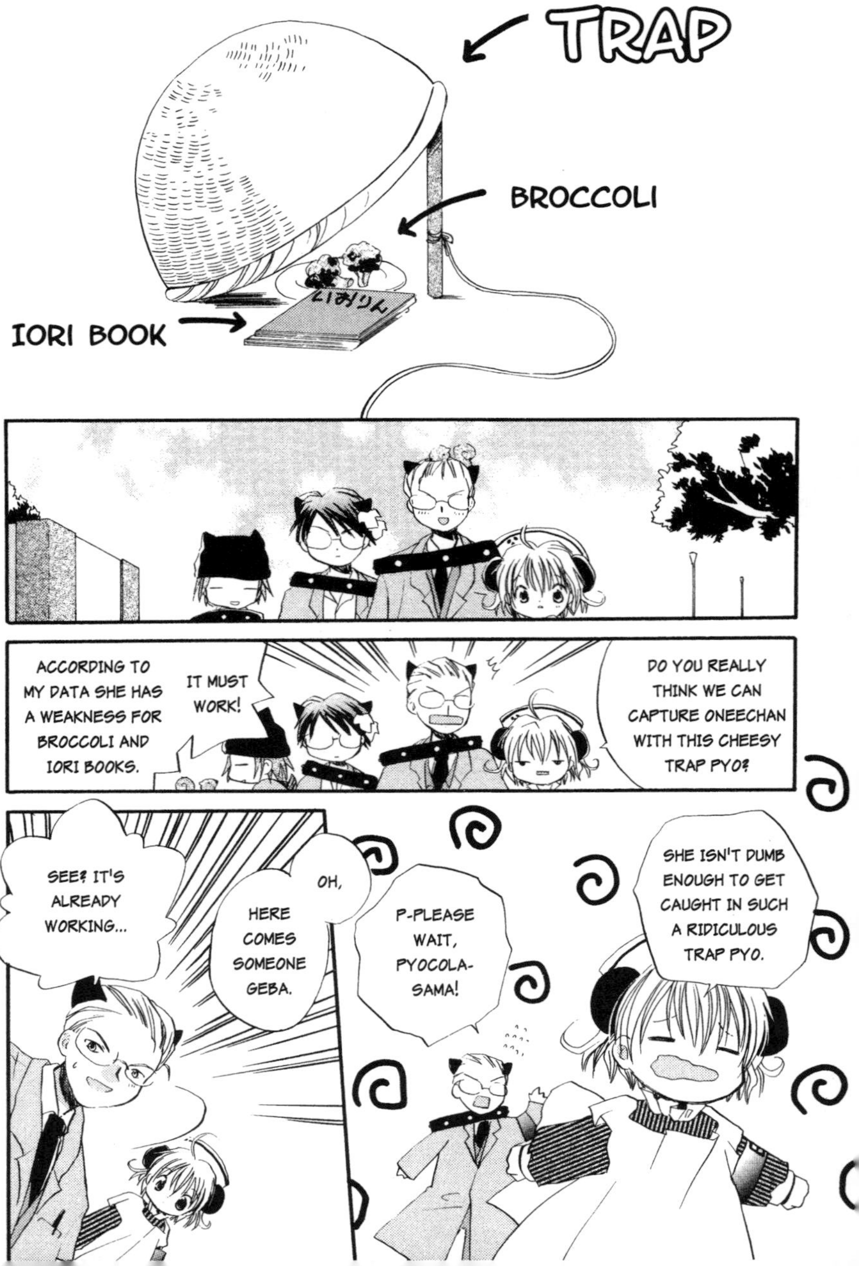
TRAP
BROCCOLI
IORI BOOK
DO YOU REALLY THINK WE CAN CAPTURE ONEECHAN WITH THIS CHEESY TRAP PYO?
IT MUST WORK!
ACCORDING TO MY DATA SHE HAS A WEAKNESS FOR BROCCOLI AND IORI BOOKS.
SHE ISN'T DUMB ENOUGH TO GET CAUGHT IN SUCH A RIDICULOUS TRAP PYO.
P-PLEASE WAIT, PYOCOLA-SAMA!
OH,
HERE COMES SOMEONE GEBA.
SEE? IT'S ALREADY WORKING...

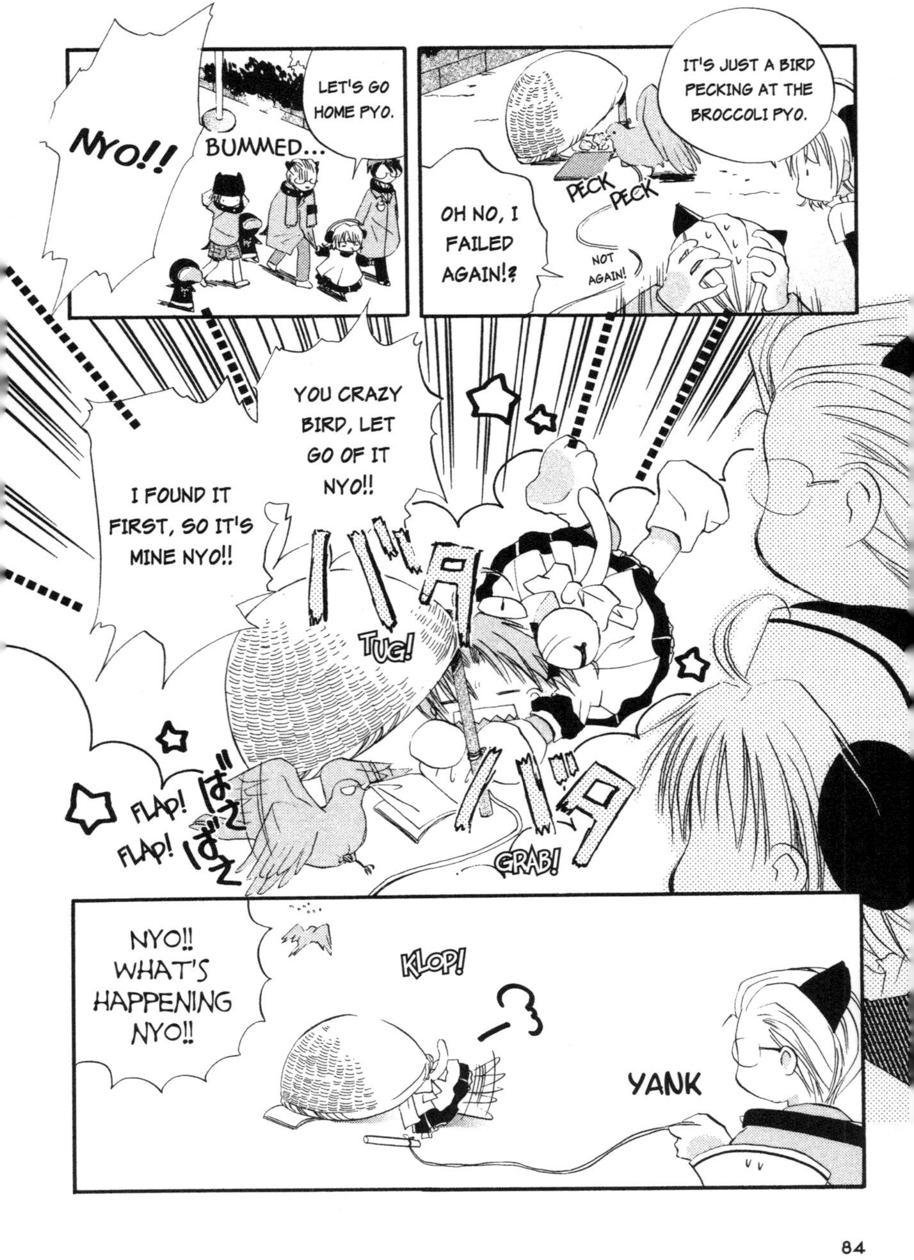
IT'S JUST A BIRD PECKING AT THE BROCCOLI PYO.
PECK PECK
OH NO, I FAILED AGAIN!?
NOT AGAIN!
LET'S GO HOME PYO.
BUMMED...
NYO!!
YOU CRAZY BIRD, LET GO OF IT NYO!!
I FOUND IT FIRST, SO IT'S MINE NYO!!
TUG!
GRAB!
ばさ ばさ
FLAP! FLAP!
KLOP!
NYO!! WHAT'S HAPPENING NYO!!
YANK

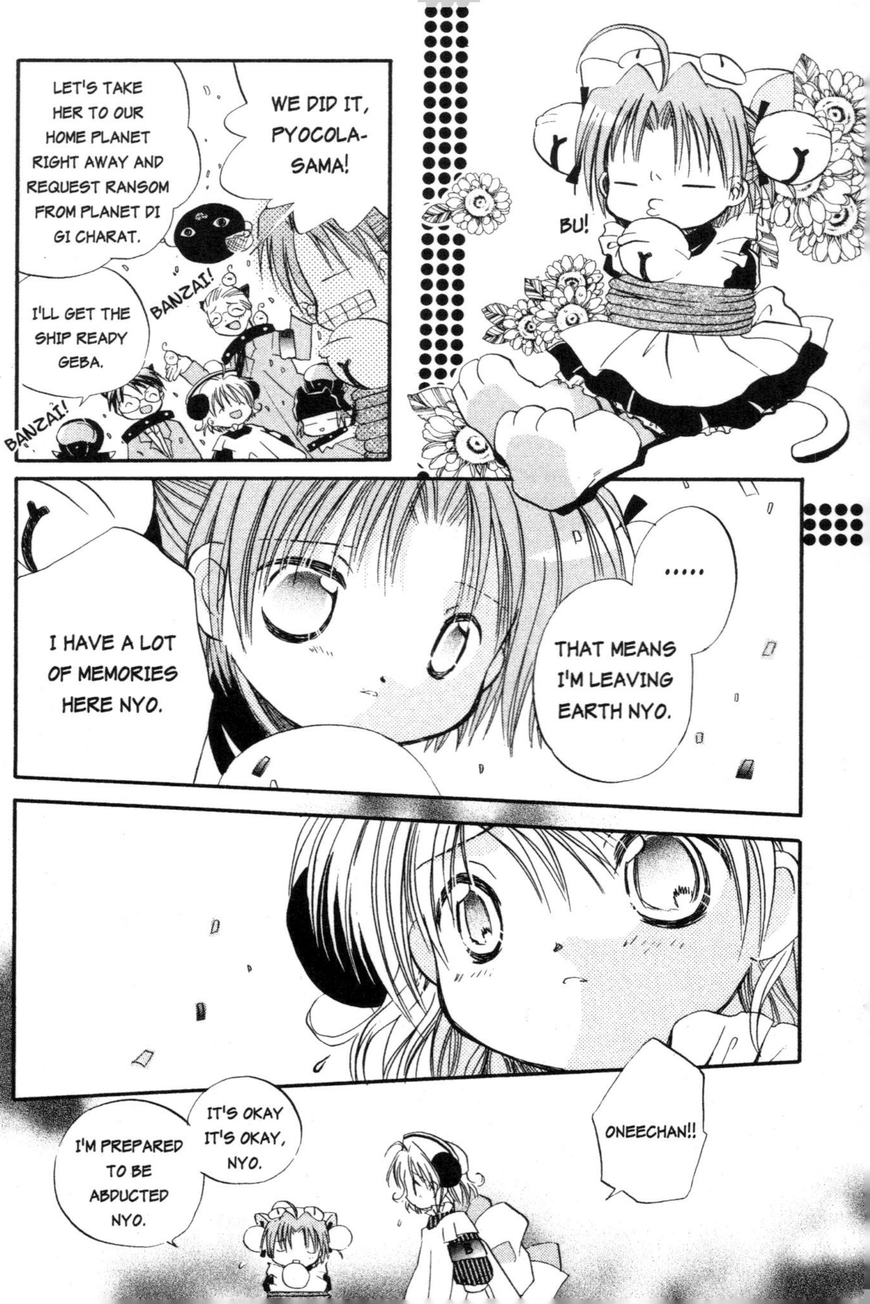
BU!
WE DID IT, PYOCOLA-SAMA!
LET'S TAKE HER TO OUR HOME PLANET RIGHT AWAY AND REQUEST RANSOM FROM PLANET DI GI CHARAT.
BANZAI!
I'LL GET THE SHIP READY GEBA.
BANZAI!
.....
THAT MEANS I'M LEAVING EARTH NYO.
I HAVE A LOT OF MEMORIES HERE NYO.
ONEECHAN!!
IT'S OKAY IT'S OKAY, NYO.
I'M PREPARED TO BE ABDUCTED NYO.

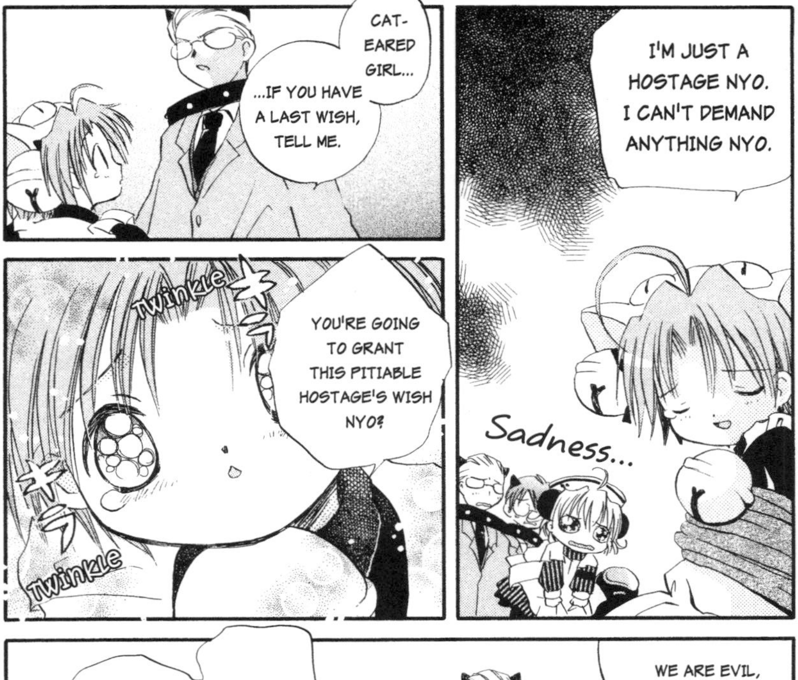
I'M JUST A HOSTAGE NYO. I CAN'T DEMAND ANYTHING NYO.
Sadness...
CAT-EARED GIRL...
...IF YOU HAVE A LAST WISH, TELL ME.
TWINKLE
YOU'RE GOING TO GRANT THIS PITIABLE HOSTAGE'S WISH NYO?
TWINKLE
WE ARE EVIL, BUT NOT DEVILS. I GUESS WE CAN GRANT YOUR REQUEST.
B
THANK YOU NYO.
YOU'RE LIKE AN ANGEL NYO.
AMEN.

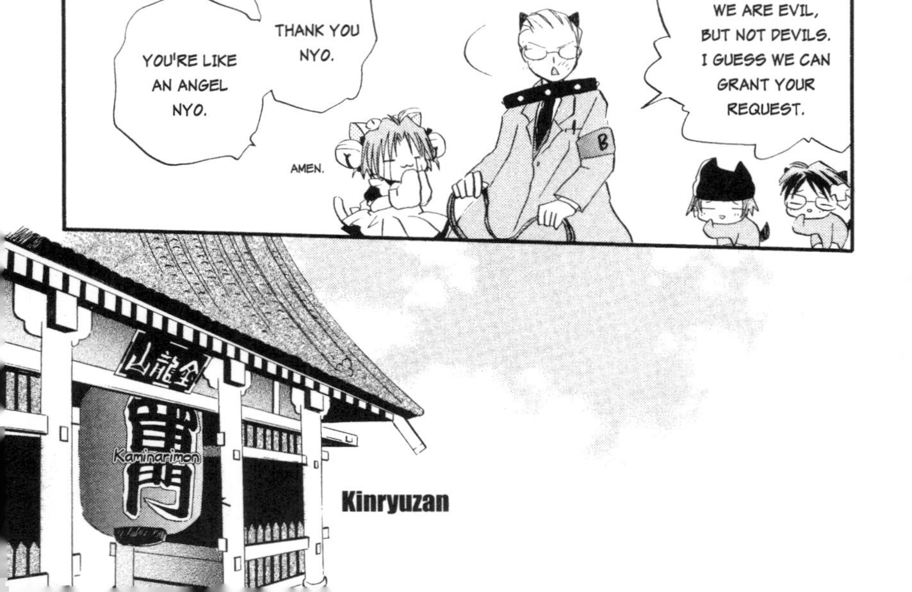
金龍山
雷門
Kaminarimon

Kinryuzan

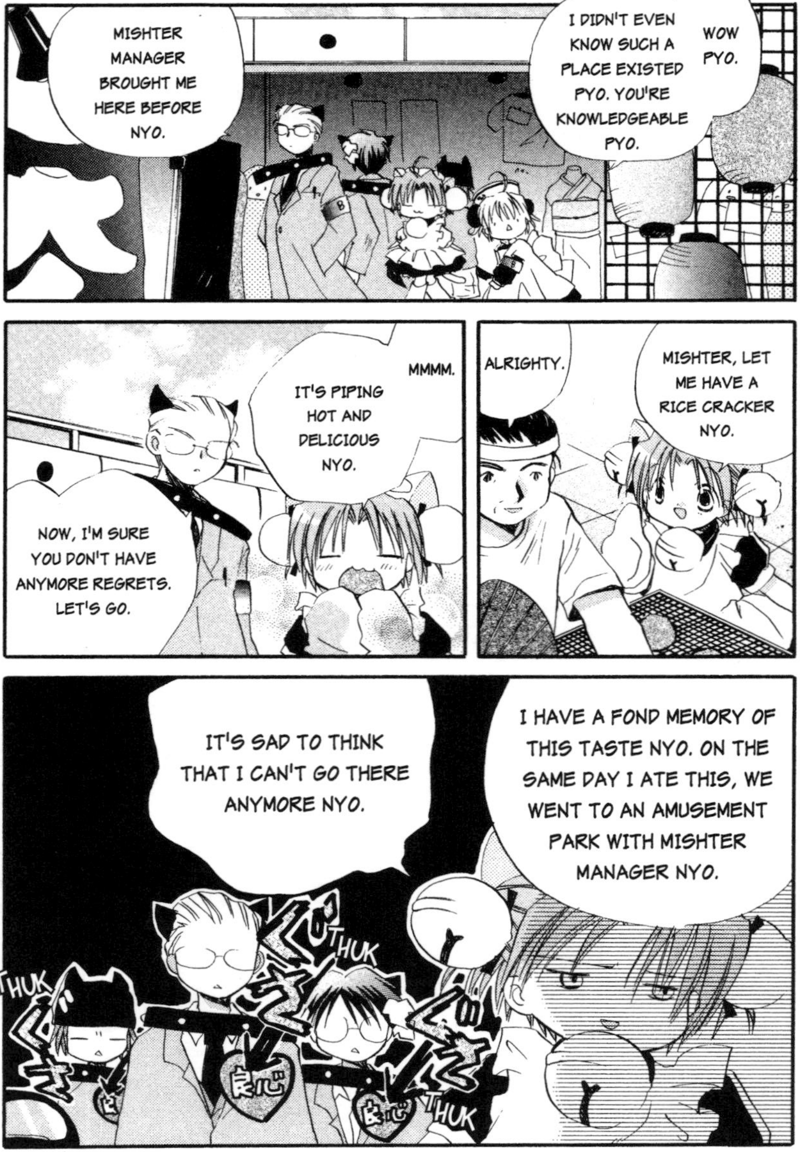
WOW PYO.
I DIDN'T EVEN KNOW SUCH A PLACE EXISTED PYO. YOU'RE KNOWLEDGEABLE PYO.
MISHTER MANAGER BROUGHT ME HERE BEFORE NYO.
MISHTER, LET ME HAVE A RICE CRACKER NYO.
ALRIGHTY.
MMMM.
IT'S PIPING HOT AND DELICIOUS NYO.
NOW, I'M SURE YOU DON'T HAVE ANYMORE REGRETS. LET'S GO.
I HAVE A FOND MEMORY OF THIS TASTE NYO. ON THE SAME DAY I ATE THIS, WE WENT TO AN AMUSEMENT PARK WITH MISHTER MANAGER NYO.
IT'S SAD TO THINK THAT I CAN'T GO THERE ANYMORE NYO.
THUK
THUK
THUK

THE HEARTS OF THE THREE: CONSCIENCE

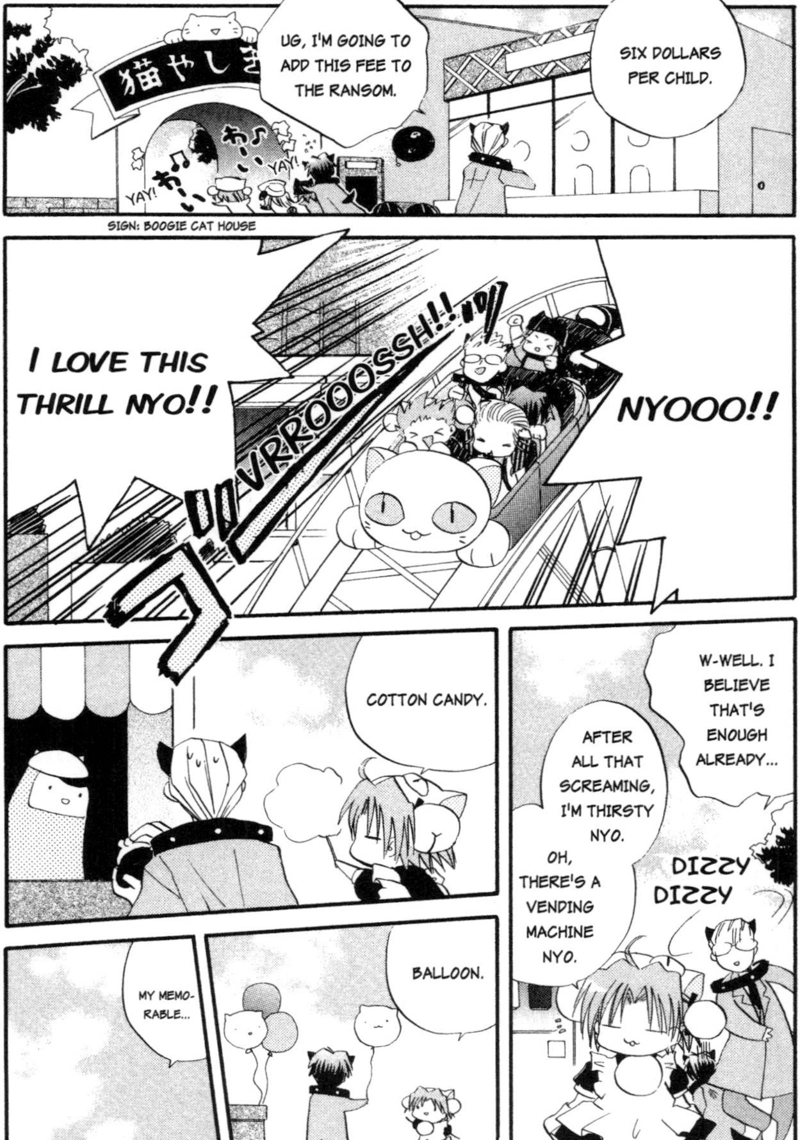
SIX DOLLARS PER CHILD.
UG, I'M GOING TO ADD THIS FEE TO THE RANSOM.
YAY!
YAY!
SIGN: BOOGIE CAT HOUSE
NYOOO!!
VRROOOSSH!!
I LOVE THIS THRILL NYO!!
W-WELL. I BELIEVE THAT'S ENOUGH ALREADY...
AFTER ALL THAT SCREAMING, I'M THIRSTY NYO.
DIZZY DIZZY
OH, THERE'S A VENDING MACHINE NYO.
COTTON CANDY.
BALLOON.
MY MEMO-RABLE...

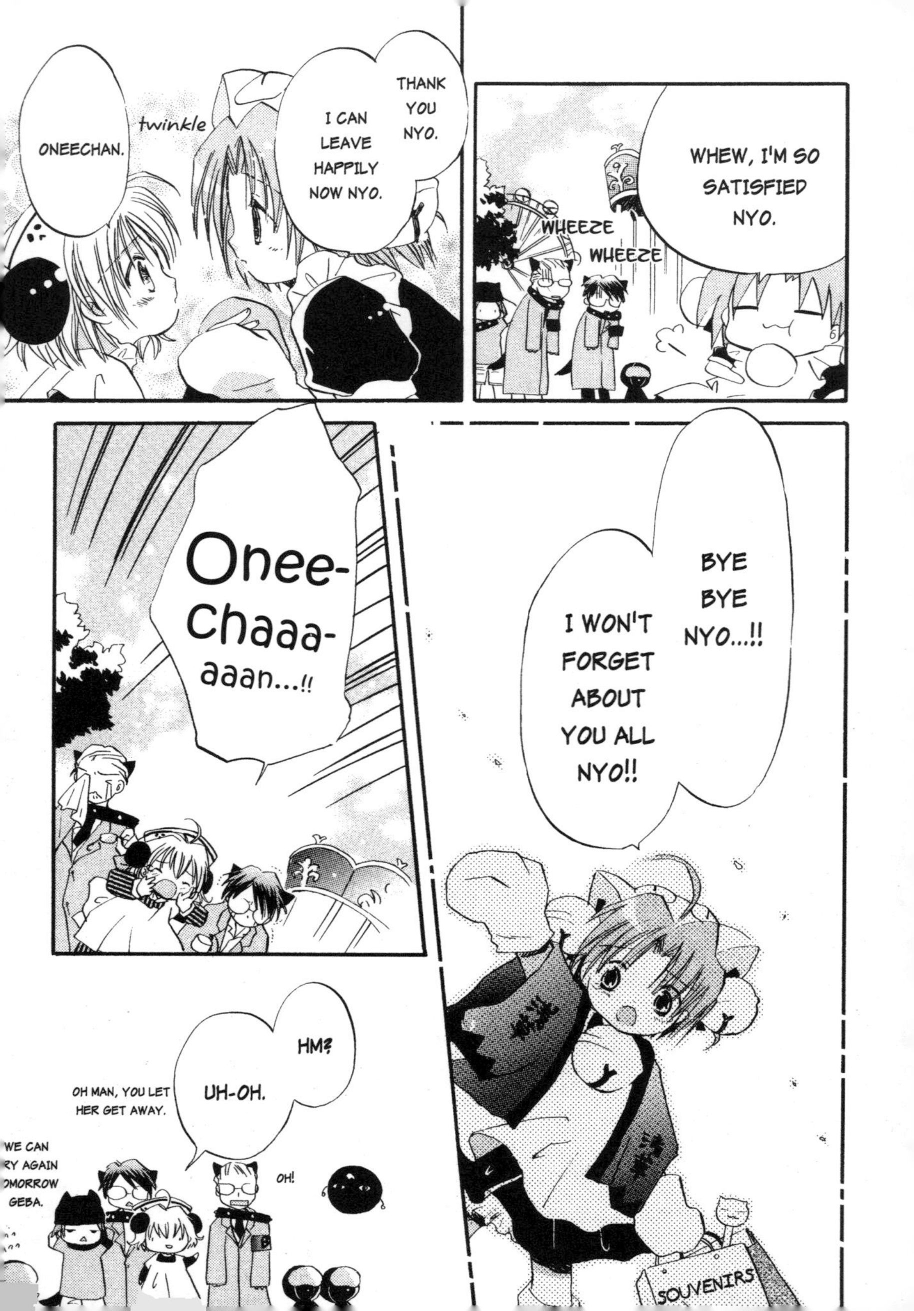
WHEW, I'M SO SATISFIED NYO.
WHEEZE WHEEZE
THANK YOU NYO.
I CAN LEAVE HAPPILY NOW NYO.
twinkle
ONEECHAN.
BYE BYE NYO...!!
I WON'T FORGET ABOUT YOU ALL NYO!!
SOUVENIRS
Onee-Chaaa-aaan...!!
HM?
UH-OH.
OH MAN, YOU LET HER GET AWAY.
OH!
WE CAN RY AGAIN OMORROW GEBA.

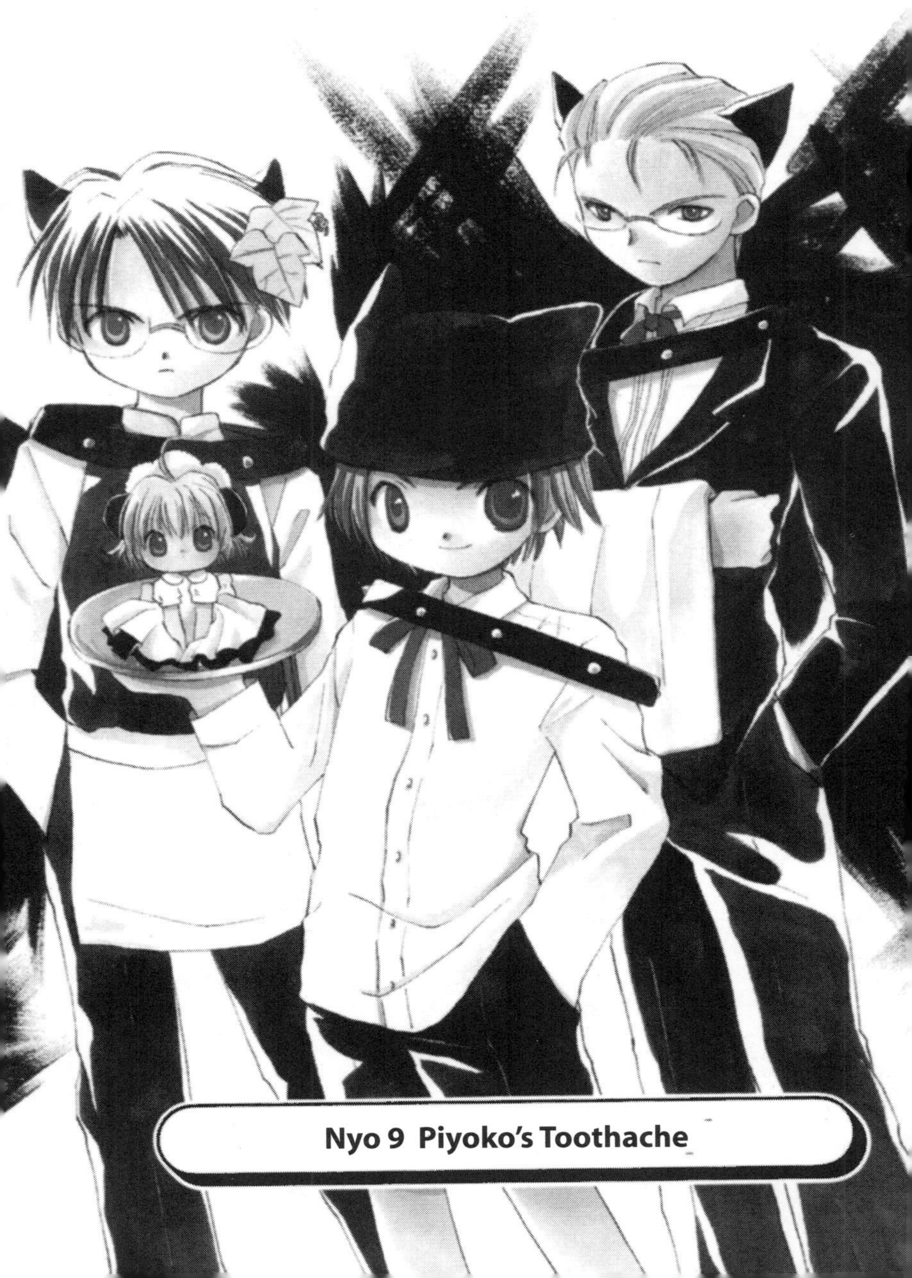
Nyo 9 Piyoko's Toothache

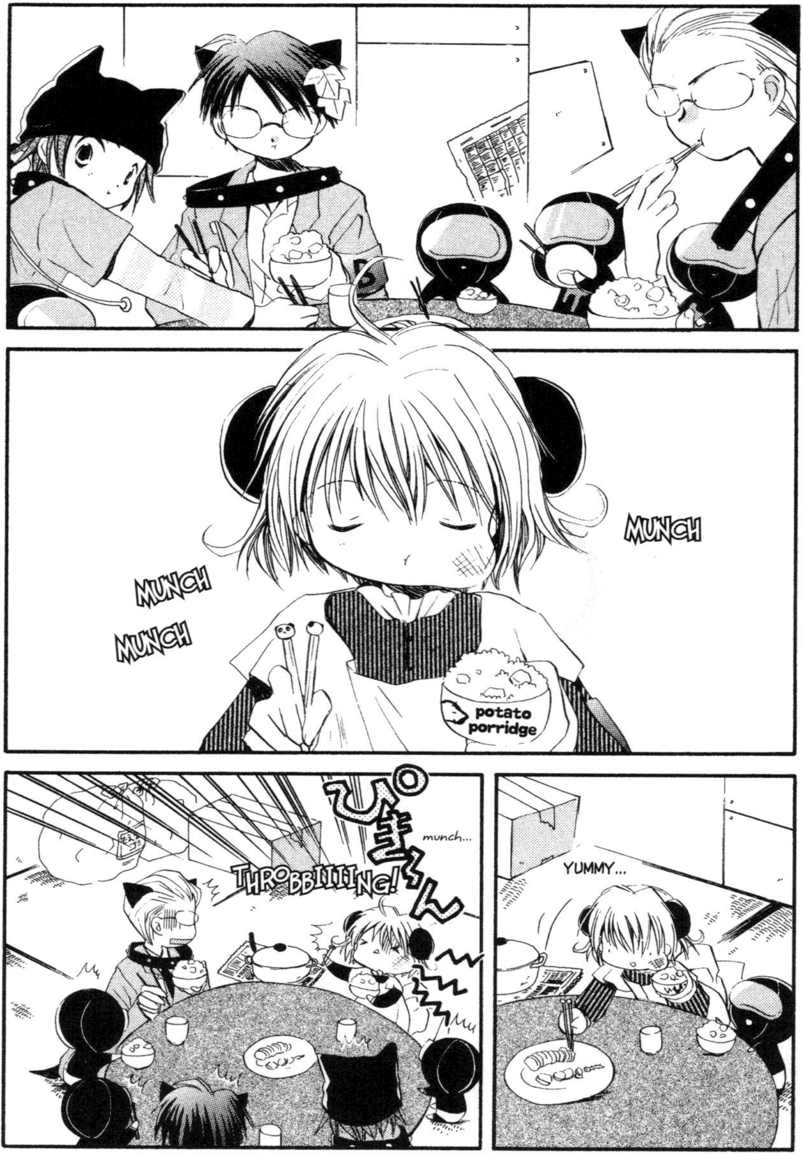
MUNCH
MUNCH
MUNCH
potato porridge
YUMMY...
munch...
THROBBIIIIING!

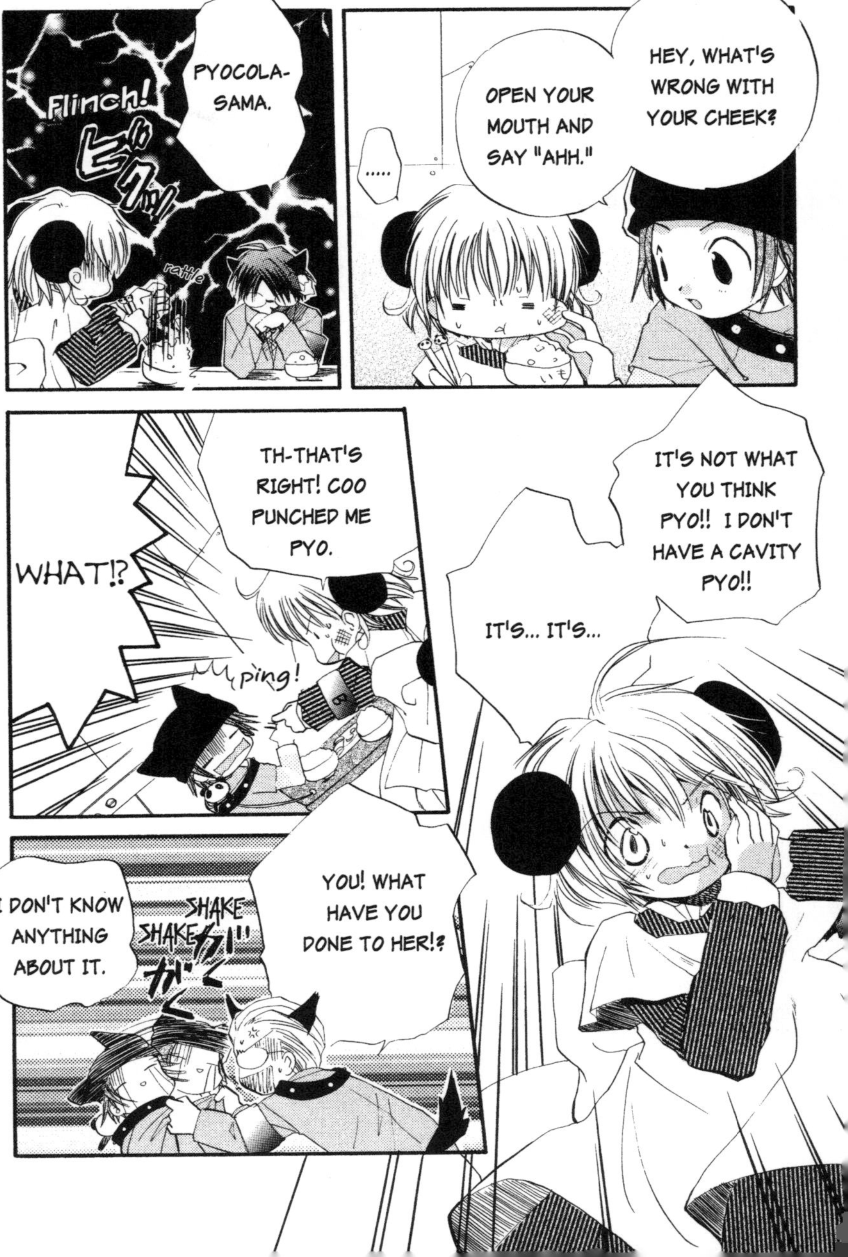
HEY, WHAT'S WRONG WITH YOUR CHEEK?
OPEN YOUR MOUTH AND SAY "AHH."
.....
PYOCOLA-SAMA.
Flinch!
rattle
IT'S NOT WHAT YOU THINK PYO!! I DON'T HAVE A CAVITY PYO!!
IT'S... IT'S...
TH-THAT'S RIGHT! COO PUNCHED ME PYO.
WHAT!?
ping!
YOU! WHAT HAVE YOU DONE TO HER!?
SHAKE SHAKE
I DON'T KNOW ANYTHING ABOUT IT.

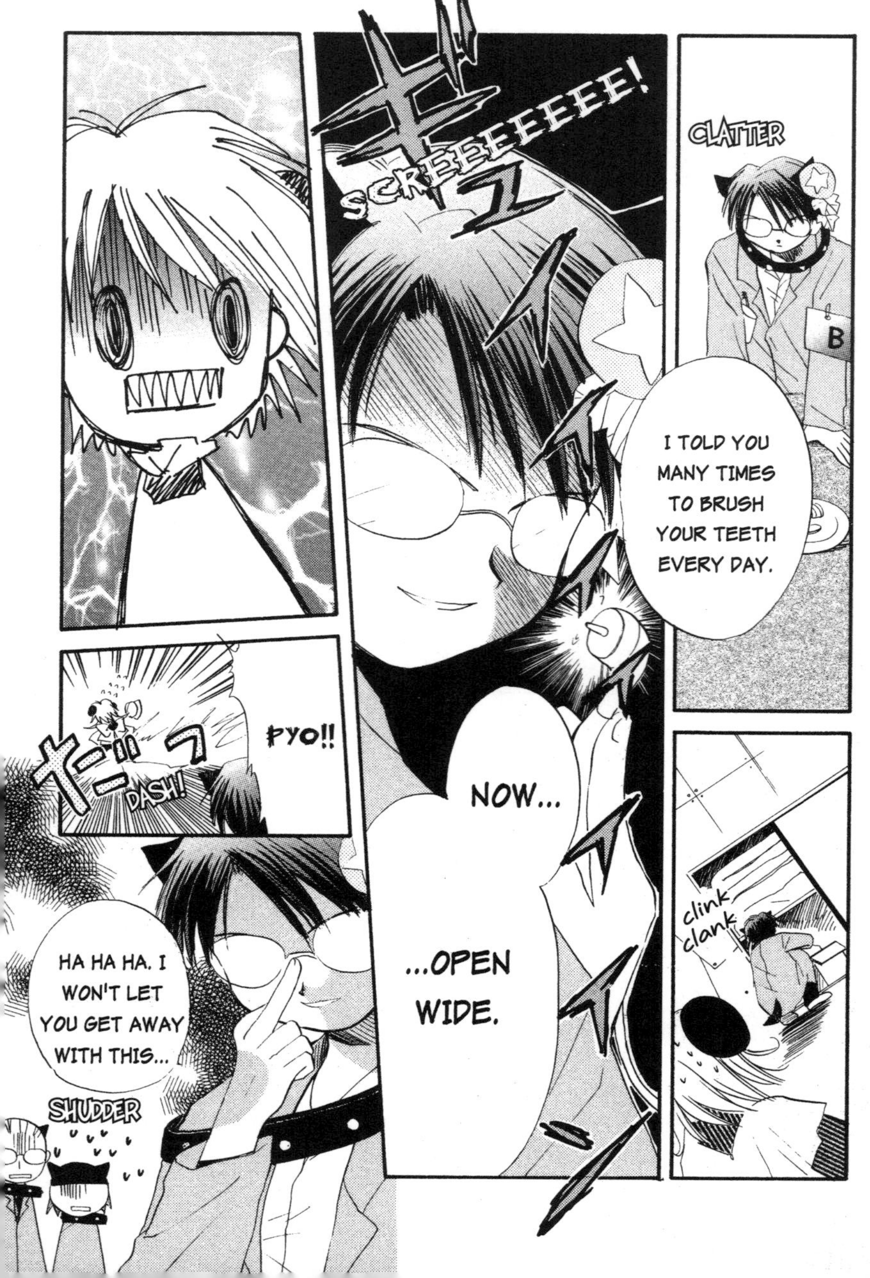
CLATTER
B
I TOLD YOU MANY TIMES TO BRUSH YOUR TEETH EVERY DAY.
clink clank
SCREEEEEEEE!
NOW...
...OPEN WIDE.
PYO!!
DASH!
HA HA HA. I WON'T LET YOU GET AWAY WITH THIS...
SHUDDER

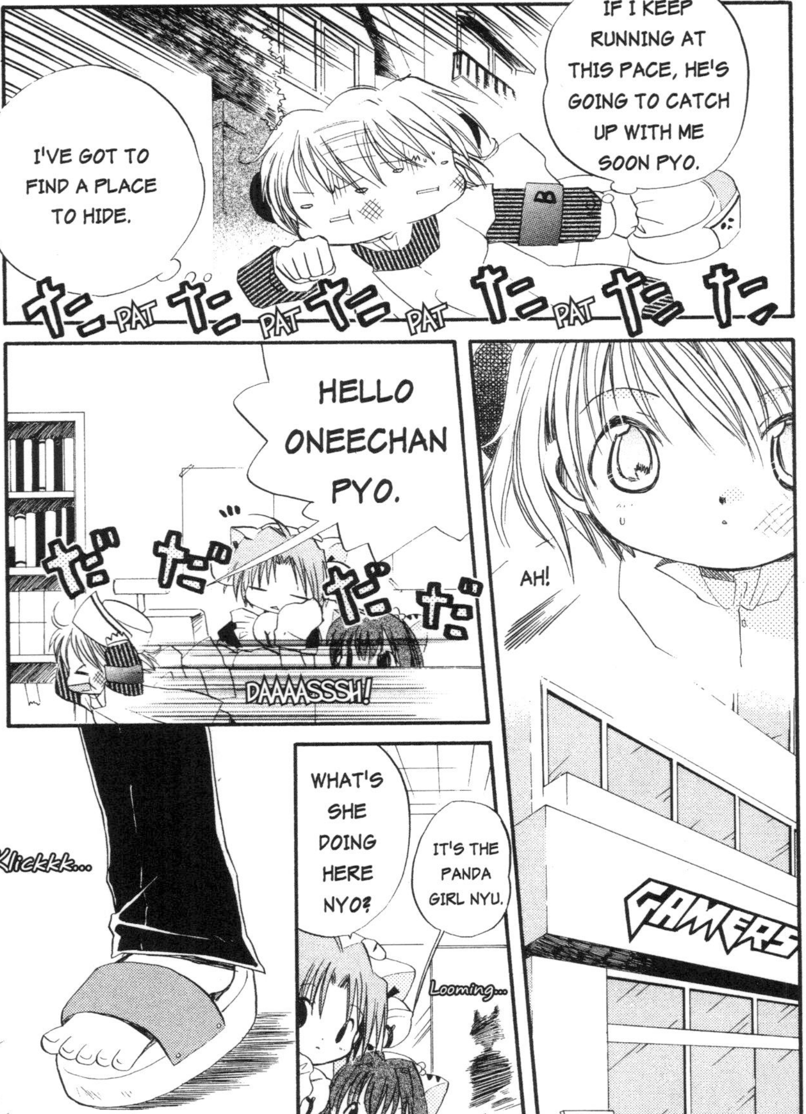

IF I KEEP RUNNING AT THIS PACE, HE'S GOING TO CATCH UP WITH ME SOON PYO.
I'VE GOT TO FIND A PLACE TO HIDE.
PAT PAT PAT PAT
AH!
HELLO ONEECHAN PYO.
DAAAASSSH!
GAMERS
WHAT'S SHE DOING HERE NYO?
IT'S THE PANDA GIRL NYU.
Looming...
Klickkk...

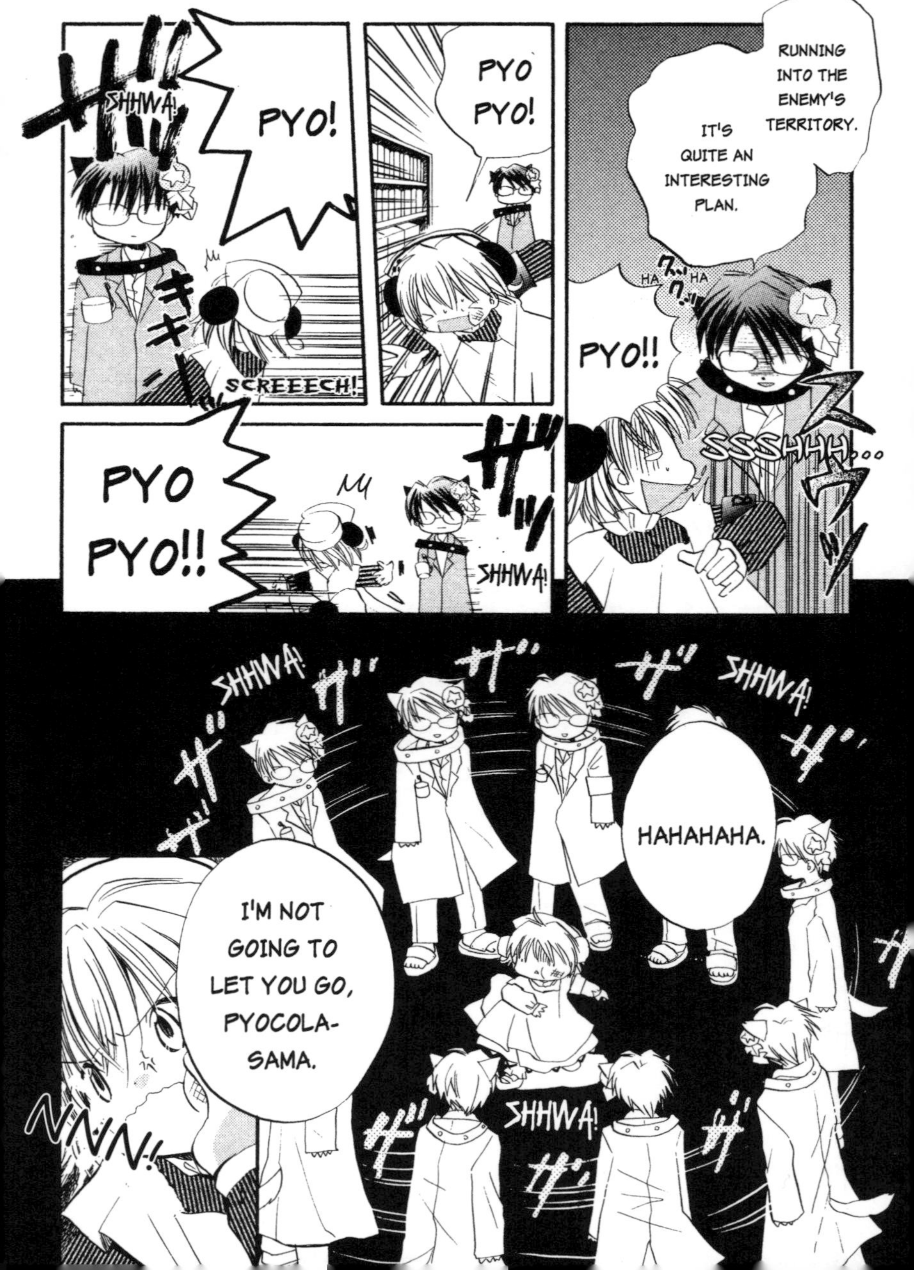
RUNNING INTO THE ENEMY'S TERRITORY.
IT'S QUITE AN INTERESTING PLAN.
HA HA
PYO!!
SSSHHH...
PYO PYO!
SHHWA!
PYO!
SCREEECH!
SHHWA!
PYO PYO!!
SHHWA!
SHHWA!
HAHAHAHA.
I'M NOT GOING TO LET YOU GO, PYOCOLA-SAMA.
SHHWA!
NNNN!

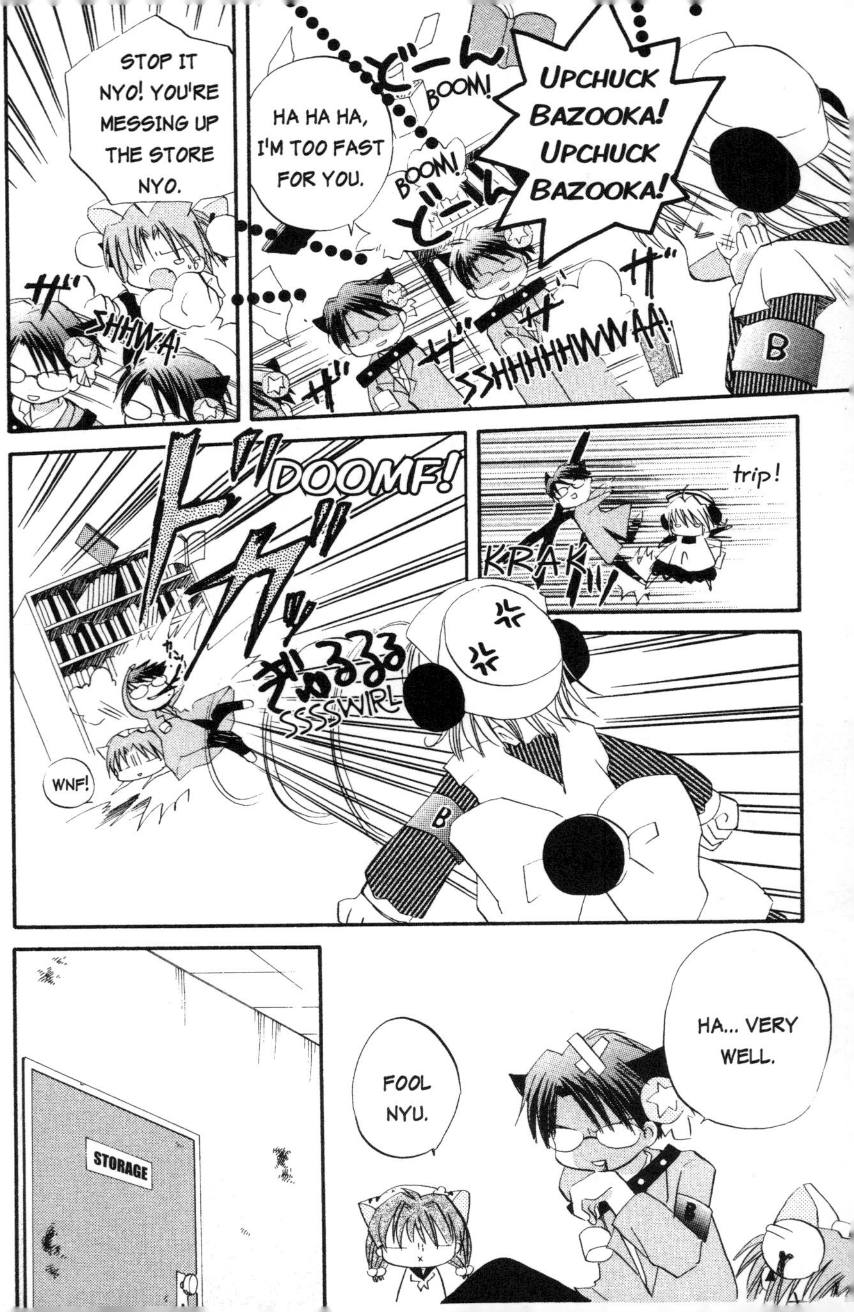
UPCHUCK BAZOOKA! UPCHUCK BAZOOKA!
BOOM!
BOOM!
HA HA HA, I'M TOO FAST FOR YOU.
SSHHHHHHWWAA!
STOP IT NYO! YOU'RE MESSING UP THE STORE NYO.
SHHWA!
trip!
KRAK
DOOMF!
SSSSWIRL
WNF!
HA... VERY WELL.
FOOL NYU.
STORAGE

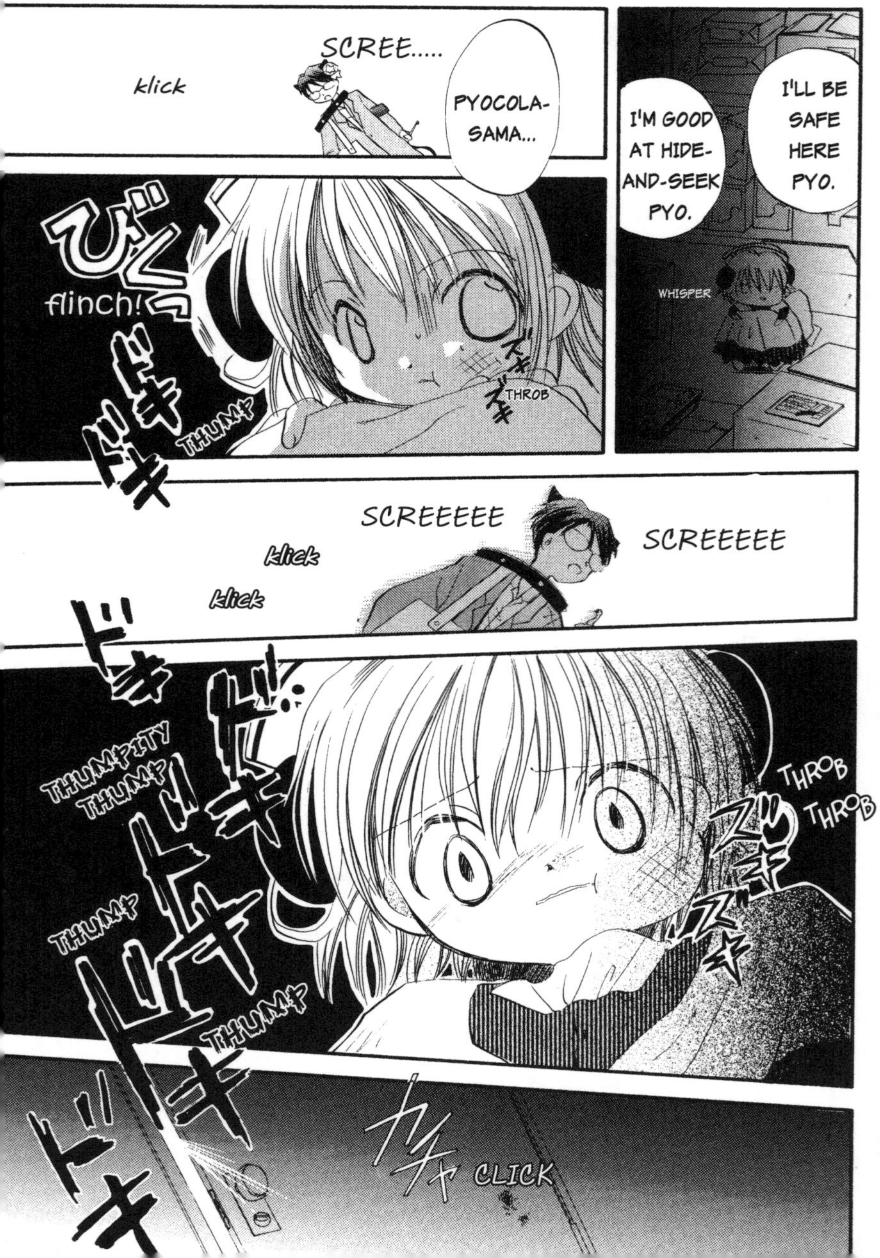
I'LL BE SAFE HERE PYO.
I'M GOOD AT HIDE-AND-SEEK PYO.
WHISPER
PYOCOLA-SAMA...
SCREE.....
klick
THROB
びくっ
flinch!
THUMP
SCREEEEEE
SCREEEEEE
klick
klick
THROB THROB
THUMPITY THUMP
THUMP
THUMP
カチャ
CLICK

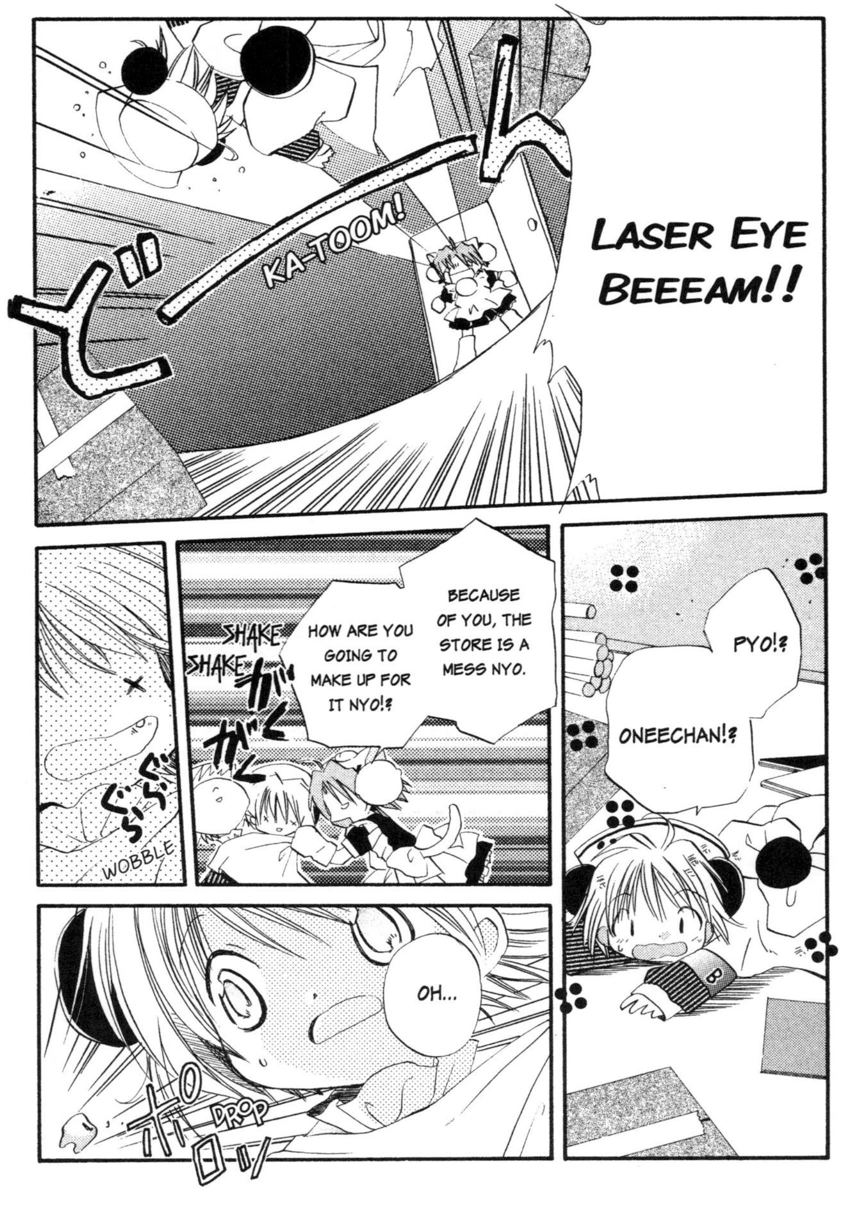
KA-TOOM!
LASER EYE BEEEAM!!
PYO!?
ONEECHAN!?
BECAUSE OF YOU, THE STORE IS A MESS NYO.
HOW ARE YOU GOING TO MAKE UP FOR IT NYO!?
SHAKE SHAKE
WOBBLE
OH...
DROP

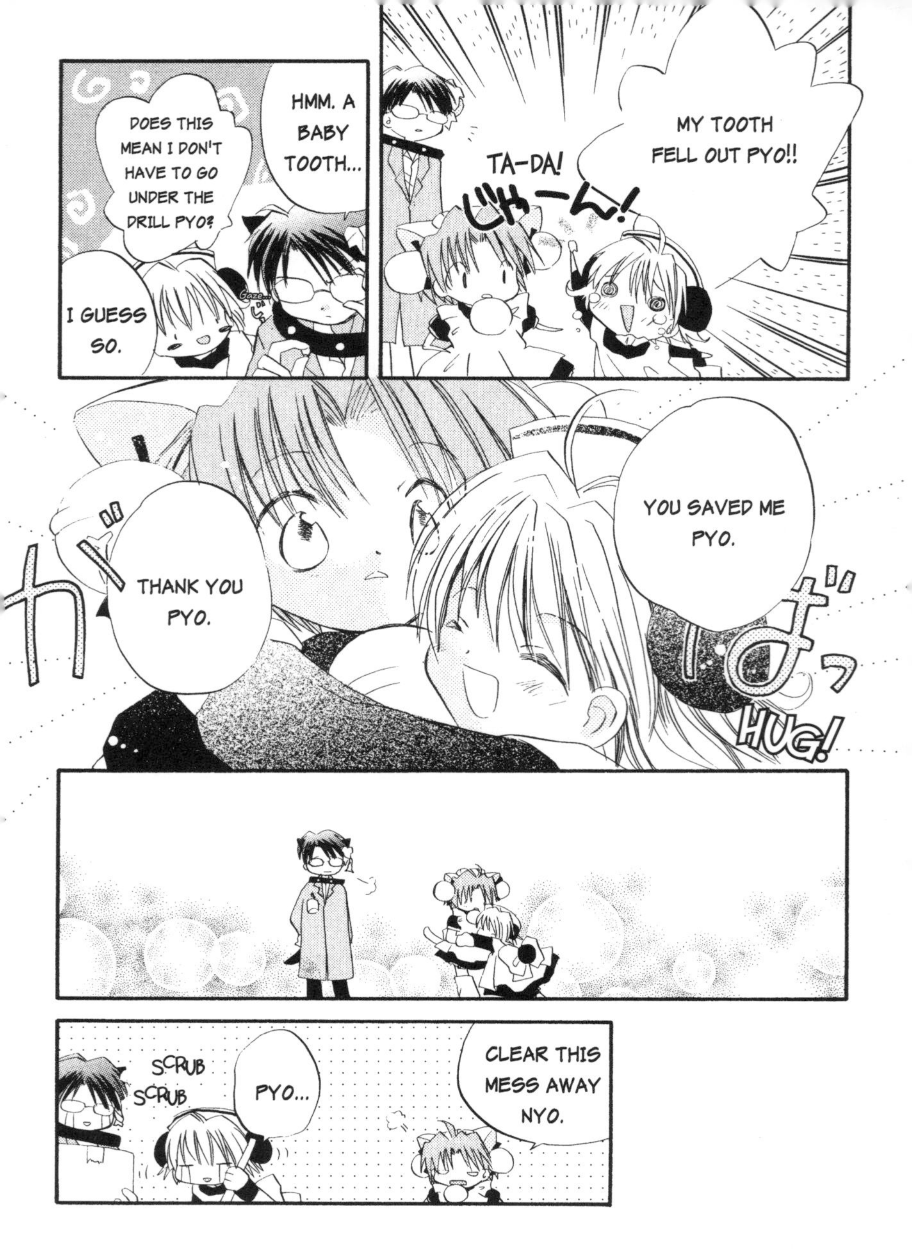
MY TOOTH FELL OUT PYO!!
TA-DA!
じゃーん!
HMM. A BABY TOOTH...
DOES THIS MEAN I DON'T HAVE TO GO UNDER THE DRILL PYO?
Gaze...
I GUESS SO.
YOU SAVED ME PYO.
HUG!
THANK YOU PYO.
CLEAR THIS MESS AWAY NYO.
PYO...
SCRUB SCRUB

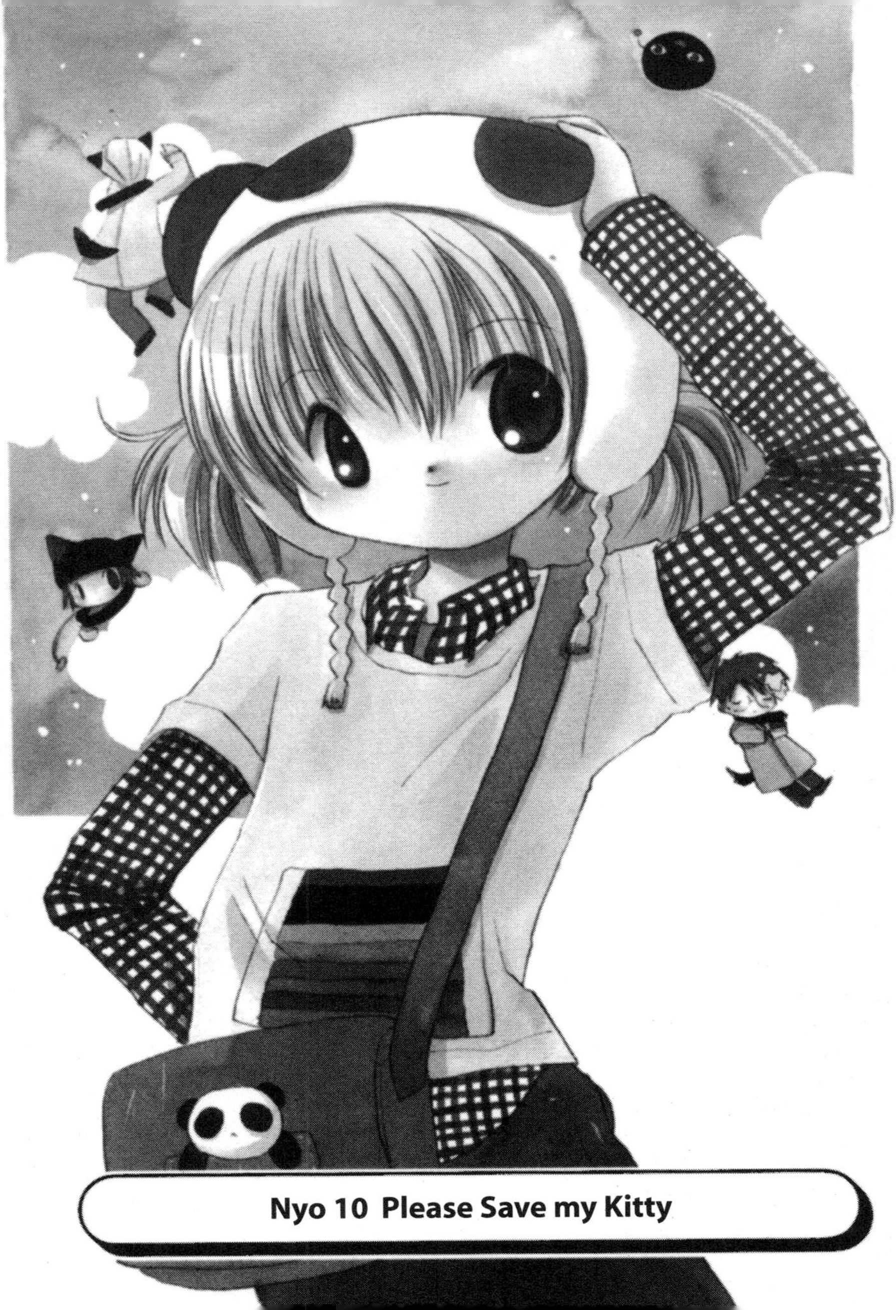

Nyo 10 Please Save my Kitty

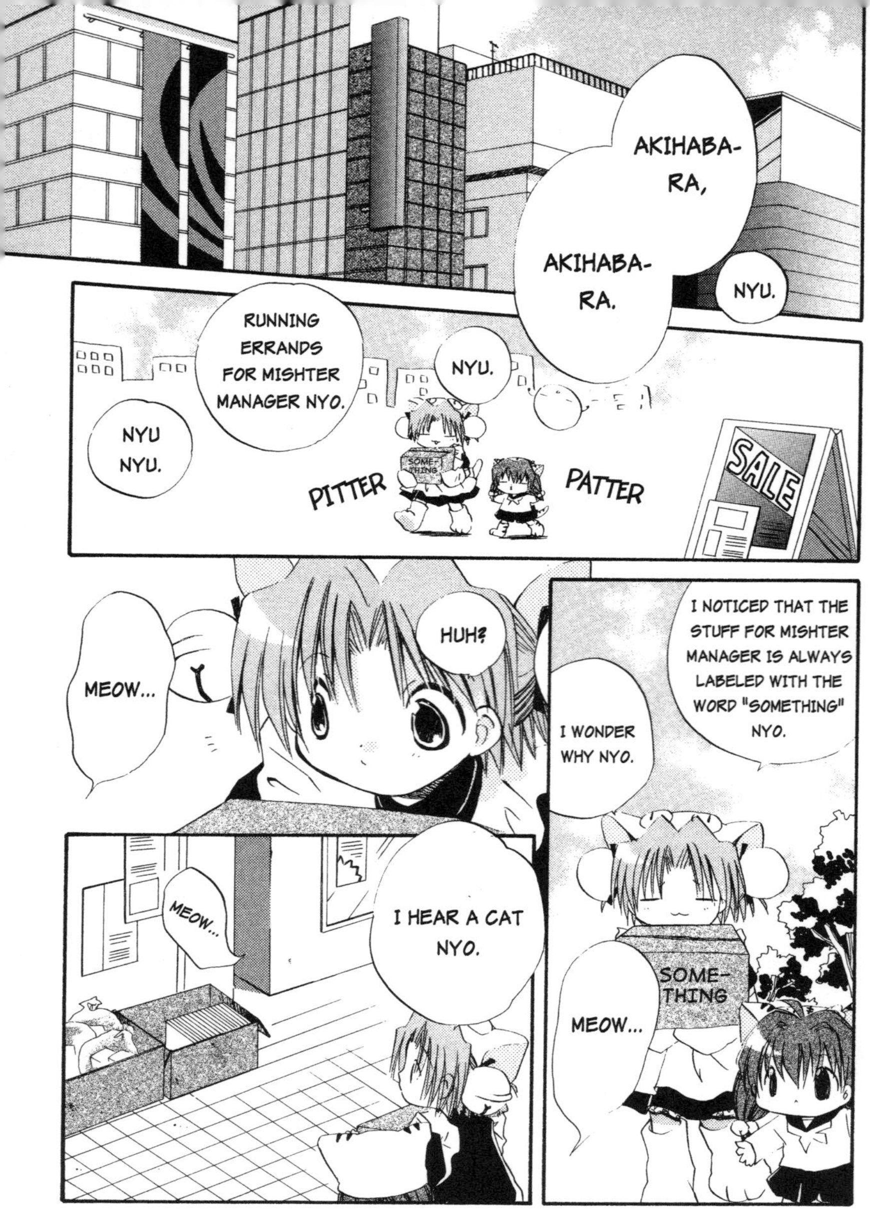
AKIHABA-RA,
AKIHABA-RA.
NYU.
RUNNING ERRANDS FOR MISHTER MANAGER NYO.
NYU.
NYU NYU.
SALE
SOME-THING
PATTER
PITTER
I NOTICED THAT THE STUFF FOR MISHTER MANAGER IS ALWAYS LABELED WITH THE WORD "SOMETHING" NYO.
I WONDER WHY NYO.
SOME-THING
MEOW...
HUH?
MEOW...
I HEAR A CAT NYO.
MEOW...

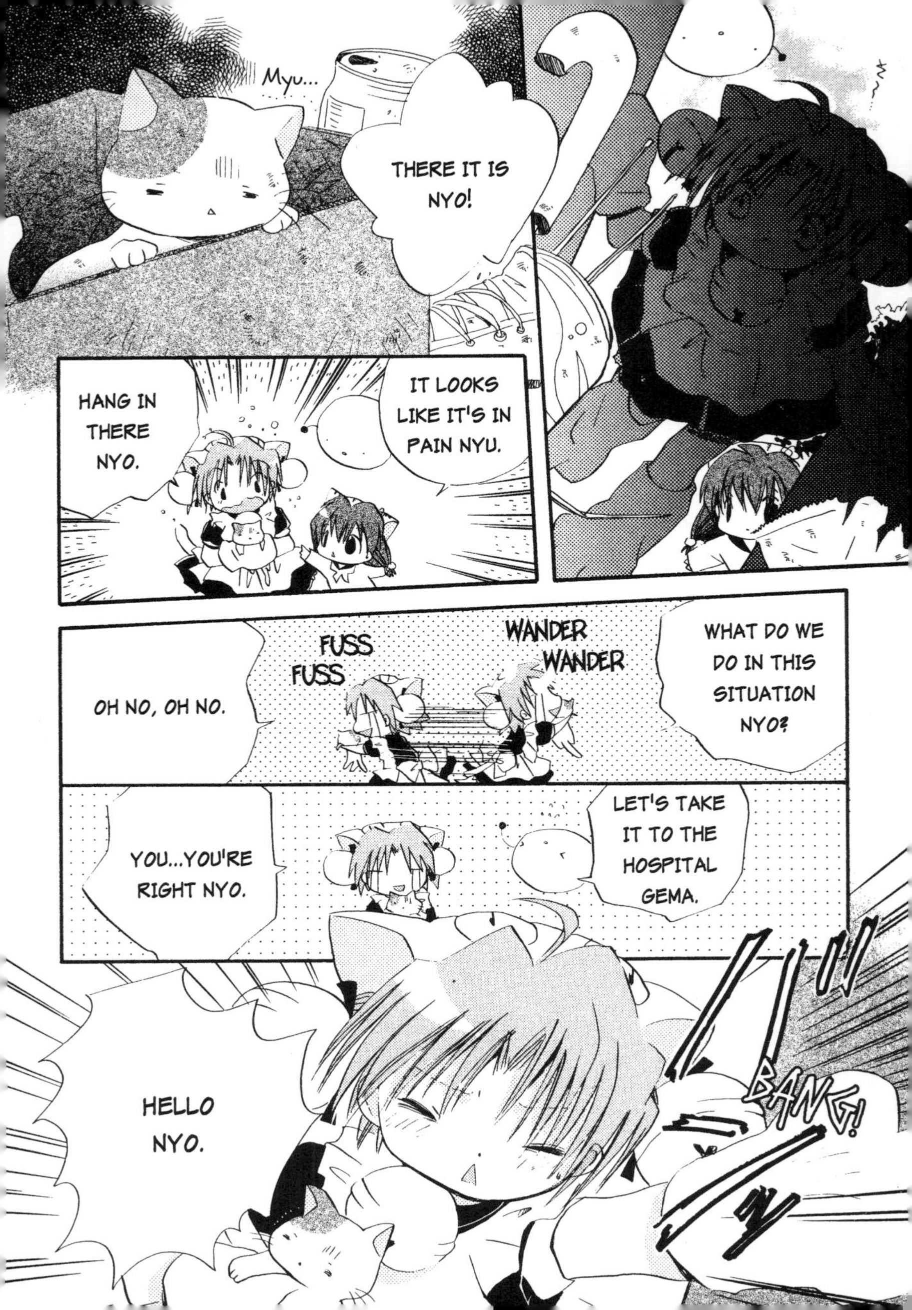
Myu...
THERE IT IS NYO!
IT LOOKS LIKE IT'S IN PAIN NYU.
HANG IN THERE NYO.
WHAT DO WE DO IN THIS SITUATION NYO?
WANDER WANDER
FUSS FUSS
OH NO, OH NO.
LET'S TAKE IT TO THE HOSPITAL GEMA.
YOU...YOU'RE RIGHT NYO.
BANG!
HELLO NYO.

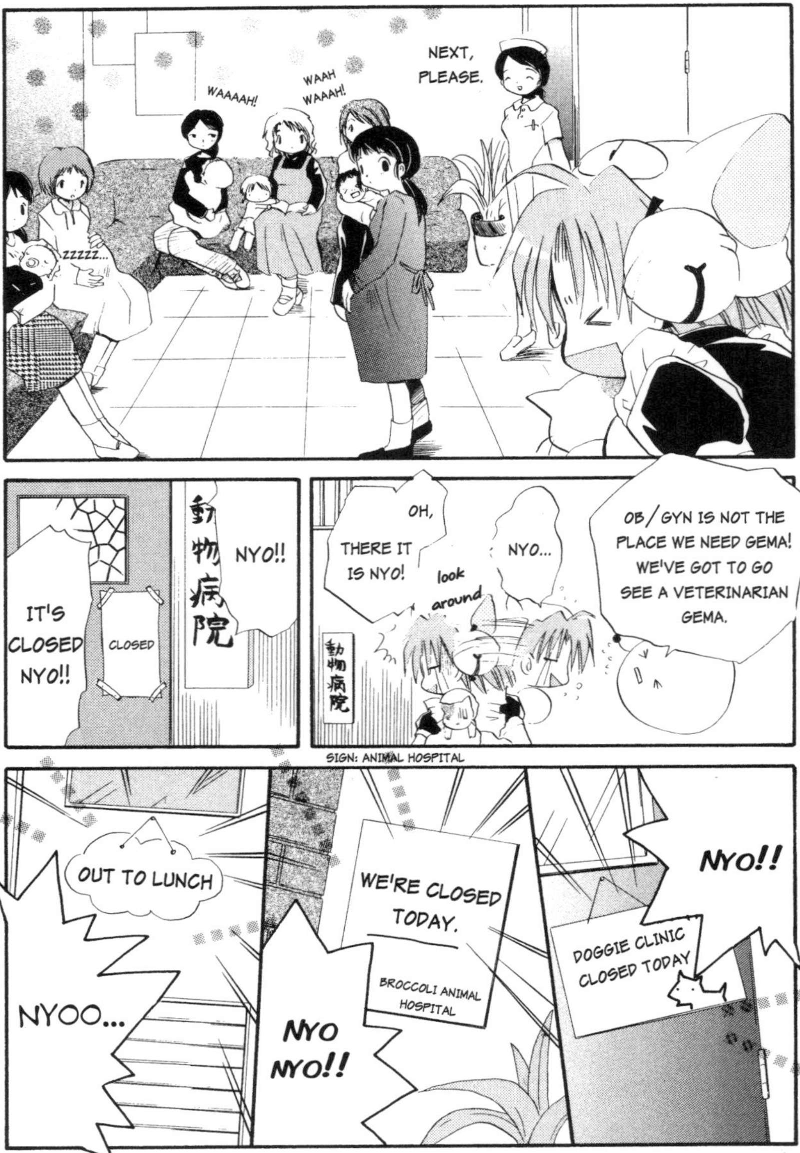
NEXT, PLEASE.
WAAH WAAAH!
WAAAAH!
ZZZZZ...
OB/GYN IS NOT THE PLACE WE NEED GEMA! WE'VE GOT TO GO SEE A VETERINARIAN GEMA.
NYO...
look around
OH, THERE IT IS NYO!
動物病院
NYO!!
動物病院
CLOSED
IT'S CLOSED NYO!!
SIGN: ANIMAL HOSPITAL
NYO!!
DOGGIE CLINIC CLOSED TODAY
WE'RE CLOSED TODAY.
BROCCOLI ANIMAL HOSPITAL
NYO NYO!!
OUT TO LUNCH
NYOO...

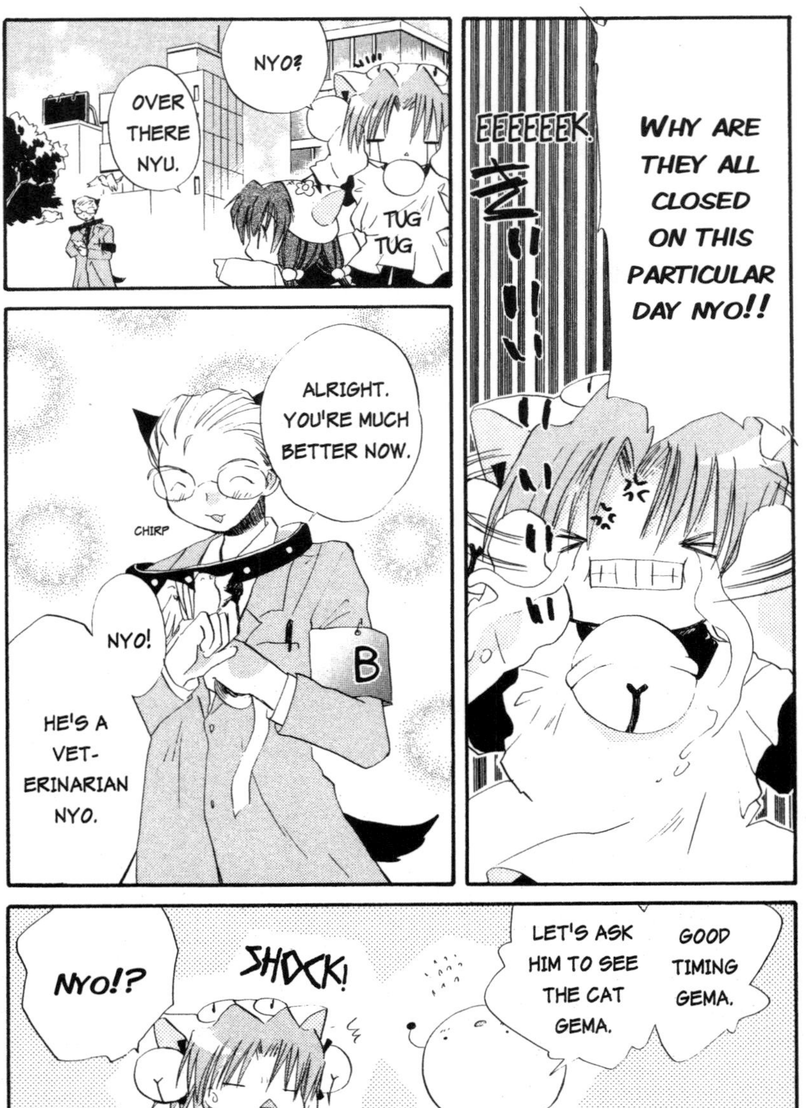
EEEEEEEK.
WHY ARE THEY ALL CLOSED ON THIS PARTICULAR DAY NYO!!
NYO?
OVER THERE NYU.
TUG TUG
ALRIGHT. YOU'RE MUCH BETTER NOW.
CHIRP
NYO!
HE'S A VET-ERINARIAN NYO.
GOOD TIMING GEMA.
LET'S ASK HIM TO SEE THE CAT GEMA.
SHOCK!
NYO!?

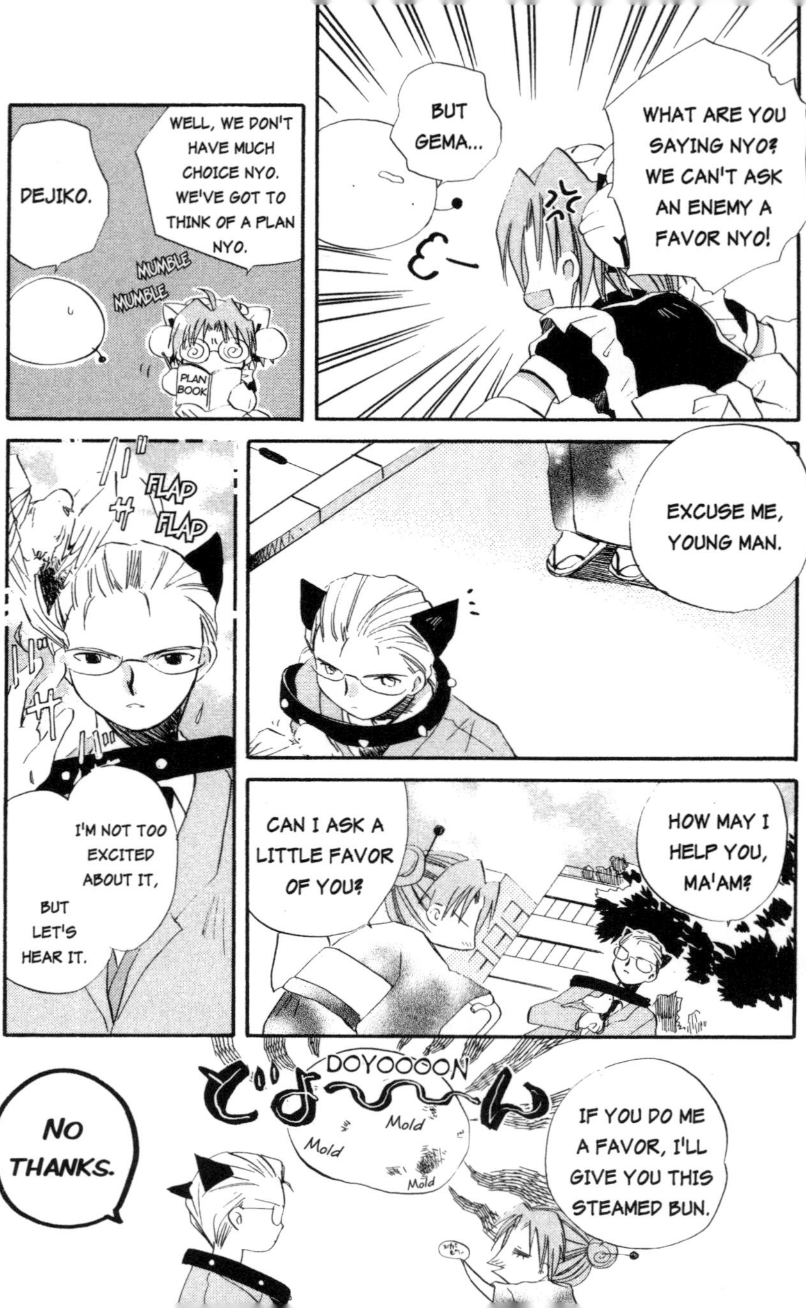
WHAT ARE YOU SAYING NYO? WE CAN'T ASK AN ENEMY A FAVOR NYO!
BUT GEMA...
WELL, WE DON'T HAVE MUCH CHOICE NYO. WE'VE GOT TO THINK OF A PLAN NYO.
DEJIKO.
MUMBLE
MUMBLE
PLAN BOOK
EXCUSE ME, YOUNG MAN.
HOW MAY I HELP YOU, MA'AM?
CAN I ASK A LITTLE FAVOR OF YOU?
FLAP
FLAP
I'M NOT TOO EXCITED ABOUT IT, BUT LET'S HEAR IT.
DOYOOOON
IF YOU DO ME A FAVOR, I'LL GIVE YOU THIS STEAMED BUN.
Mold
Mold
Mold
NO THANKS.

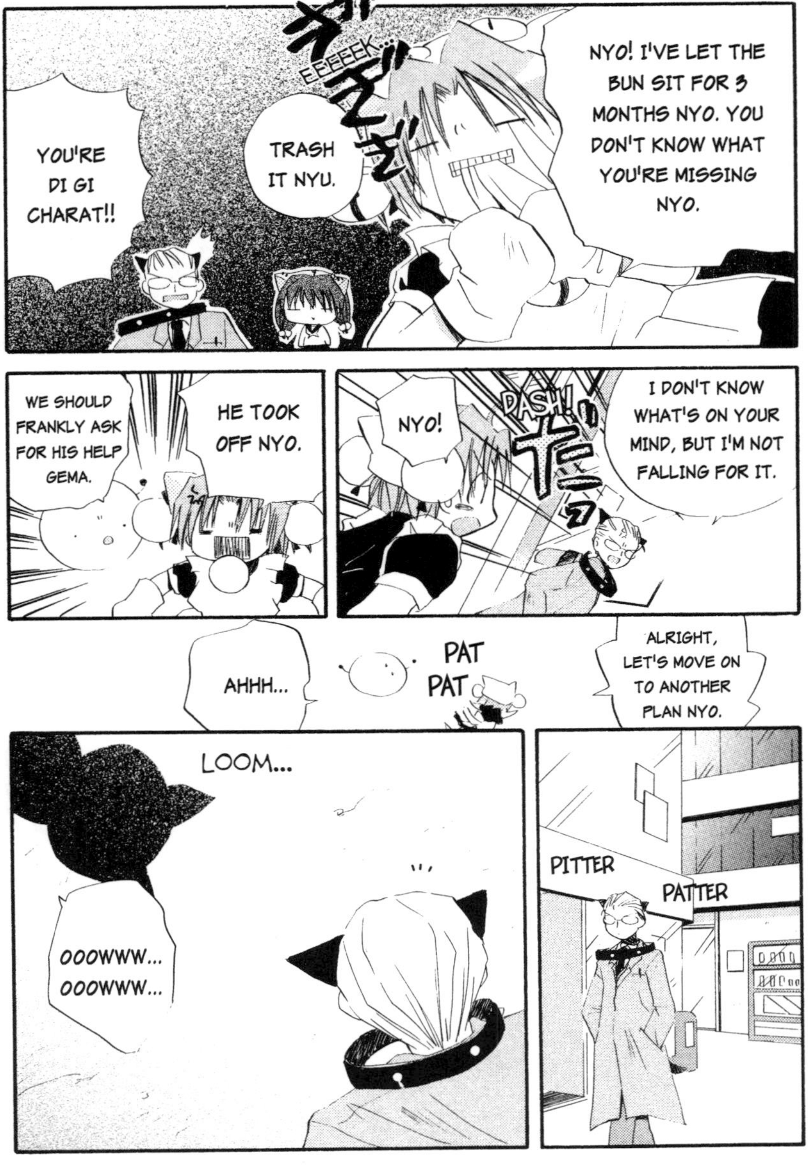
NYO! I'VE LET THE BUN SIT FOR 3 MONTHS NYO. YOU DON'T KNOW WHAT YOU'RE MISSING NYO.
EEEEEK...
TRASH IT NYU.
YOU'RE DI GI CHARAT!!
I DON'T KNOW WHAT'S ON YOUR MIND, BUT I'M NOT FALLING FOR IT.
DASH!
NYO!
HE TOOK OFF NYO.
WE SHOULD FRANKLY ASK FOR HIS HELP GEMA.
ALRIGHT, LET'S MOVE ON TO ANOTHER PLAN NYO.
PAT PAT
AHHH...
PITTER
PATTER
LOOM...
OOOWWW... OOOWWW...

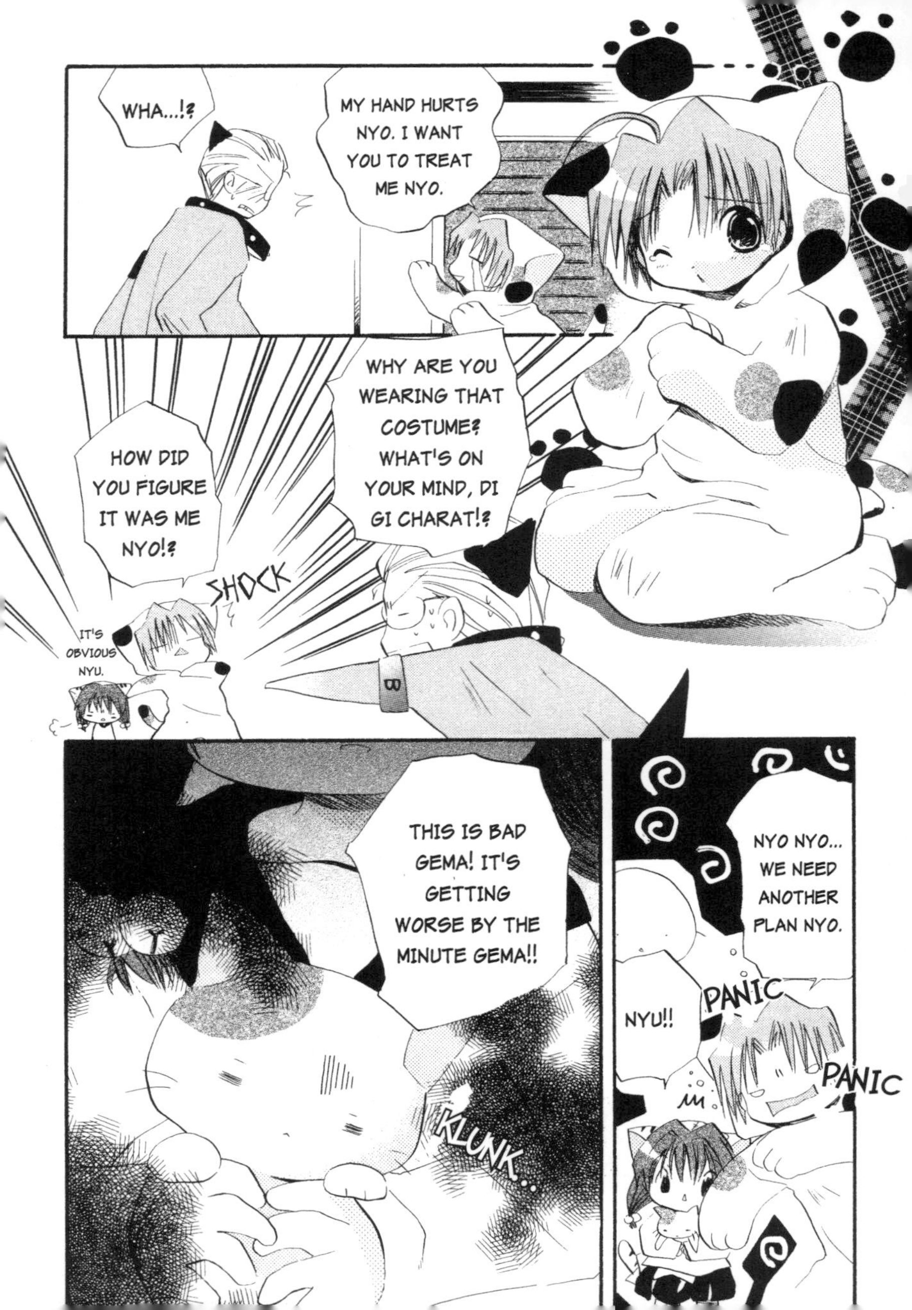
MY HAND HURTS NYO. I WANT YOU TO TREAT ME NYO.
WHA...!?
WHY ARE YOU WEARING THAT COSTUME? WHAT'S ON YOUR MIND, DI GI CHARAT!?
HOW DID YOU FIGURE IT WAS ME NYO!?
SHOCK
IT'S OBVIOUS NYU.
NYO NYO... WE NEED ANOTHER PLAN NYO.
PANIC
NYU!!
PANIC
THIS IS BAD GEMA! IT'S GETTING WORSE BY THE MINUTE GEMA!!
KLUNK...

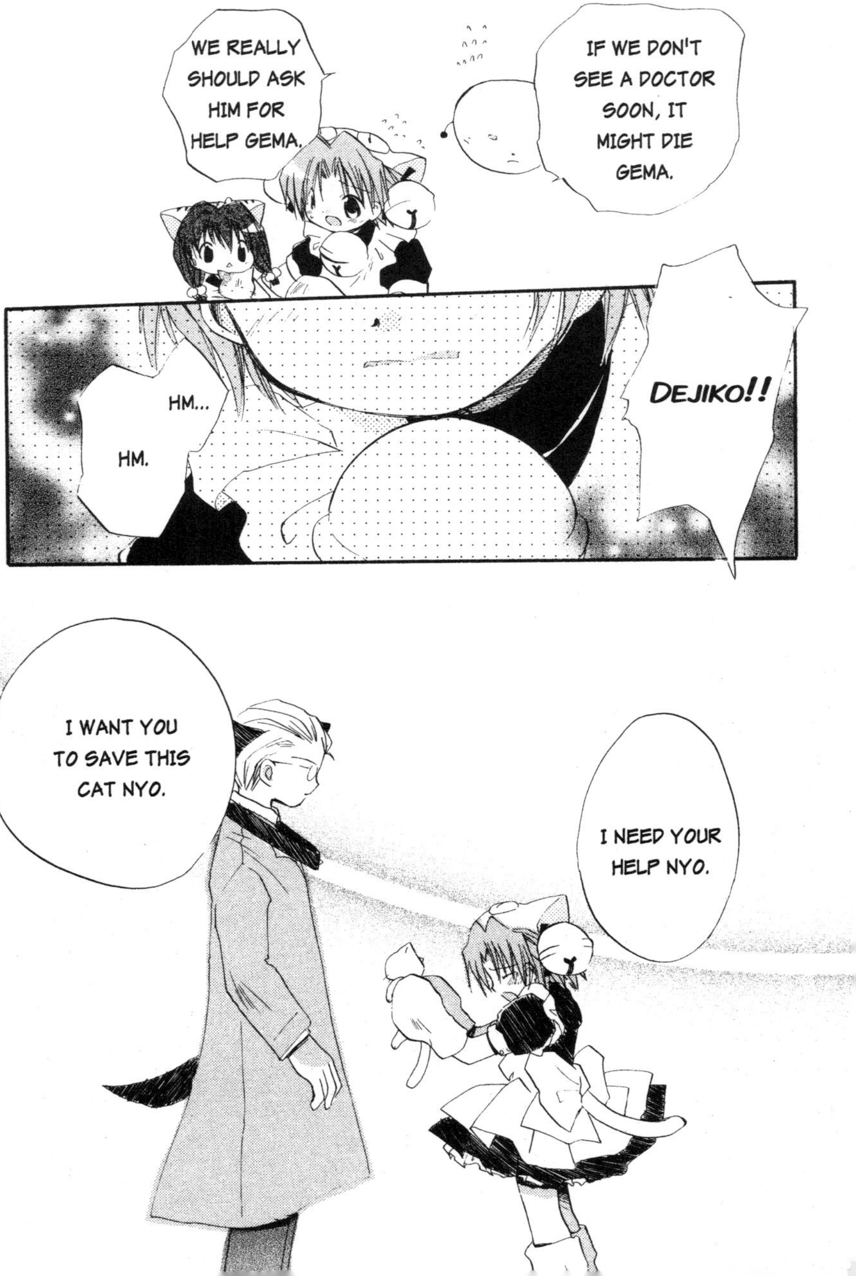
IF WE DON'T SEE A DOCTOR SOON, IT MIGHT DIE GEMA.
WE REALLY SHOULD ASK HIM FOR HELP GEMA.
DEJIKO!!
HM...
HM.
I WANT YOU TO SAVE THIS CAT NYO.
I NEED YOUR HELP NYO.

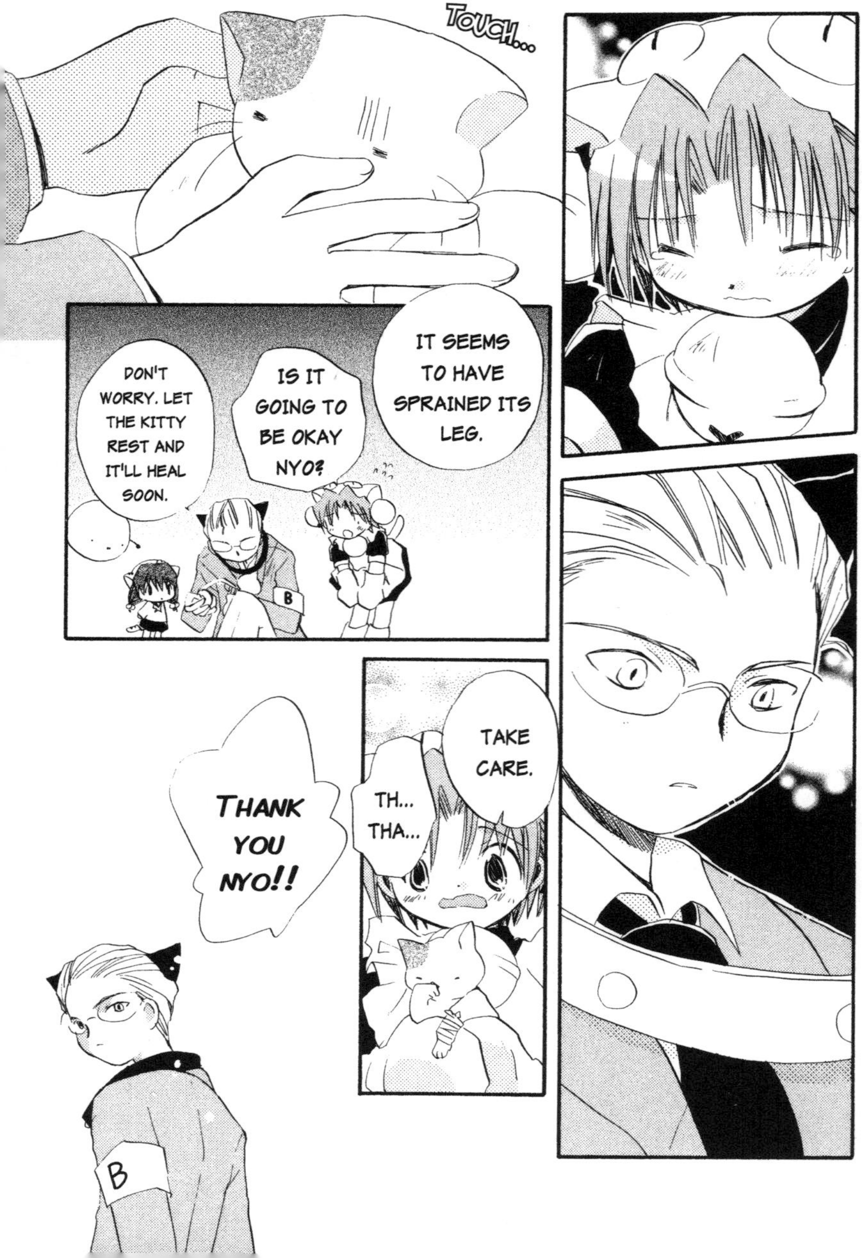
TOUCH...
IT SEEMS TO HAVE SPRAINED ITS LEG.
IS IT GOING TO BE OKAY NYO?
DON'T WORRY. LET THE KITTY REST AND IT'LL HEAL SOON.
TAKE CARE.
TH... THA...
THANK YOU NYO!!

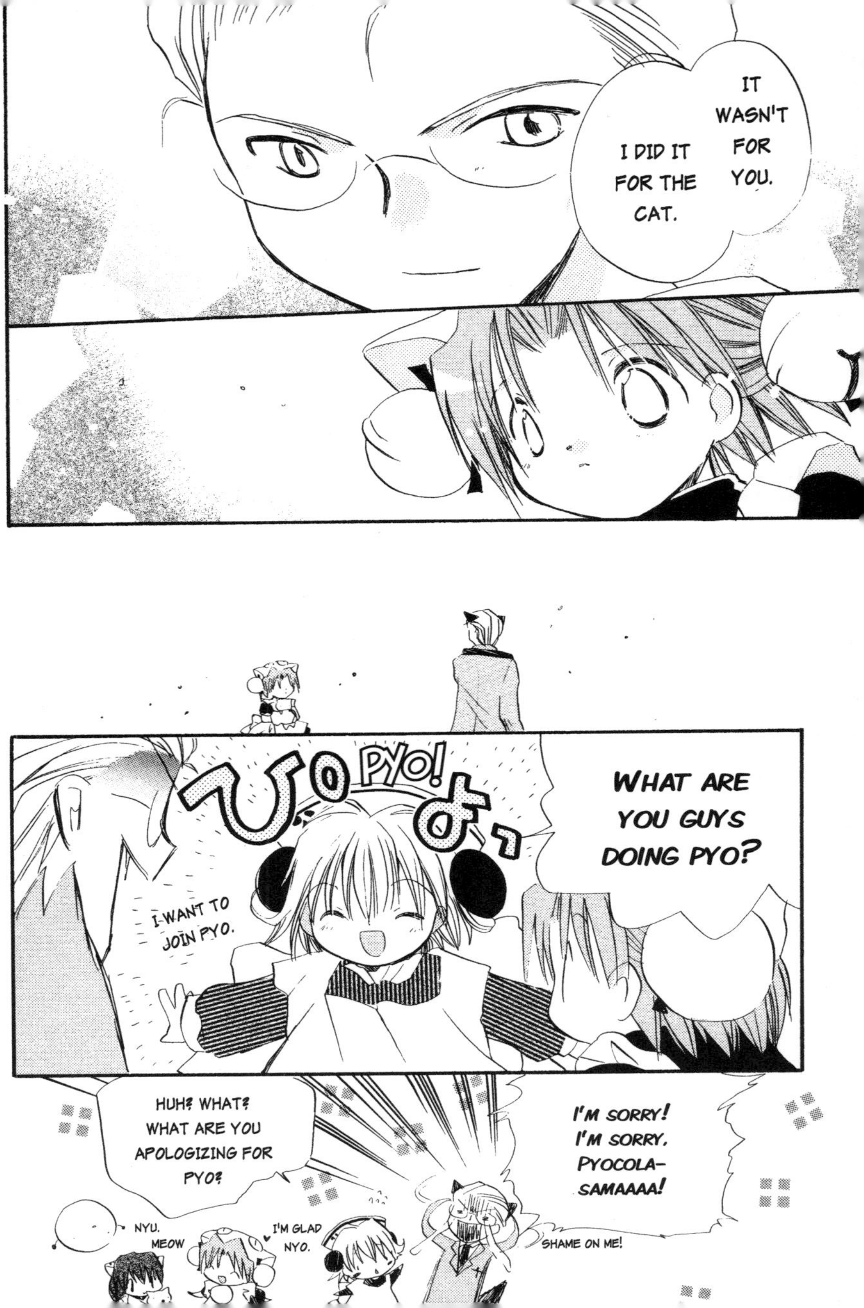
IT WASN'T FOR YOU.
I DID IT FOR THE CAT.
WHAT ARE YOU GUYS DOING PYO?
PYO!
I-WANT TO JOIN PYO.
I'M SORRY! I'M SORRY, PYOCOLA-SAMAAAA!
SHAME ON ME!
HUH? WHAT? WHAT ARE YOU APOLOGIZING FOR PYO?
I'M GLAD NYO.
NYU. MEOW

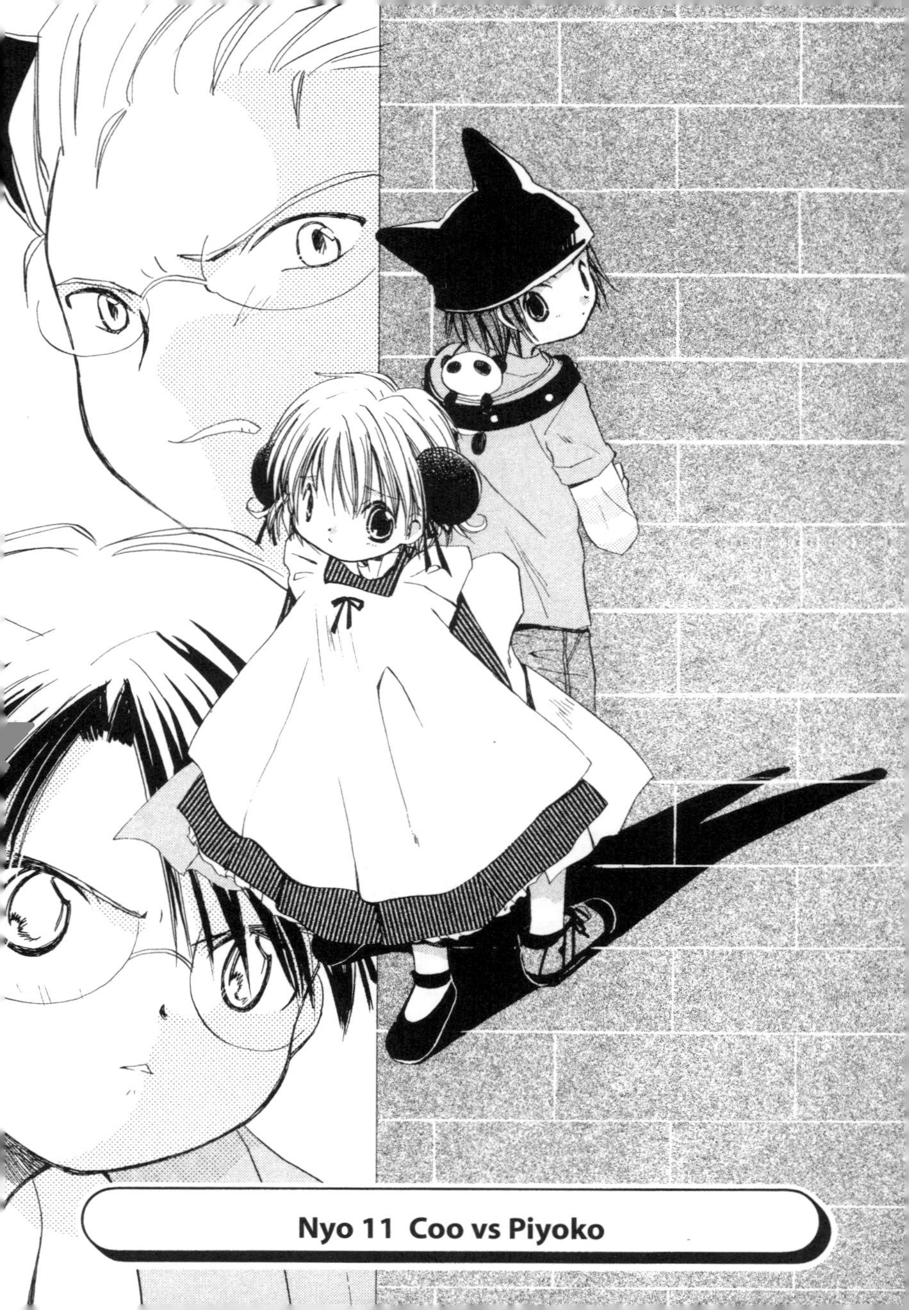

Nyo 11 Coo vs Piyoko

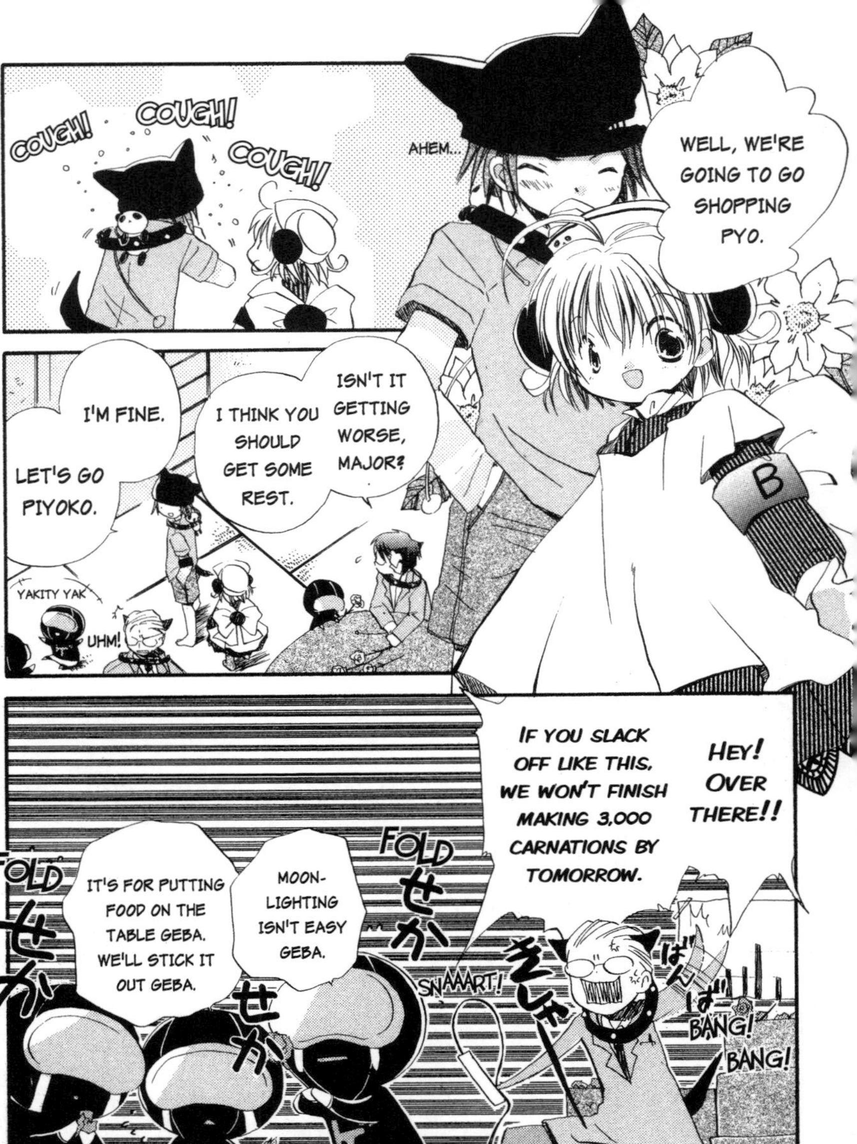
AHEM...
WELL, WE'RE GOING TO GO SHOPPING PYO.
COUGH! COUGH! COUGH!
ISN'T IT GETTING WORSE, MAJOR?
I THINK YOU SHOULD GET SOME REST.
I'M FINE.
LET'S GO PIYOKO.
YAKITY YAK
UHM!
HEY! OVER THERE!!
IF YOU SLACK OFF LIKE THIS, WE WON'T FINISH MAKING 3,000 CARNATIONS BY TOMORROW.
BANG! BANG!
SNAAART!
FOLD せか
MOON-LIGHTING ISN'T EASY GEBA.
せか
IT'S FOR PUTTING FOOD ON THE TABLE GEBA. WE'LL STICK IT OUT GEBA.
FOLD せか

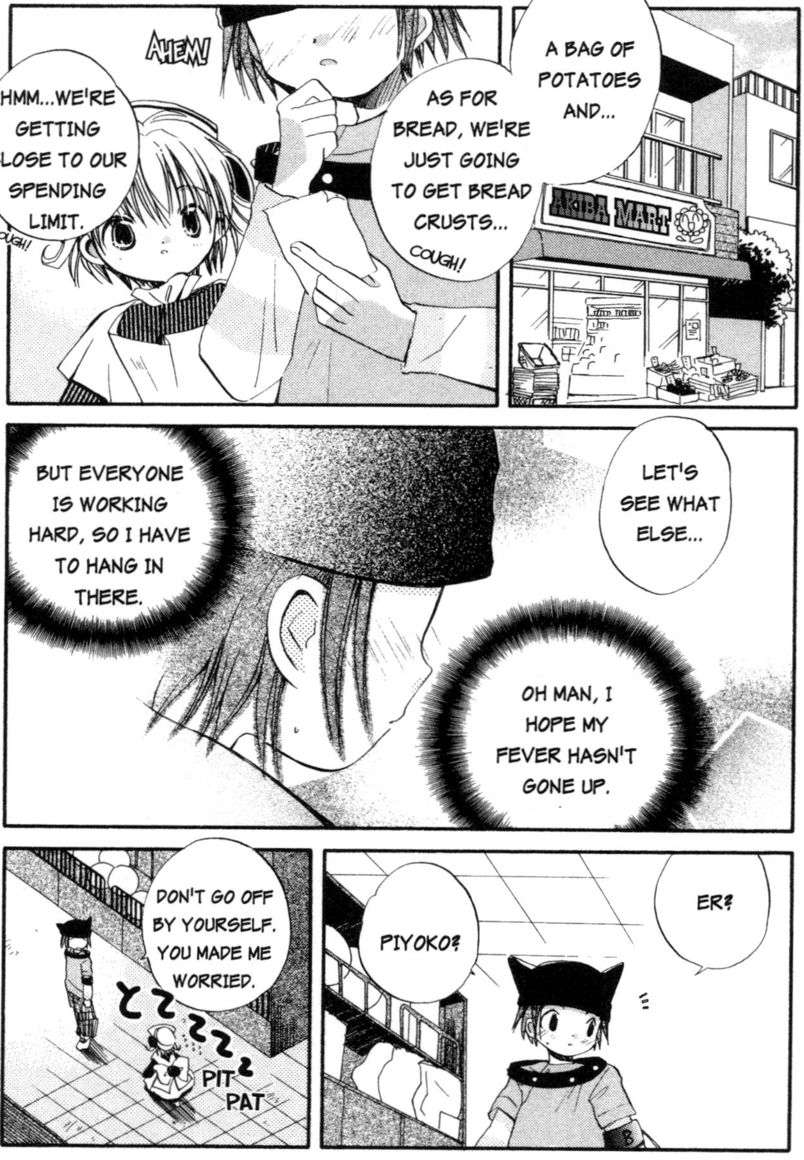
A BAG OF POTATOES AND...
AS FOR BREAD, WE'RE JUST GOING TO GET BREAD CRUSTS...
COUGH!
AHEM!
HMM...WE'RE GETTING CLOSE TO OUR SPENDING LIMIT.
COUGH!
AKIBA MART
LET'S SEE WHAT ELSE...
BUT EVERYONE IS WORKING HARD, SO I HAVE TO HANG IN THERE.
OH MAN, I HOPE MY FEVER HASN'T GONE UP.
ER?
PIYOKO?
DON'T GO OFF BY YOURSELF. YOU MADE ME WORRIED.
PIT PAT

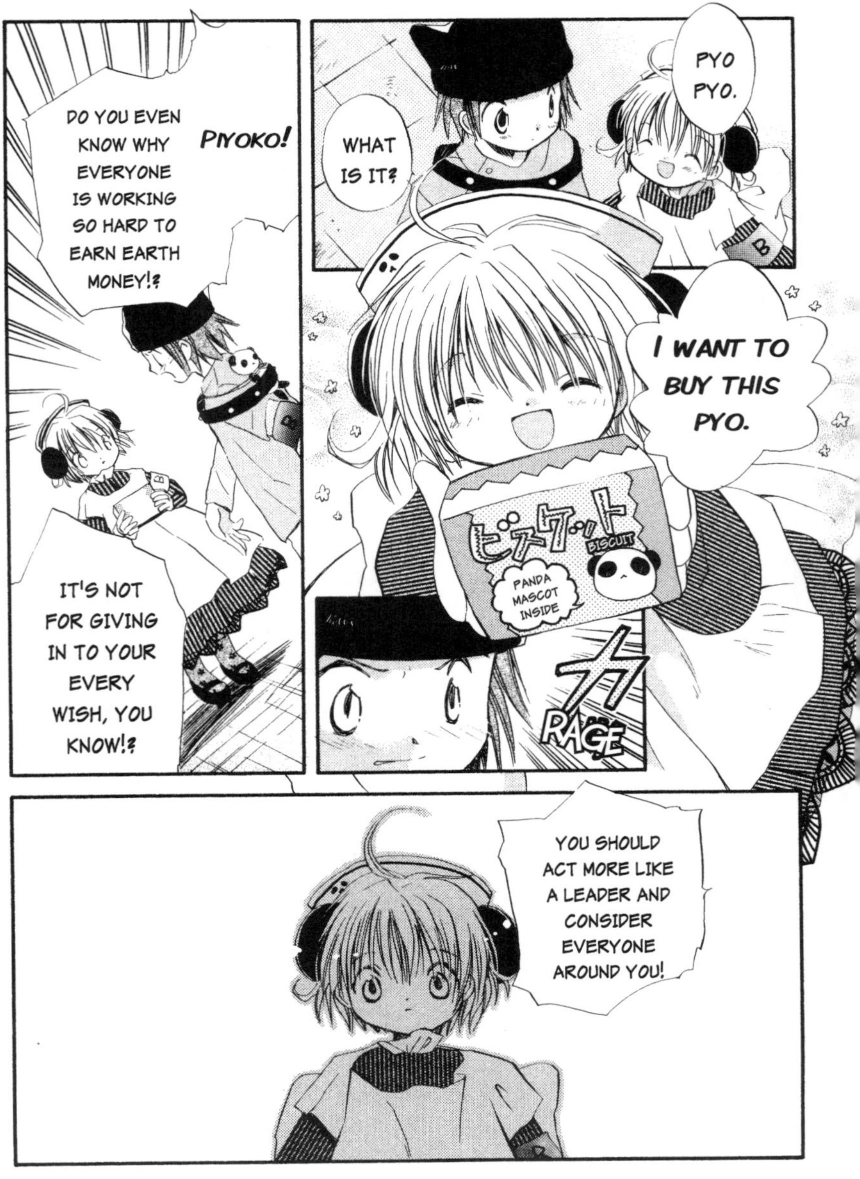
PYO PYO.
WHAT IS IT?
I WANT TO BUY THIS PYO.
ビスケット
BISCUIT
PANDA MASCOT INSIDE
RAGE
PIYOKO!
DO YOU EVEN KNOW WHY EVERYONE IS WORKING SO HARD TO EARN EARTH MONEY!?
IT'S NOT FOR GIVING IN TO YOUR EVERY WISH, YOU KNOW!?
YOU SHOULD ACT MORE LIKE A LEADER AND CONSIDER EVERYONE AROUND YOU!

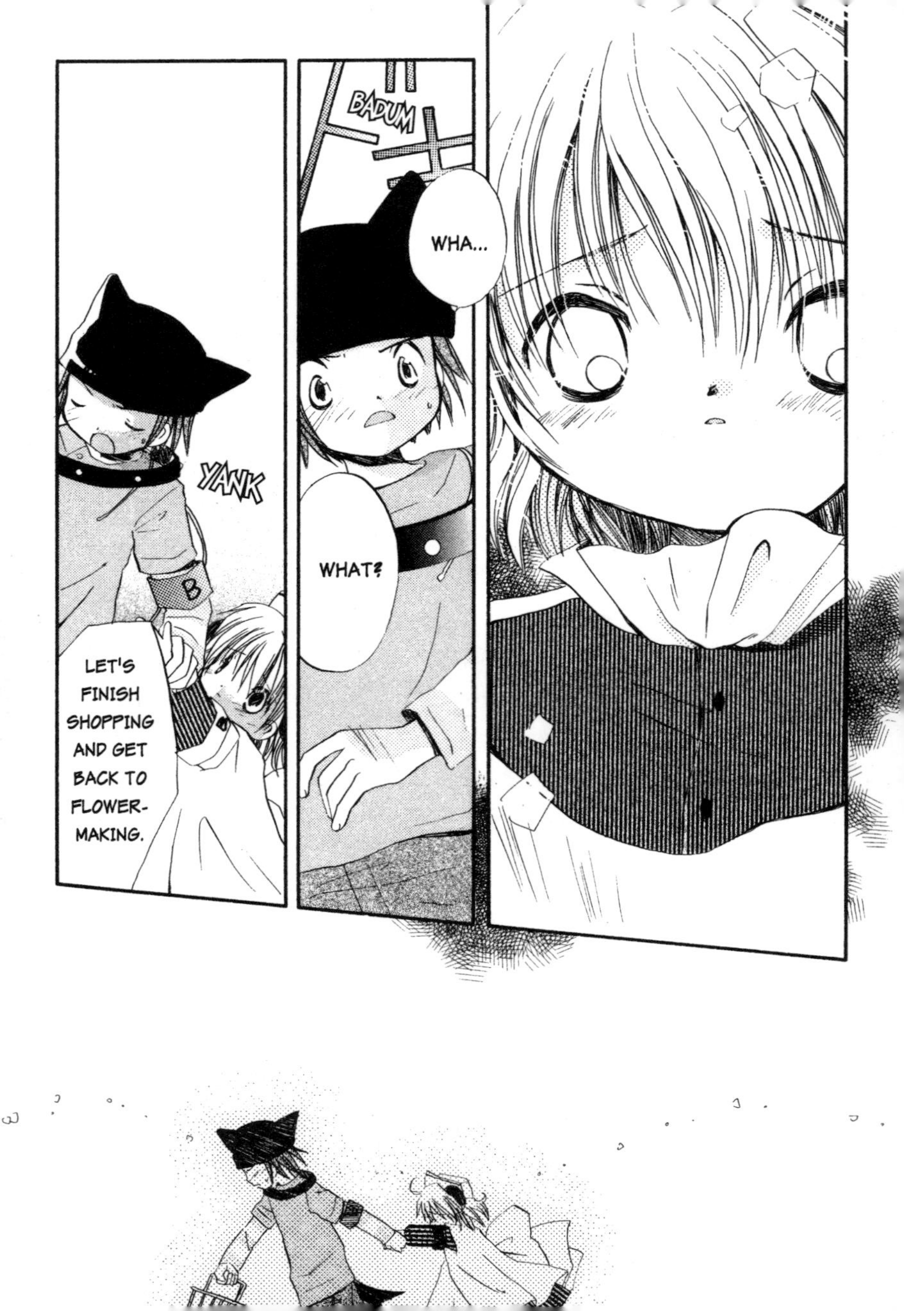
BADUM
WHA...
WHAT?
YANK
LET'S FINISH SHOPPING AND GET BACK TO FLOWER-MAKING.

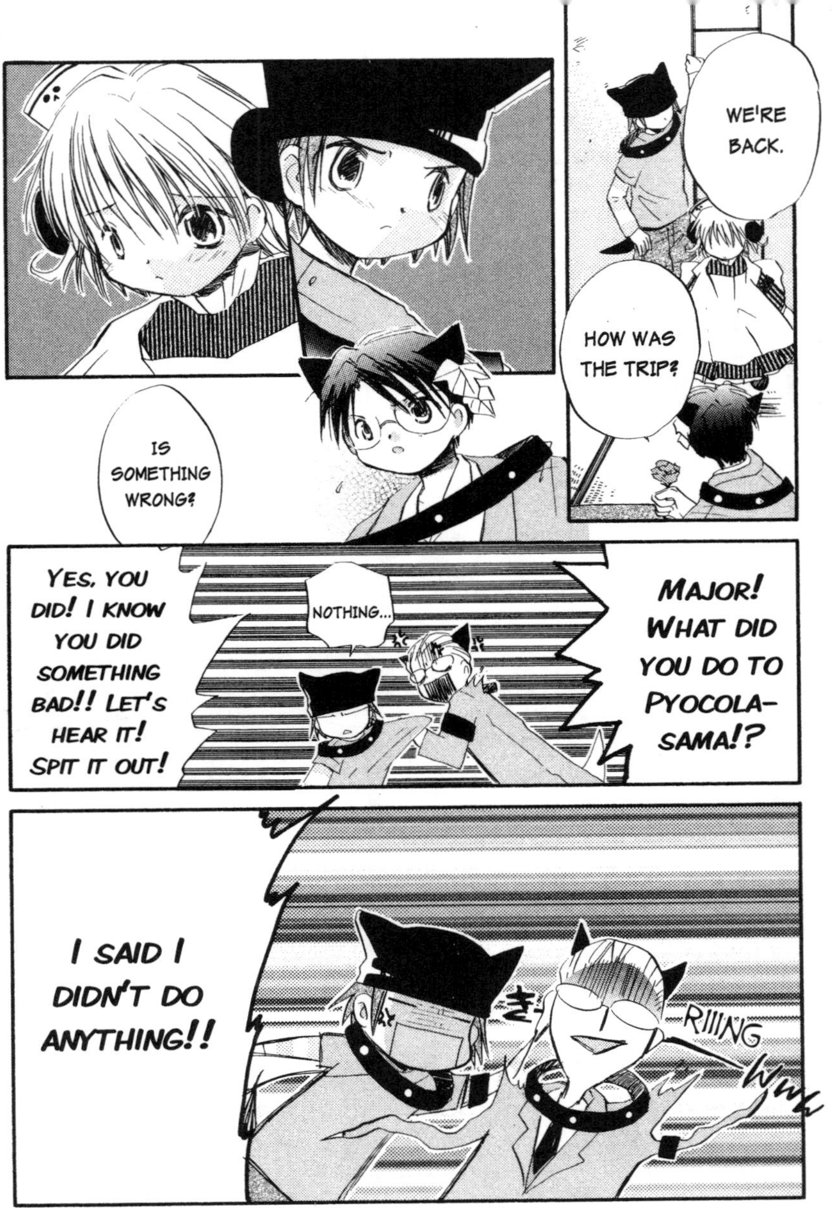
WE'RE BACK.
HOW WAS THE TRIP?
IS SOMETHING WRONG?
MAJOR! WHAT DID YOU DO TO PYOCOLA-SAMA!?
NOTHING...
YES, YOU DID! I KNOW YOU DID SOMETHING BAD!! LET'S HEAR IT! SPIT IT OUT!
I SAID I DIDN'T DO ANYTHING!!
RIIING

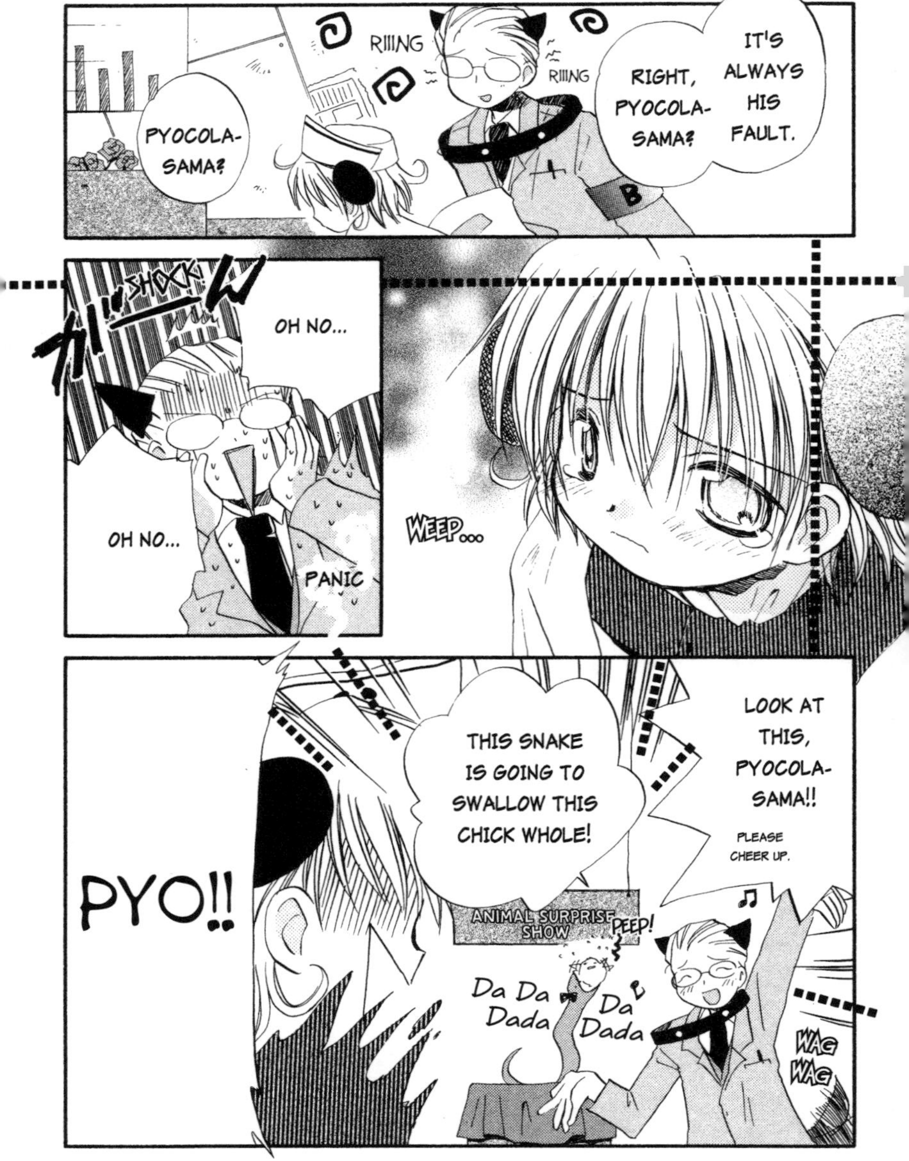
IT'S ALWAYS HIS FAULT.
RIGHT, PYOCOLA-SAMA?
RIIING
RIIING
PYOCOLA-SAMA?
WEEP...
SHOCK!
OH NO...
OH NO...
PANIC
LOOK AT THIS, PYOCOLA-SAMA!!
PLEASE CHEER UP.
THIS SNAKE IS GOING TO SWALLOW THIS CHICK WHOLE!
WAG WAG
PEEP!
ANIMAL SURPRISE SHOW
Da Dada
Da Da Dada
PYO!!

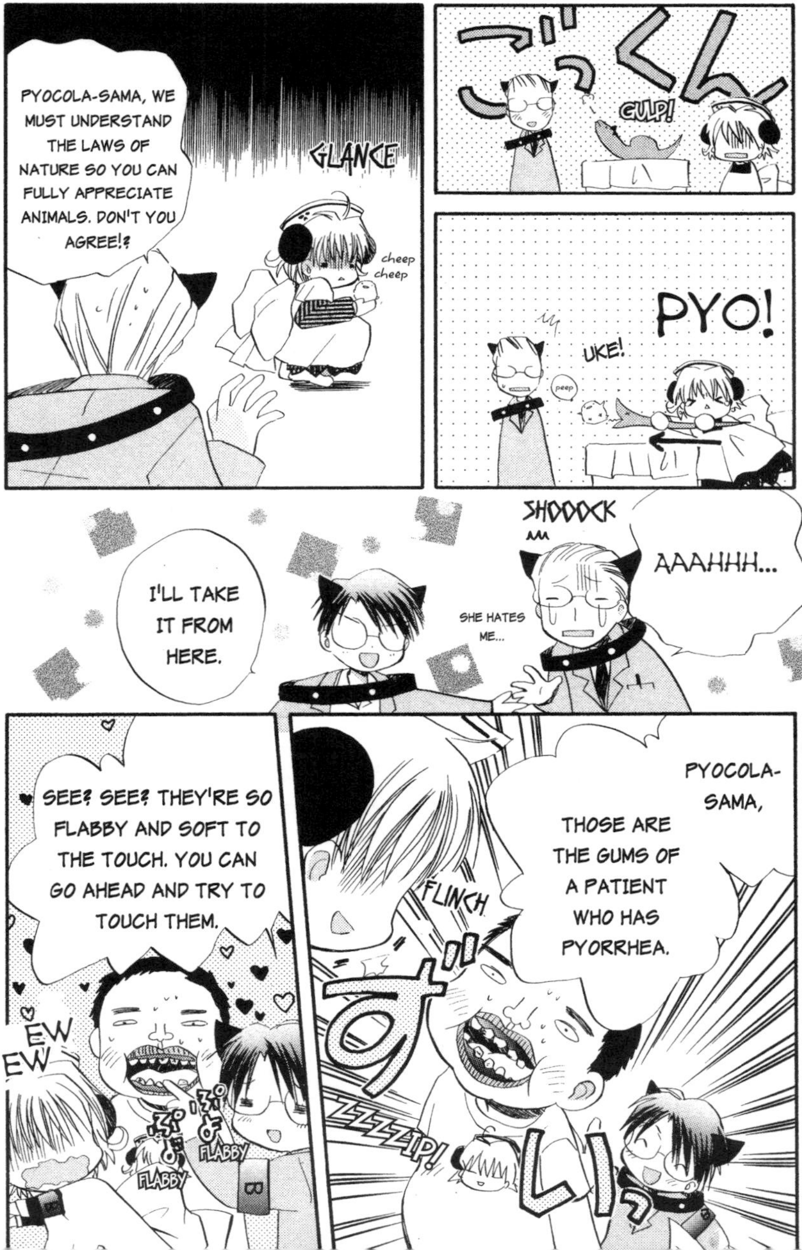
ごっくん
GULP!
PYO!
UKE!
peep
PYOCOLA-SAMA, WE MUST UNDERSTAND THE LAWS OF NATURE SO YOU CAN FULLY APPRECIATE ANIMALS. DON'T YOU AGREE!?
GLANCE
cheep cheep
SHOOOCK
AAAHHH...
SHE HATES ME...
I'LL TAKE IT FROM HERE.
PYOCOLA-SAMA,
THOSE ARE THE GUMS OF A PATIENT WHO HAS PYORRHEA.
FLINCH
ずっ
ZZZZZIP!
しっ
SEE? SEE? THEY'RE SO FLABBY AND SOFT TO THE TOUCH. YOU CAN GO AHEAD AND TRY TO TOUCH THEM.
EW EW
ぷよぷよ
FLABBY
FLABBY

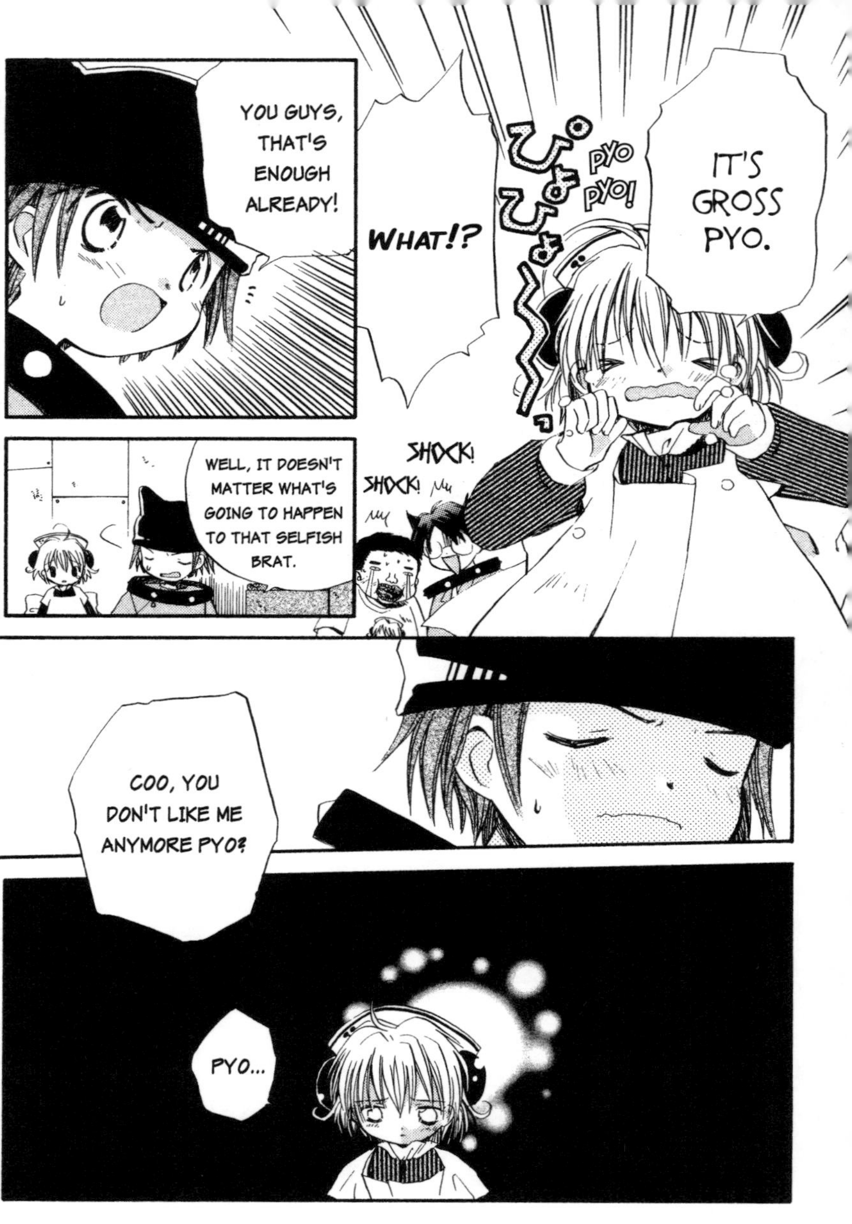
IT'S GROSS PYO.
PYO PYO!
WHAT!?
SHOCK! SHOCK!
YOU GUYS, THAT'S ENOUGH ALREADY!
WELL, IT DOESN'T MATTER WHAT'S GOING TO HAPPEN TO THAT SELFISH BRAT.
COO, YOU DON'T LIKE ME ANYMORE PYO?
PYO...

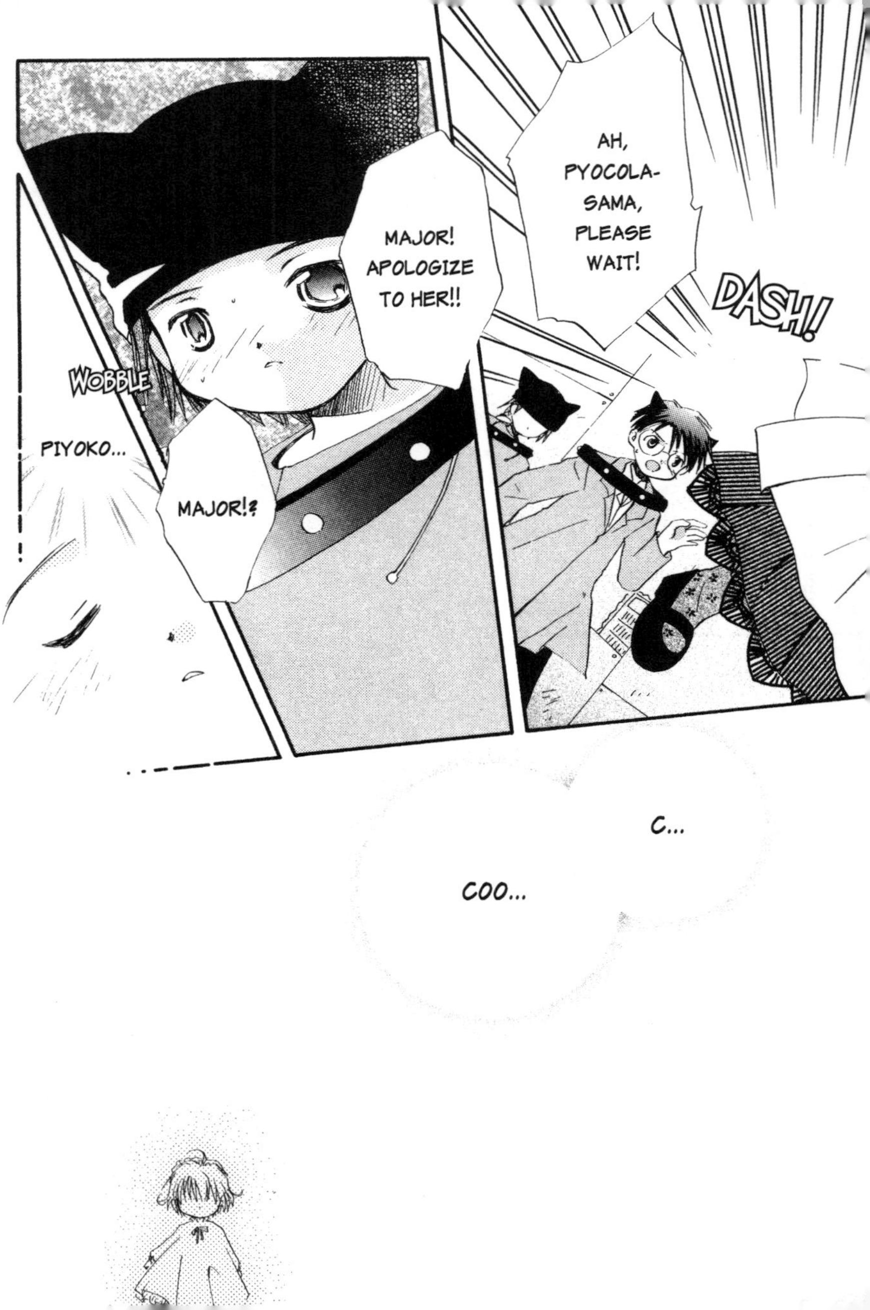
AH, PYOCOLA-SAMA, PLEASE WAIT!
DASH!
MAJOR! APOLOGIZE TO HER!!
MAJOR!?
WOBBLE
PIYOKO...
C...
COO...

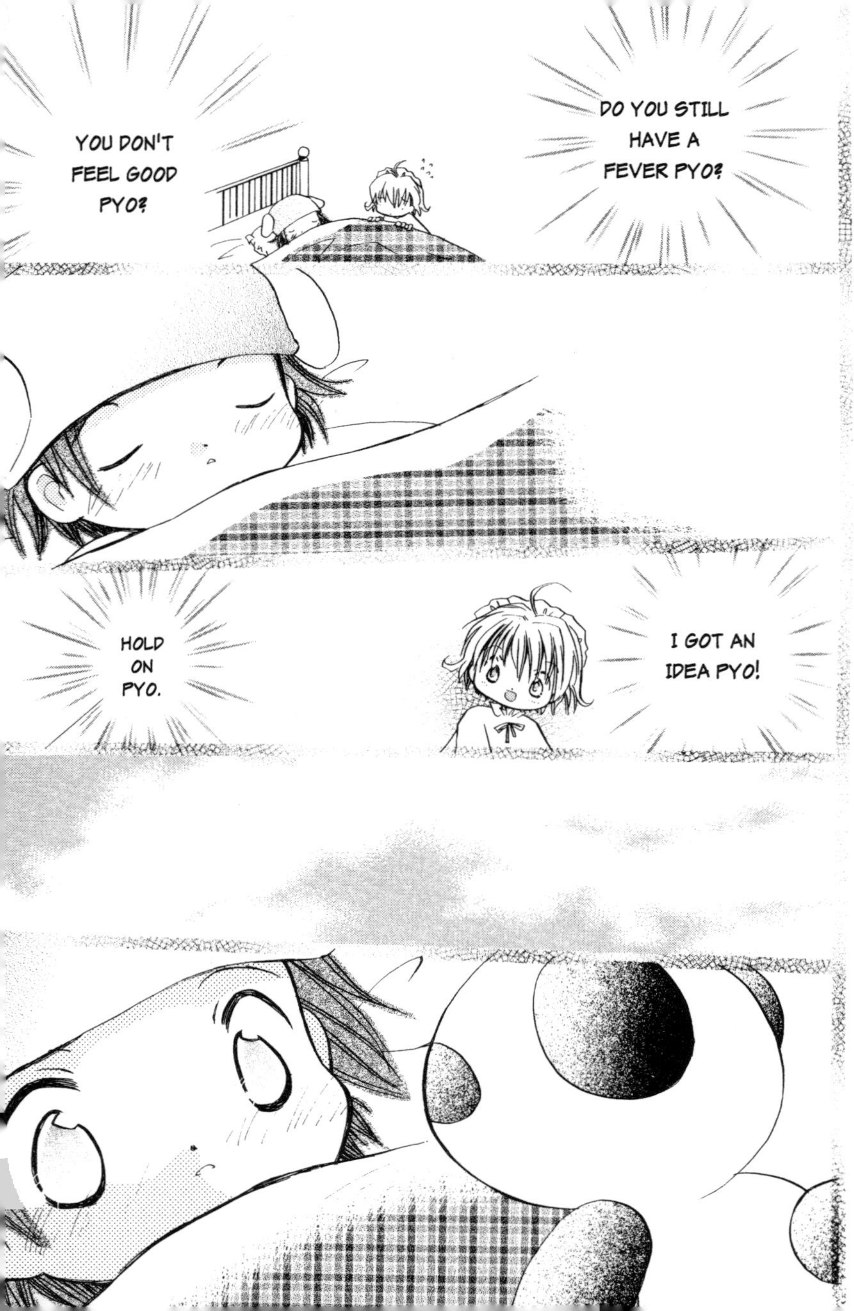
DO YOU STILL HAVE A FEVER PYO?
YOU DON'T FEEL GOOD PYO?
I GOT AN IDEA PYO!
HOLD ON PYO.

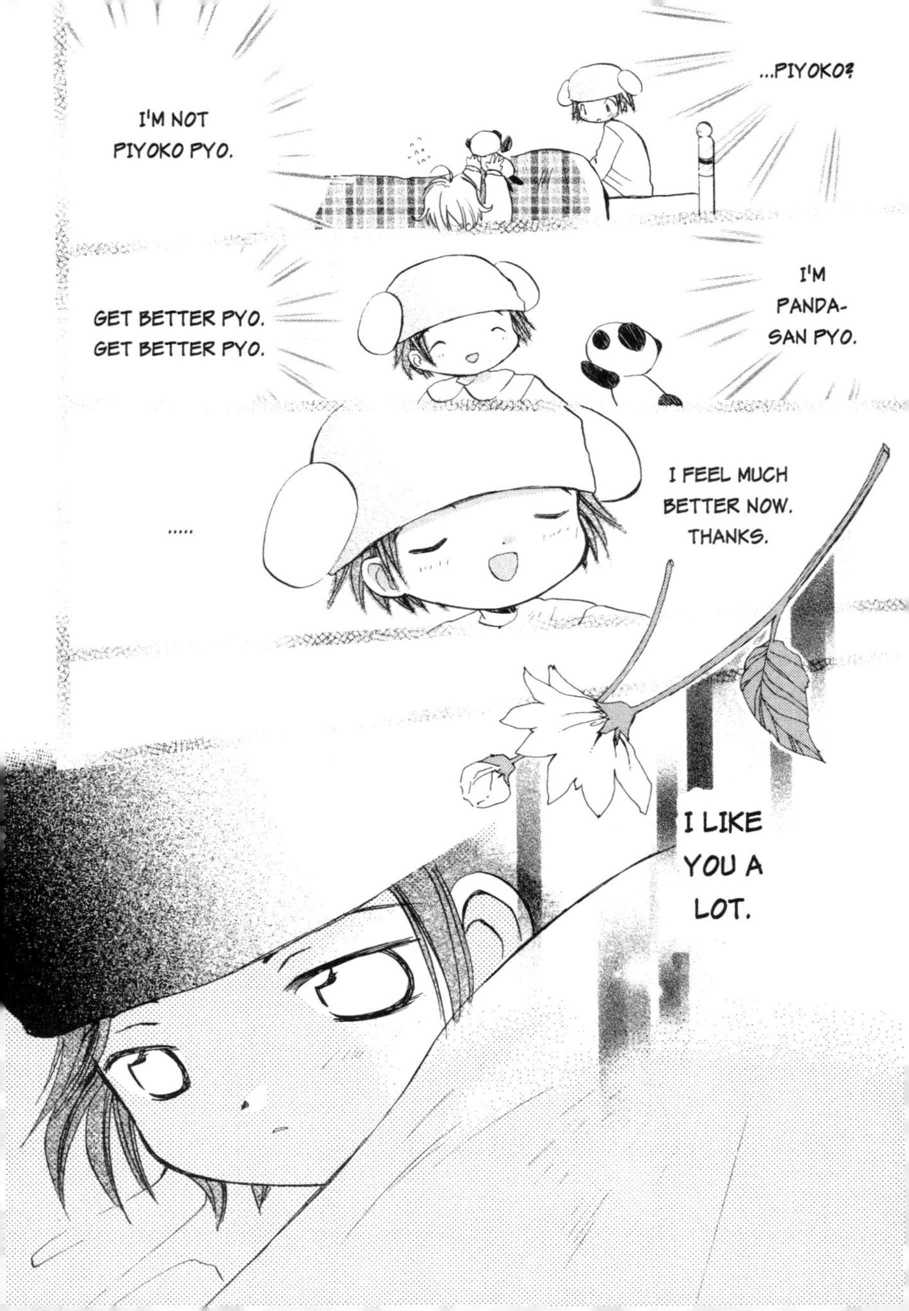
...PIYOKO?
I'M NOT PIYOKO PYO.
I'M PANDA-SAN PYO.
GET BETTER PYO. GET BETTER PYO.
I FEEL MUCH BETTER NOW. THANKS.
.....
I LIKE YOU A LOT.

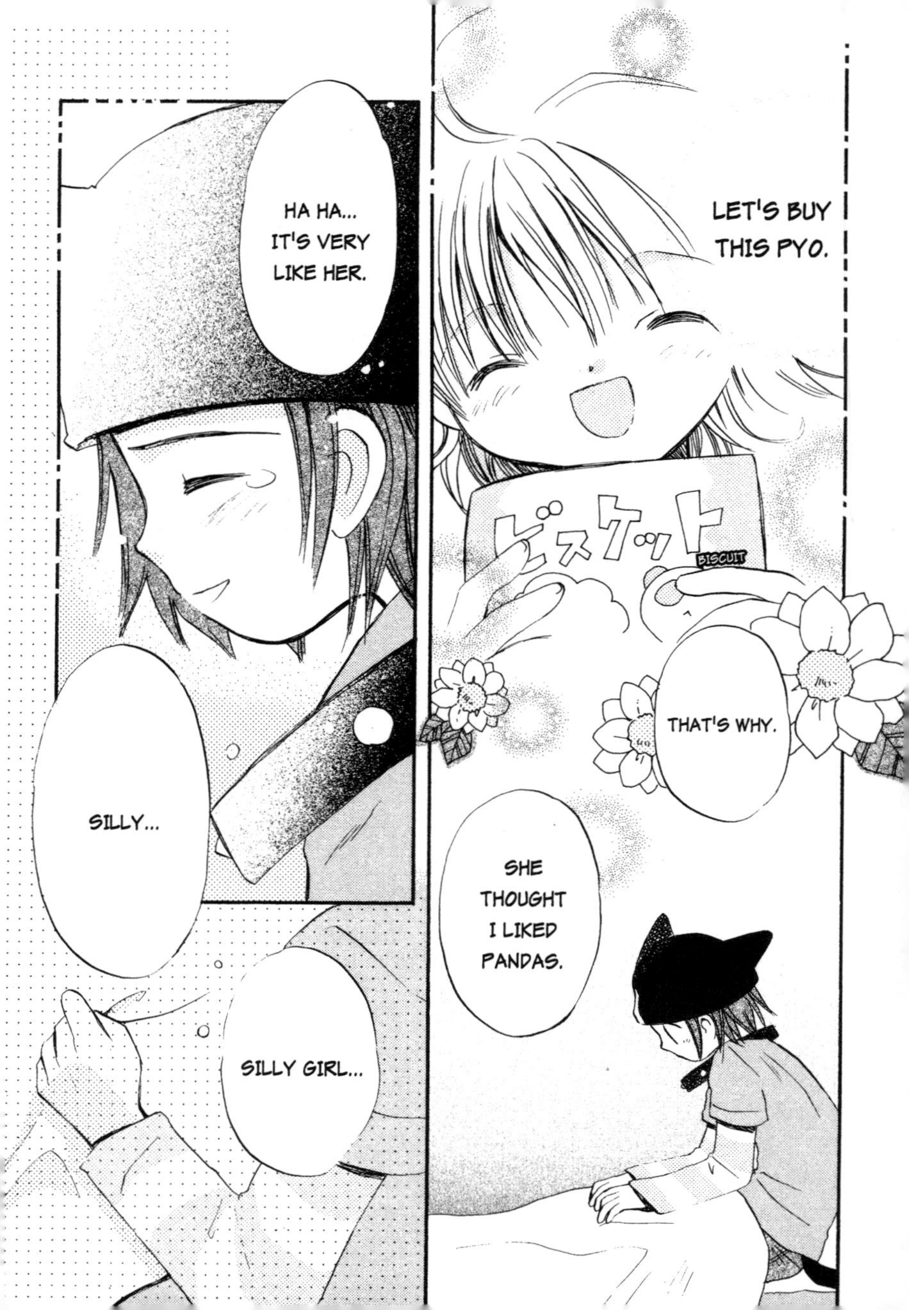
LET'S BUY THIS PYO.
ビスケット
BISCUIT
THAT'S WHY.
SHE THOUGHT I LIKED PANDAS.
HA HA... IT'S VERY LIKE HER.
SILLY...
SILLY GIRL...

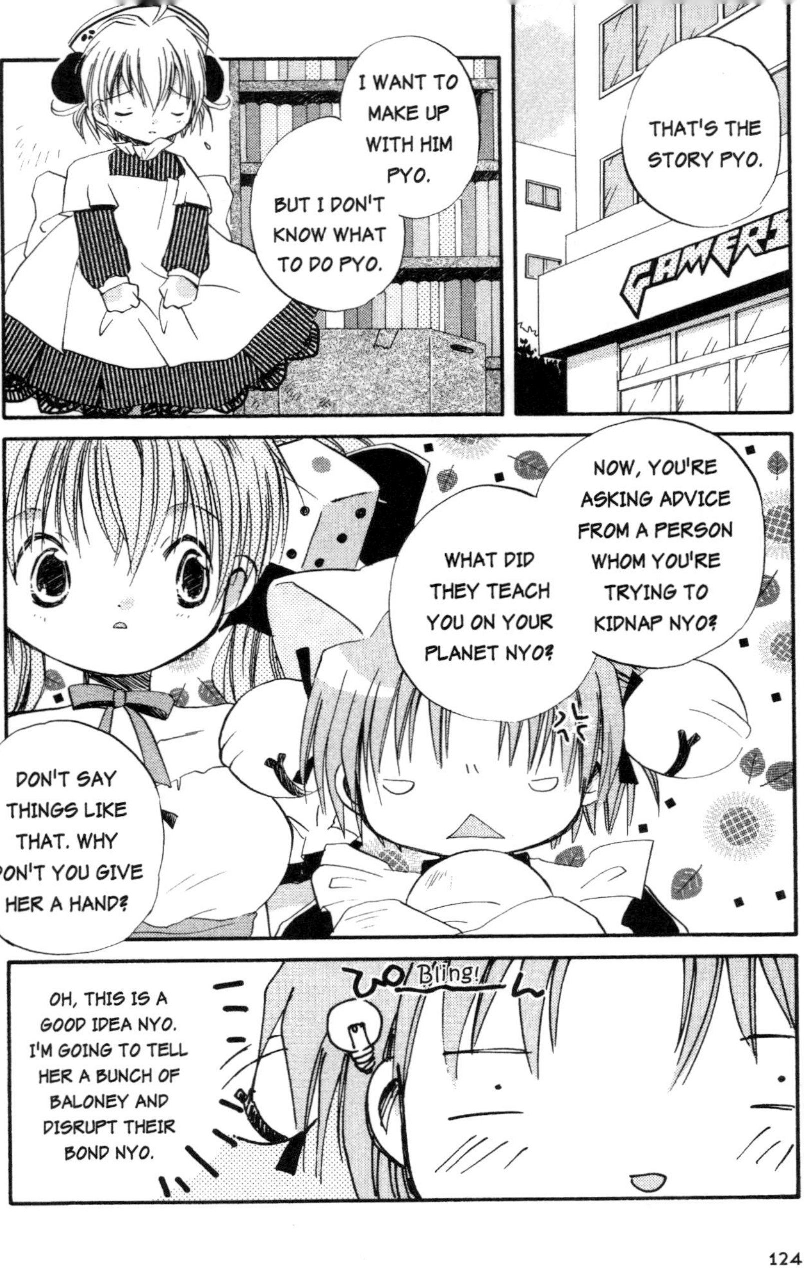
THAT'S THE STORY PYO.
I WANT TO MAKE UP WITH HIM PYO.
BUT I DON'T KNOW WHAT TO DO PYO.
NOW, YOU'RE ASKING ADVICE FROM A PERSON WHOM YOU'RE TRYING TO KIDNAP NYO?
WHAT DID THEY TEACH YOU ON YOUR PLANET NYO?
DON'T SAY THINGS LIKE THAT. WHY DON'T YOU GIVE HER A HAND?
Bling!
OH, THIS IS A GOOD IDEA NYO. I'M GOING TO TELL HER A BUNCH OF BALONEY AND DISRUPT THEIR BOND NYO.

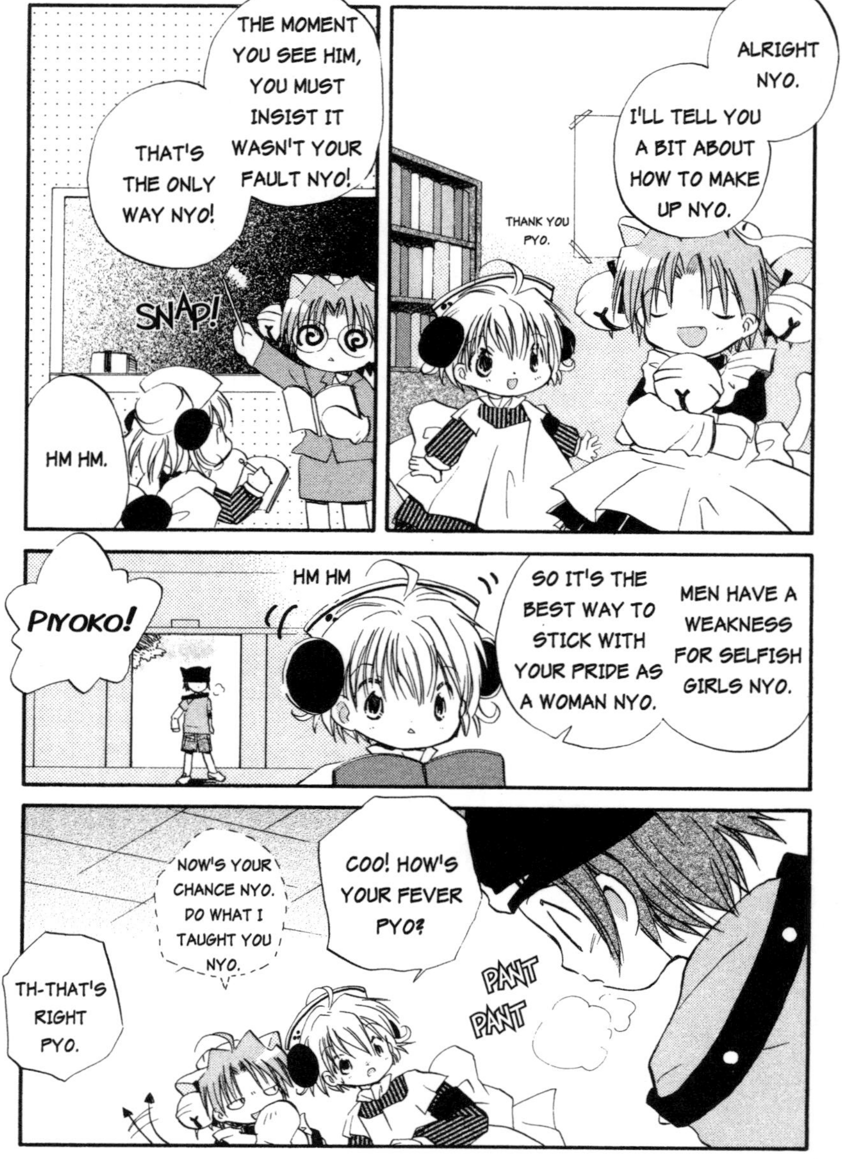
ALRIGHT NYO.
I'LL TELL YOU A BIT ABOUT HOW TO MAKE UP NYO.
THANK YOU PYO.
THE MOMENT YOU SEE HIM, YOU MUST INSIST IT WASN'T YOUR FAULT NYO!
THAT'S THE ONLY WAY NYO!
SNAP!
HM HM.
MEN HAVE A WEAKNESS FOR SELFISH GIRLS NYO.
SO IT'S THE BEST WAY TO STICK WITH YOUR PRIDE AS A WOMAN NYO.
HM HM
PIYOKO!
COO! HOW'S YOUR FEVER PYO?
PANT PANT
NOW'S YOUR CHANCE NYO. DO WHAT I TAUGHT YOU NYO.
TH-THAT'S RIGHT PYO.

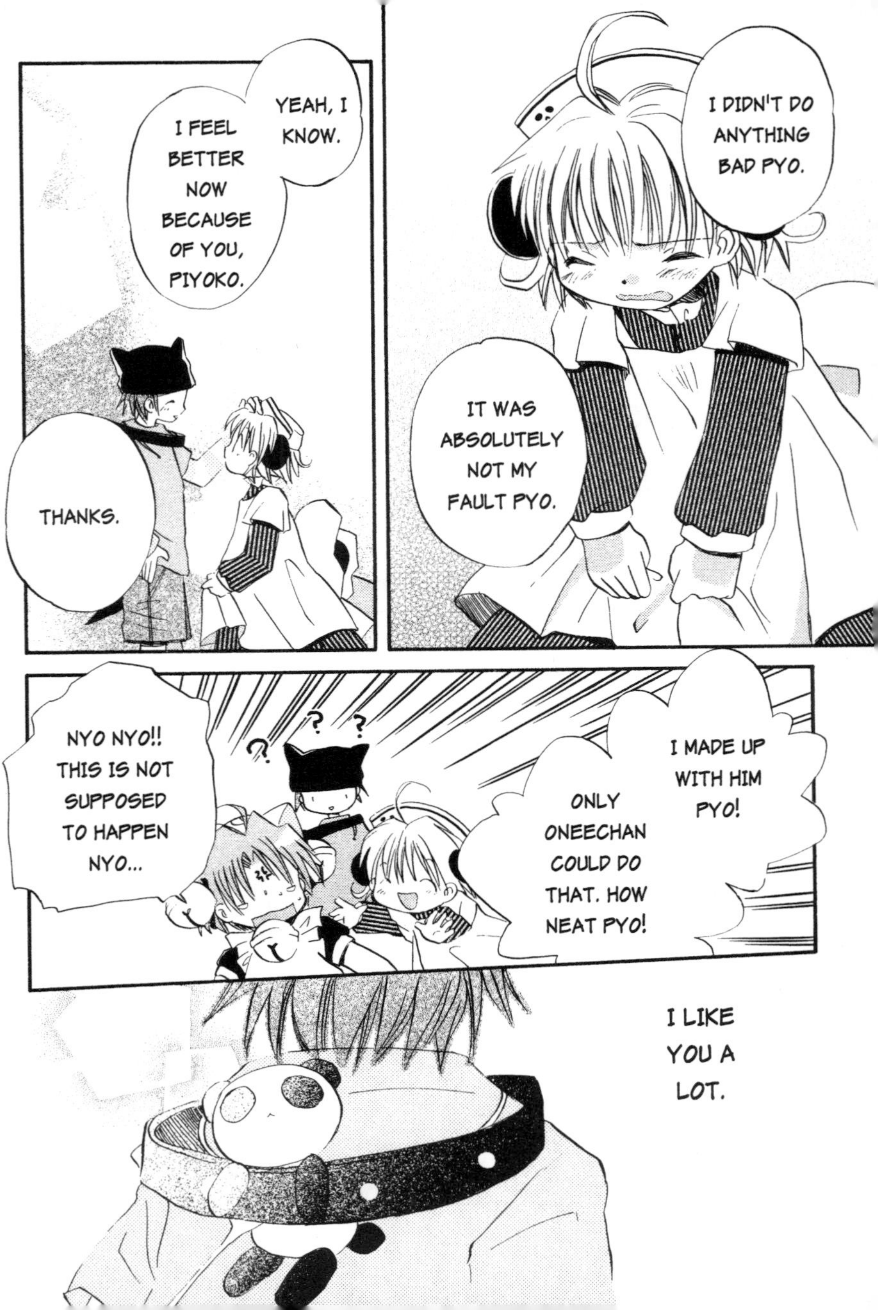
I DIDN'T DO ANYTHING BAD PYO.
IT WAS ABSOLUTELY NOT MY FAULT PYO.
YEAH, I KNOW.
I FEEL BETTER NOW BECAUSE OF YOU, PIYOKO.
THANKS.
I MADE UP WITH HIM PYO!
ONLY ONEECHAN COULD DO THAT. HOW NEAT PYO!
? ? ?
NYO NYO!! THIS IS NOT SUPPOSED TO HAPPEN NYO...
I LIKE YOU A LOT.

Nyo 12 Let's Train with Piyoko

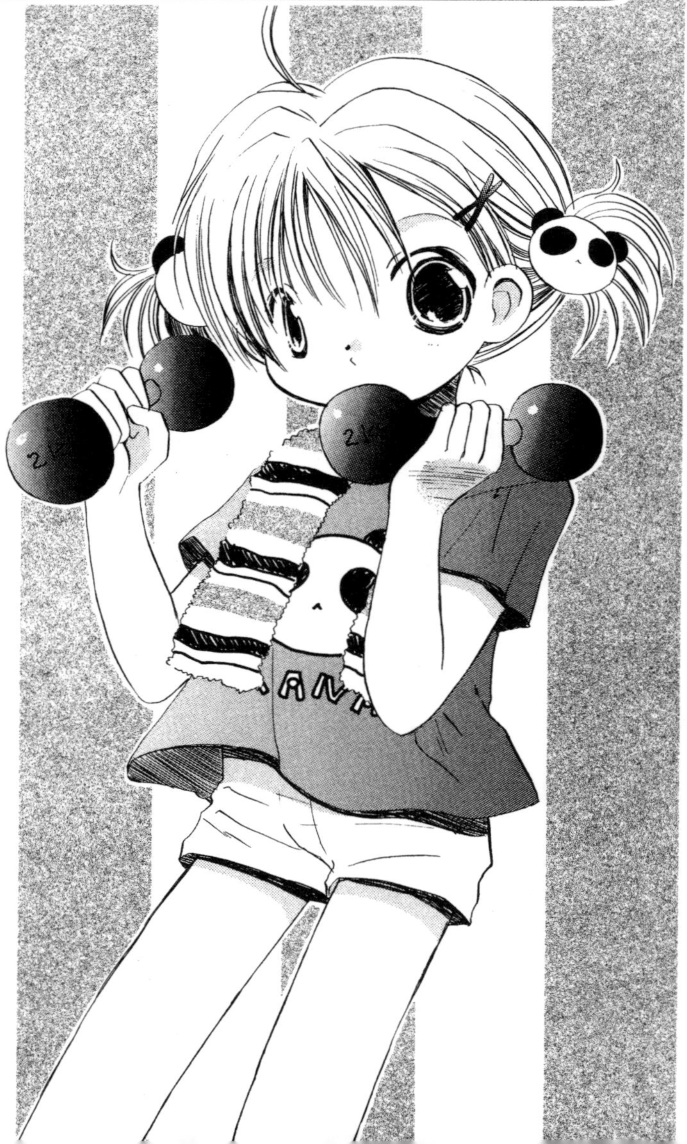

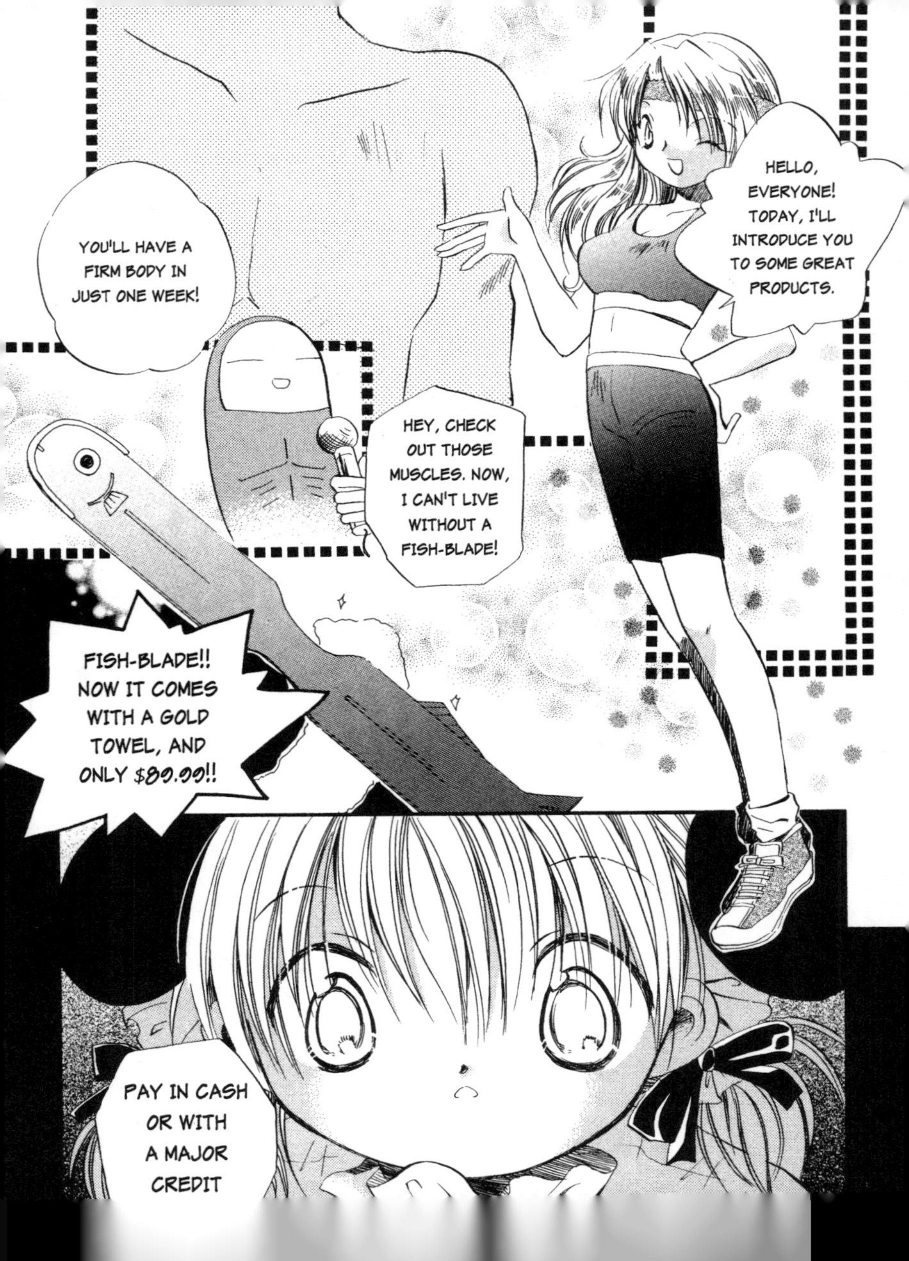
HELLO, EVERYONE! TODAY, I'LL INTRODUCE YOU TO SOME GREAT PRODUCTS.
YOU'LL HAVE A FIRM BODY IN JUST ONE WEEK!
HEY, CHECK OUT THOSE MUSCLES. NOW, I CAN'T LIVE WITHOUT A FISH-BLADE!
FISH-BLADE!! NOW IT COMES WITH A GOLD TOWEL, AND ONLY $89.99!!
PAY IN CASH OR WITH A MAJOR CREDIT

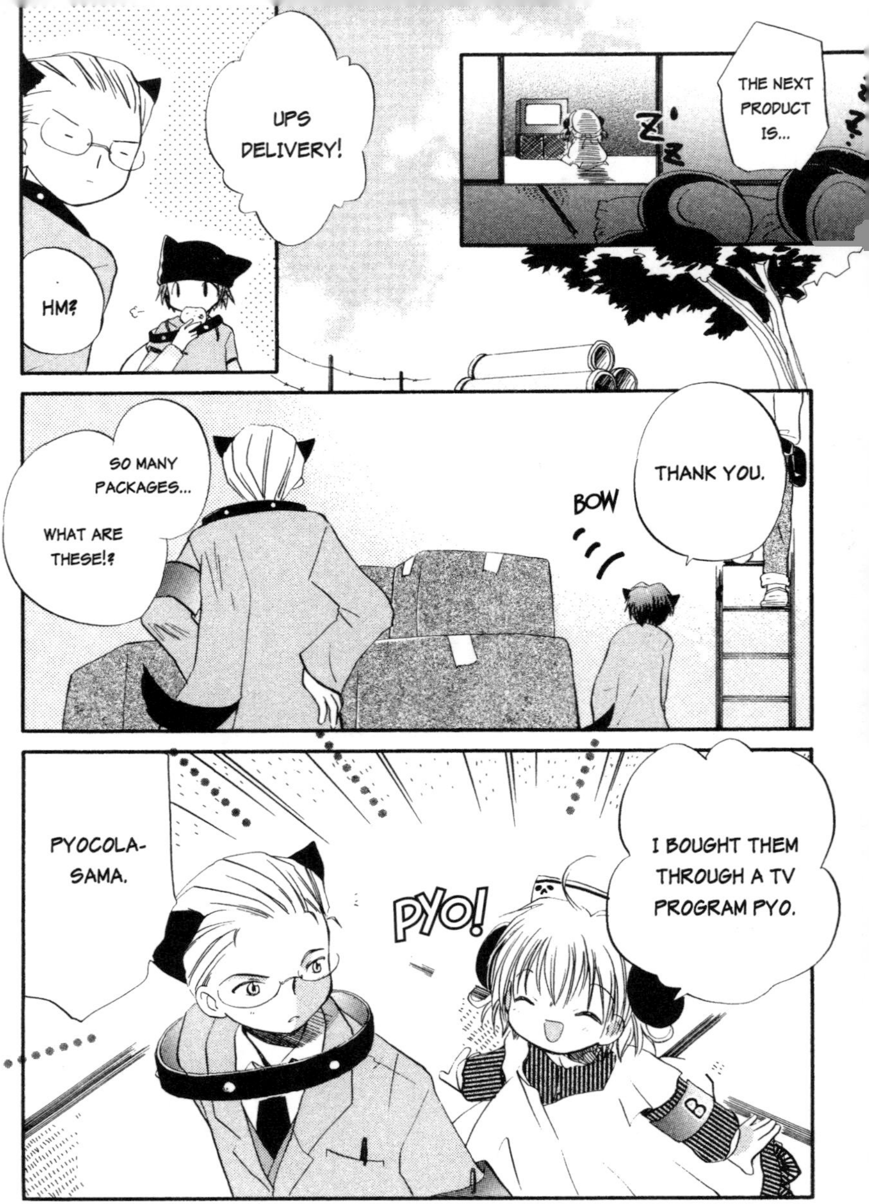
THE NEXT PRODUCT IS...
UPS DELIVERY!
HM?
THANK YOU.
BOW
SO MANY PACKAGES...
WHAT ARE THESE!?
I BOUGHT THEM THROUGH A TV PROGRAM PYO.
PYO!
PYOCOLA-SAMA.

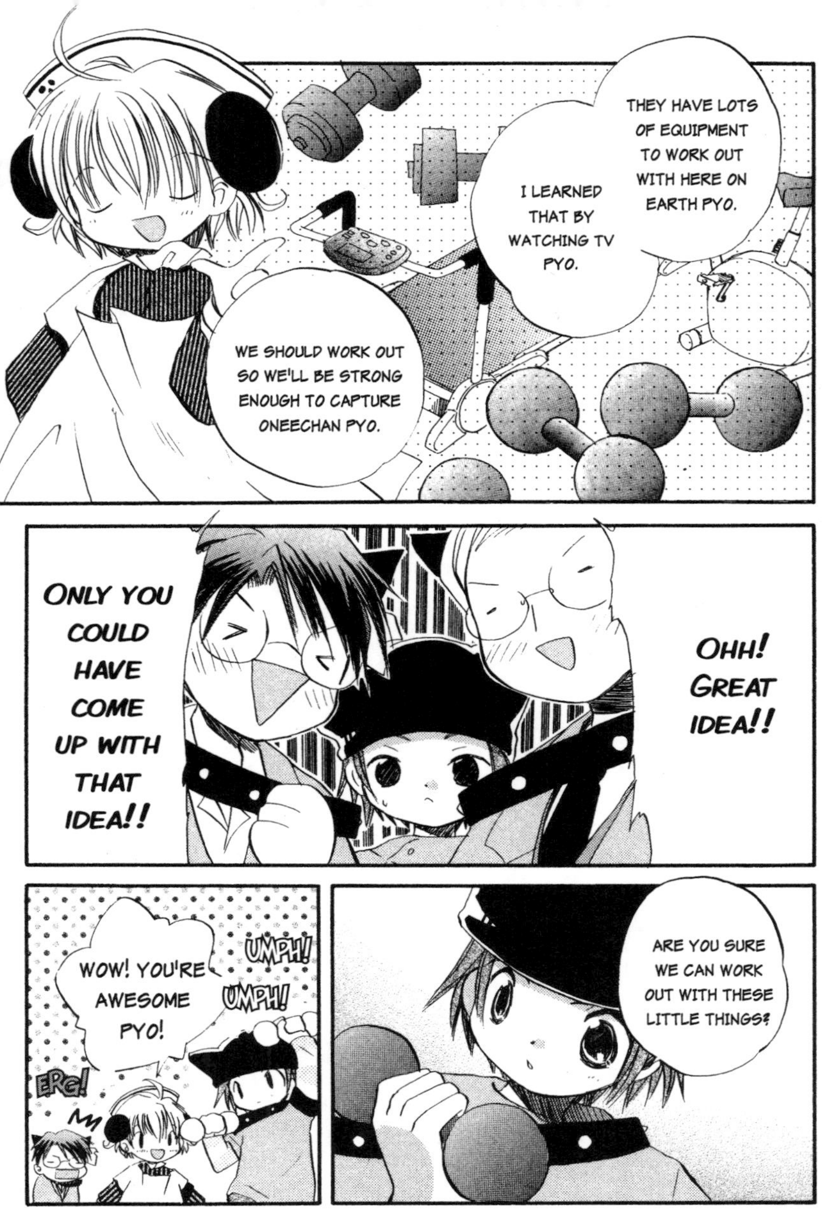
THEY HAVE LOTS OF EQUIPMENT TO WORK OUT WITH HERE ON EARTH PYO.
I LEARNED THAT BY WATCHING TV PYO.
WE SHOULD WORK OUT SO WE'LL BE STRONG ENOUGH TO CAPTURE ONEECHAN PYO.
OHH! GREAT IDEA!!
ONLY YOU COULD HAVE COME UP WITH THAT IDEA!!
ARE YOU SURE WE CAN WORK OUT WITH THESE LITTLE THINGS?
UMPH!
UMPH!
WOW! YOU'RE AWESOME PYO!
ERG!

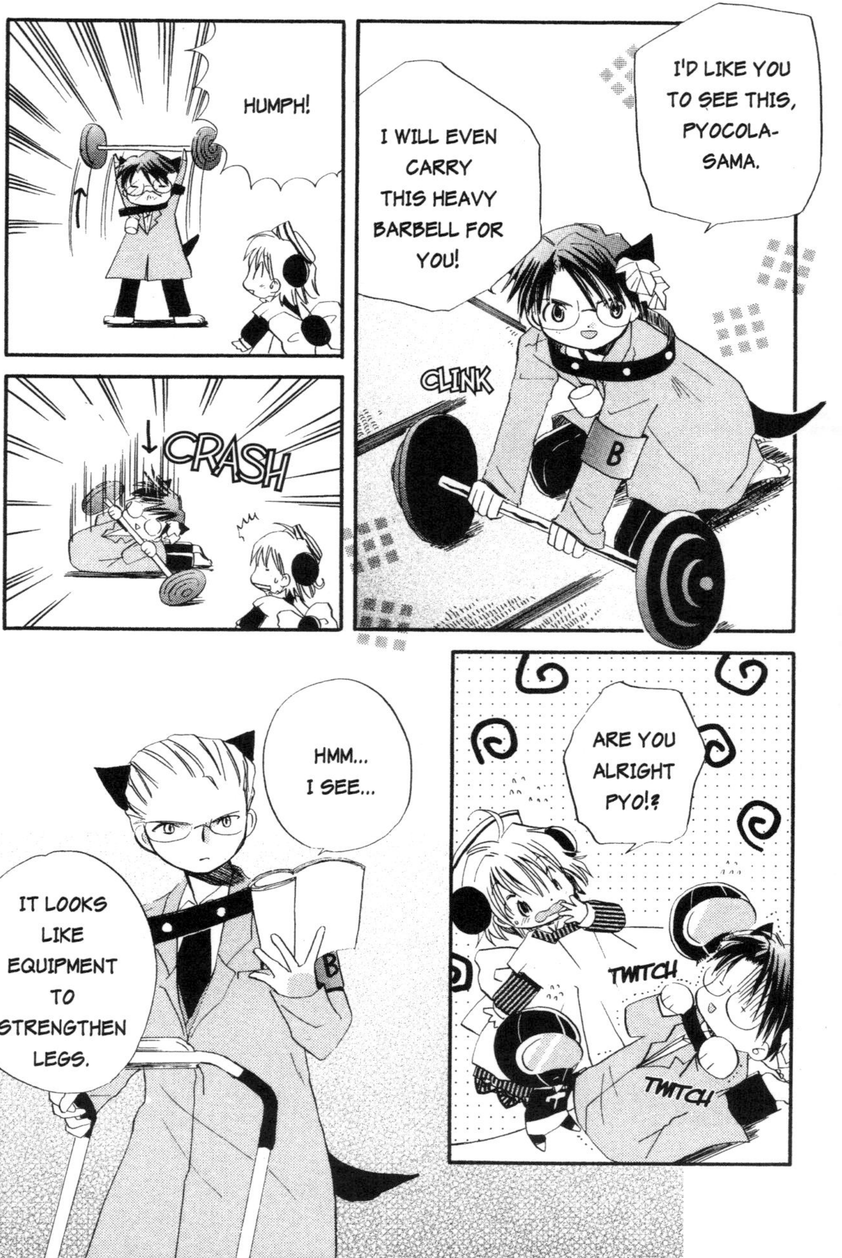
I'D LIKE YOU TO SEE THIS, PYOCOLA-SAMA.
I WILL EVEN CARRY THIS HEAVY BARBELL FOR YOU!
CLINK
HUMPH!
CRASH
ARE YOU ALRIGHT PYO!?
TWITCH
TWITCH
HMM... I SEE...
IT LOOKS LIKE EQUIPMENT TO STRENGTHEN LEGS.

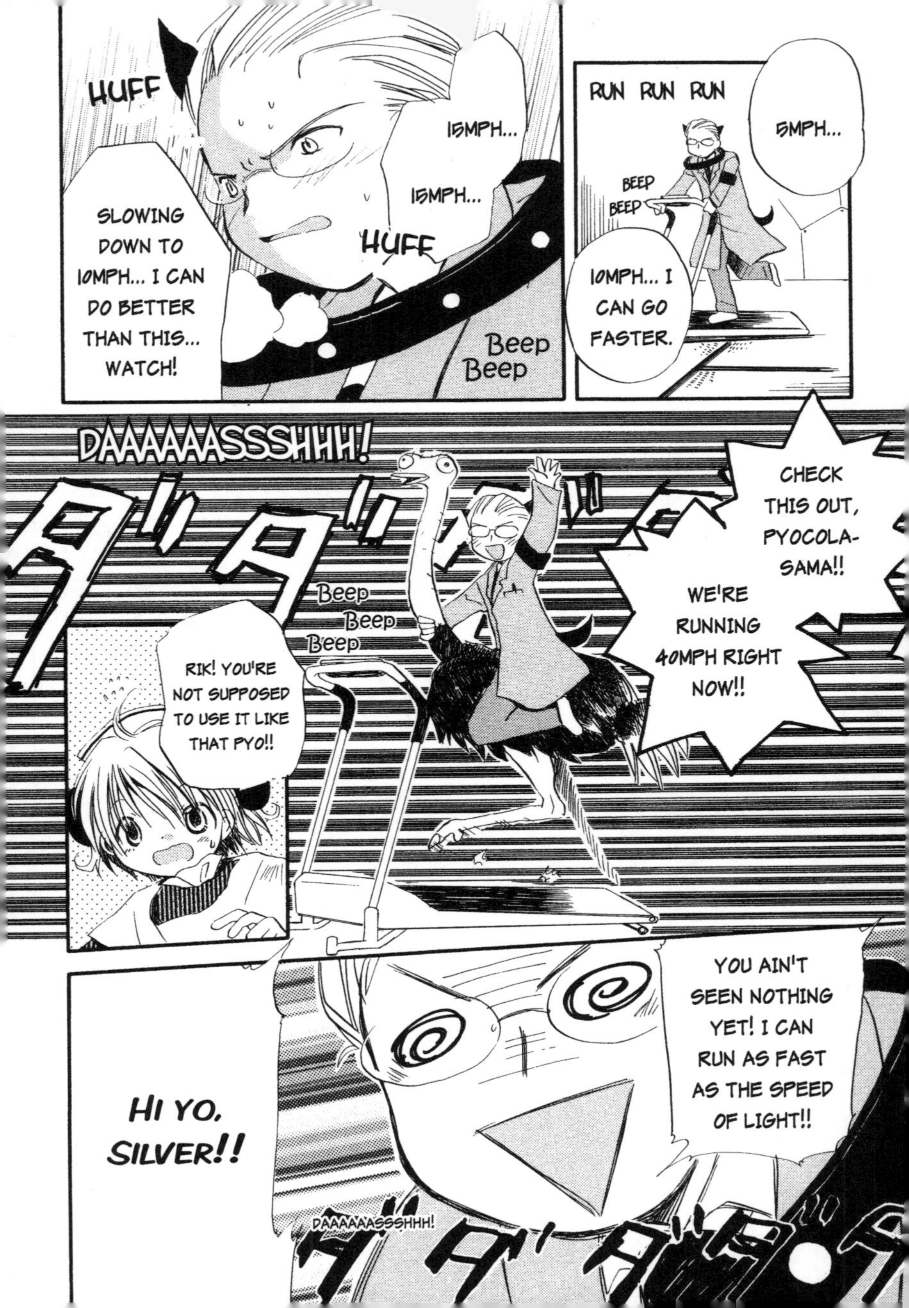
RUN RUN RUN
5MPH...
BEEP BEEP
10MPH... I CAN GO FASTER.
15MPH...
HUFF
15MPH...
HUFF
SLOWING DOWN TO 10MPH... I CAN DO BETTER THAN THIS... WATCH!
Beep Beep
DAAAAAASSSHHH!
CHECK THIS OUT, PYOCOLA-SAMA!!
WE'RE RUNNING 40MPH RIGHT NOW!!
Beep Beep Beep
RIK! YOU'RE NOT SUPPOSED TO USE IT LIKE THAT PYO!!
YOU AIN'T SEEN NOTHING YET! I CAN RUN AS FAST AS THE SPEED OF LIGHT!!
HI YO, SILVER!!
DAAAAAASSSHHH!

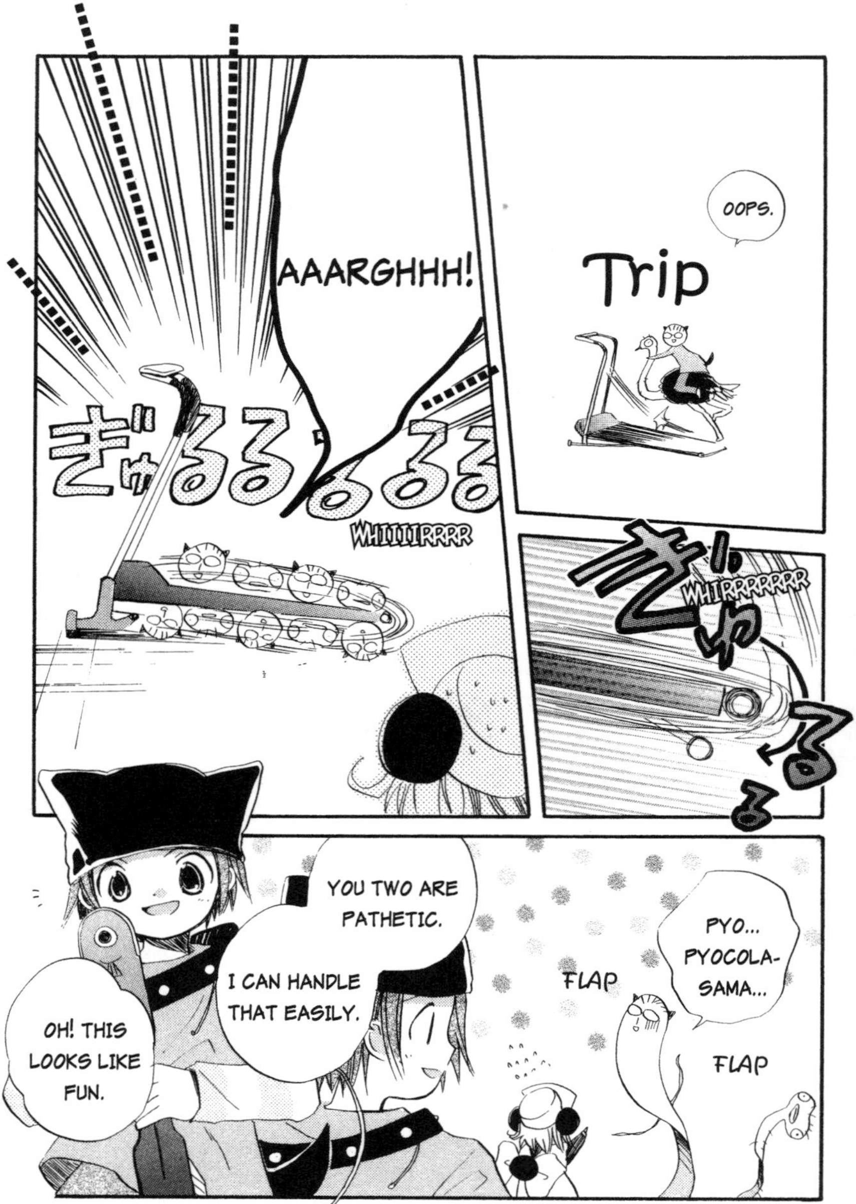
OOPS.
Trip
ぎゅるる
WHIRRRRRRR
AAARGHHH!
ぎゅるるるる
WHIIIIRRRR
PYO... PYOCOLA-SAMA...
FLAP
FLAP
YOU TWO ARE PATHETIC.
I CAN HANDLE THAT EASILY.
OH! THIS LOOKS LIKE FUN.

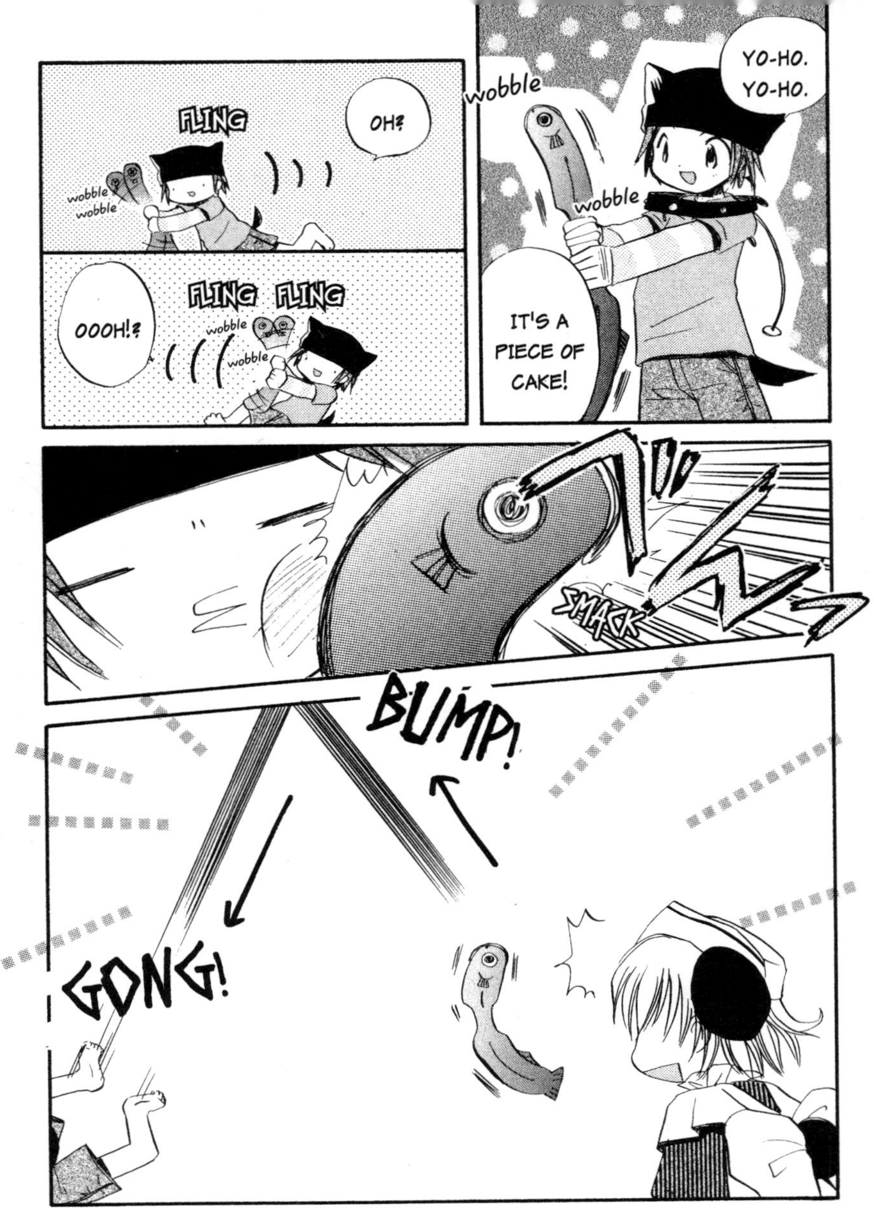
YO-HO. YO-HO.
wobble
wobble
IT'S A PIECE OF CAKE!
OH?
FLING
wobble wobble
FLING FLING
OOOH!?
wobble
wobble
SMACK
BUMP!
GONG!

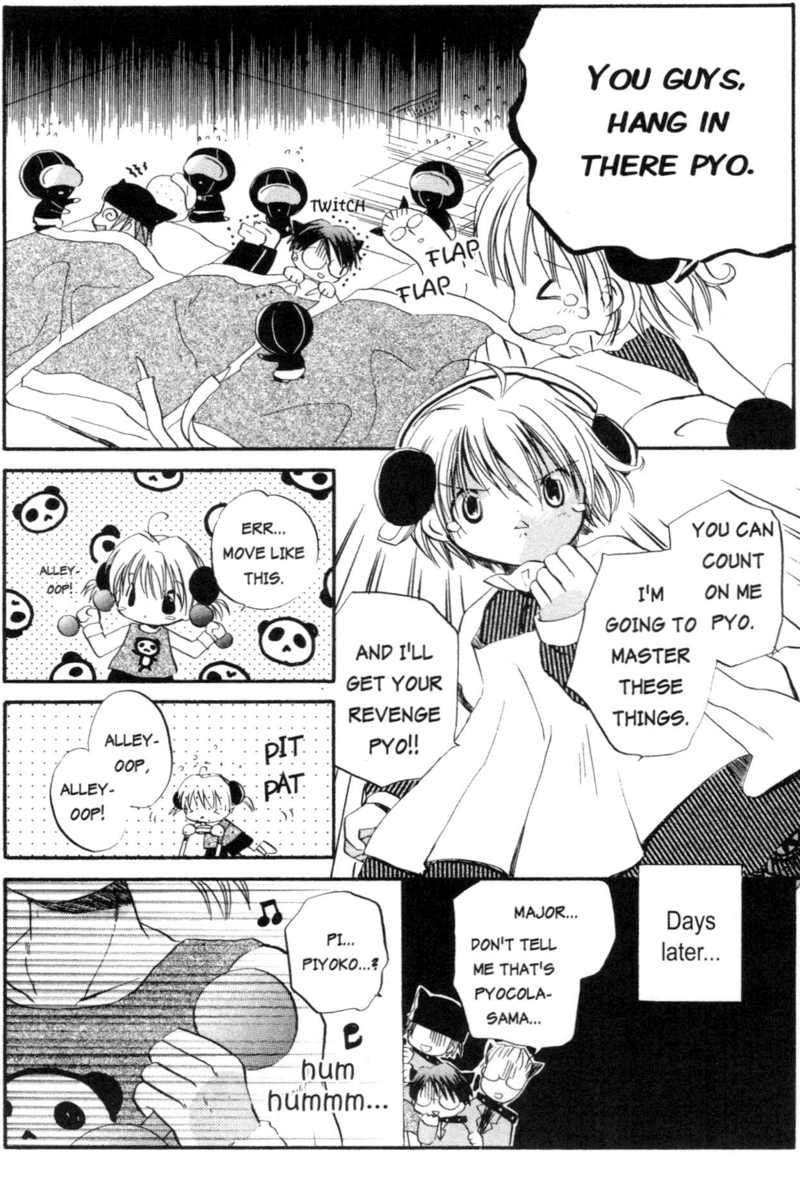
YOU GUYS, HANG IN THERE PYO.
TWITCH
FLAP
FLAP
YOU CAN COUNT ON ME PYO.
I'M GOING TO MASTER THESE THINGS.
AND I'LL GET YOUR REVENGE PYO!!
ERR... MOVE LIKE THIS.
ALLEY-OOP!
ALLEY-OOP,
ALLEY-OOP!
PIT PAT
Days later...
MAJOR...
DON'T TELL ME THAT'S PYOCOLA-SAMA...
PI... PIYOKO...?
hum hummm...

A Day in the Life of
the Black Gema Gema Gang
6:00 PM Night meeting

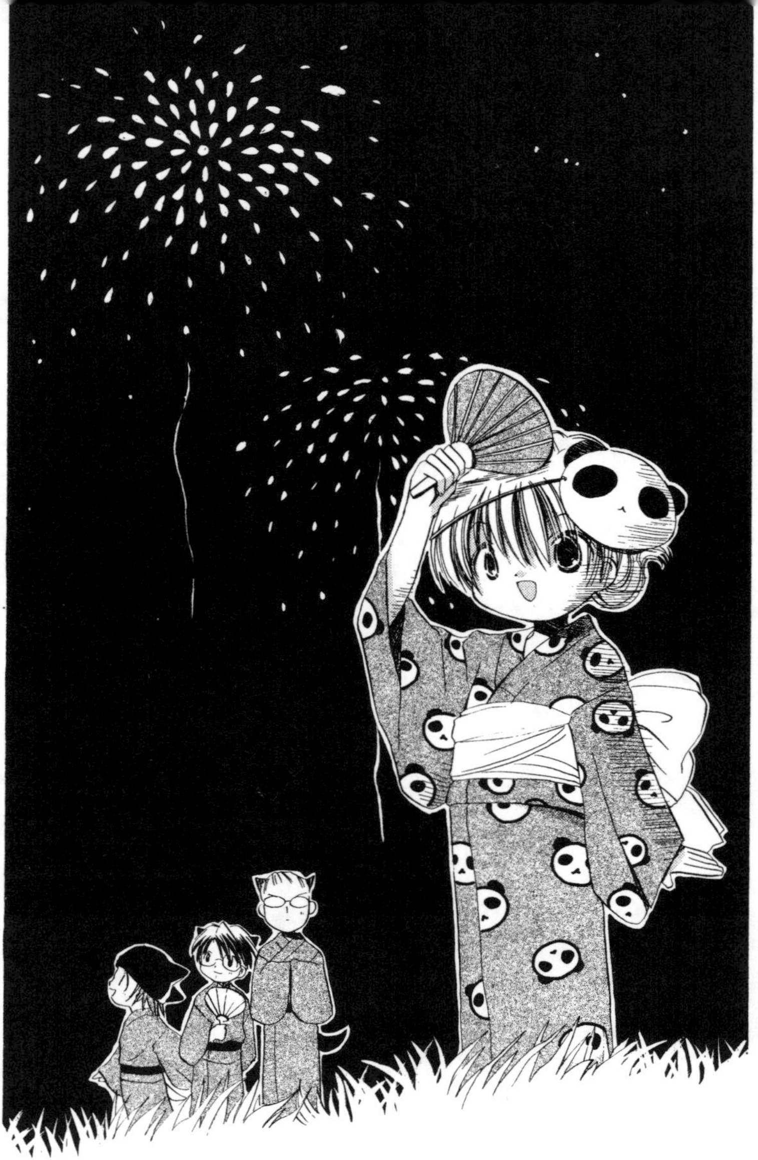

Nyo 13 Summer Festival

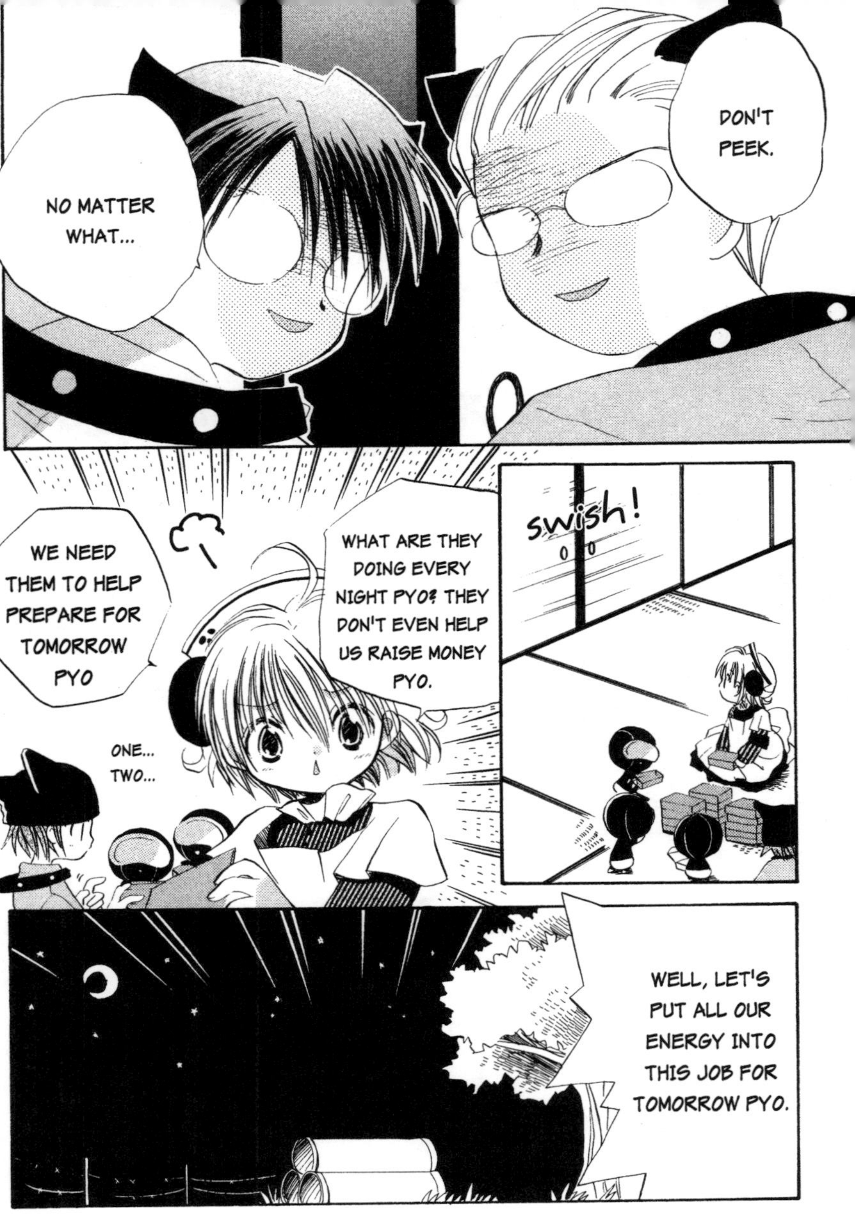
DON'T PEEK.
NO MATTER WHAT...
swish!
WHAT ARE THEY DOING EVERY NIGHT PYO? THEY DON'T EVEN HELP US RAISE MONEY PYO.
WE NEED THEM TO HELP PREPARE FOR TOMORROW PYO
ONE... TWO...
WELL, LET'S PUT ALL OUR ENERGY INTO THIS JOB FOR TOMORROW PYO.

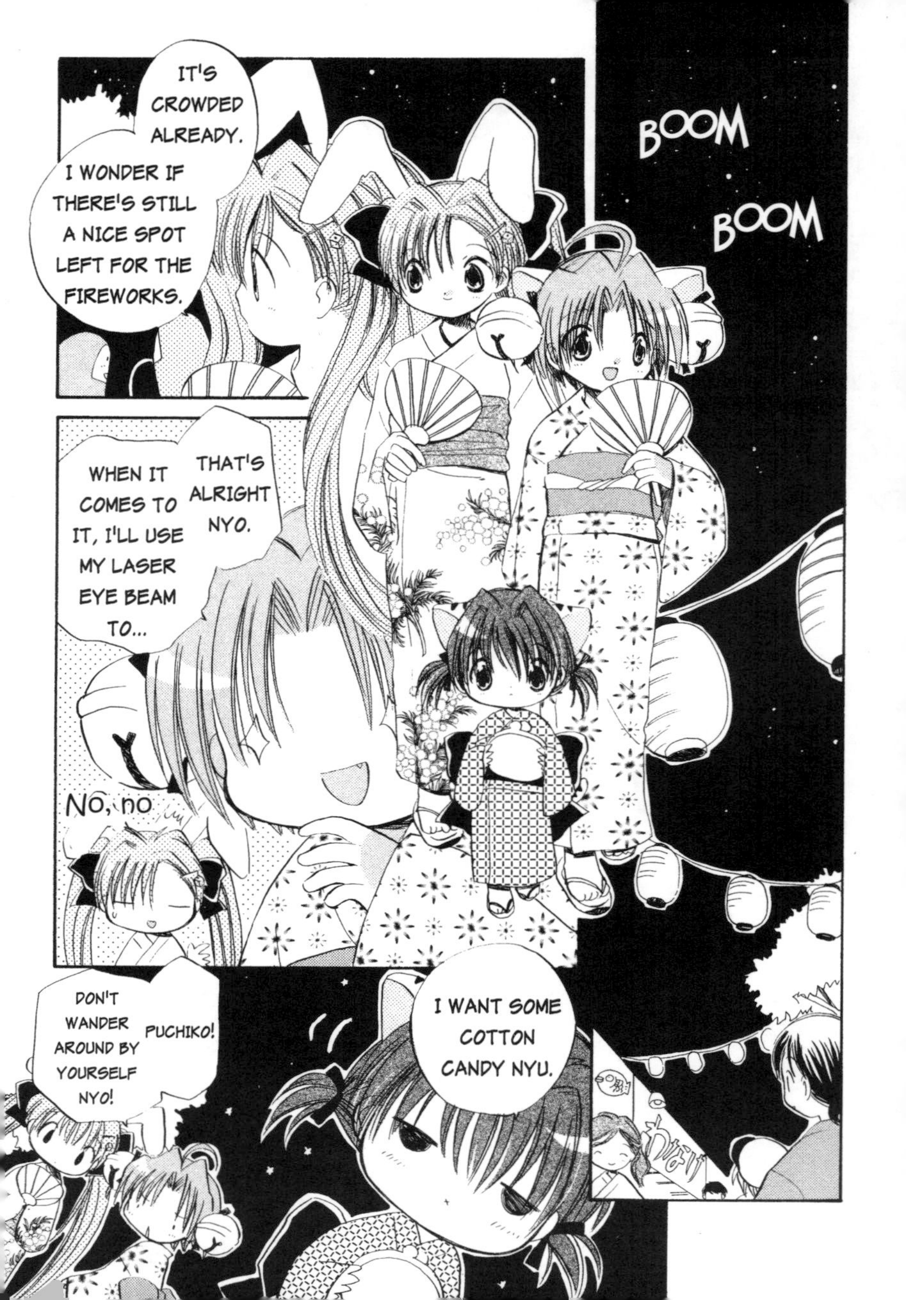
BOOM
BOOM
IT'S CROWDED ALREADY.
I WONDER IF THERE'S STILL A NICE SPOT LEFT FOR THE FIREWORKS.
THAT'S ALRIGHT NYO.
WHEN IT COMES TO IT, I'LL USE MY LASER EYE BEAM TO...
No, no
I WANT SOME COTTON CANDY NYU.
PUCHIKO!
DON'T WANDER AROUND BY YOURSELF NYO!

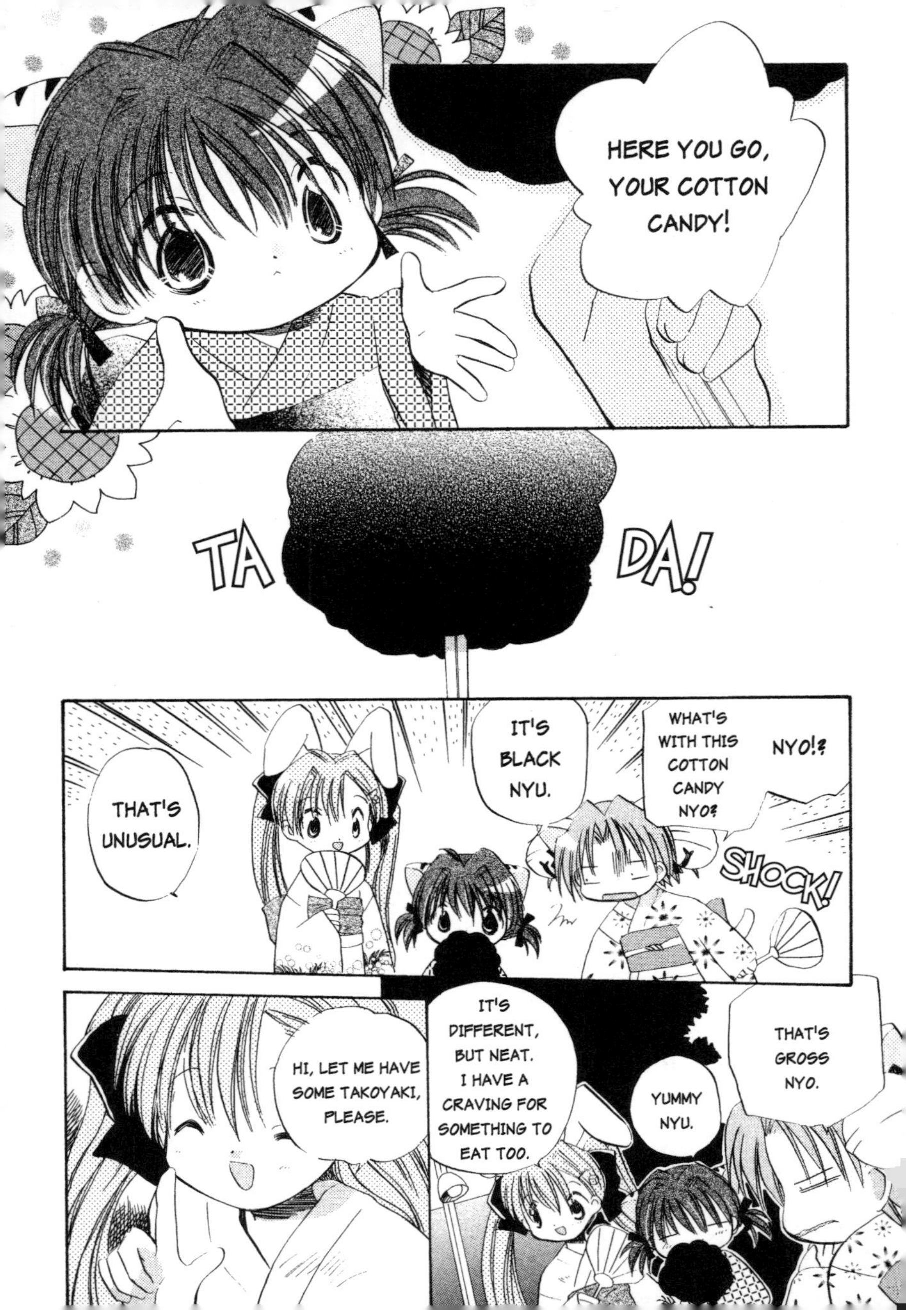
HERE YOU GO, YOUR COTTON CANDY!
TA DA!
NYO!?
WHAT'S WITH THIS COTTON CANDY NYO?
SHOCK!
IT'S BLACK NYU.
THAT'S UNUSUAL.
THAT'S GROSS NYO.
YUMMY NYU.
IT'S DIFFERENT, BUT NEAT. I HAVE A CRAVING FOR SOMETHING TO EAT TOO.
HI, LET ME HAVE SOME TAKOYAKI, PLEASE.

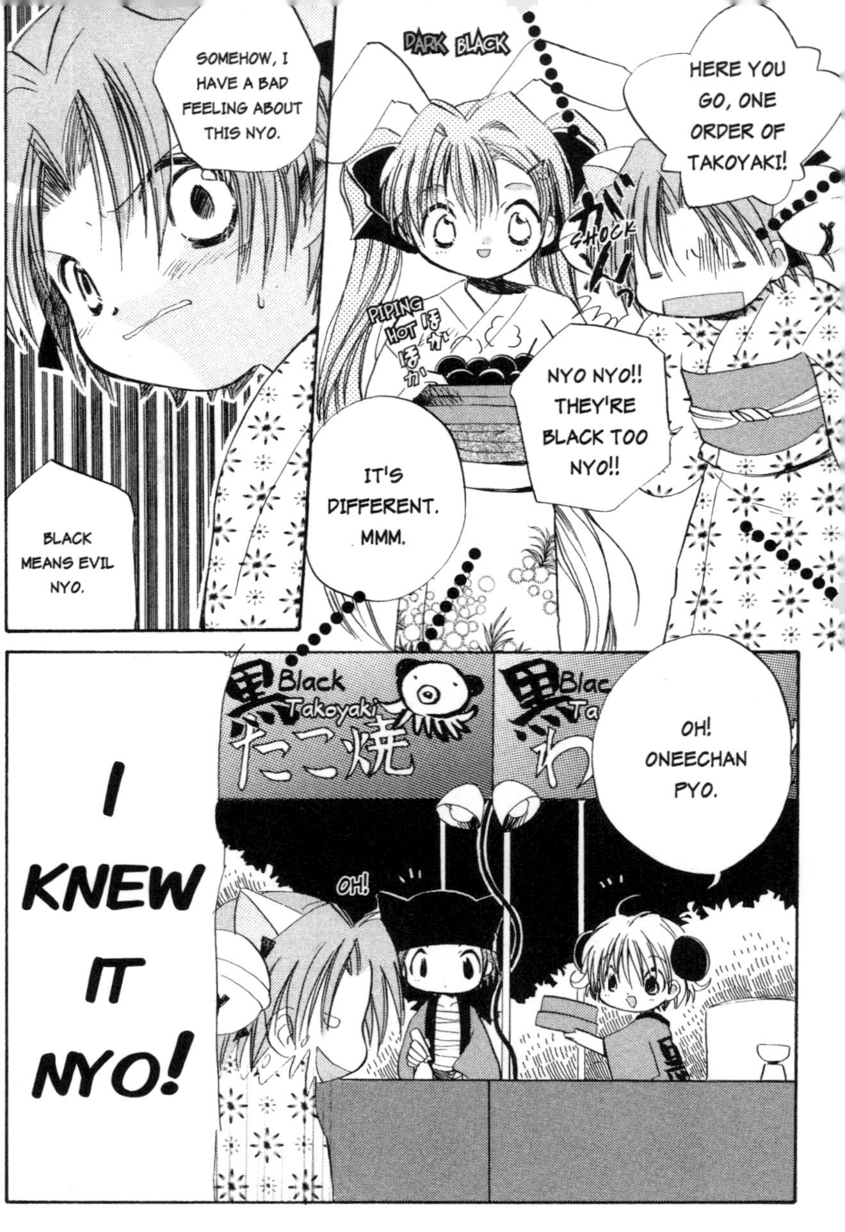
DARK BLACK
HERE YOU GO, ONE ORDER OF TAKOYAKI!
SHOCK
PIPING HOT ほかほか
NYO NYO!! THEY'RE BLACK TOO NYO!!
IT'S DIFFERENT. MMM.
SOMEHOW, I HAVE A BAD FEELING ABOUT THIS NYO.
BLACK MEANS EVIL NYO.
黒 Black Takoyaki たこ焼
OH! ONEECHAN PYO.
OH!
I KNEW IT NYO!

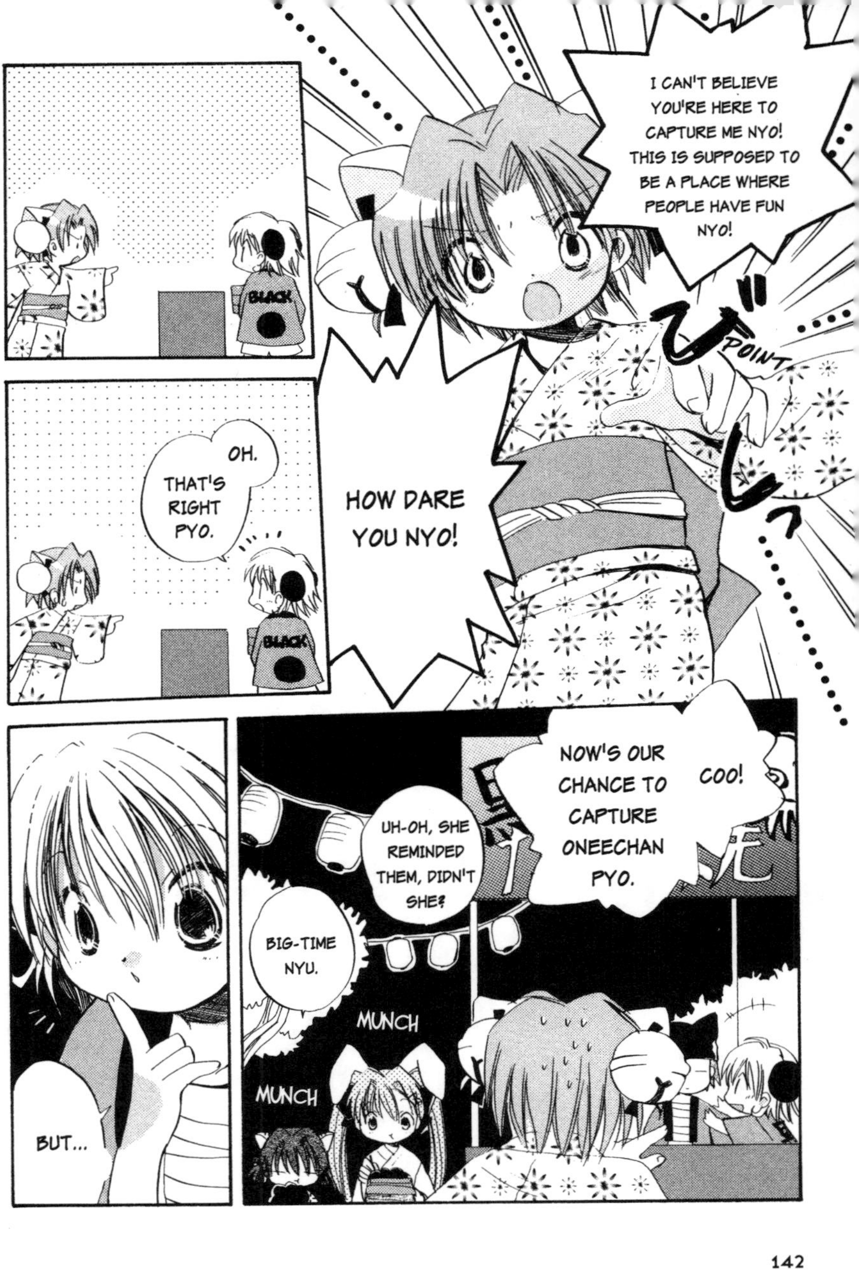
I CAN'T BELIEVE YOU'RE HERE TO CAPTURE ME NYO! THIS IS SUPPOSED TO BE A PLACE WHERE PEOPLE HAVE FUN NYO!
POINT
HOW DARE YOU NYO!
BLACK
OH.
THAT'S RIGHT PYO.
BLACK
NOW'S OUR CHANCE TO CAPTURE ONEECHAN PYO.
COO!
UH-OH, SHE REMINDED THEM, DIDN'T SHE?
BIG-TIME NYU.
MUNCH
MUNCH
BUT...

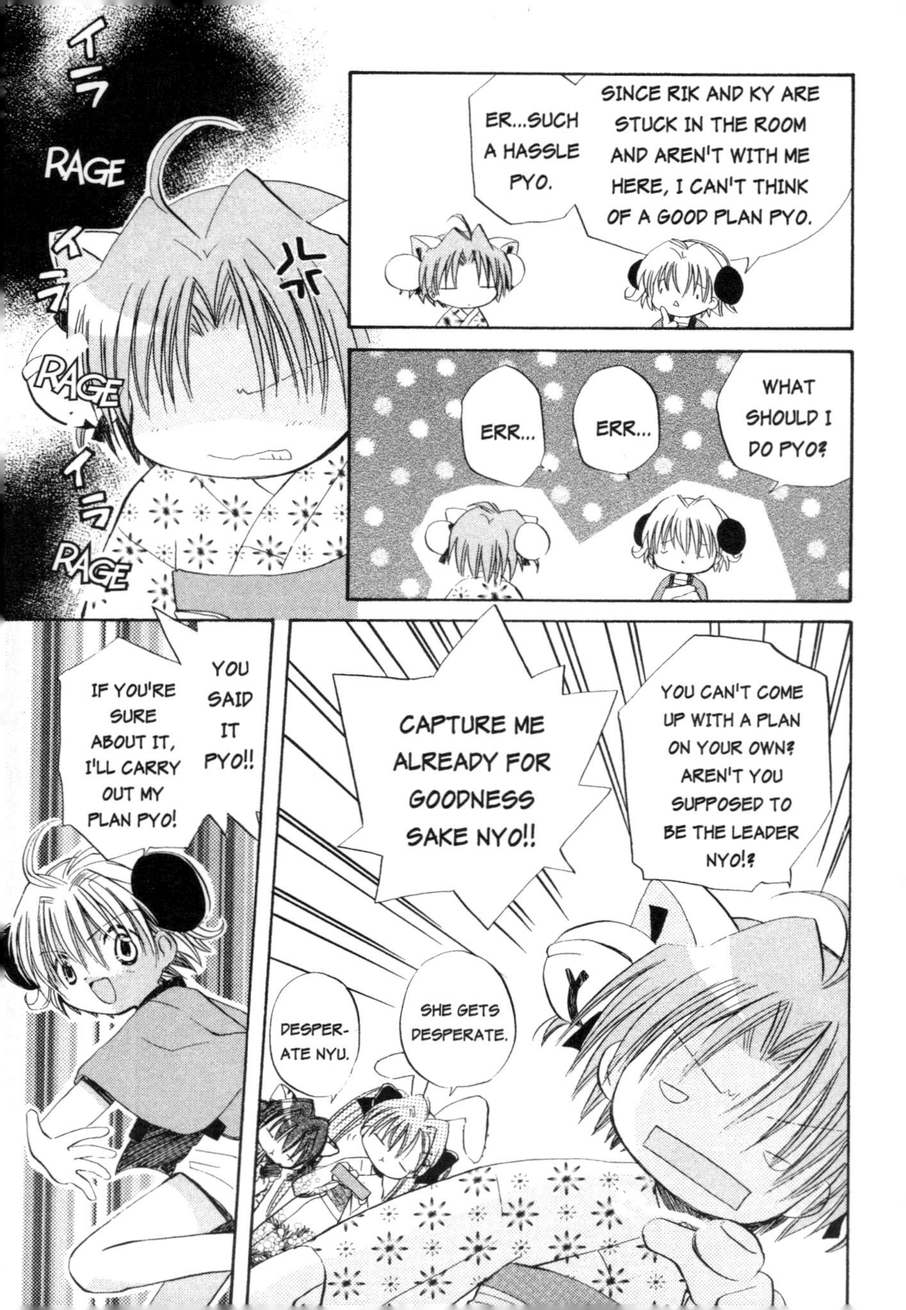
SINCE RIK AND KY ARE STUCK IN THE ROOM AND AREN'T WITH ME HERE, I CAN'T THINK OF A GOOD PLAN PYO.
ER...SUCH A HASSLE PYO.
WHAT SHOULD I DO PYO?
ERR...
ERR...
イラ
RAGE
イラ
RAGE
イラ
RAGE
YOU CAN'T COME UP WITH A PLAN ON YOUR OWN? AREN'T YOU SUPPOSED TO BE THE LEADER NYO!?
CAPTURE ME ALREADY FOR GOODNESS SAKE NYO!!
SHE GETS DESPERATE.
DESPER-ATE NYU.
YOU SAID IT PYO!!
IF YOU'RE SURE ABOUT IT, I'LL CARRY OUT MY PLAN PYO!

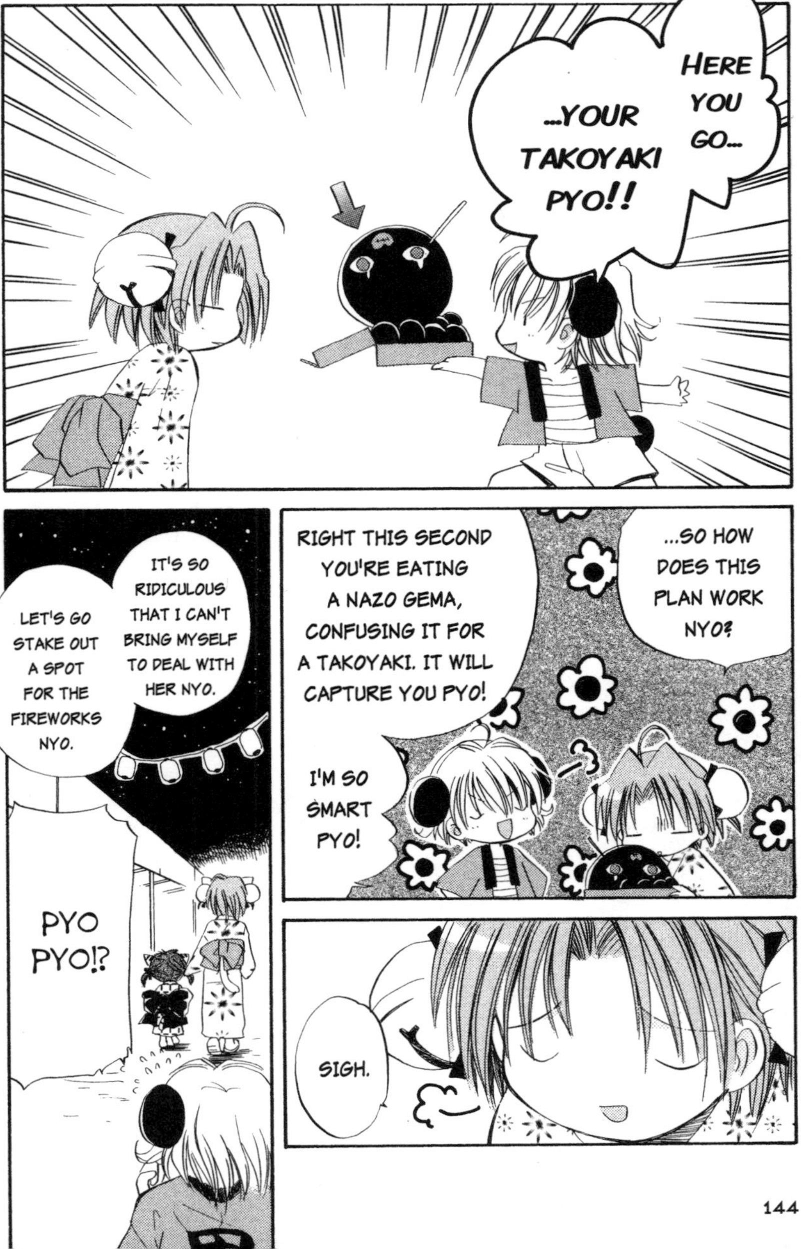
HERE YOU GO...
...YOUR TAKOYAKI PYO!!
...SO HOW DOES THIS PLAN WORK NYO?
RIGHT THIS SECOND YOU'RE EATING A NAZO GEMA, CONFUSING IT FOR A TAKOYAKI. IT WILL CAPTURE YOU PYO!
I'M SO SMART PYO!
SIGH.
IT'S SO RIDICULOUS THAT I CAN'T BRING MYSELF TO DEAL WITH HER NYO.
LET'S GO STAKE OUT A SPOT FOR THE FIREWORKS NYO.
PYO PYO!?

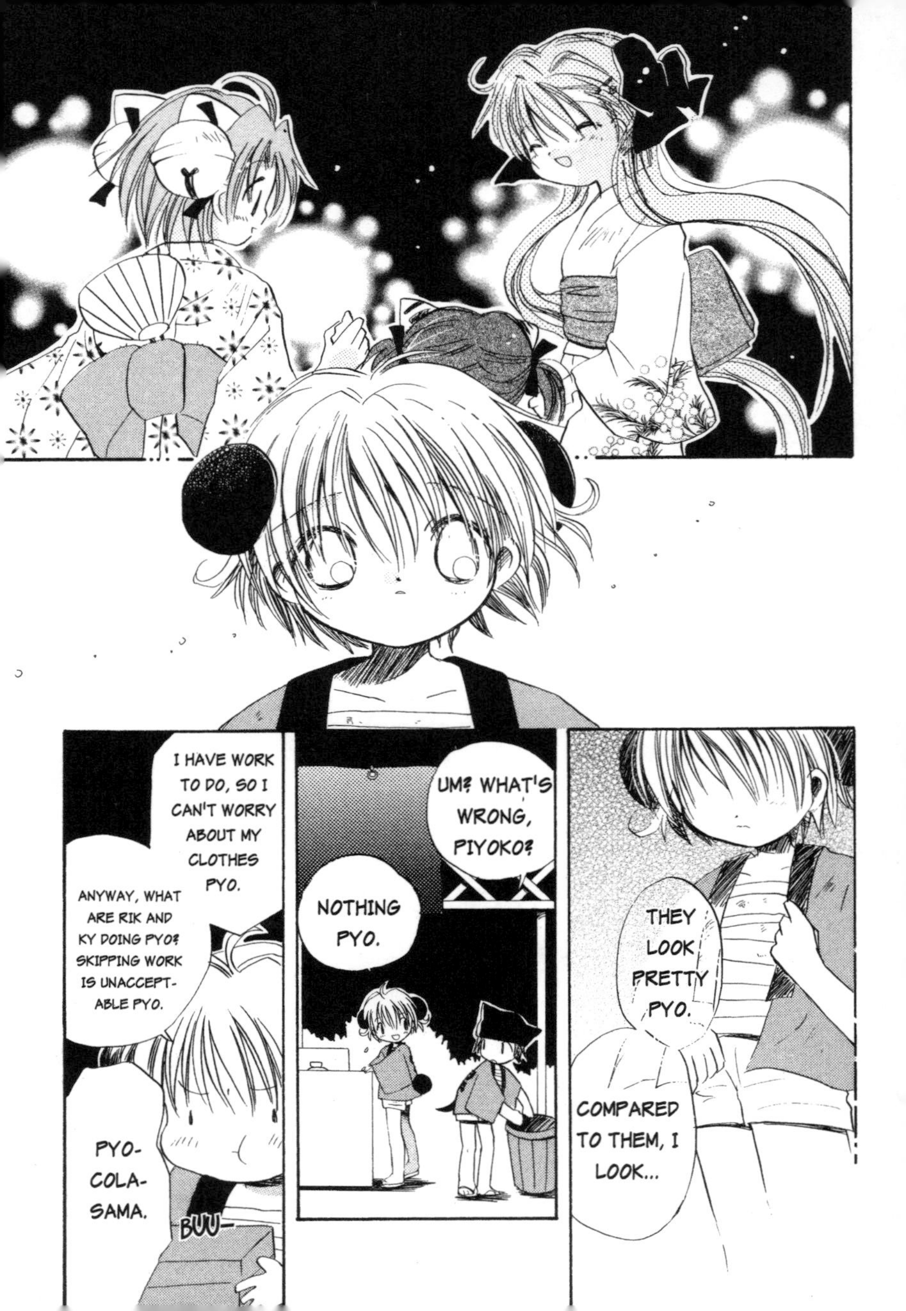
THEY LOOK PRETTY PYO.
COMPARED TO THEM, I LOOK...
UM? WHAT'S WRONG, PIYOKO?
NOTHING PYO.
I HAVE WORK TO DO, SO I CAN'T WORRY ABOUT MY CLOTHES PYO.
ANYWAY, WHAT ARE RIK AND KY DOING PYO? SKIPPING WORK IS UNACCEPTABLE PYO.
PYO-COLA-SAMA.
BUU-

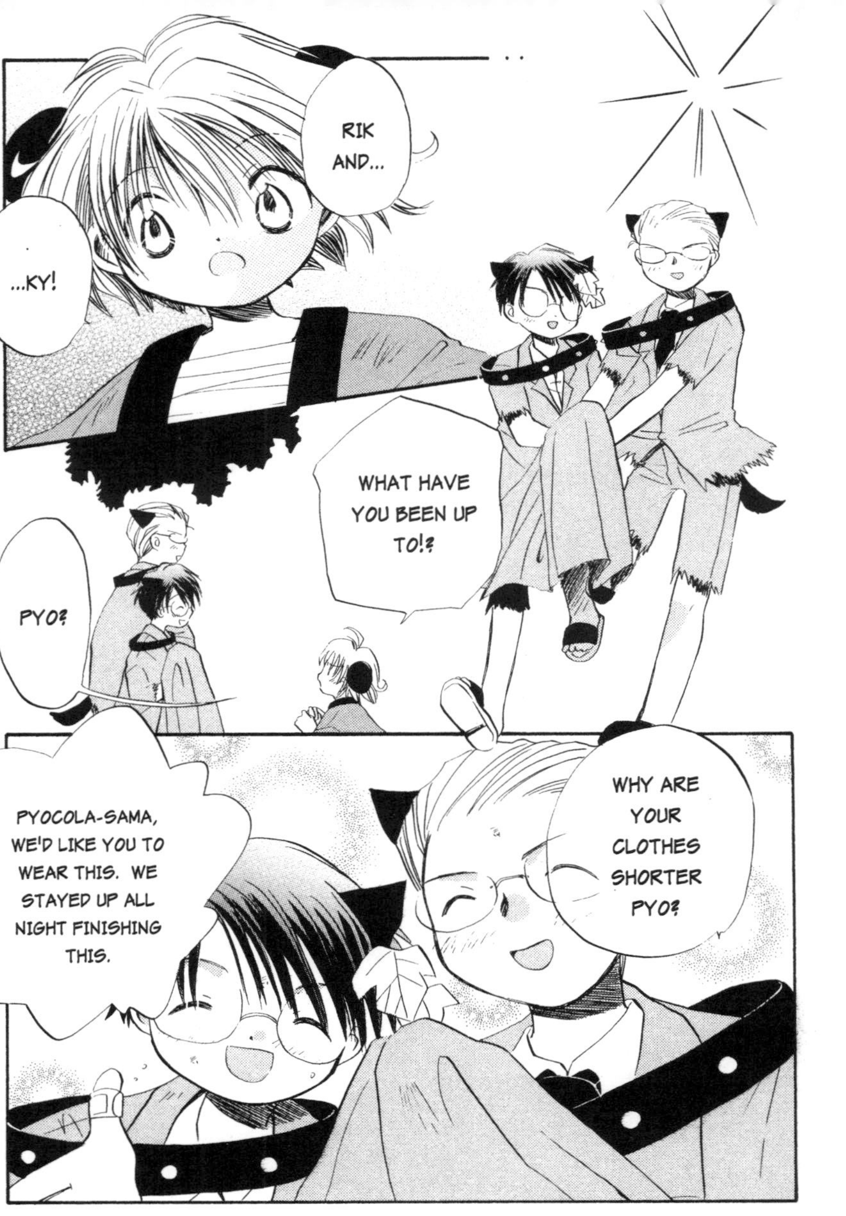

RIK AND...
...KY!
WHAT HAVE YOU BEEN UP TO!?
PYO?
WHY ARE YOUR CLOTHES SHORTER PYO?
PYOCOLA-SAMA, WE'D LIKE YOU TO WEAR THIS. WE STAYED UP ALL NIGHT FINISHING THIS.

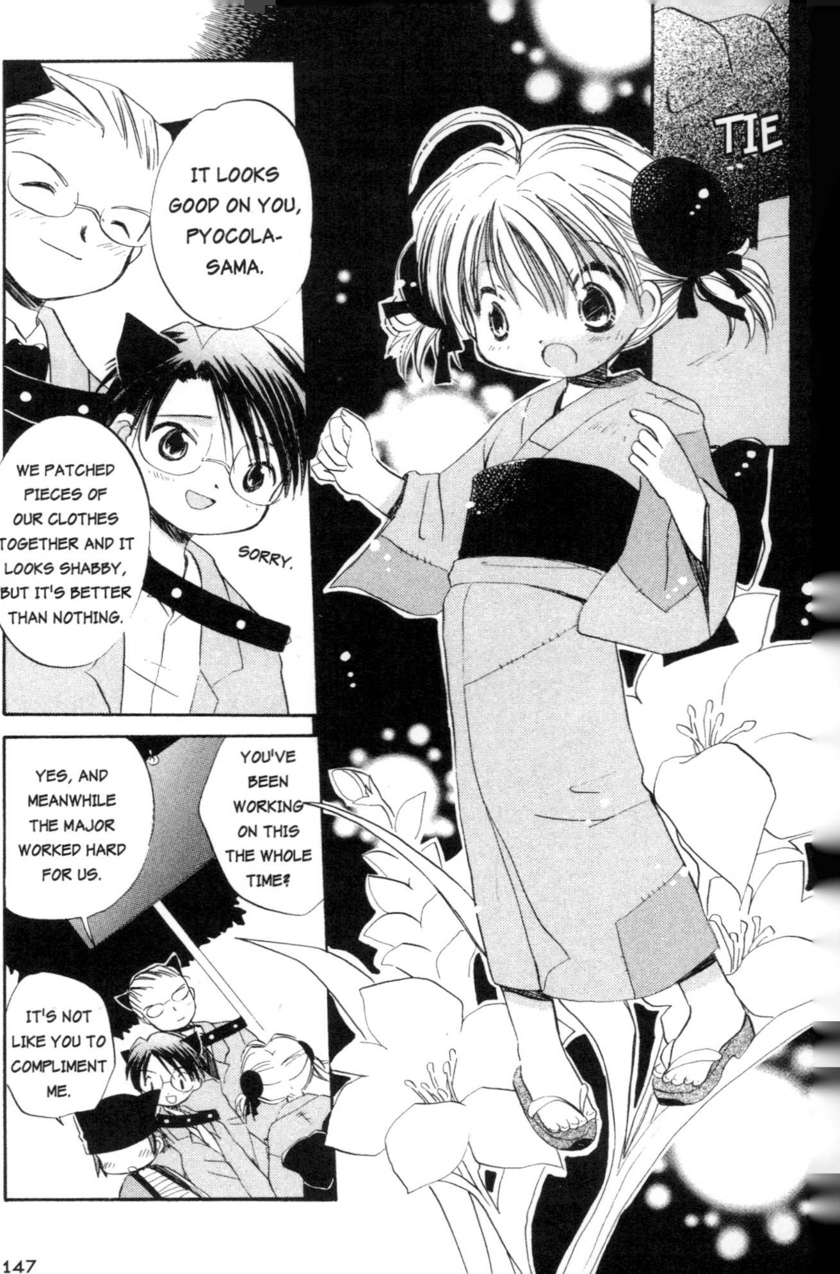
TIE
IT LOOKS GOOD ON YOU, PYOCOLA-SAMA.
WE PATCHED PIECES OF OUR CLOTHES TOGETHER AND IT LOOKS SHABBY, BUT IT'S BETTER THAN NOTHING.
SORRY.
YOU'VE BEEN WORKING ON THIS THE WHOLE TIME?
YES, AND MEANWHILE THE MAJOR WORKED HARD FOR US.
IT'S NOT LIKE YOU TO COMPLIMENT ME.

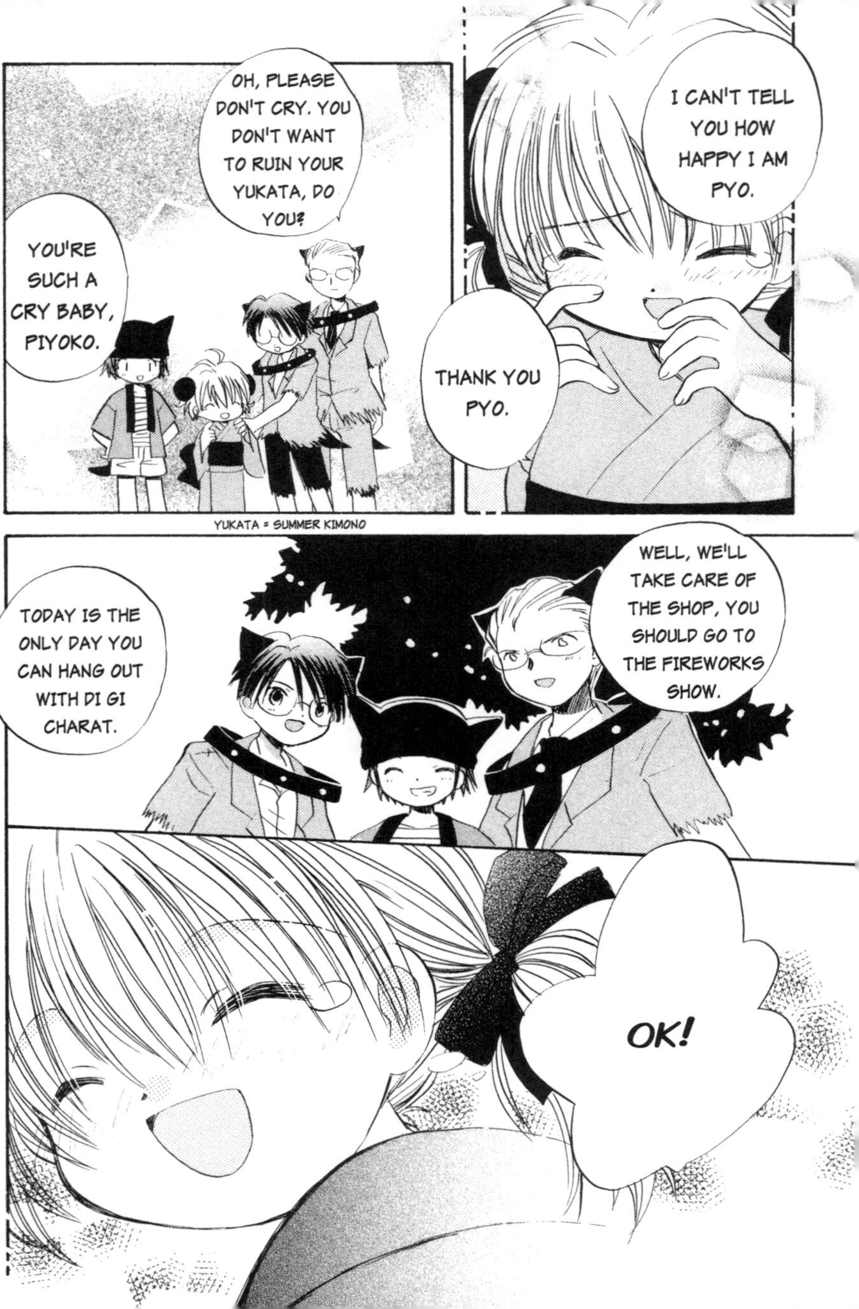
I CAN'T TELL YOU HOW HAPPY I AM PYO.
THANK YOU PYO.
OH, PLEASE DON'T CRY. YOU DON'T WANT TO RUIN YOUR YUKATA, DO YOU?
YOU'RE SUCH A CRY BABY, PIYOKO.
YUKATA = SUMMER KIMONO
WELL, WE'LL TAKE CARE OF THE SHOP, YOU SHOULD GO TO THE FIREWORKS SHOW.
TODAY IS THE ONLY DAY YOU CAN HANG OUT WITH DI GI CHARAT.
OK!

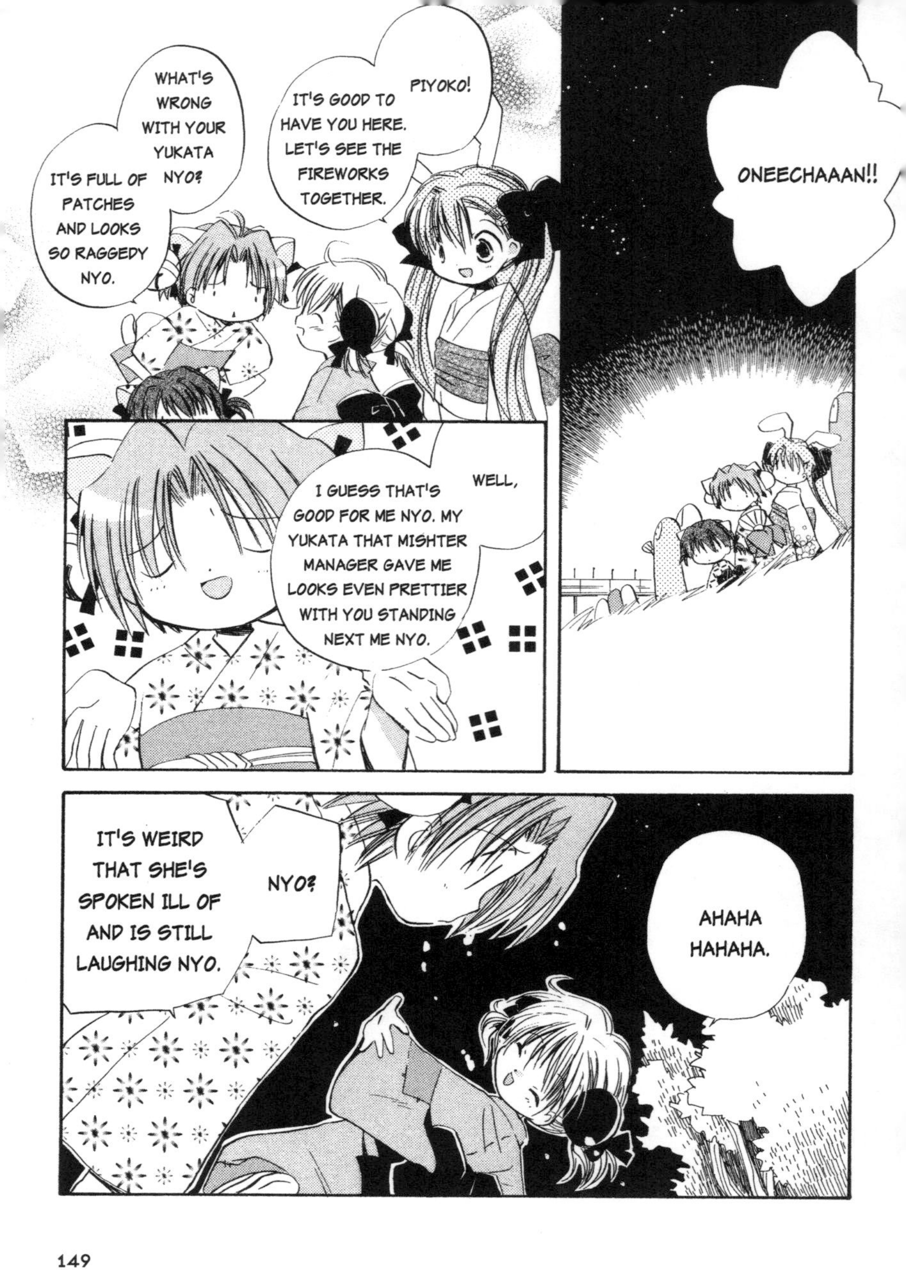
ONEECHAAAN!!
PIYOKO!
IT'S GOOD TO HAVE YOU HERE. LET'S SEE THE FIREWORKS TOGETHER.
WHAT'S WRONG WITH YOUR YUKATA NYO?
IT'S FULL OF PATCHES AND LOOKS SO RAGGEDY NYO.
WELL,
I GUESS THAT'S GOOD FOR ME NYO. MY YUKATA THAT MISHTER MANAGER GAVE ME LOOKS EVEN PRETTIER WITH YOU STANDING NEXT ME NYO.
AHAHA HAHAHA.
NYO?
IT'S WEIRD THAT SHE'S SPOKEN ILL OF AND IS STILL LAUGHING NYO.

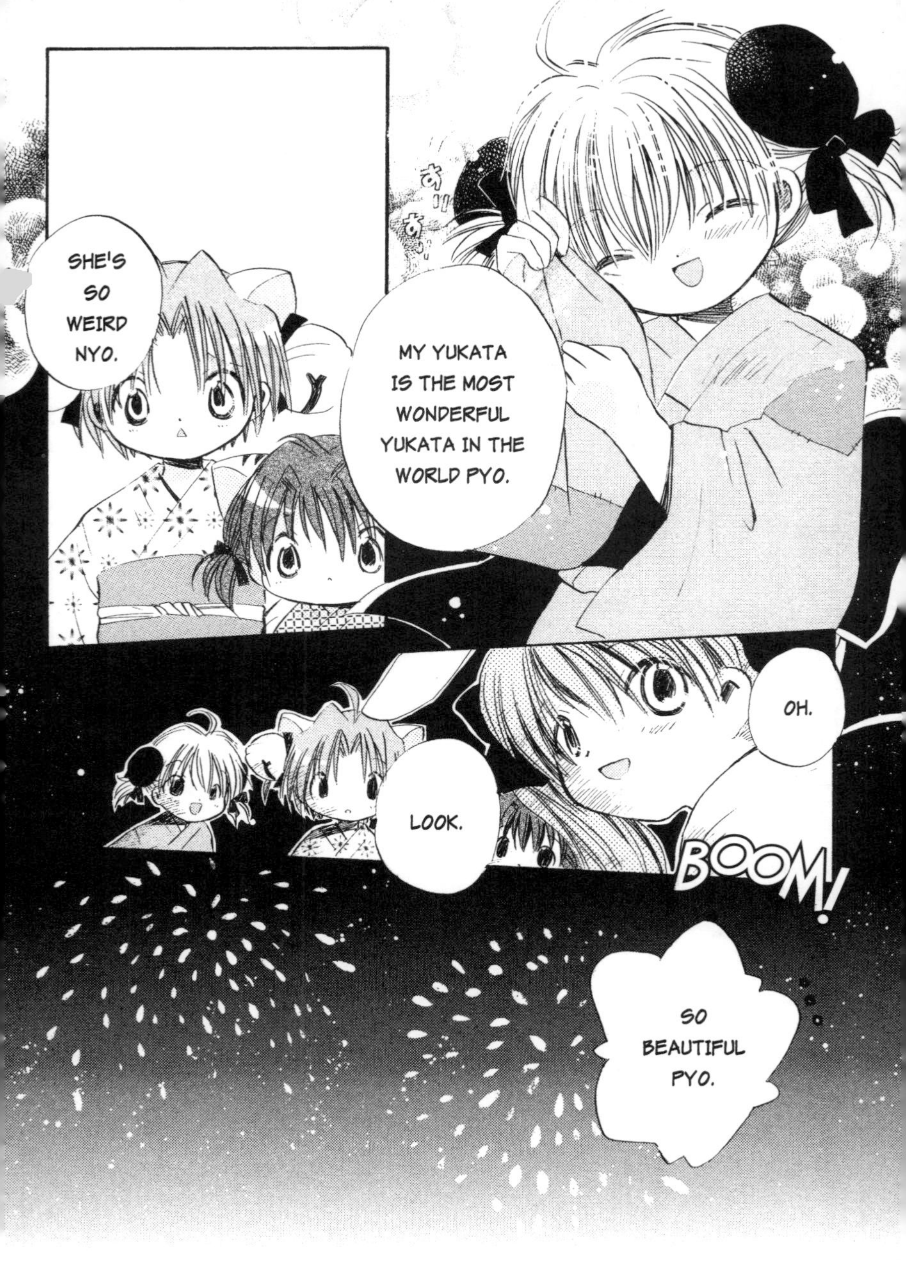
MY YUKATA IS THE MOST WONDERFUL YUKATA IN THE WORLD PYO.
SHE'S SO WEIRD NYO.
OH.
LOOK.
BOOM!
SO BEAUTIFUL PYO.

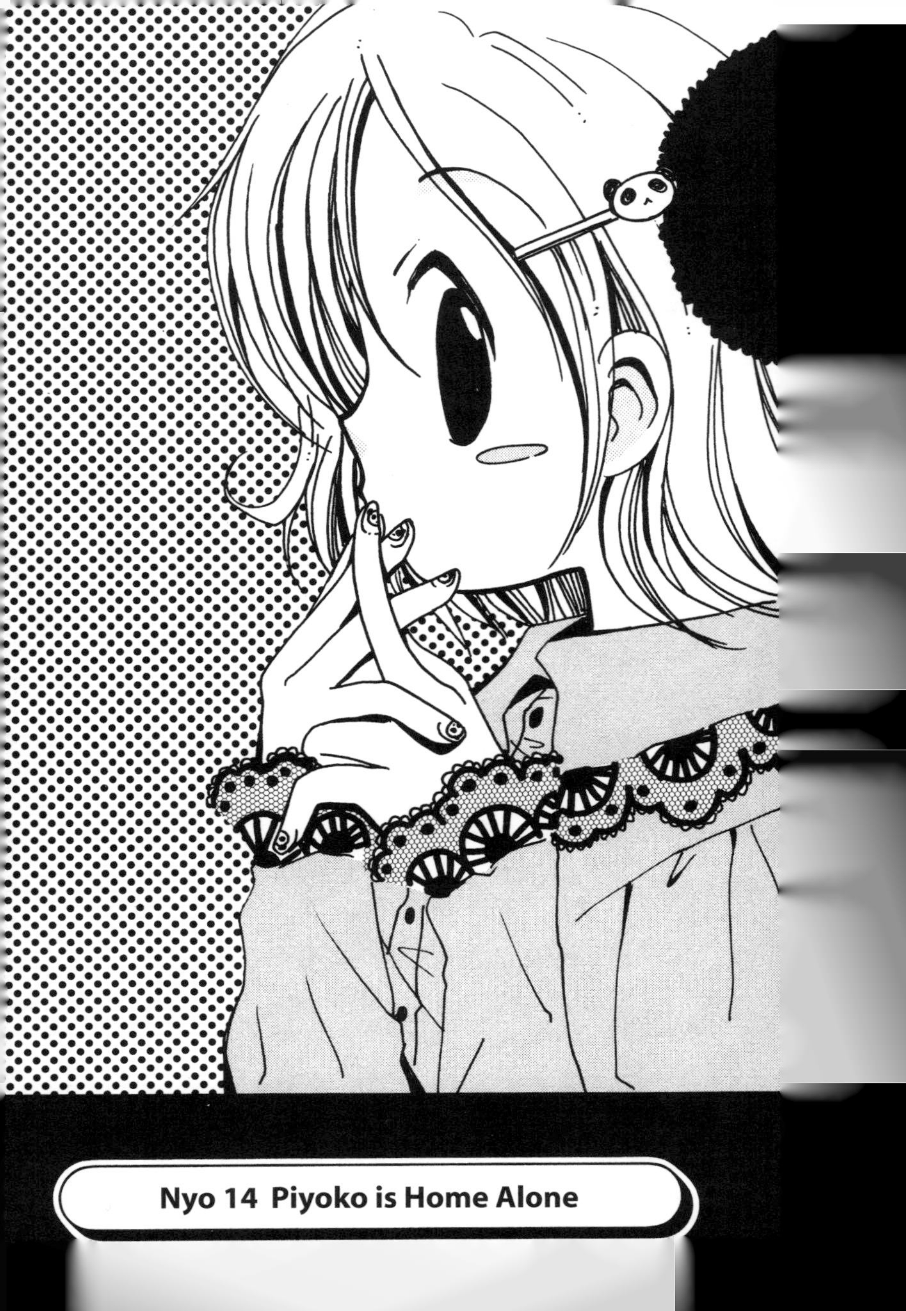

Nyo 14 Piyoko is Home Alone

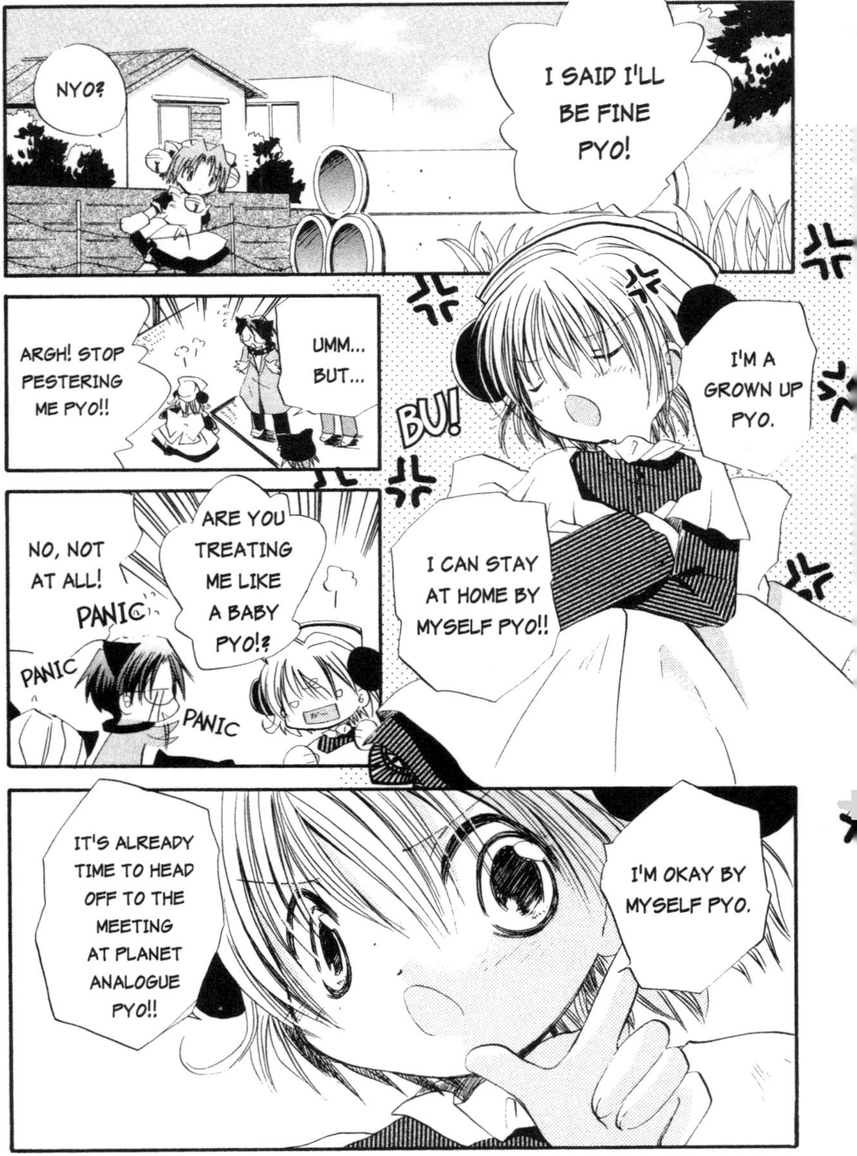
I SAID I'LL BE FINE PYO!
NYO?
BU!
I'M A GROWN UP PYO.
I CAN STAY AT HOME BY MYSELF PYO!!
UMM... BUT...
ARGH! STOP PESTERING ME PYO!!
ARE YOU TREATING ME LIKE A BABY PYO!?
NO, NOT AT ALL!
PANIC
PANIC
PANIC
I'M OKAY BY MYSELF PYO.
IT'S ALREADY TIME TO HEAD OFF TO THE MEETING AT PLANET ANALOGUE PYO!!

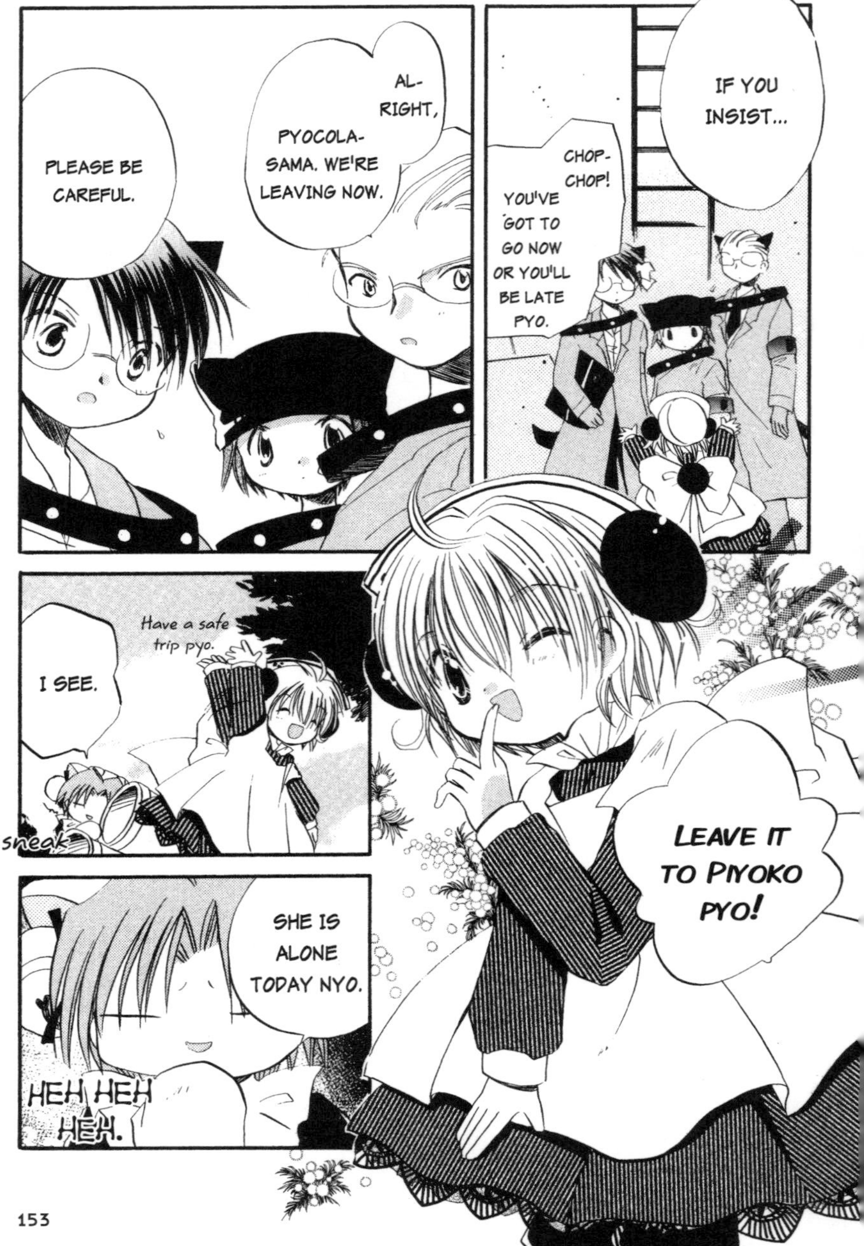
IF YOU INSIST...
CHOP-CHOP!
YOU'VE GOT TO GO NOW OR YOU'LL BE LATE PYO.
AL-RIGHT,
PYOCOLA-SAMA. WE'RE LEAVING NOW.
PLEASE BE CAREFUL.
LEAVE IT TO PIYOKO PYO!
Have a safe trip pyo.
I SEE.
sneak
SHE IS ALONE TODAY NYO.
HEH HEH HEH.

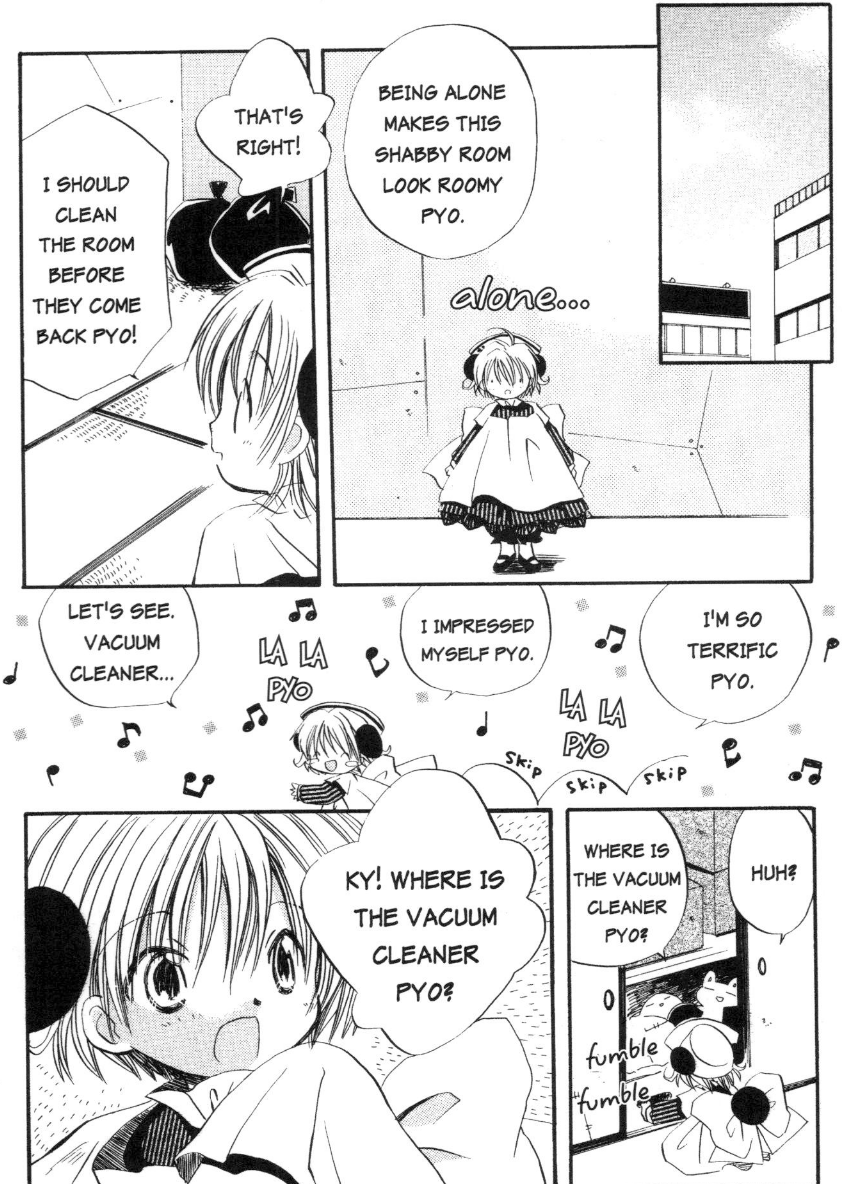
BEING ALONE MAKES THIS SHABBY ROOM LOOK ROOMY PYO.
alone...
THAT'S RIGHT!
I SHOULD CLEAN THE ROOM BEFORE THEY COME BACK PYO!
I'M SO TERRIFIC PYO.
LA LA PYO
I IMPRESSED MYSELF PYO.
LA LA PYO
LET'S SEE. VACUUM CLEANER...
skip skip skip
HUH?
WHERE IS THE VACUUM CLEANER PYO?
fumble fumble
KY! WHERE IS THE VACUUM CLEANER PYO?

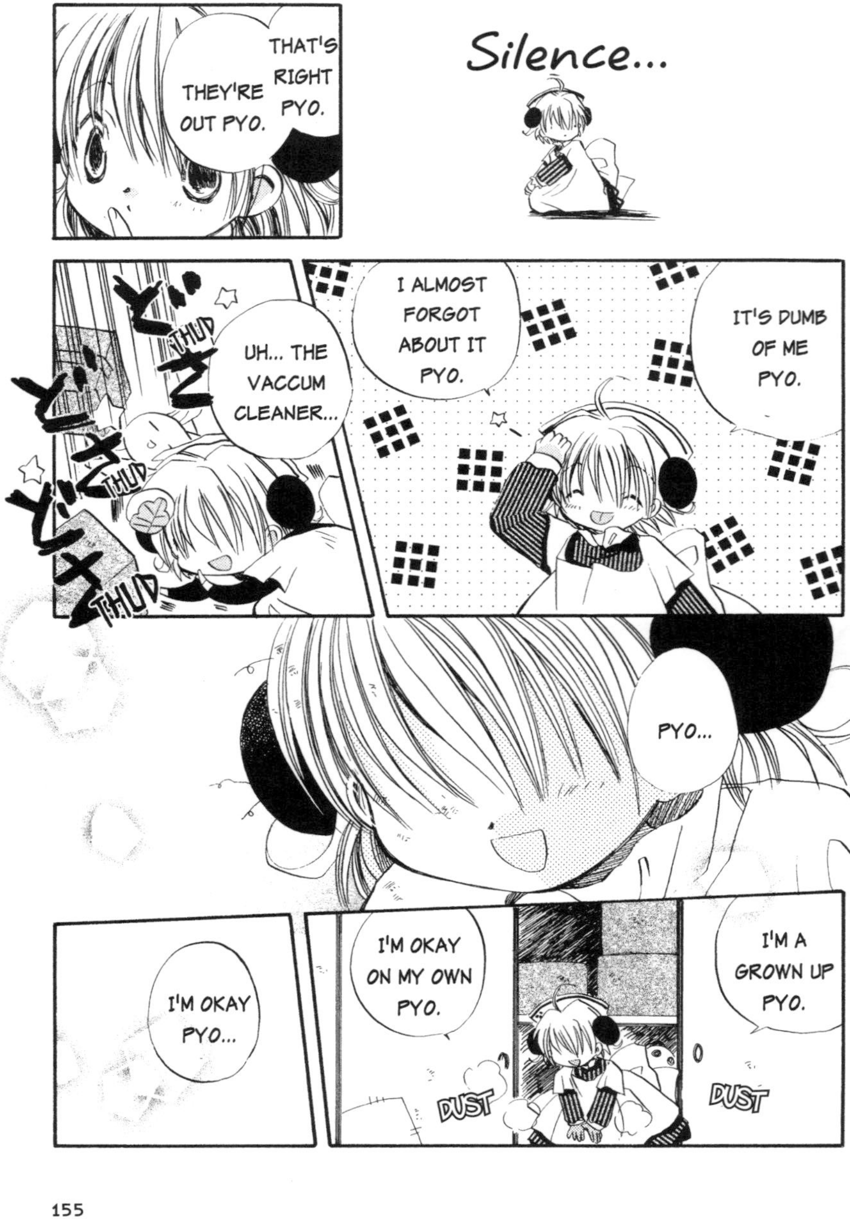
Silence...
THAT'S RIGHT PYO.
THEY'RE OUT PYO.
IT'S DUMB OF ME PYO.
I ALMOST FORGOT ABOUT IT PYO.
UH... THE VACCUM CLEANER...
THUD
THUD
THUD
PYO...
I'M A GROWN UP PYO.
I'M OKAY ON MY OWN PYO.
DUST
DUST
I'M OKAY PYO...

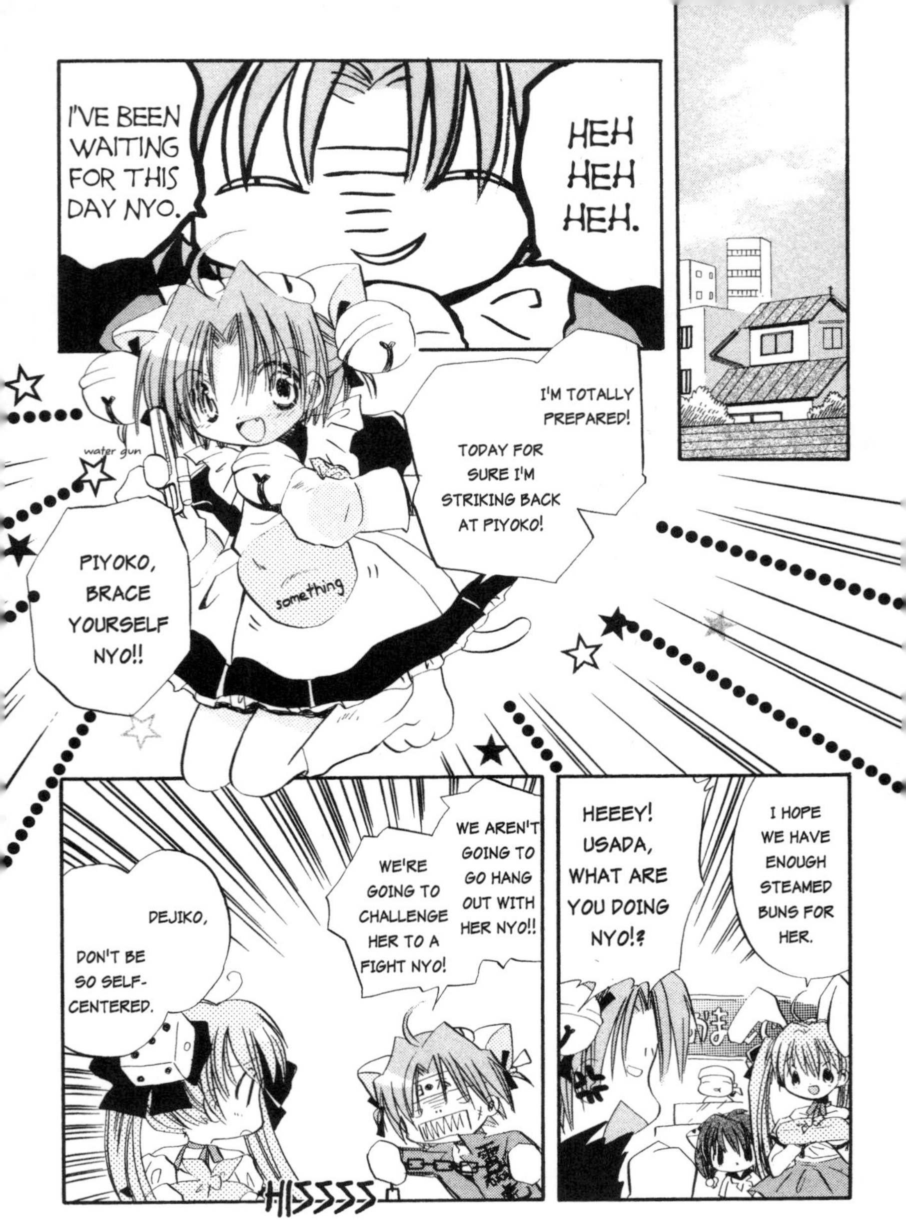
HEH HEH HEH.
I'VE BEEN WAITING FOR THIS DAY NYO.
I'M TOTALLY PREPARED!
TODAY FOR SURE I'M STRIKING BACK AT PIYOKO!
water gun
something
PIYOKO, BRACE YOURSELF NYO!!
I HOPE WE HAVE ENOUGH STEAMED BUNS FOR HER.
HEEEY! USADA, WHAT ARE YOU DOING NYO!?
WE AREN'T GOING TO GO HANG OUT WITH HER NYO!!
WE'RE GOING TO CHALLENGE HER TO A FIGHT NYO!
DEJIKO,
DON'T BE SO SELF-CENTERED.
HISSSSS

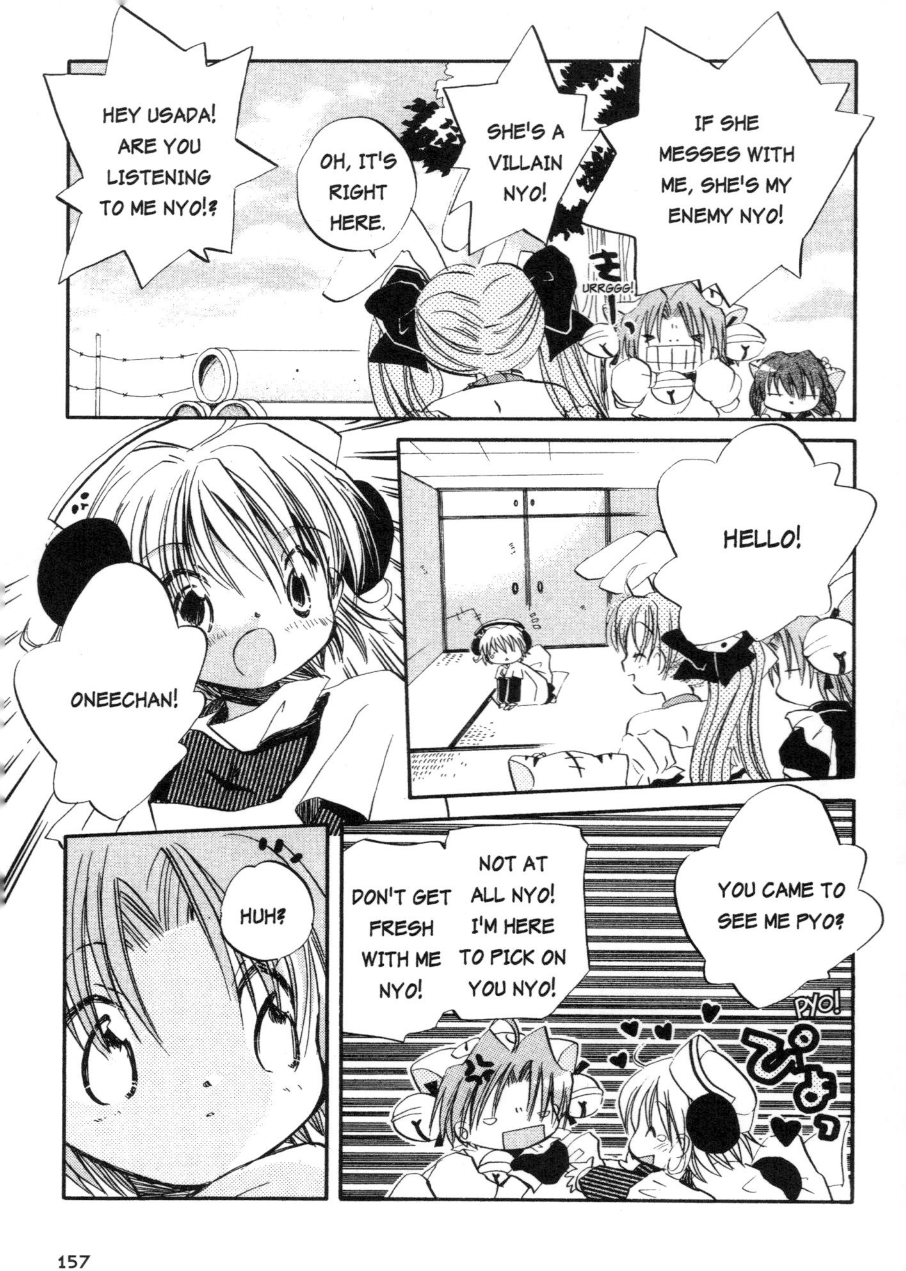
IF SHE MESSES WITH ME, SHE'S MY ENEMY NYO!
SHE'S A VILLAIN NYO!
URRGGG!
OH, IT'S RIGHT HERE.
HEY USADA! ARE YOU LISTENING TO ME NYO!?
HELLO!
ONEECHAN!
YOU CAME TO SEE ME PYO?
PYO!
NOT AT ALL NYO! I'M HERE TO PICK ON YOU NYO!
DON'T GET FRESH WITH ME NYO!
HUH?

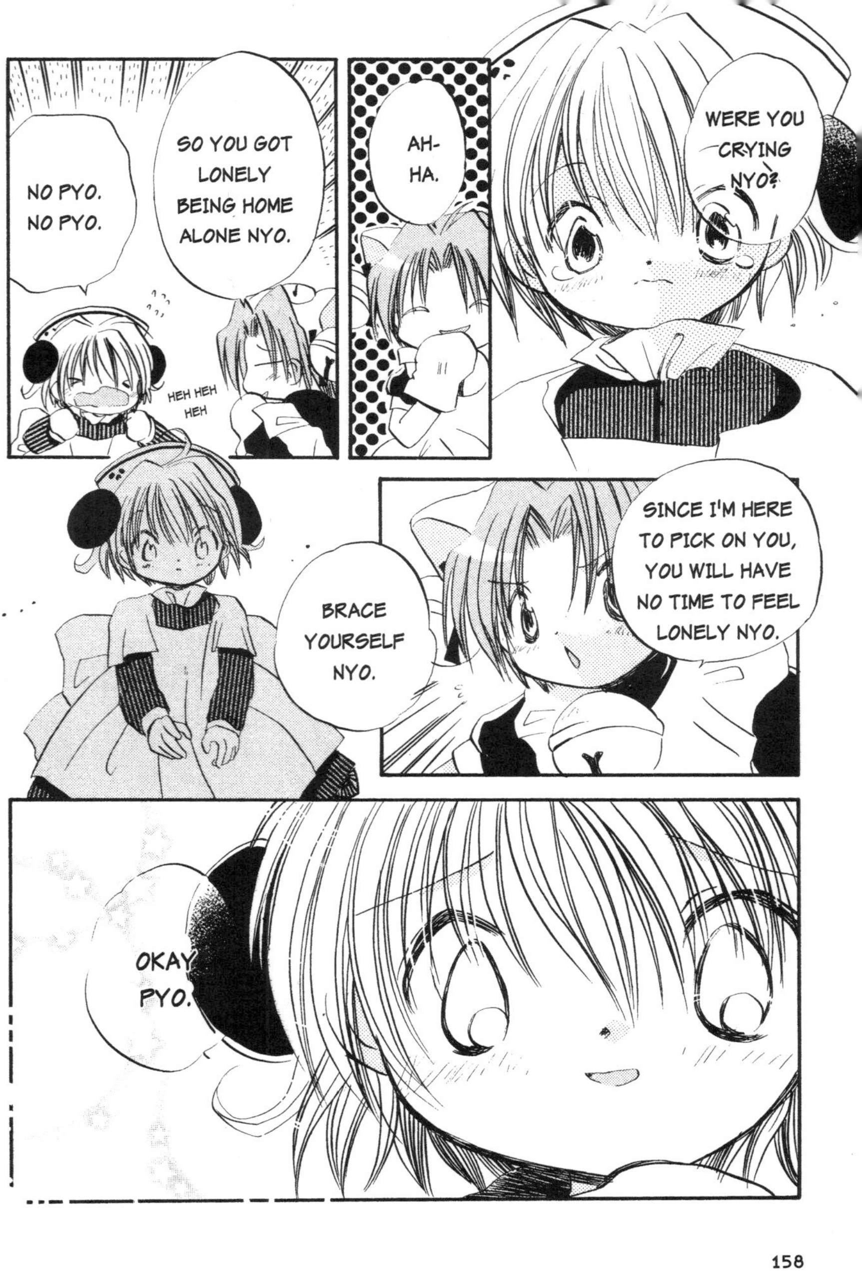
WERE YOU CRYING NYO?
AH-HA.
SO YOU GOT LONELY BEING HOME ALONE NYO.
NO PYO. NO PYO.
HEH HEH HEH
SINCE I'M HERE TO PICK ON YOU, YOU WILL HAVE NO TIME TO FEEL LONELY NYO.
BRACE YOURSELF NYO.
OKAY PYO.

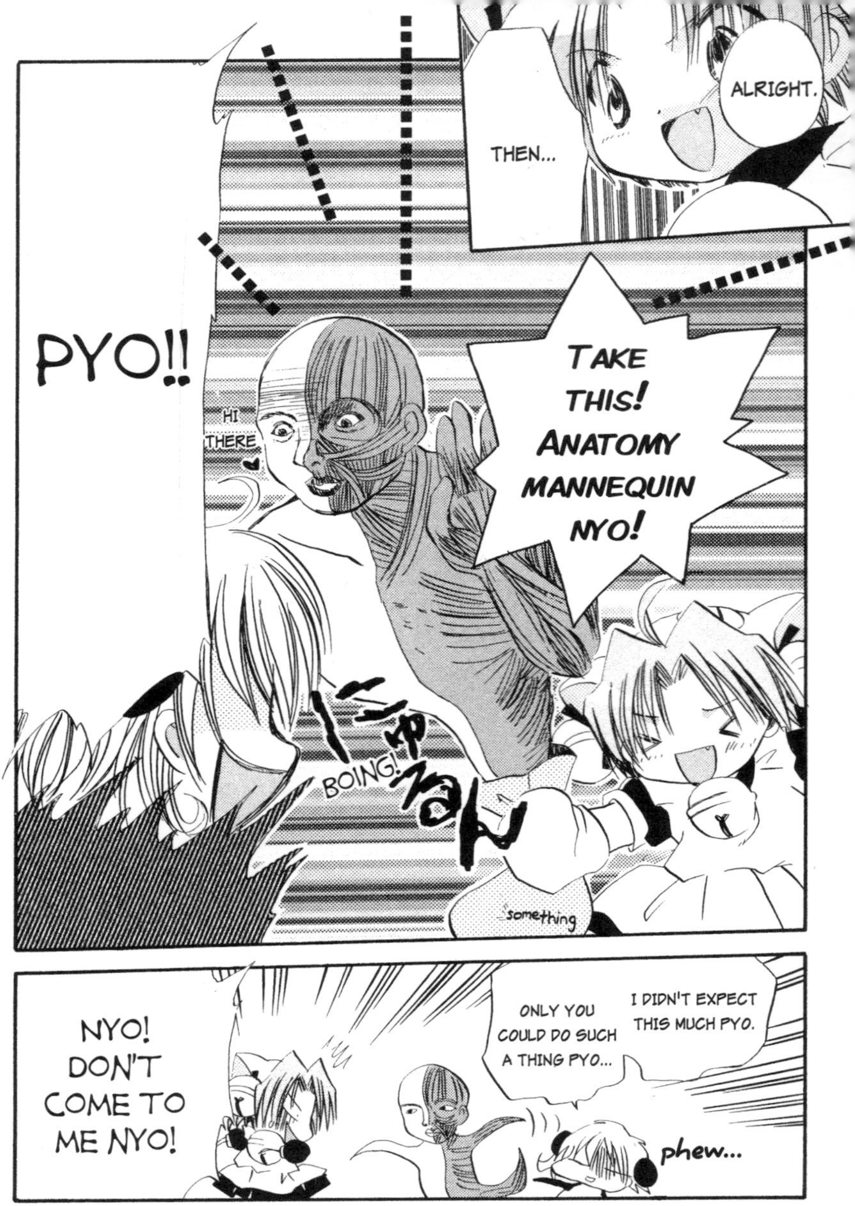
ALRIGHT.
THEN...
TAKE THIS! ANATOMY MANNEQUIN NYO!
PYO!!
HI THERE
BOING!
something
I DIDN'T EXPECT THIS MUCH PYO.
ONLY YOU COULD DO SUCH A THING PYO...
phew...
NYO! DON'T COME TO ME NYO!

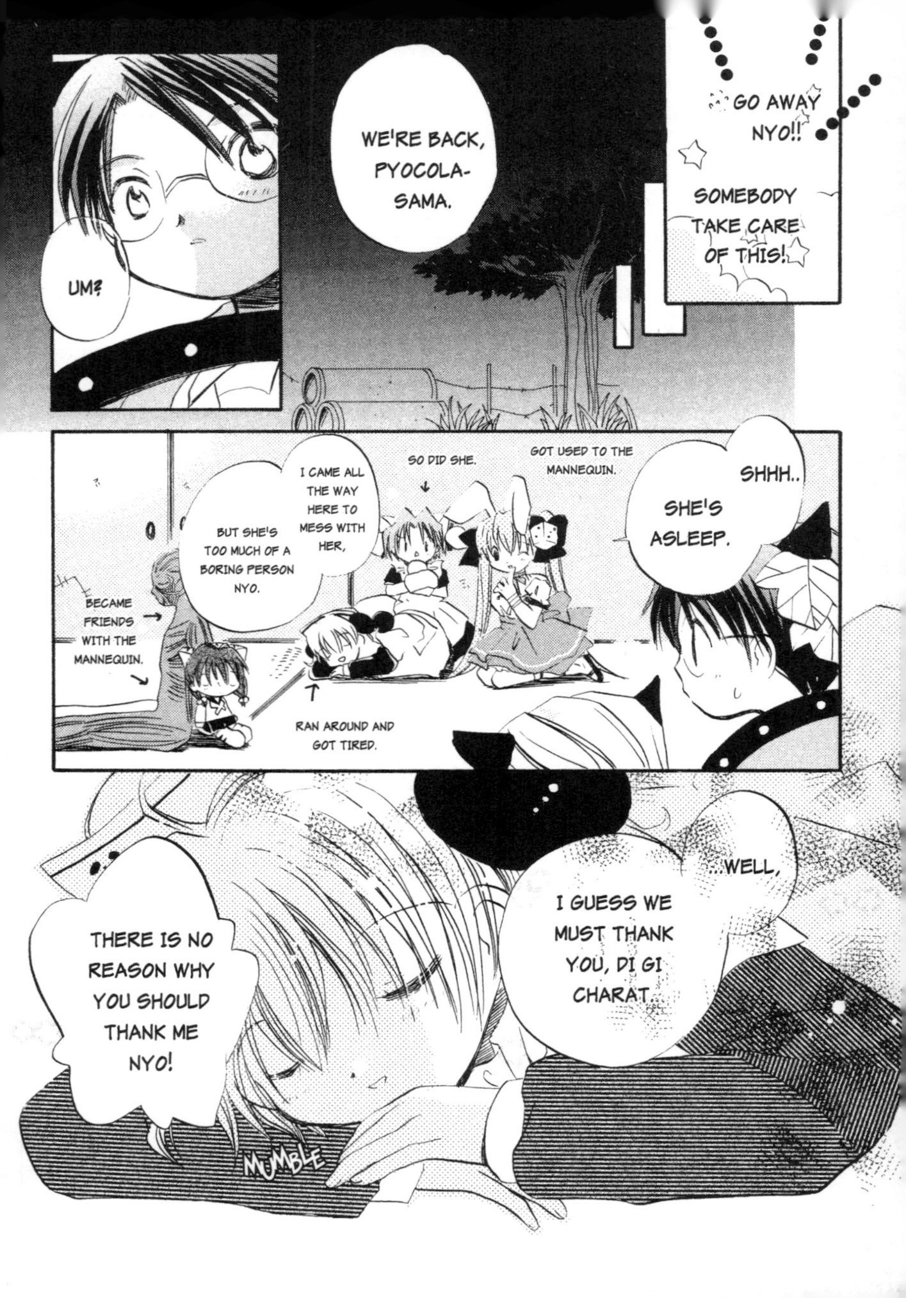
GO AWAY NYO!!
SOMEBODY TAKE CARE OF THIS!
WE'RE BACK, PYOCOLA-SAMA.
UM?
SHHH..
SHE'S ASLEEP.
GOT USED TO THE MANNEQUIN.
SO DID SHE.
I CAME ALL THE WAY HERE TO MESS WITH HER,
BUT SHE'S TOO MUCH OF A BORING PERSON NYO.
RAN AROUND AND GOT TIRED.
BECAME FRIENDS WITH THE MANNEQUIN.
...WELL,
I GUESS WE MUST THANK YOU, DI GI CHARAT.
THERE IS NO REASON WHY YOU SHOULD THANK ME NYO!
MUMBLE

Planet Analogue

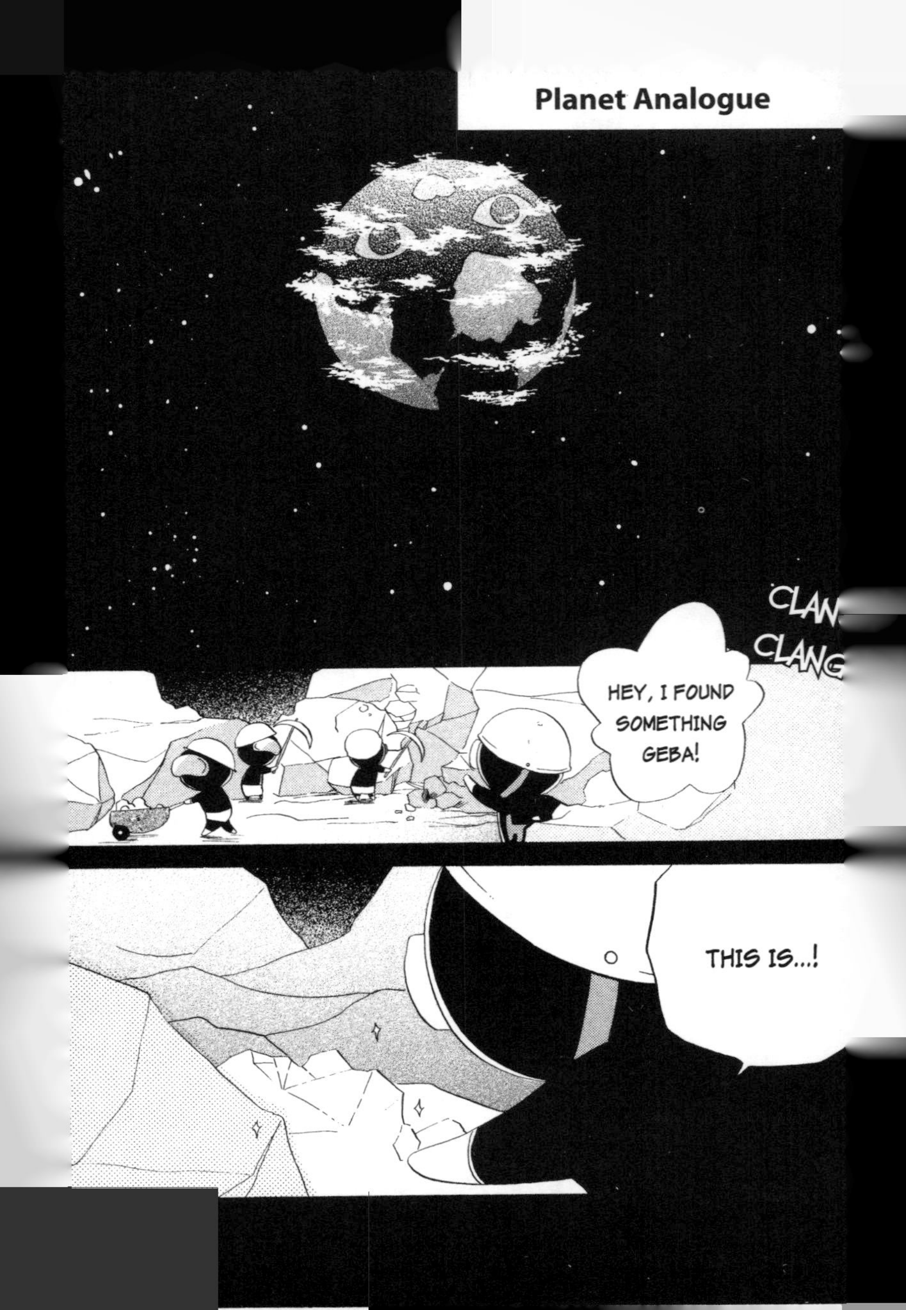
CLANG
CLANG
HEY, I FOUND SOMETHING GEBA!
THIS IS...!

Nyo 15 Planet Analogue Strikes it Rich!

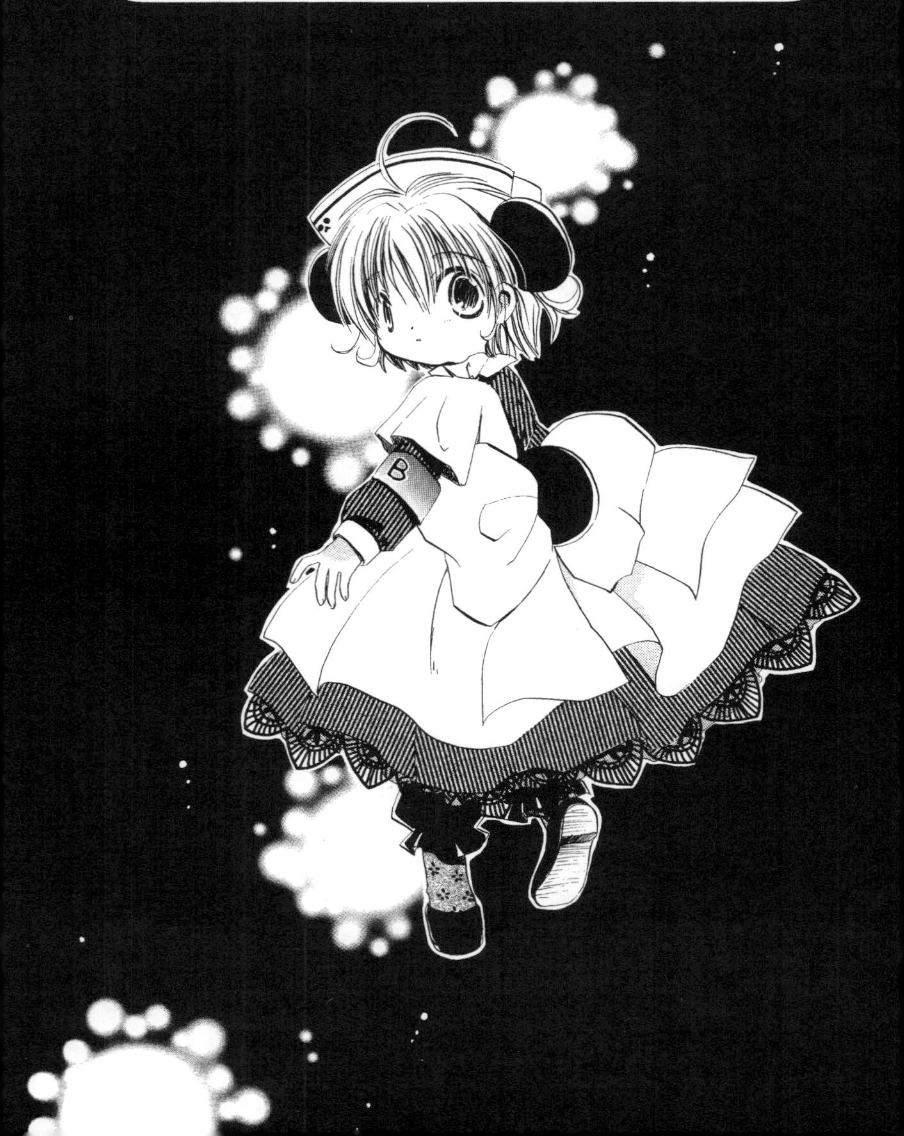

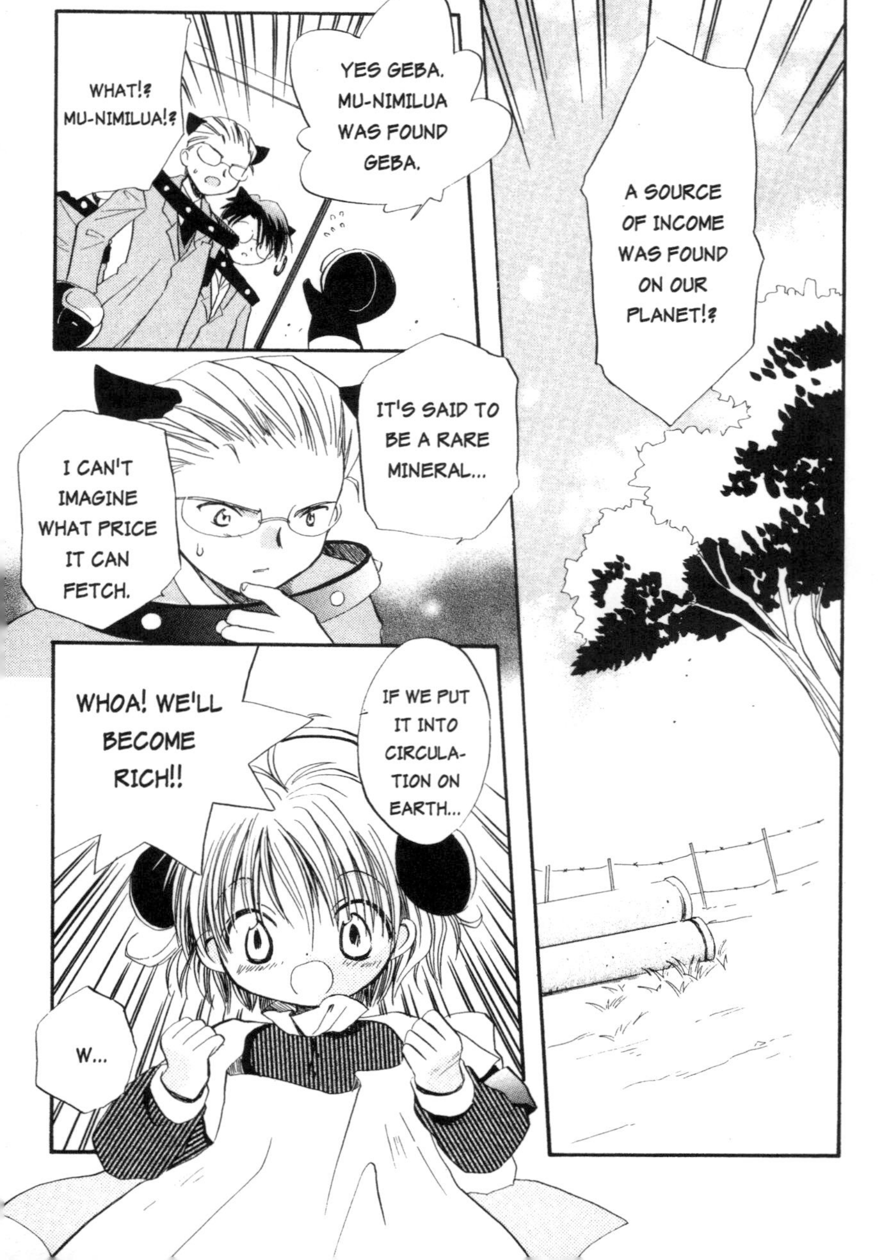
A SOURCE OF INCOME WAS FOUND ON OUR PLANET!?
YES GEBA. MU-NIMILUA WAS FOUND GEBA.
WHAT!? MU-NIMILUA!?
IT'S SAID TO BE A RARE MINERAL...
I CAN'T IMAGINE WHAT PRICE IT CAN FETCH.
IF WE PUT IT INTO CIRCULA-TION ON EARTH...
WHOA! WE'LL BECOME RICH!!
W...

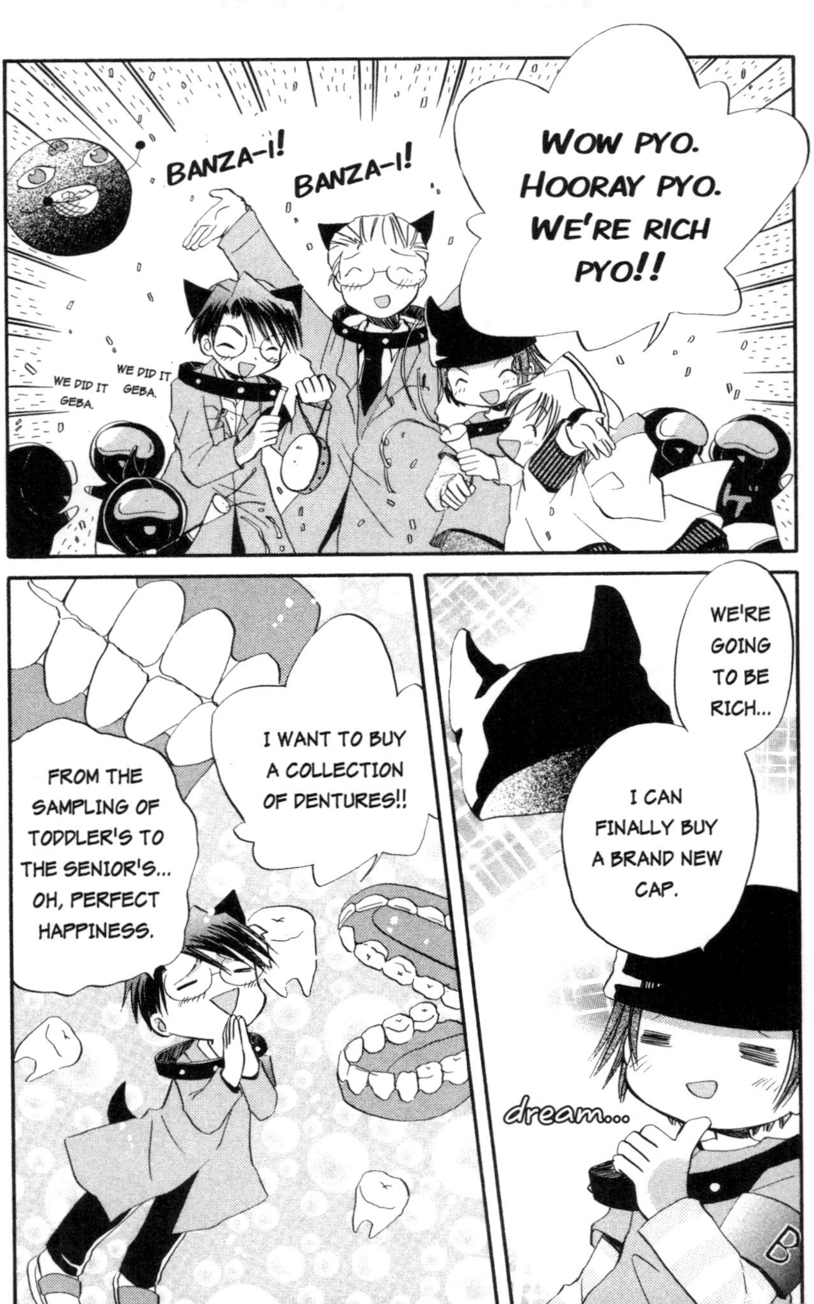
WOW PYO. HOORAY PYO. WE'RE RICH PYO!!
BANZA-I!
BANZA-I!
WE DID IT GEBA.
WE DID IT GEBA.
WE'RE GOING TO BE RICH...
I CAN FINALLY BUY A BRAND NEW CAP.
dream...
I WANT TO BUY A COLLECTION OF DENTURES!!
FROM THE SAMPLING OF TODDLER'S TO THE SENIOR'S... OH, PERFECT HAPPINESS.

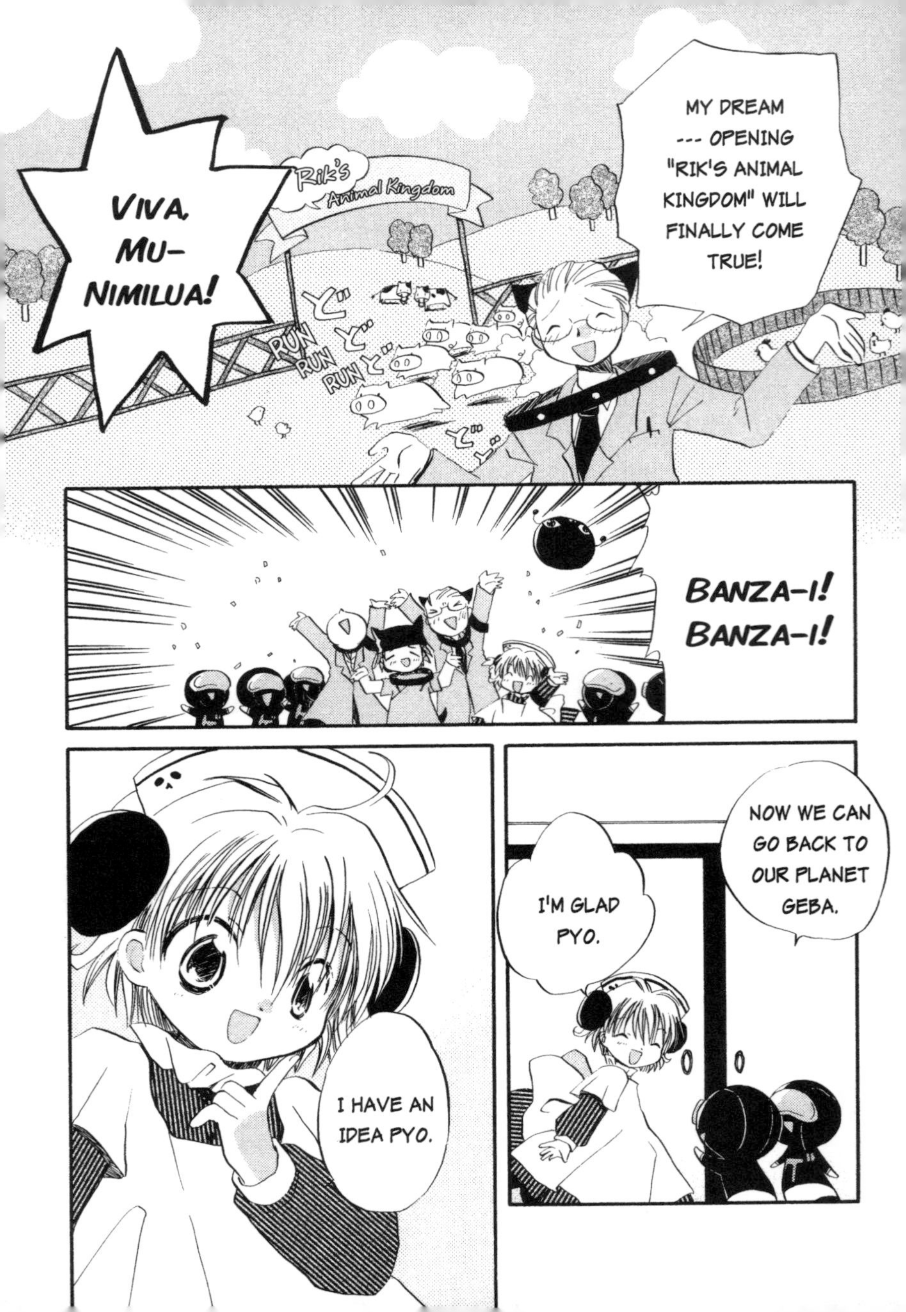
MY DREAM --- OPENING "RIK'S ANIMAL KINGDOM" WILL FINALLY COME TRUE!
Rik's Animal Kingdom
RUN RUN RUN
VIVA, MU-NIMILUA!
BANZA-I! BANZA-I!
NOW WE CAN GO BACK TO OUR PLANET GEBA.
I'M GLAD PYO.
I HAVE AN IDEA PYO.

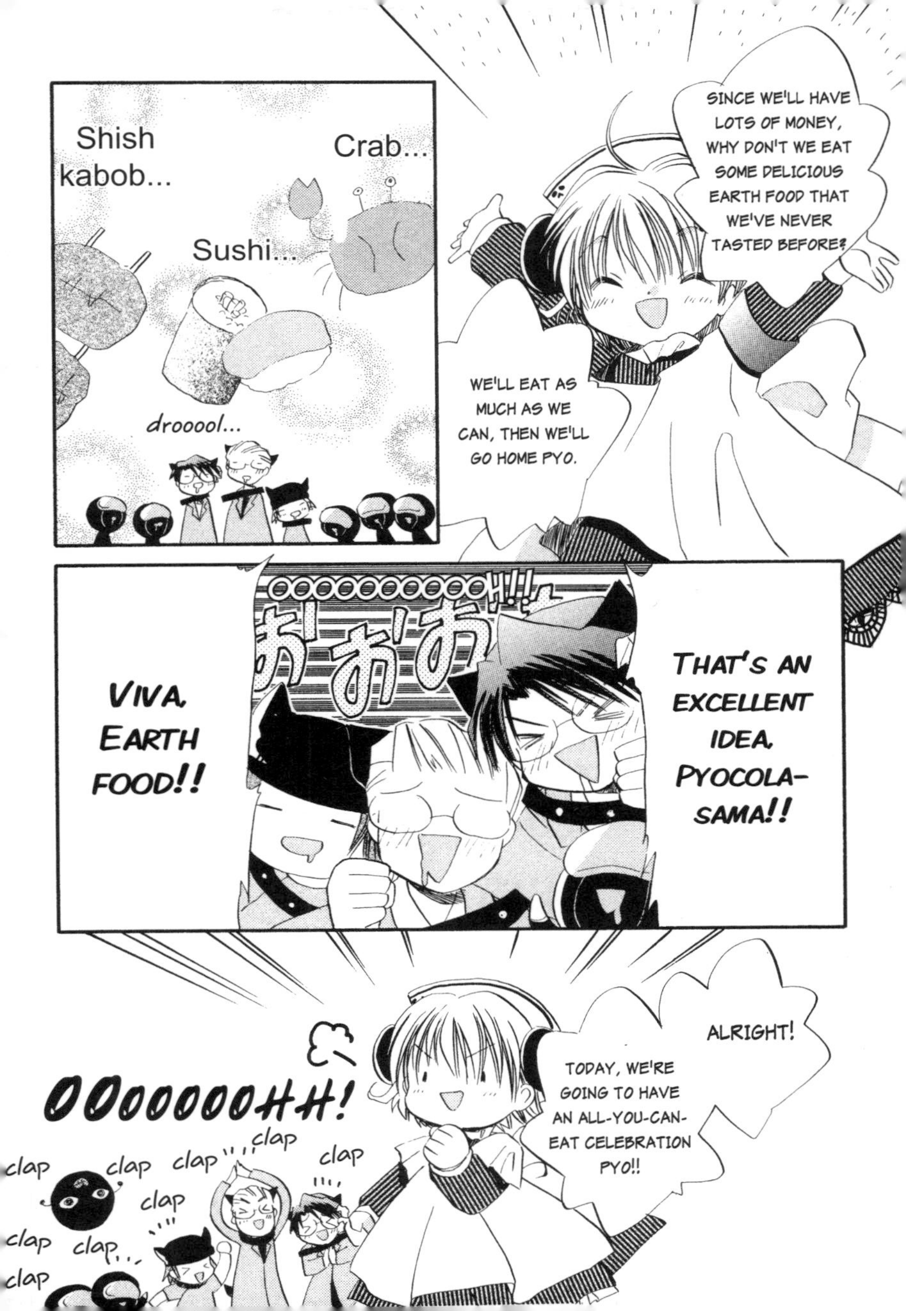
SINCE WE'LL HAVE LOTS OF MONEY, WHY DON'T WE EAT SOME DELICIOUS EARTH FOOD THAT WE'VE NEVER TASTED BEFORE?
WE'LL EAT AS MUCH AS WE CAN, THEN WE'LL GO HOME PYO.
Crab...
Shish kabob...
Sushi...
droooool...
OOOOOOOOOOOH!!!
お!お!お!
THAT'S AN EXCELLENT IDEA, PYOCOLA-SAMA!!
VIVA, EARTH FOOD!!
ALRIGHT!
TODAY, WE'RE GOING TO HAVE AN ALL-YOU-CAN-EAT CELEBRATION PYO!!
OOOOOOOHH!
clap
clap
clap
clap
clap
clap
clap
clap
clap

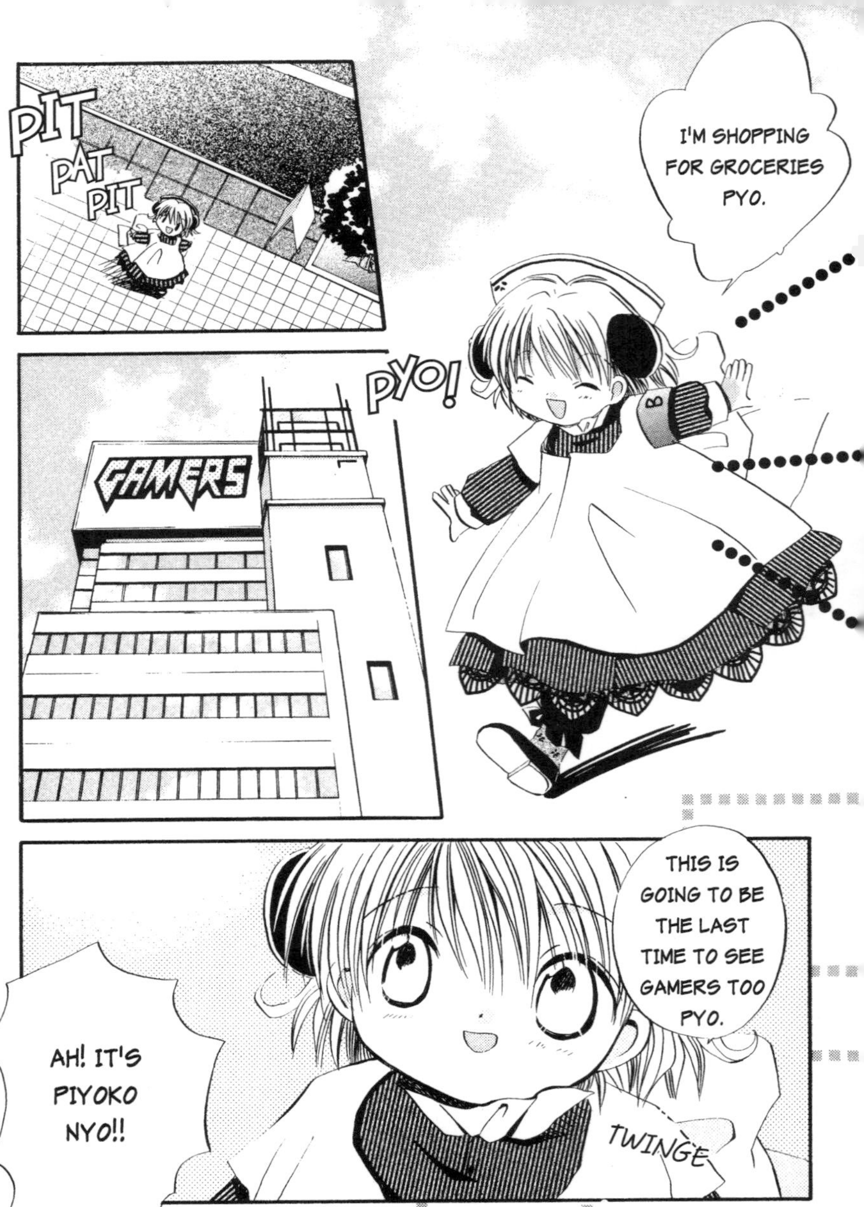
I'M SHOPPING FOR GROCERIES PYO.
PYO!
PIT PAT PIT
GAMERS
THIS IS GOING TO BE THE LAST TIME TO SEE GAMERS TOO PYO.
TWINGE
AH! IT'S PIYOKO NYO!!

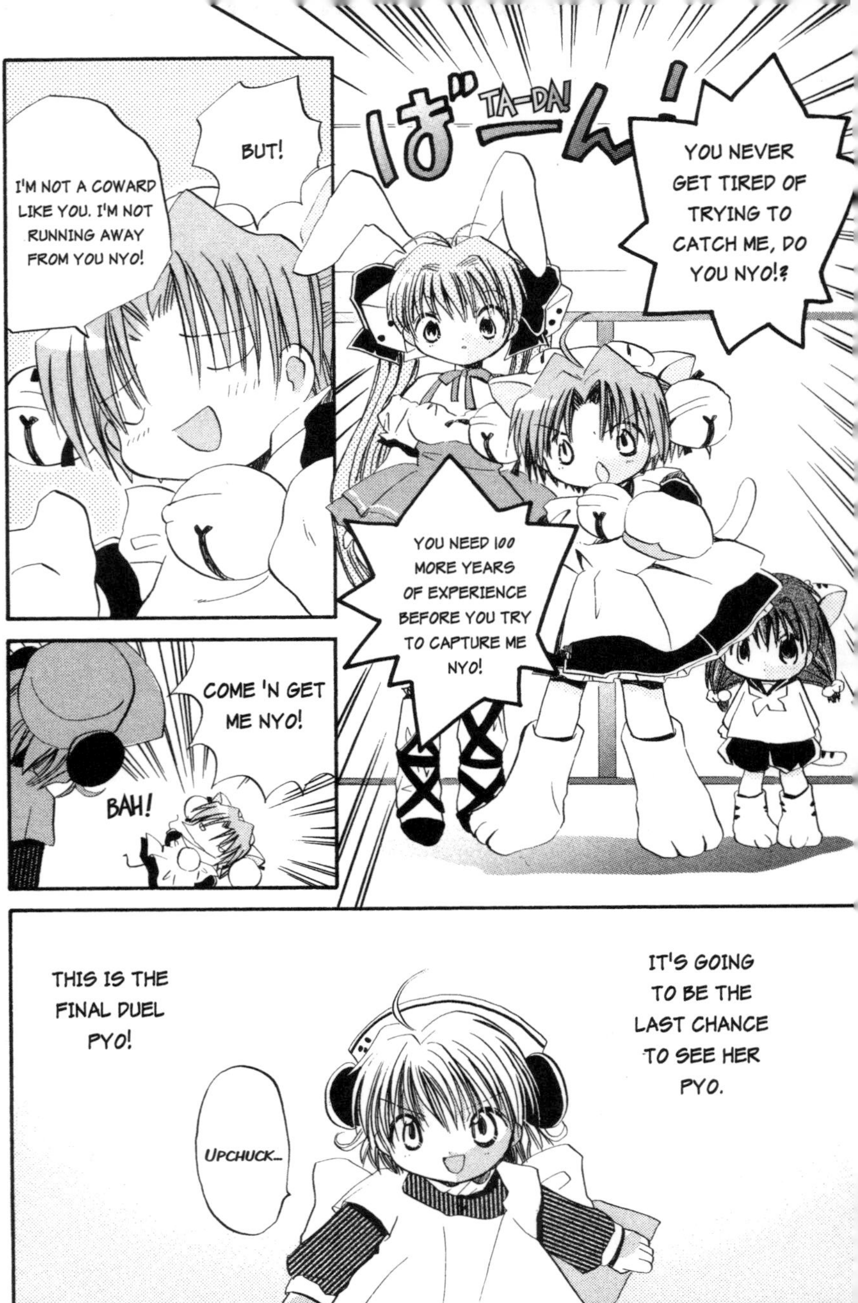
ばーん!
TA-DA!
YOU NEVER GET TIRED OF TRYING TO CATCH ME, DO YOU NYO!?
YOU NEED 100 MORE YEARS OF EXPERIENCE BEFORE YOU TRY TO CAPTURE ME NYO!
BUT!
I'M NOT A COWARD LIKE YOU. I'M NOT RUNNING AWAY FROM YOU NYO!
COME 'N GET ME NYO!
BAH!
IT'S GOING TO BE THE LAST CHANCE TO SEE HER PYO.
THIS IS THE FINAL DUEL PYO!
UPCHUCK...

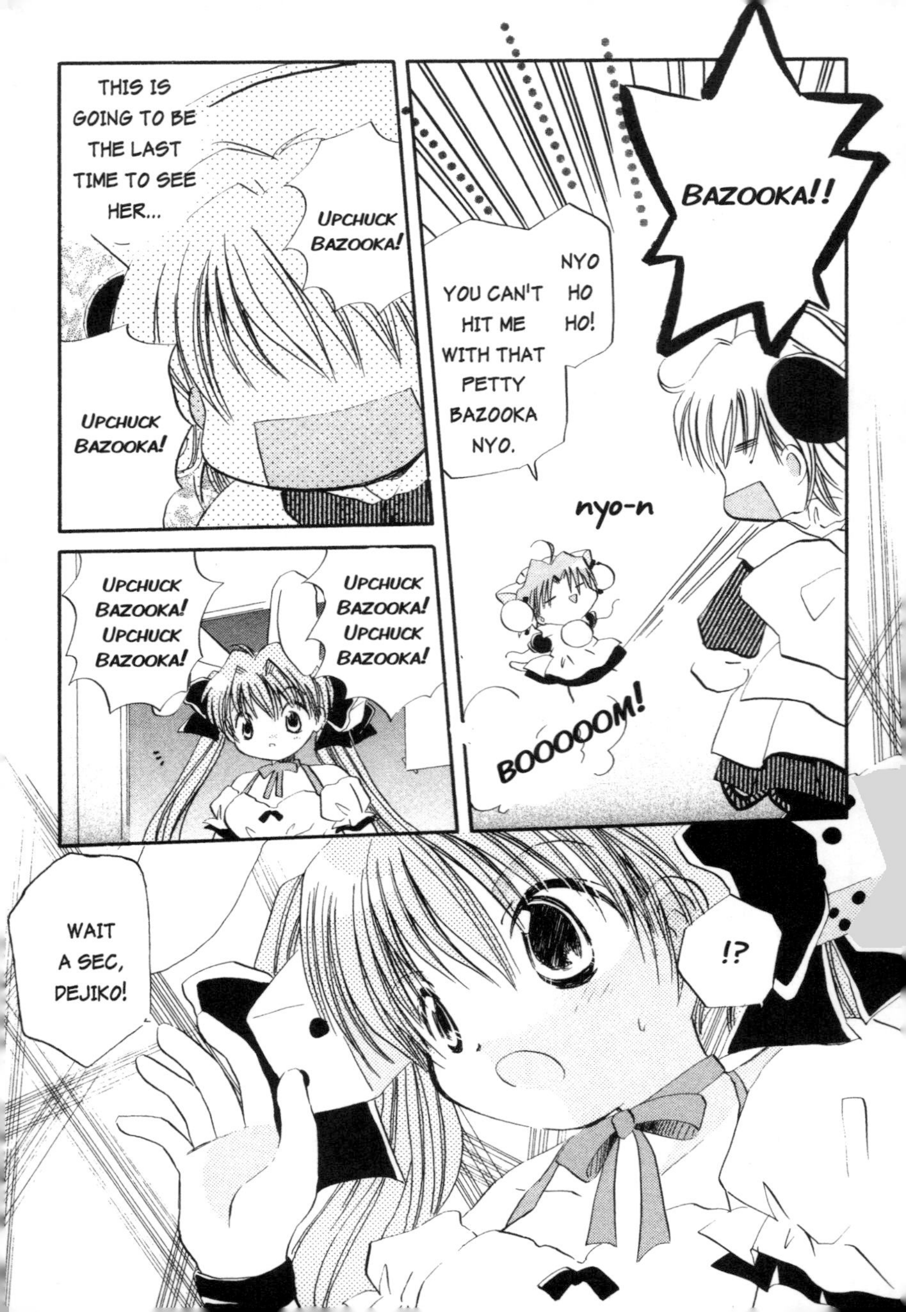

BAZOOKA!!
NYO HO HO! YOU CAN'T HIT ME WITH THAT PETTY BAZOOKA NYO.
nyo-n
BOOOOOM!
THIS IS GOING TO BE THE LAST TIME TO SEE HER...
UPCHUCK BAZOOKA!
UPCHUCK BAZOOKA!
UPCHUCK BAZOOKA! UPCHUCK BAZOOKA!
UPCHUCK BAZOOKA! UPCHUCK BAZOOKA!
!?
WAIT A SEC, DEJIKO!

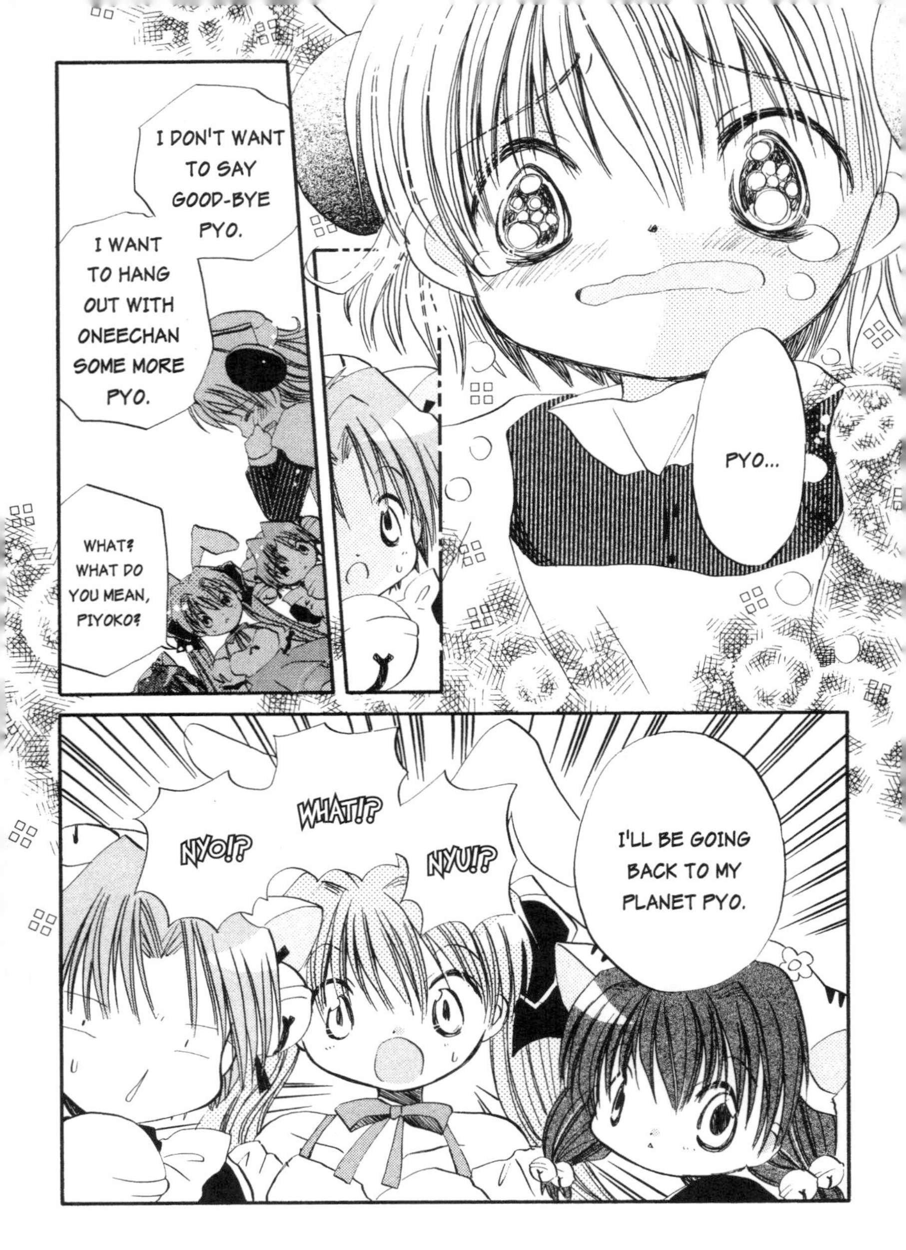
PYO...
I DON'T WANT TO SAY GOOD-BYE PYO.
I WANT TO HANG OUT WITH ONEECHAN SOME MORE PYO.
WHAT? WHAT DO YOU MEAN, PIYOKO?
I'LL BE GOING BACK TO MY PLANET PYO.
NYU!?
WHAT!?
NYO!?

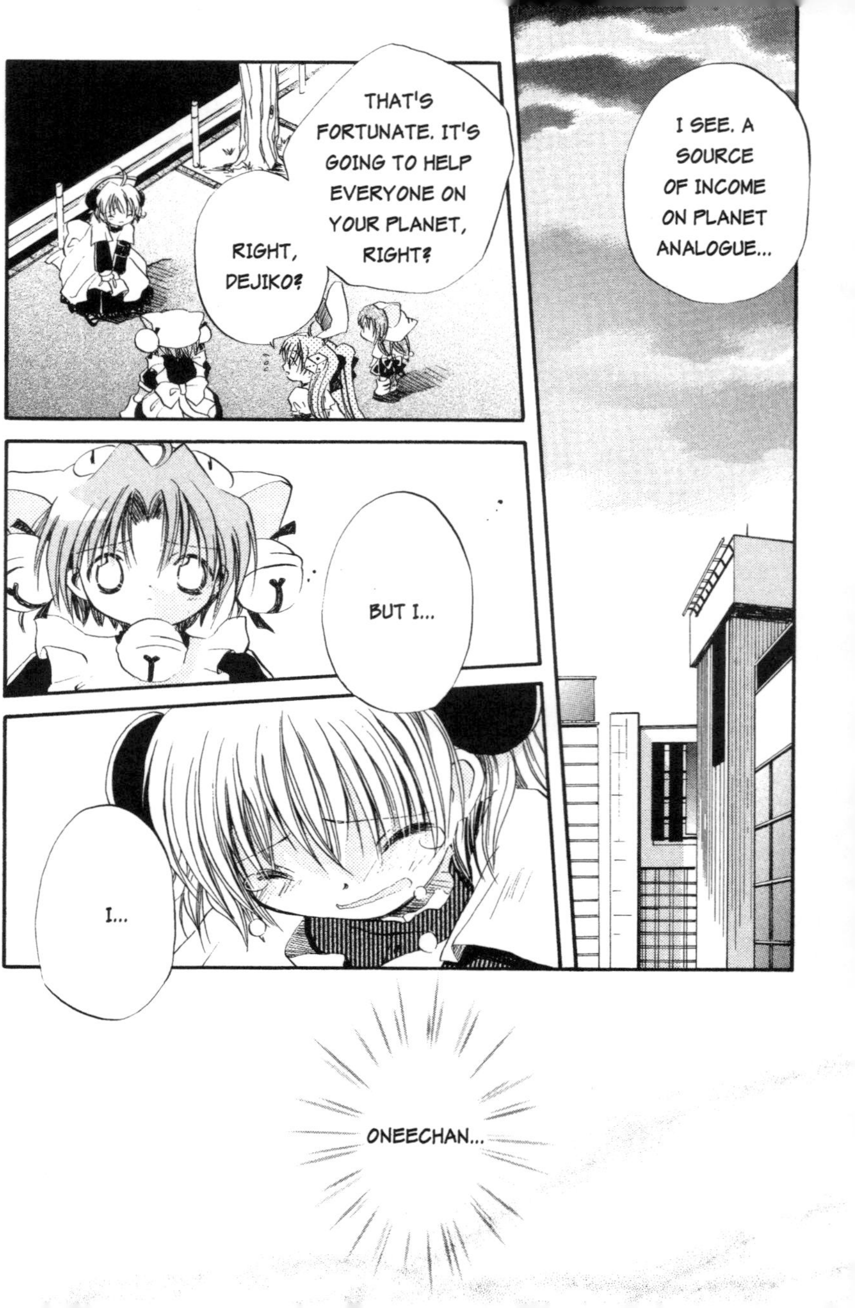
I SEE. A SOURCE OF INCOME ON PLANET ANALOGUE...
THAT'S FORTUNATE. IT'S GOING TO HELP EVERYONE ON YOUR PLANET, RIGHT?
RIGHT, DEJIKO?
BUT I...
I...
ONEECHAN...

Nyo 16 Good-bye Piyoko

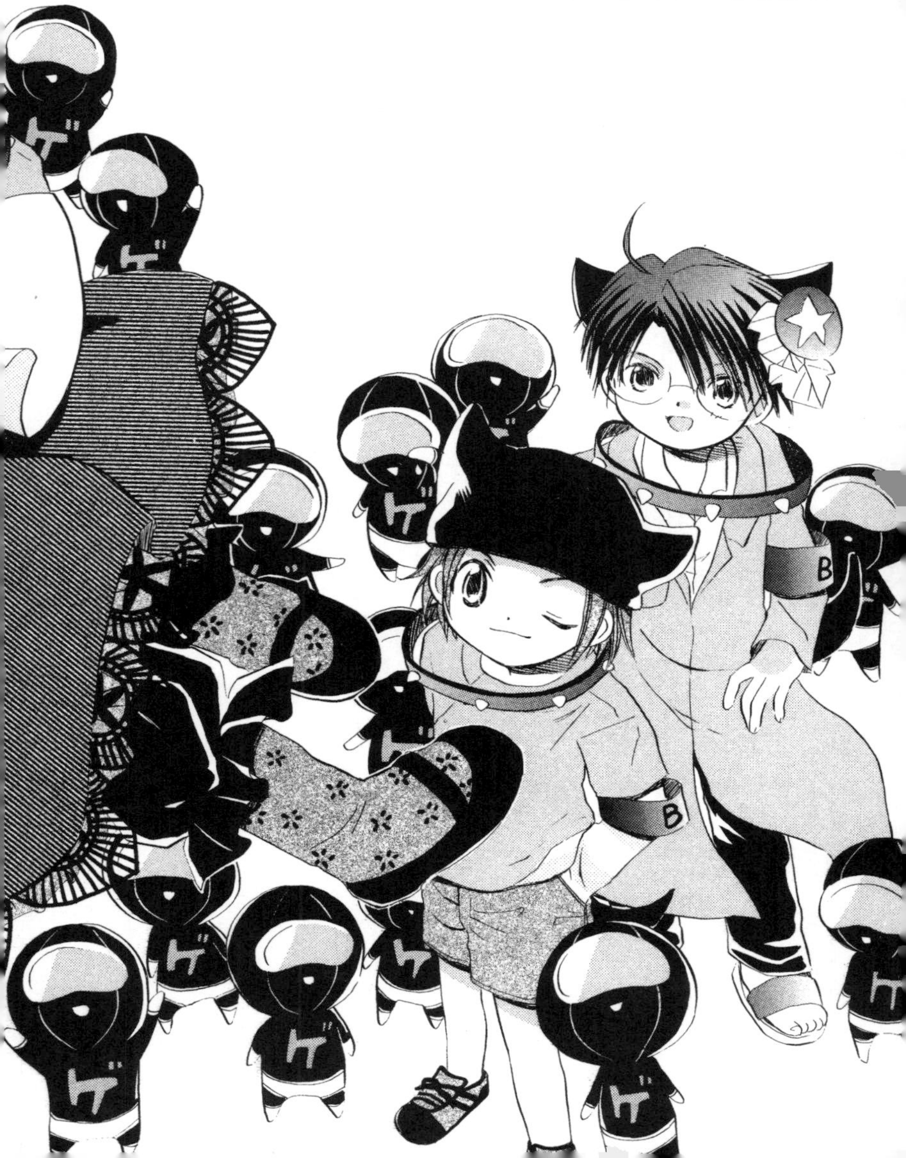

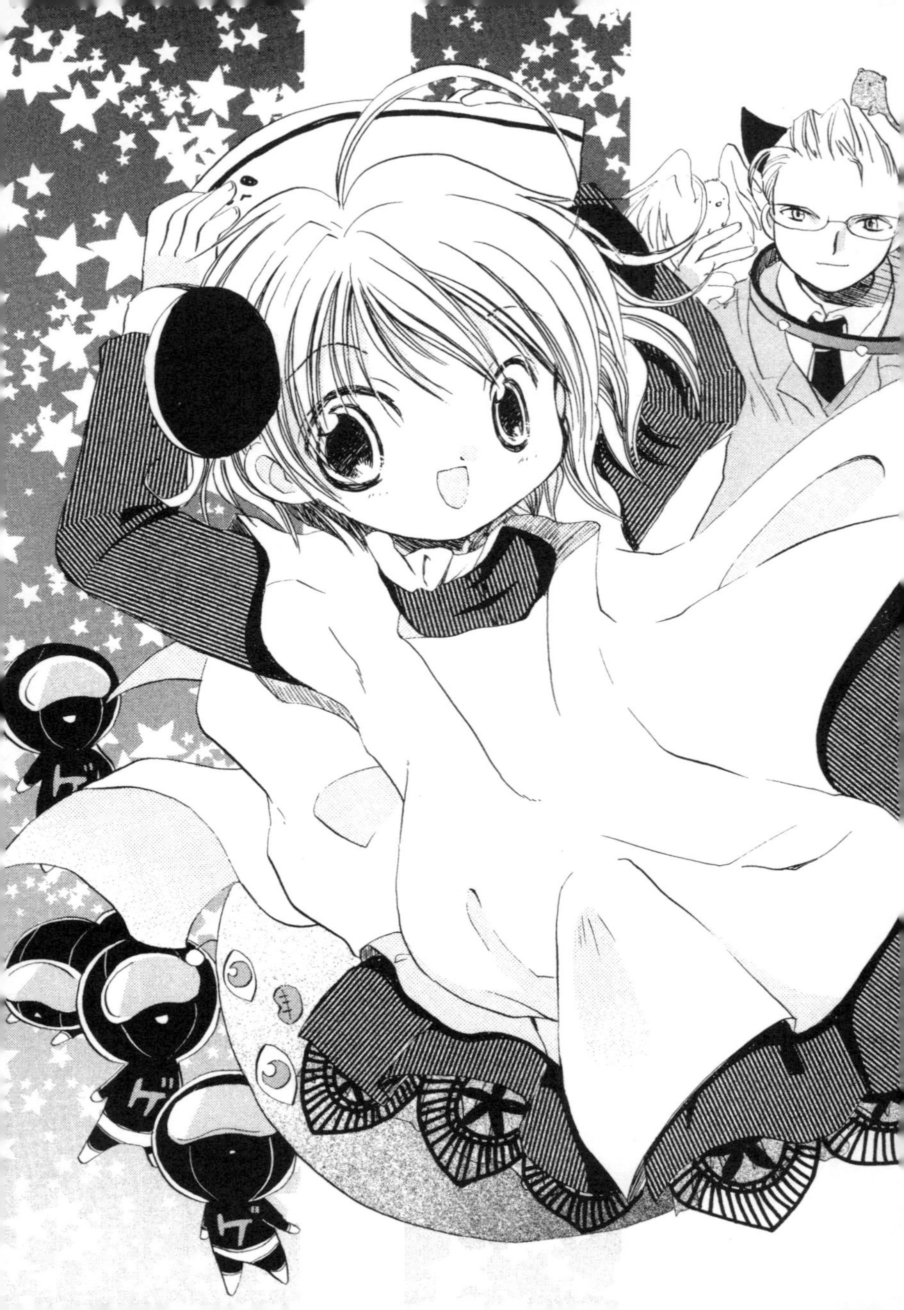

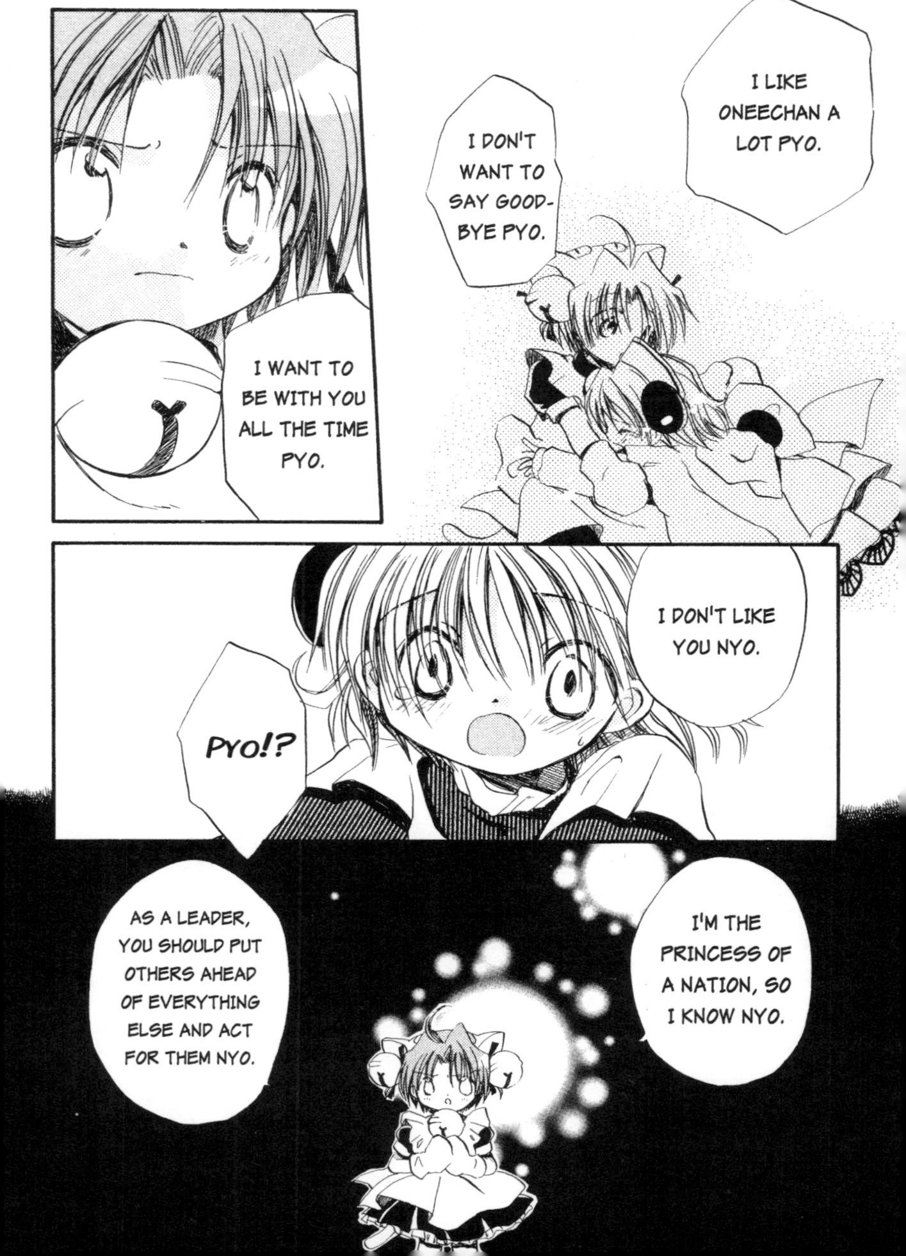
I LIKE ONEECHAN A LOT PYO.
I DON'T WANT TO SAY GOOD-BYE PYO.
I WANT TO BE WITH YOU ALL THE TIME PYO.
I DON'T LIKE YOU NYO.
PYO!?
I'M THE PRINCESS OF A NATION, SO I KNOW NYO.
AS A LEADER, YOU SHOULD PUT OTHERS AHEAD OF EVERYTHING ELSE AND ACT FOR THEM NYO.

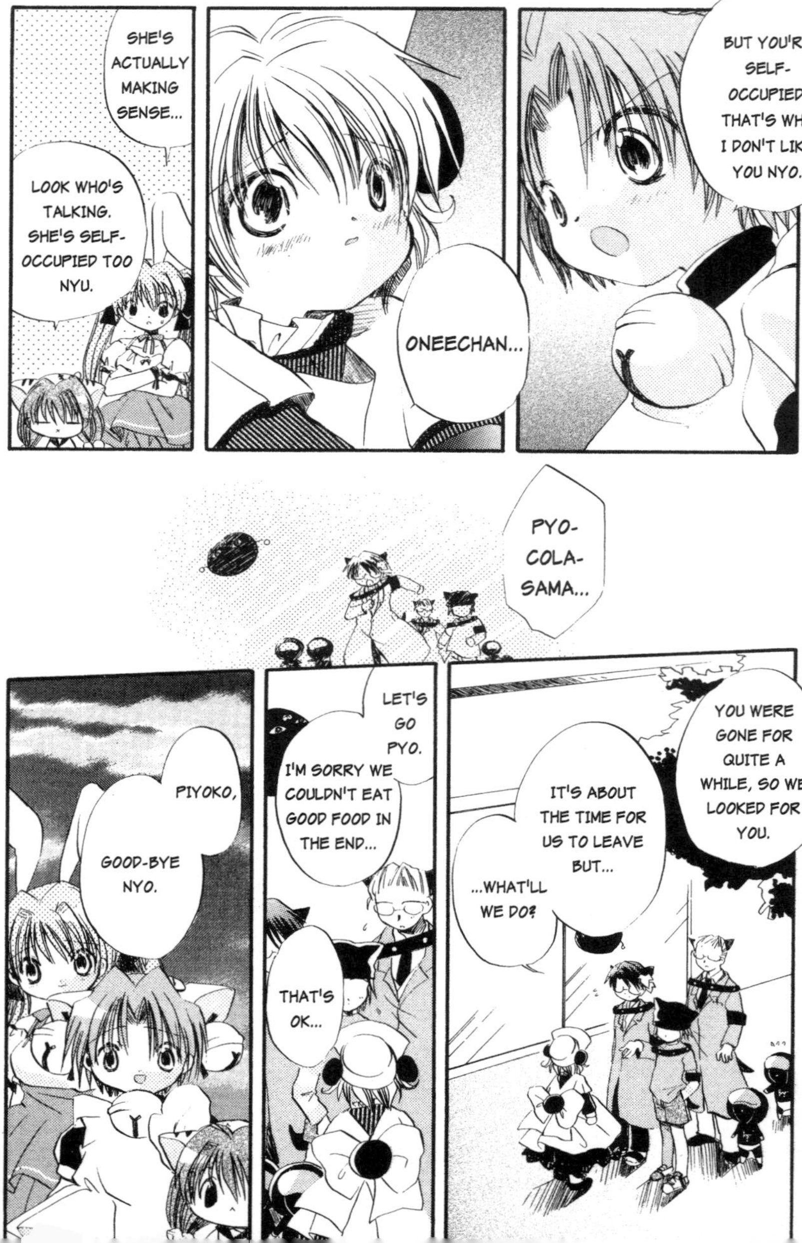
BUT YOU'RE SELF-OCCUPIED. THAT'S WHY I DON'T LIKE YOU NYO.
ONEECHAN...
SHE'S ACTUALLY MAKING SENSE...
LOOK WHO'S TALKING. SHE'S SELF-OCCUPIED TOO NYU.
PYO-COLA-SAMA...
YOU WERE GONE FOR QUITE A WHILE, SO WE LOOKED FOR YOU.
IT'S ABOUT THE TIME FOR US TO LEAVE BUT...
...WHAT'LL WE DO?
LET'S GO PYO.
I'M SORRY WE COULDN'T EAT GOOD FOOD IN THE END...
THAT'S OK...
PIYOKO,
GOOD-BYE NYO.

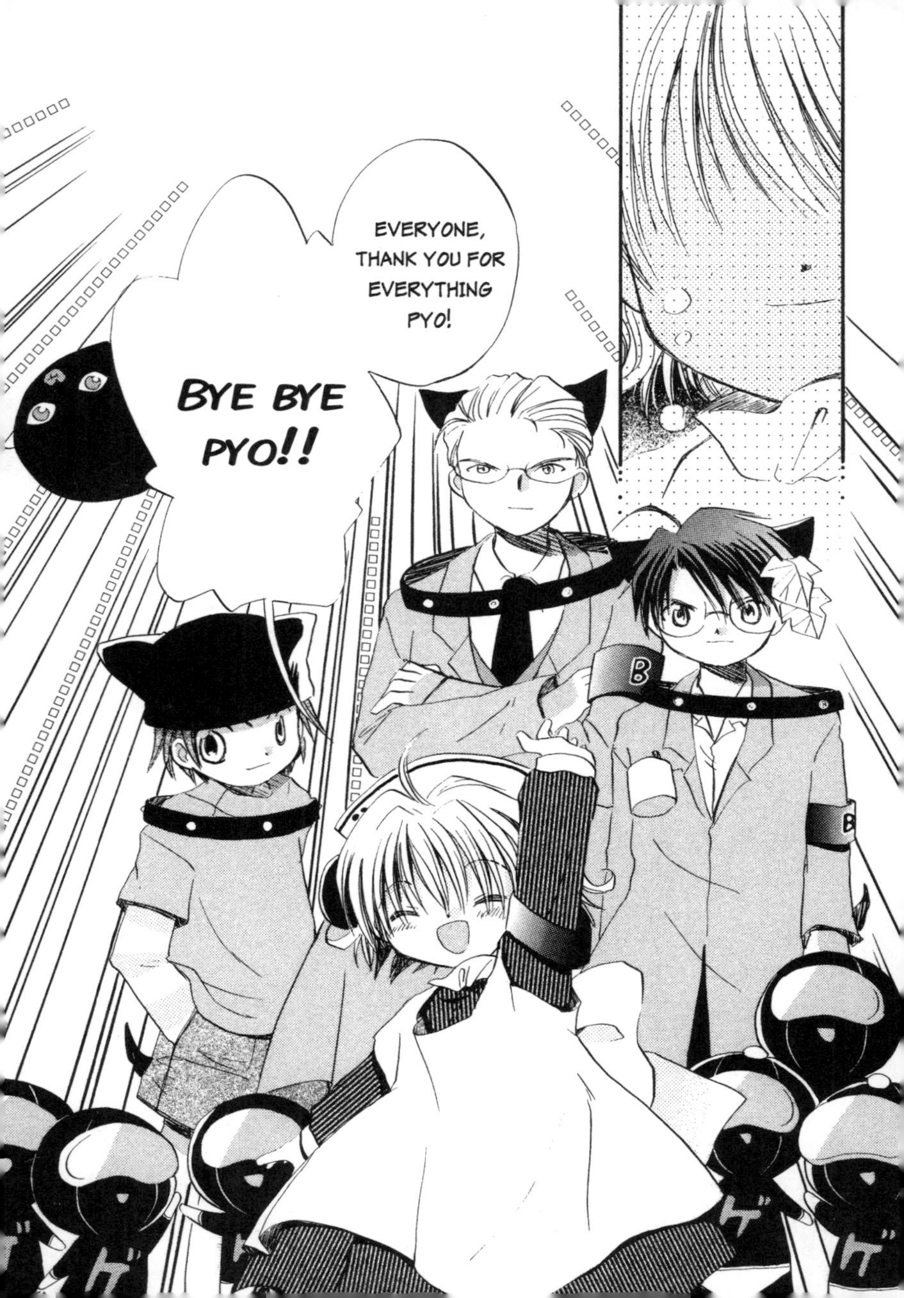
EVERYONE, THANK YOU FOR EVERYTHING PYO!
BYE BYE PYO!!

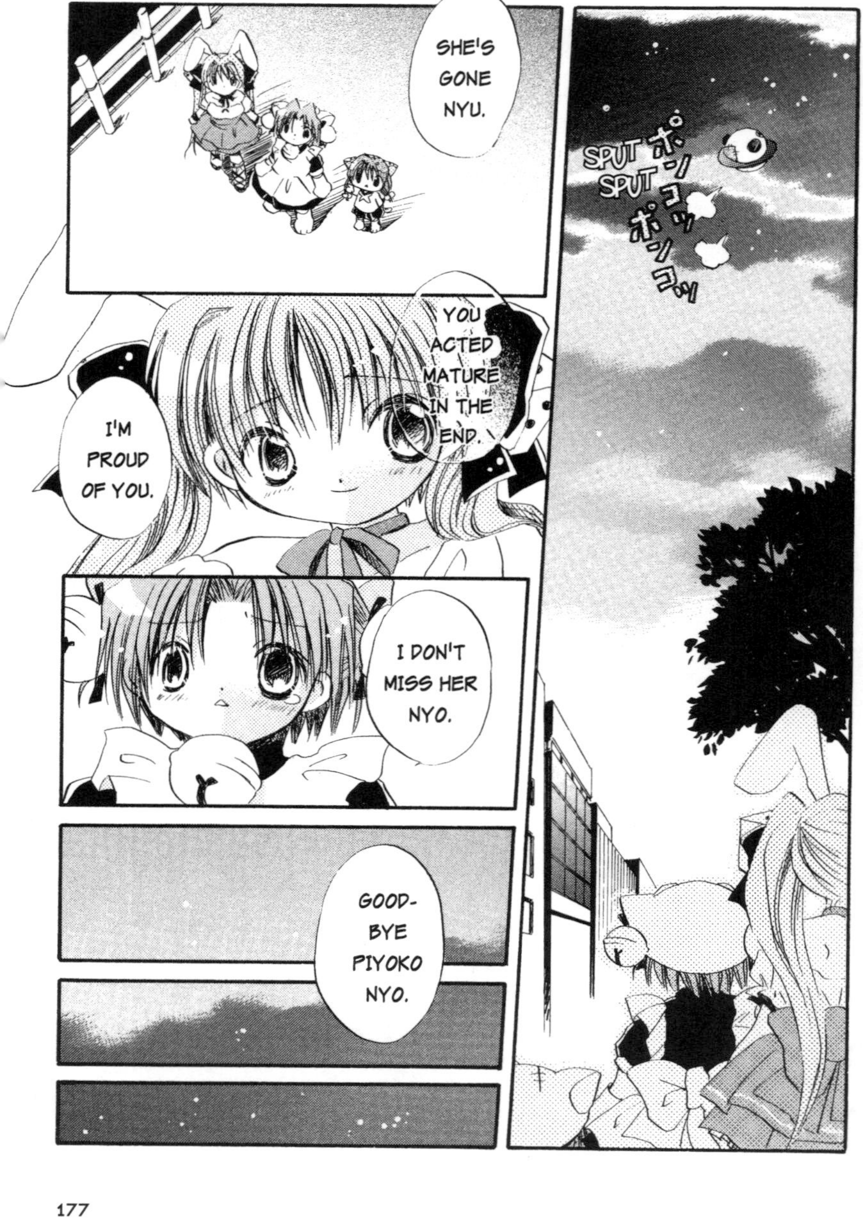
SPUT SPUT
ポンコッ ポンコッ
SHE'S GONE NYU.
YOU ACTED MATURE IN THE END.
I'M PROUD OF YOU.
I DON'T MISS HER NYO.
GOOD-BYE PIYOKO NYO.

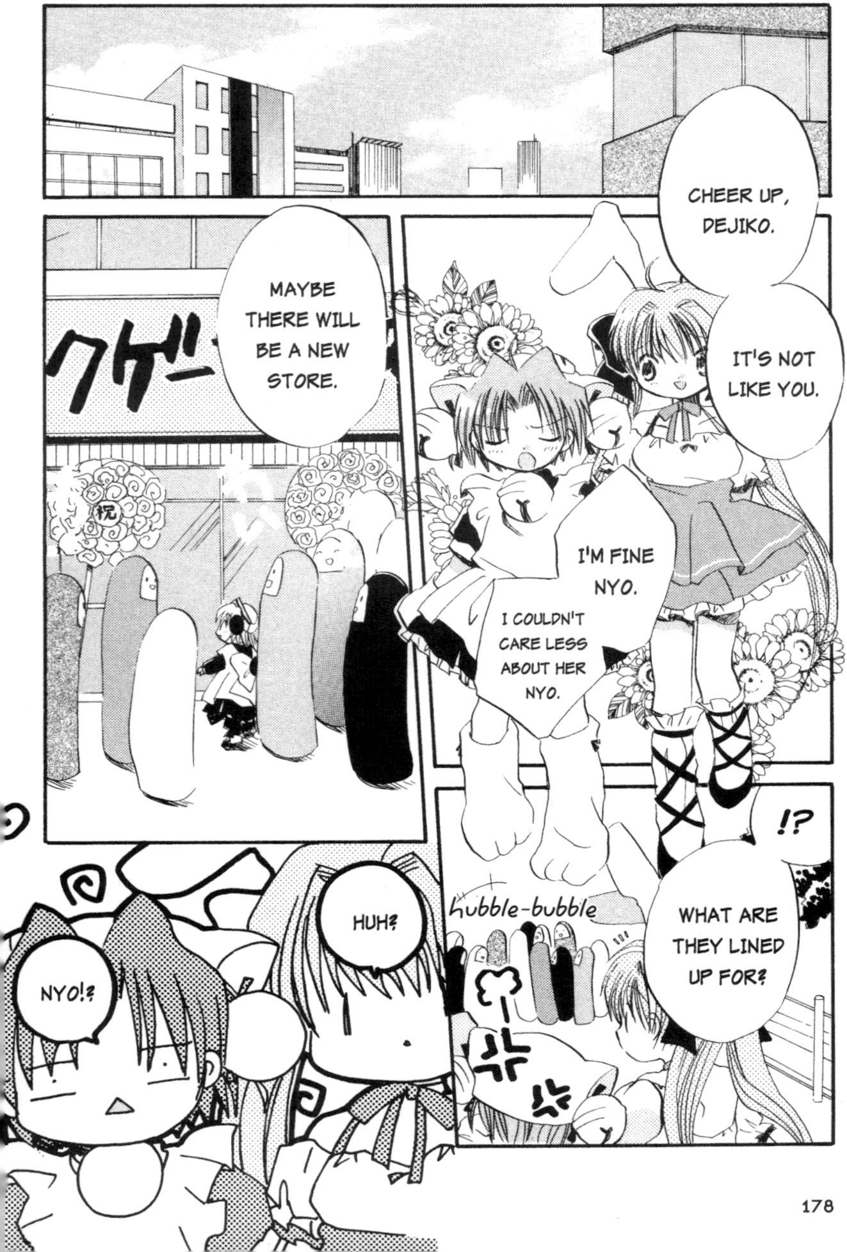
CHEER UP, DEJIKO.
IT'S NOT LIKE YOU.
I'M FINE NYO.
I COULDN'T CARE LESS ABOUT HER NYO.
MAYBE THERE WILL BE A NEW STORE.
祝
!?
WHAT ARE THEY LINED UP FOR?
bubble-bubble
HUH?
NYO!?

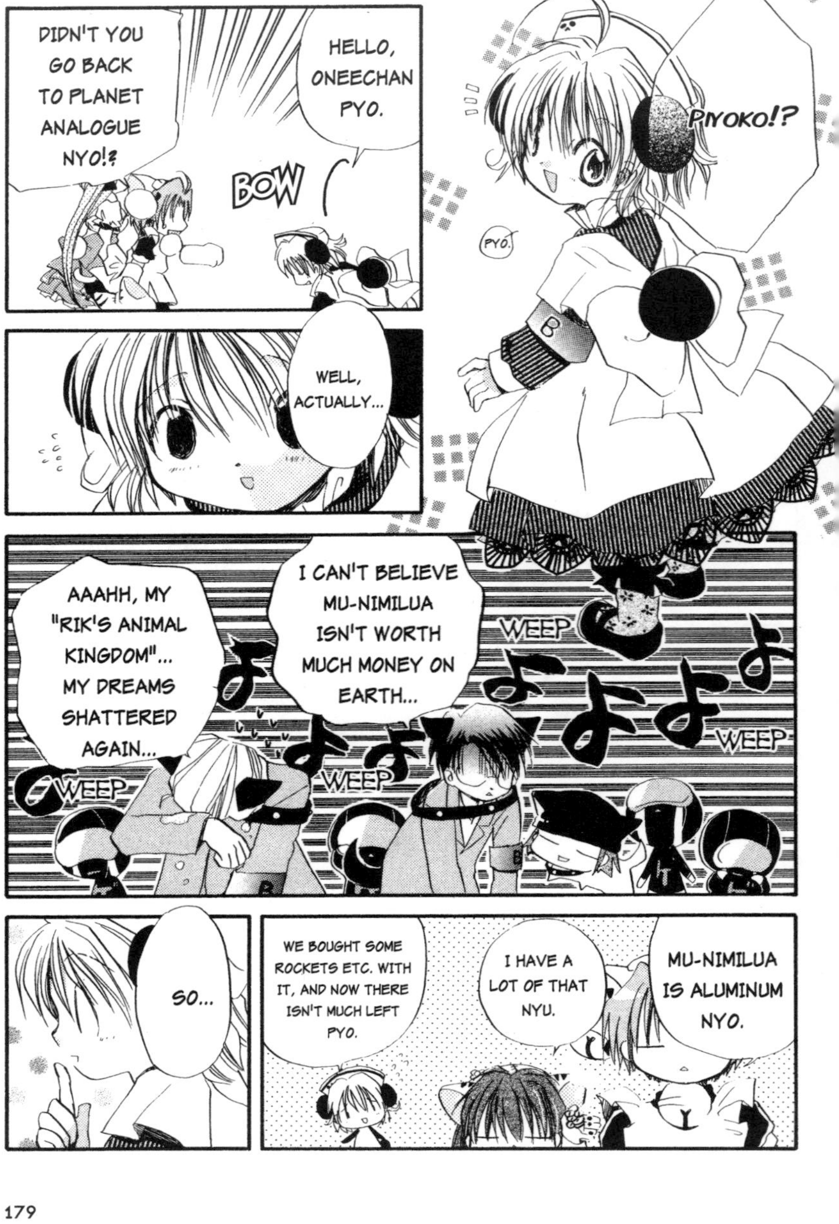
PIYOKO!?
PYO.
HELLO, ONEECHAN PYO.
BOW
DIDN'T YOU GO BACK TO PLANET ANALOGUE NYO!?
WELL, ACTUALLY...
I CAN'T BELIEVE MU-NIMILUA ISN'T WORTH MUCH MONEY ON EARTH...
WEEP
WEEP
AAAHH, MY "RIK'S ANIMAL KINGDOM"... MY DREAMS SHATTERED AGAIN...
WEEP
WEEP
MU-NIMILUA IS ALUMINUM NYO.
I HAVE A LOT OF THAT NYU.
WE BOUGHT SOME ROCKETS ETC. WITH IT, AND NOW THERE ISN'T MUCH LEFT PYO.
SO...

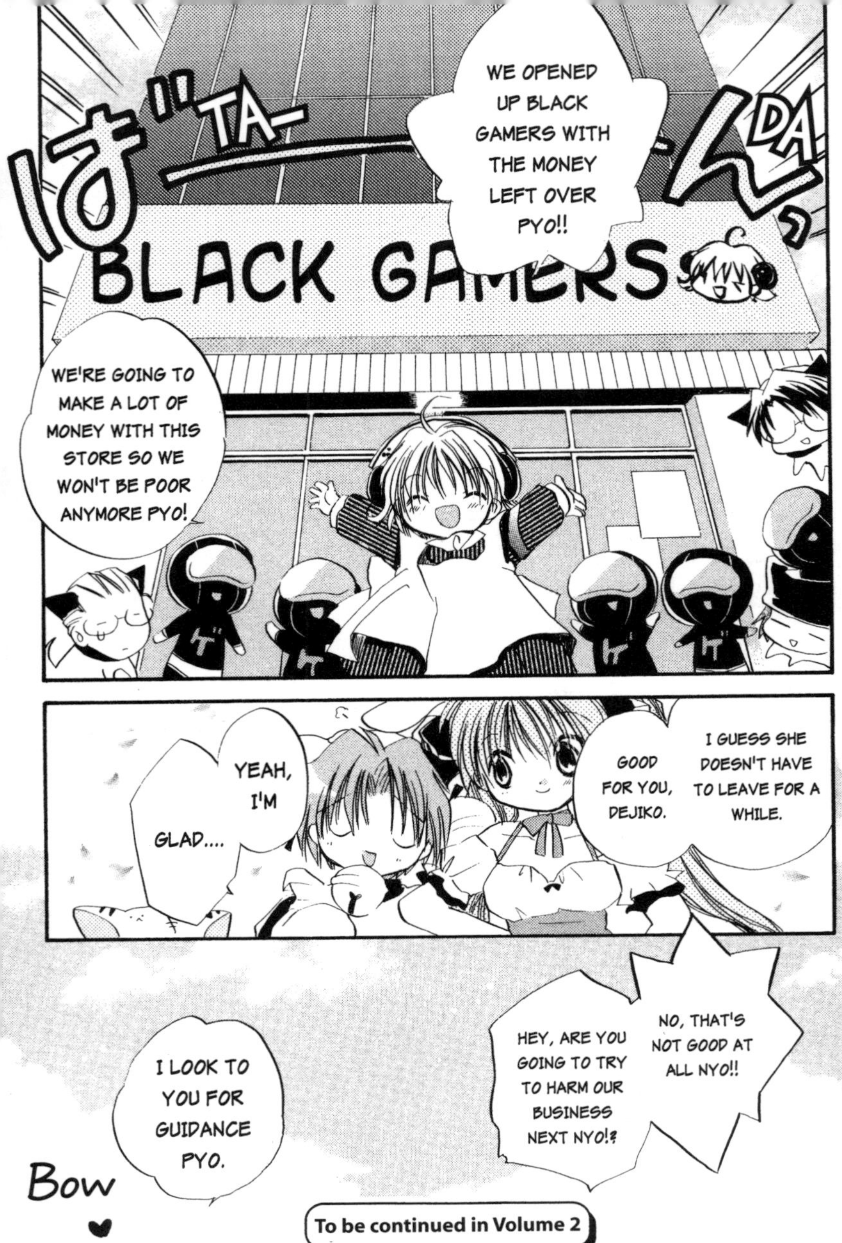
ば―ん TA-DA
WE OPENED UP BLACK GAMERS WITH THE MONEY LEFT OVER PYO!!
BLACK GAMERS
WE'RE GOING TO MAKE A LOT OF MONEY WITH THIS STORE SO WE WON'T BE POOR ANYMORE PYO!
I GUESS SHE DOESN'T HAVE TO LEAVE FOR A WHILE.
GOOD FOR YOU, DEJIKO.
YEAH, I'M GLAD....
NO, THAT'S NOT GOOD AT ALL NYO!!
HEY, ARE YOU GOING TO TRY TO HARM OUR BUSINESS NEXT NYO!?
I LOOK TO YOU FOR GUIDANCE PYO.
Bow

To be continued in Volume 2

**A Day in the Life of
the Black Gema Gema Gang**
8:30 PM  Piyoko goes to bed

TRANSLATION NOTES

pg. 12 Akihabara – An electronic district in Tokyo, Japan. The Gamers store where Dejiko & others work is located in Akihabara.

pg. 12 Gamers – A chain of Japanese anime merchandise stores operated by BROCCOLI. The first US Gamers store opened in Los Angeles in 2001 (http://retail.animegamers.com).

pg. 23 Oneechan – Literally "older sister," but can be used to address an older female one is close to. Piyoko calls Dejiko "oneechan," because Dejiko is older.

pg. 25 Fireworks – The customers think fireworks are lively and that there might be a festival because fireworks are used for celebration throughout the year.

pg. 27 Tamaya – Japanese people say "Tamaya" when a big firework goes up. This is a tradition originating from the Edo Period, when two firework makers known as Tamaya and Kagiya competed to make the best fireworks. The two would put up fireworks and yell out their names "Tamaya!" and "Kagiya!" every time their work went up.

pg. 46 Shikao – "Shika" means "deer" in Japanese. "O" is a male name ending, written as the kanji for "male." Rik's friend is named Shikao because he's a male deer.

pg. 50 Pipes in undeveloped land – An empty plot of land always has large pipes stacked on it in manga. This comes from *Doraemon*, a popular children's manga & anime, where the kids from the show would hang out in an empty plot of land & sit on top of the large pipes.

pg. 60 Kuromame (Japanese sweet black beans) – A popular side dish eaten during New Year's celebrations. People are supposed to eat a bean for each year of their age.

pg. 67 Praying w/ paper-wand – In Shinto, a white paper wand purifies the item it is waved at.

pg. 67 Mochi – Japanese sweet rice cakes that are usually made around the time of the New Year.

pg. 83 Iori book – Dejiko is a fan of Iori from the video game series *King of Fighters*. The Black Gema Gema Gang try to catch Dejiko by luring her with an Iori doujinshi, or self-published comic book.

TRANSLATION NOTES

pg. 86 Kinryuzan/Kaminarimon – Kinryuzan is a revered Buddhist temple in Tokyo, Japan. It was founded in the 7th century A.D. to enshrine a statue of Kannon, the Goddess of Mercy, which was discovered by two fishermen. A large red lantern with the words "Kaminarimon," or "Thunder Gate," stands at the entrance of the temple.

pg. 89 Dejiko wearing a happi coat – A souvenir of Kaminarimon and other shrines.

pg. 128 Fish-blade – A parody on Body-Blade fitness equipment.

pg. 138 Don't peek – Rik and Ky make reference to Tsuru no Ongaeshi, or The Grateful Crane. It is a Japanese folktale about an old couple who rescues a crane caught in a trap. A few days later, during a blizzard, a young woman visits their home and asks to stay with them. Learning that the old couple has a loom, the young woman asks them if she can weave cloth for them. The only condition she gives them is to never look inside the room while she weaves. The young woman makes beautiful cloth and the old couple is able to sell it and become wealthy. But the couple notices that the young woman grows weaker as she weaves the cloth everyday. Concerned, they take a peek into the room and see a crane pulling its feathers and weaving them into the cloth. The crane turns into the young woman and tells them that they broke their promise, so she must go back to the mountains.

pg. 141 Takoyaki – A fried ball of dough with a small piece of octopus inside.

pg. 148 Yukata – A summer version of the kimono. It's made out of lighter cloth and has no lining.

Leave it to Piyoko!™

2

DELUXE
Di Gi CHARAT
Leave it to Piyoko!
2
by Hina.

BLACK GAMERS OPENS!

NAZO GEMA FALLS IN LOVE WITH GEMA?

DEJIKO IS NOW A GUY?

LOOK FOR LEAVE IT TO PIYOKO VOLUME 2, COMING SOON TO YOUR LOCAL BOOKSTORES!

THE FOLLOWING PAGES ARE A SNEAK PEEK OF WHAT'S COMING!

DEJIKO WILL RULE THIS MANGA NYO!
But it's my manga pyo...

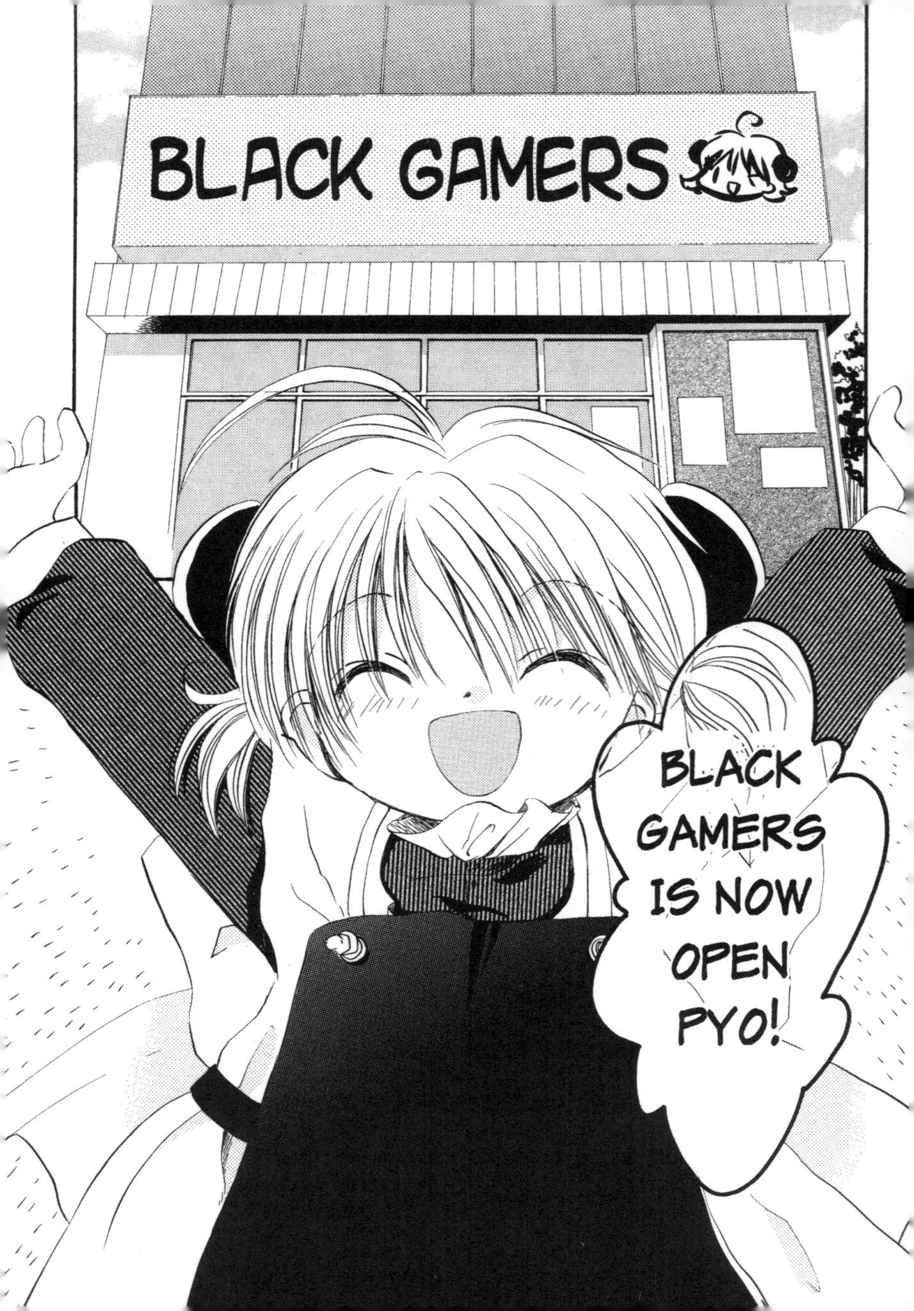
BLACK GAMERS
BLACK GAMERS IS NOW OPEN PYO!

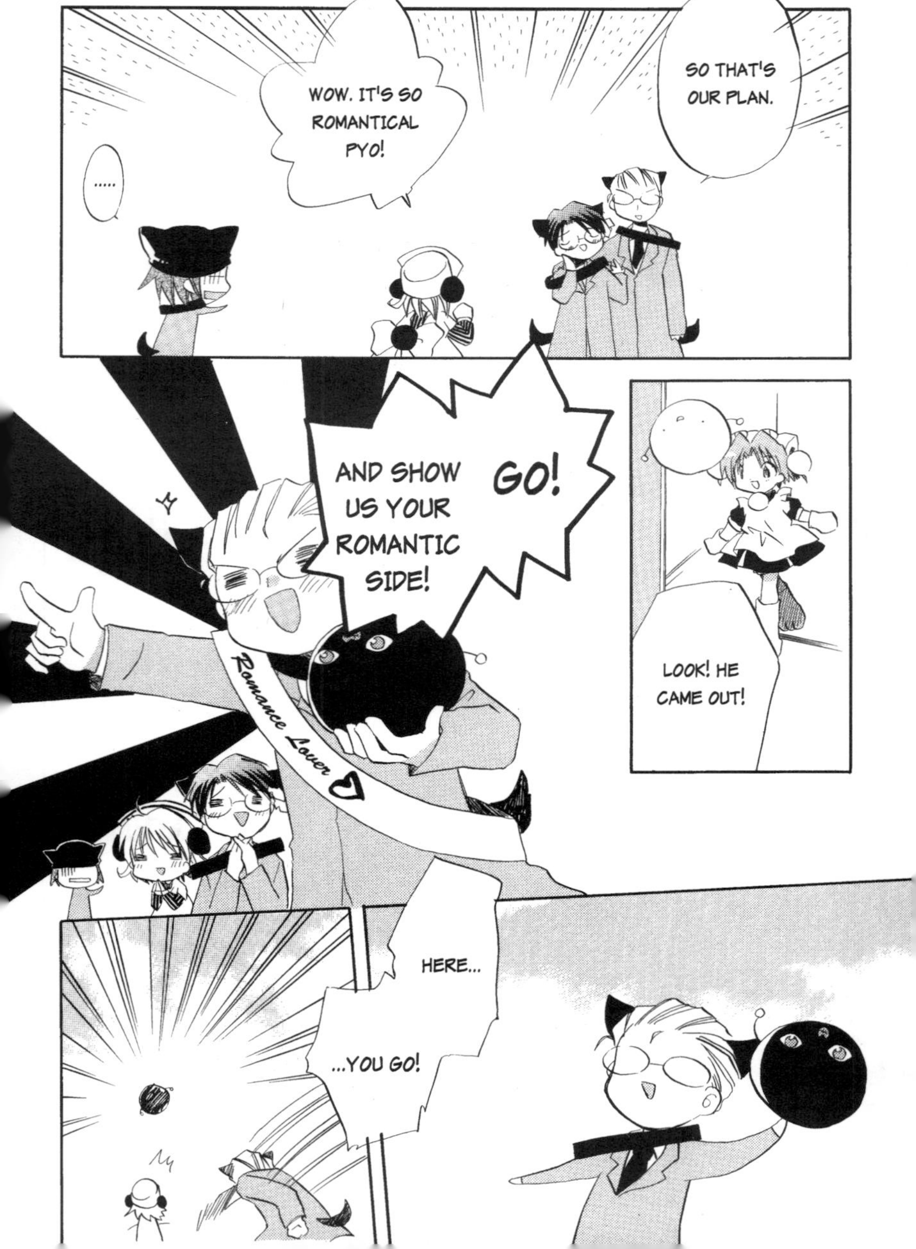
SO THAT'S OUR PLAN.
WOW. IT'S SO ROMANTICAL PYO!
......
LOOK! HE CAME OUT!
GO!
AND SHOW US YOUR ROMANTIC SIDE!
Romance Lover
HERE...
...YOU GO!

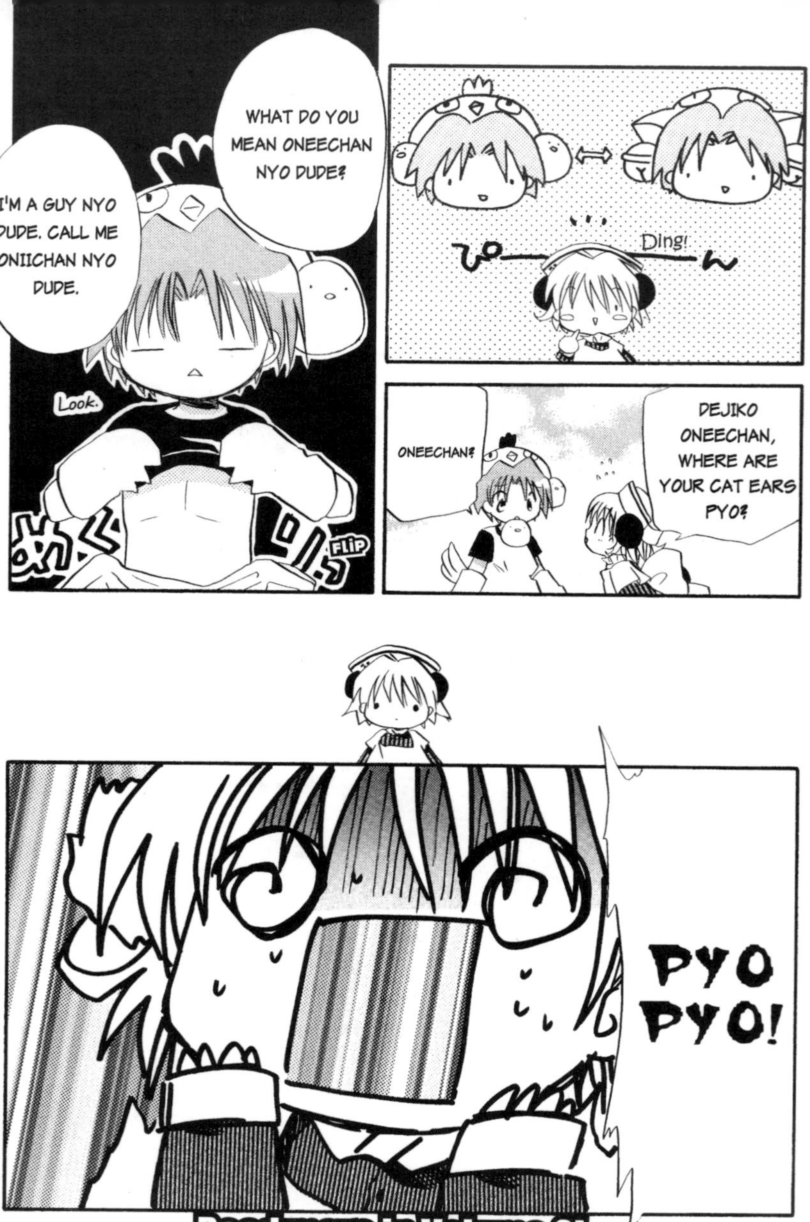

Ding!
DEJIKO ONEECHAN, WHERE ARE YOUR CAT EARS PYO?
ONEECHAN?
WHAT DO YOU MEAN ONEECHAN NYO DUDE?
I'M A GUY NYO DUDE. CALL ME ONIICHAN NYO DUDE.
Look.
FLIP
PYO PYO!

Read more in Volume 2!

GALLERY

Warrior Piyoko
Di Gi Charat CCG Part 1
Card No. 55

Illust. by Hina.

GALLERY

Paladin Puchiko
Di Gi Charat CCG Part 2
Card No. 174

Illust. by Hina.

GALLERY

Cowgirl Dejiko
Di Gi Charat CCG Part 1
Card No. 7

Illust. by Hina.

GALLERY

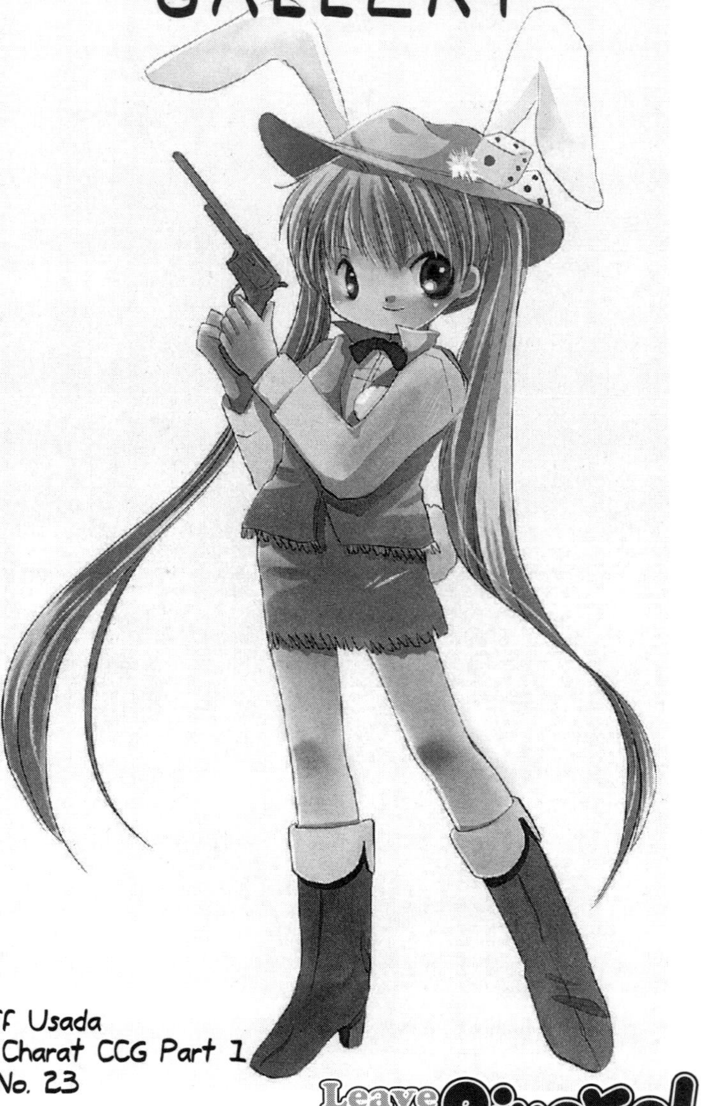
Leave it to Piyoko!™

Sheriff Usada
Di Gi Charat CCG Part 1
Card No. 23

Illust. by Hina.

BLACK GEMA GEMA STAMP OF APPROVAL

PLEASE SUPPORT THE BLACK GEMA GEMA GANG!

CONTINUED ON NEXT PAGE

THE BLACK GEMA GEMA GANG SUPPORT FUND

In order to continue with their plans to save Planet Analogue, the poor Black Gema Gema Gang first needs food in their tummies! How can an evil organization survive without money?

That's why they need your help. Buying Black Gema Gema Gang merchandise from Anime Gamers supports the troops that have worked so hard at capturing Princess Di Gi Charat. Maybe one day, with your help, they can succeed!

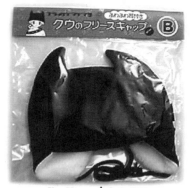

zipper holders

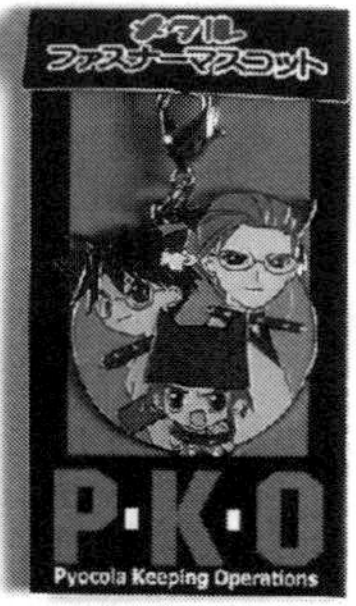
ファスナーマスコット
P·K·O
Pyocola Keeping Operations

PKO
$4.95

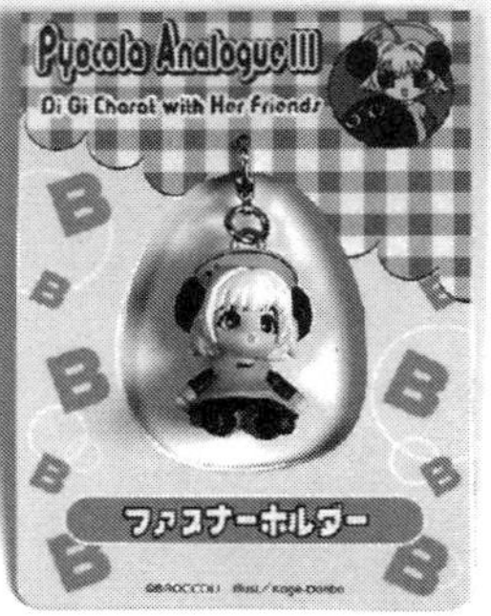
Pyocola Analogue III
Di Gi Charat with Her Friends
ファスナーホルダー

Piyoko
mascot
$4.50

cellphone straps

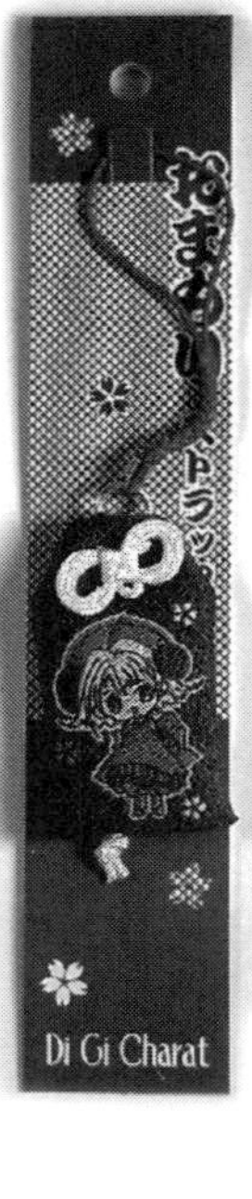
Di Gi Charat

Piyoko
charm
$7.95

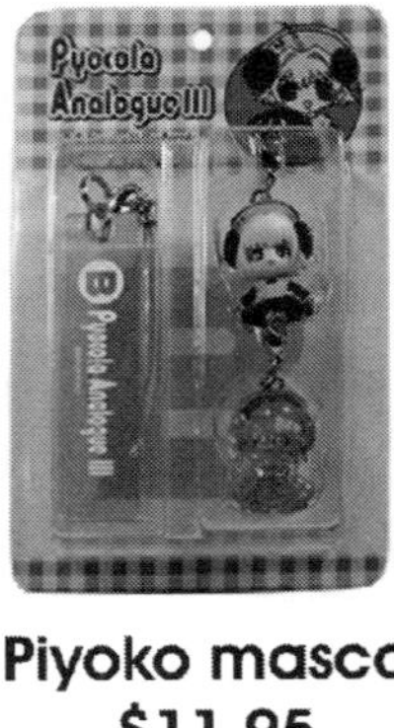
Pyocola
Analogue III
Pyocola Analogue III

Piyoko mascot
$11.95

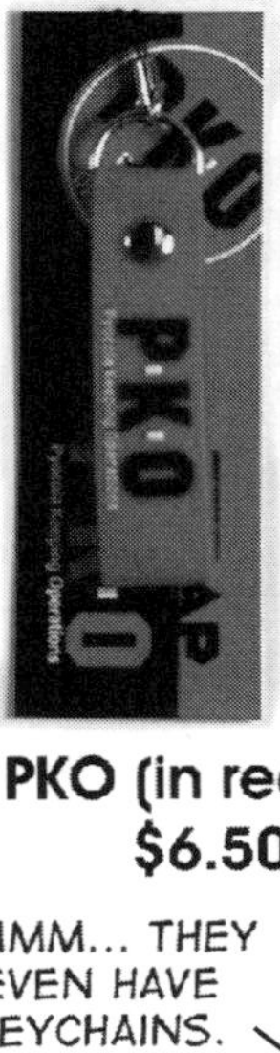
PKO

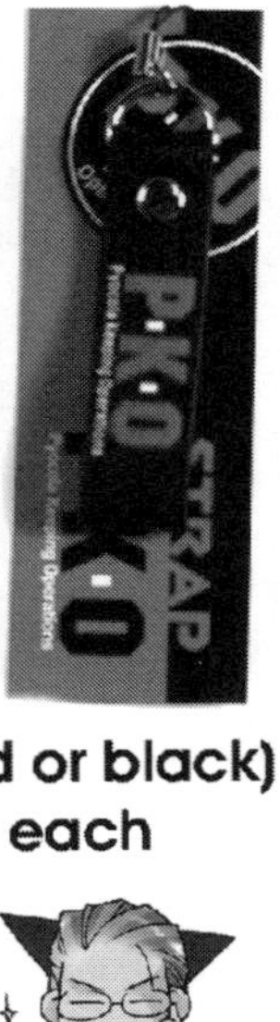
PKO
STRAP

PKO (in red or black)
$6.50 each

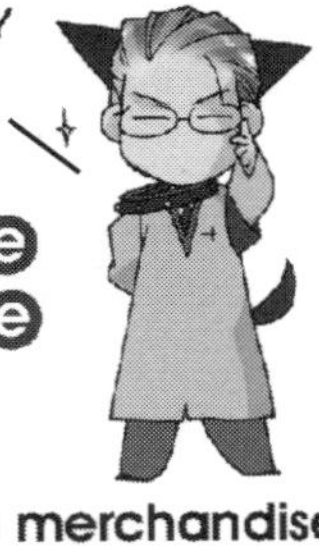
HMMM... THEY
EVEN HAVE
KEYCHAINS.

There's even more accessories on the website!

Get your ~~Di Gi Charat~~ Black Gema Gema Gang merchandise at:

www.animegamers.com

stationery items

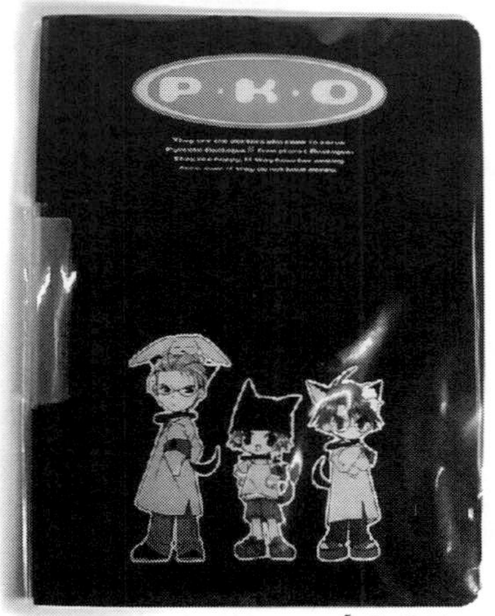
P·K·O

PKO folder - $6.95

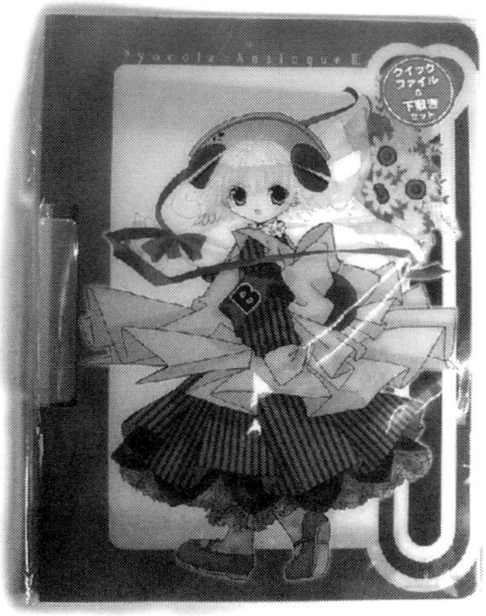

Piyoko folder and pencil board set - $9.95

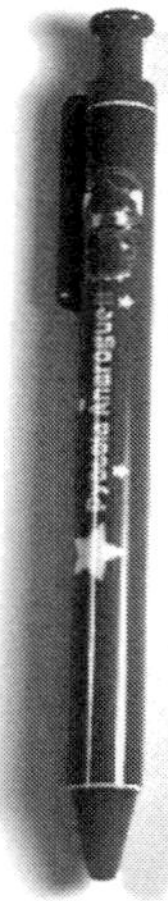

Piyoko red pen $2.60

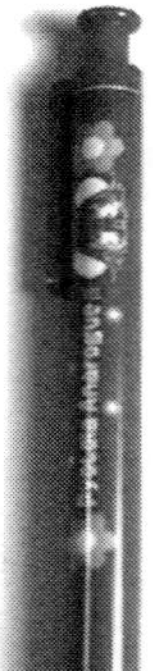

Piyoko red lead pencil $2.60

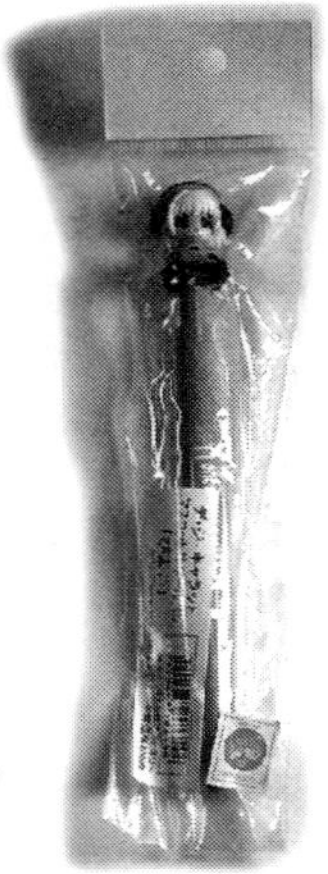

Piyoko mascot pen $5.25

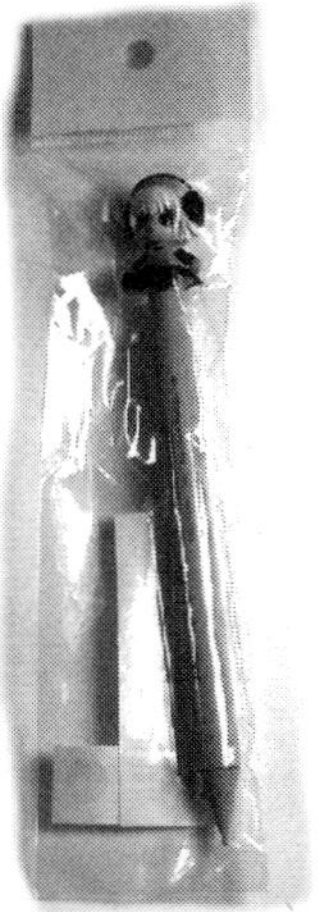

Piyoko mascot lead pencil $5.25

Get your ~~Di Gi Charat~~ Black Gema Gema Gang merchandise at:

www.animegamers.com

BROCCOLI BOOKS

READ ⁞ POINT ∷ CLICK ⁝

www.bro-usa.com

After reading some Broccoli Books manga, why not look for more on the web? Check out the latest news, upcoming releases, character profiles, synopses, manga previews, production blog and fan art!

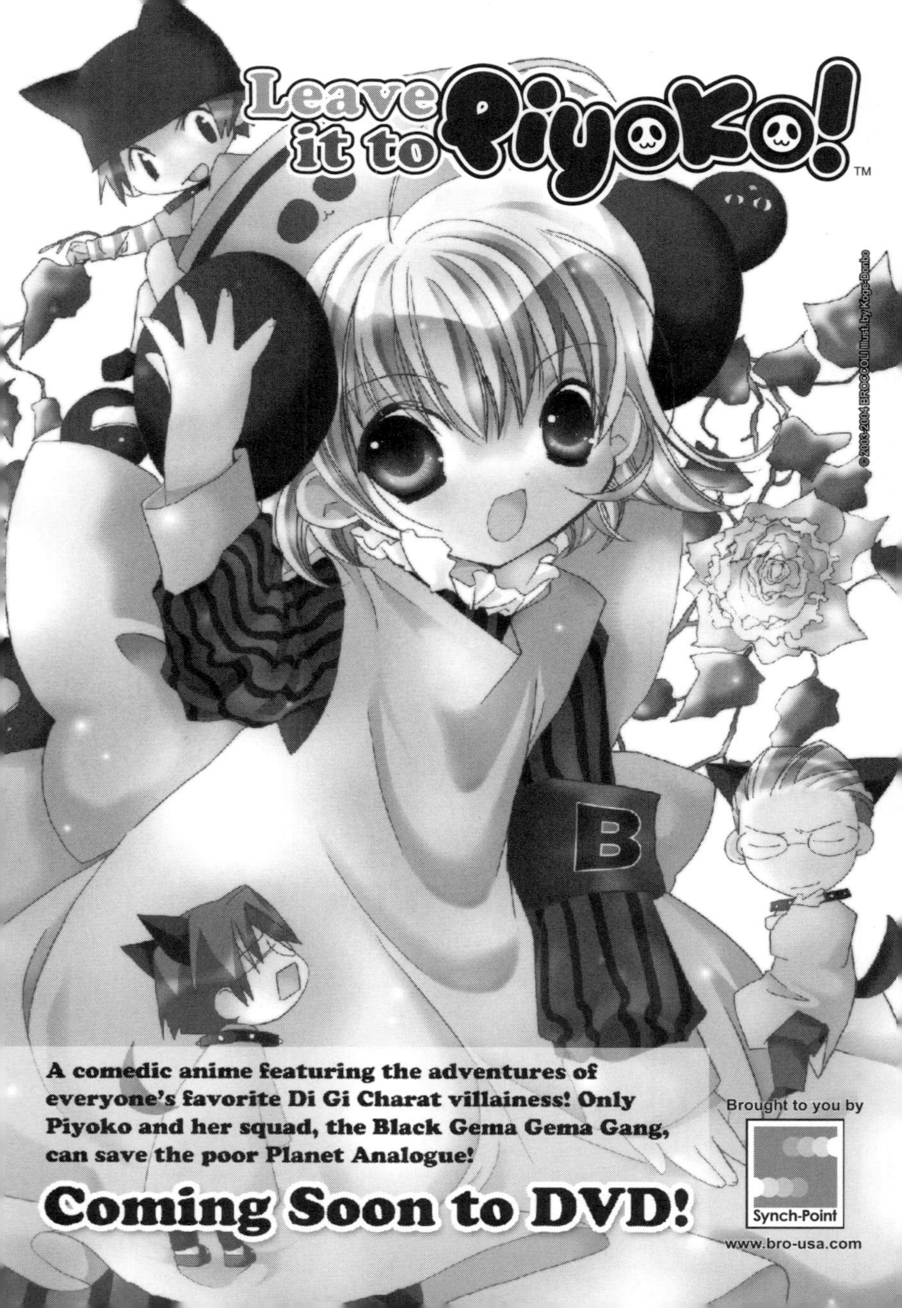
Leave it to Piyoko!
™
© 2003-2004 BROCCOLI Illust. by Koge-Donbo
A comedic anime featuring the adventures of everyone's favorite Di Gi Charat villainess! Only Piyoko and her squad, the Black Gema Gema Gang, can save the poor Planet Analogue!
Coming Soon to DVD!
Brought to you by
Synch-Point
www.bro-usa.com

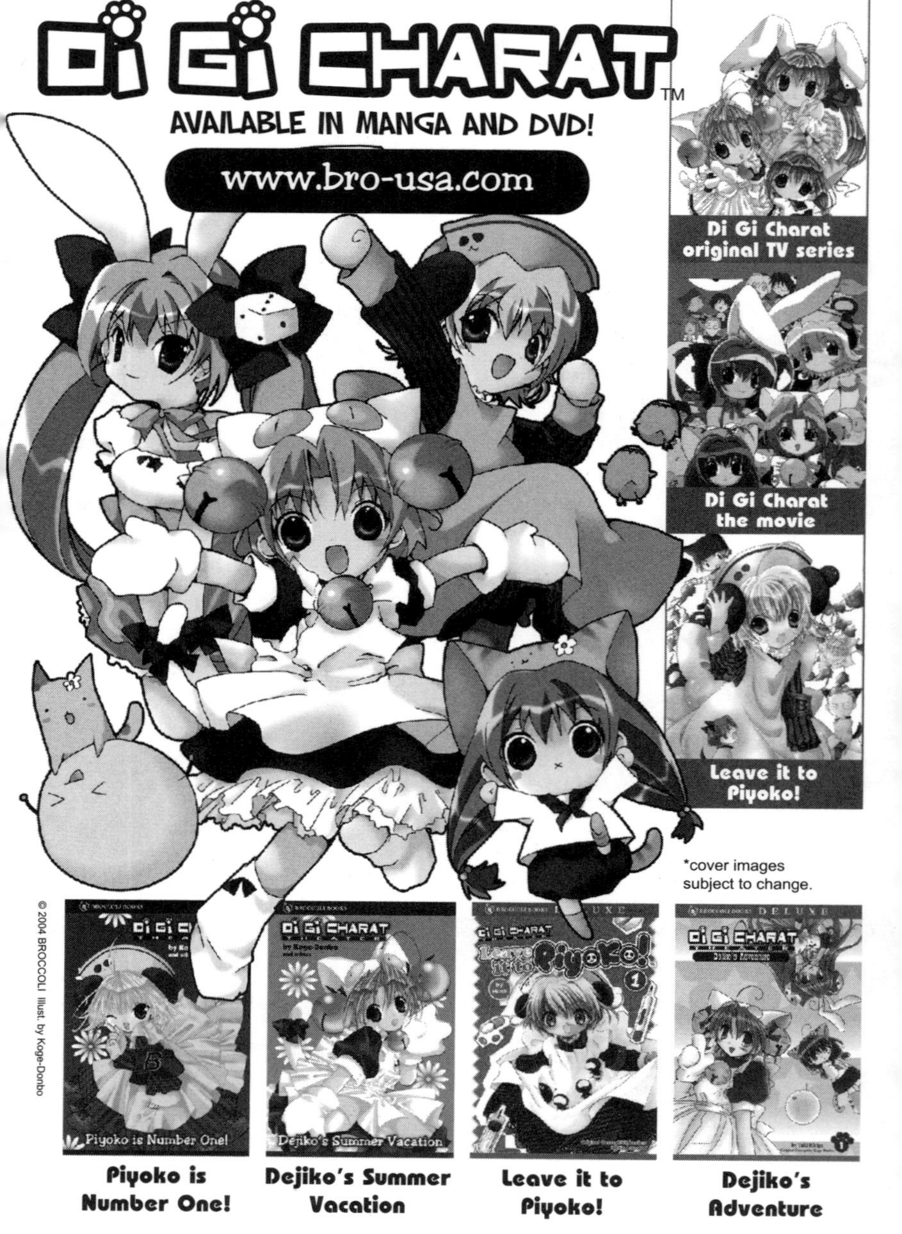
DI GI CHARAT™
AVAILABLE IN MANGA AND DVD!
www.bro-usa.com
Di Gi Charat original TV series
Di Gi Charat the movie
Leave it to Piyoko!
*cover images subject to change.
© 2004 BROCCOLI Illust. by Koge-Donbo
Piyoko is Number One!
Piyoko is Number One!
Dejiko's Summer Vacation
Dejiko's Summer Vacation
Leave it to Piyoko!
Dejiko's Adventure

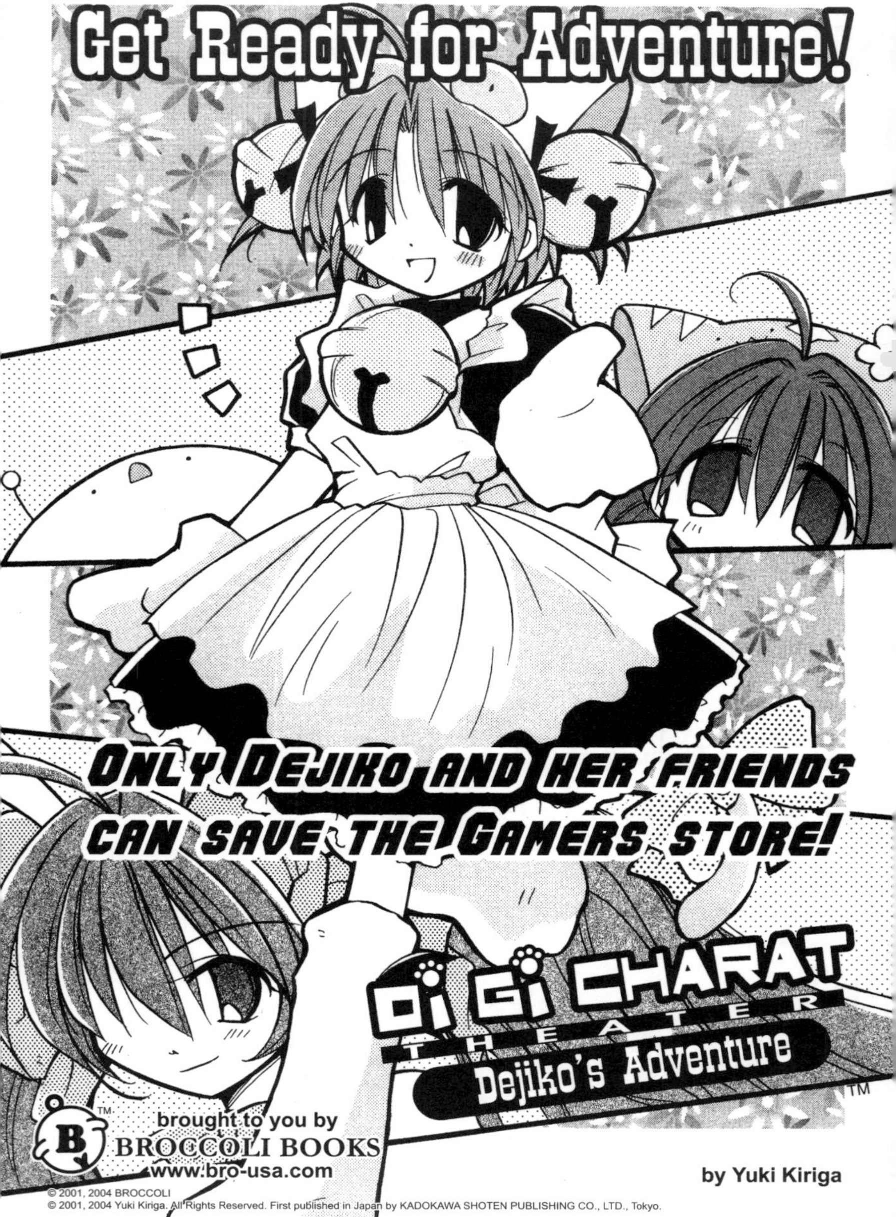

Get Ready for Adventure!
ONLY DEJIKO AND HER FRIENDS CAN SAVE THE GAMERS STORE!
DI GI CHARAT THEATER
Dejiko's Adventure
TM
brought to you by
BROCCOLI BOOKS
www.bro-usa.com
by Yuki Kiriga

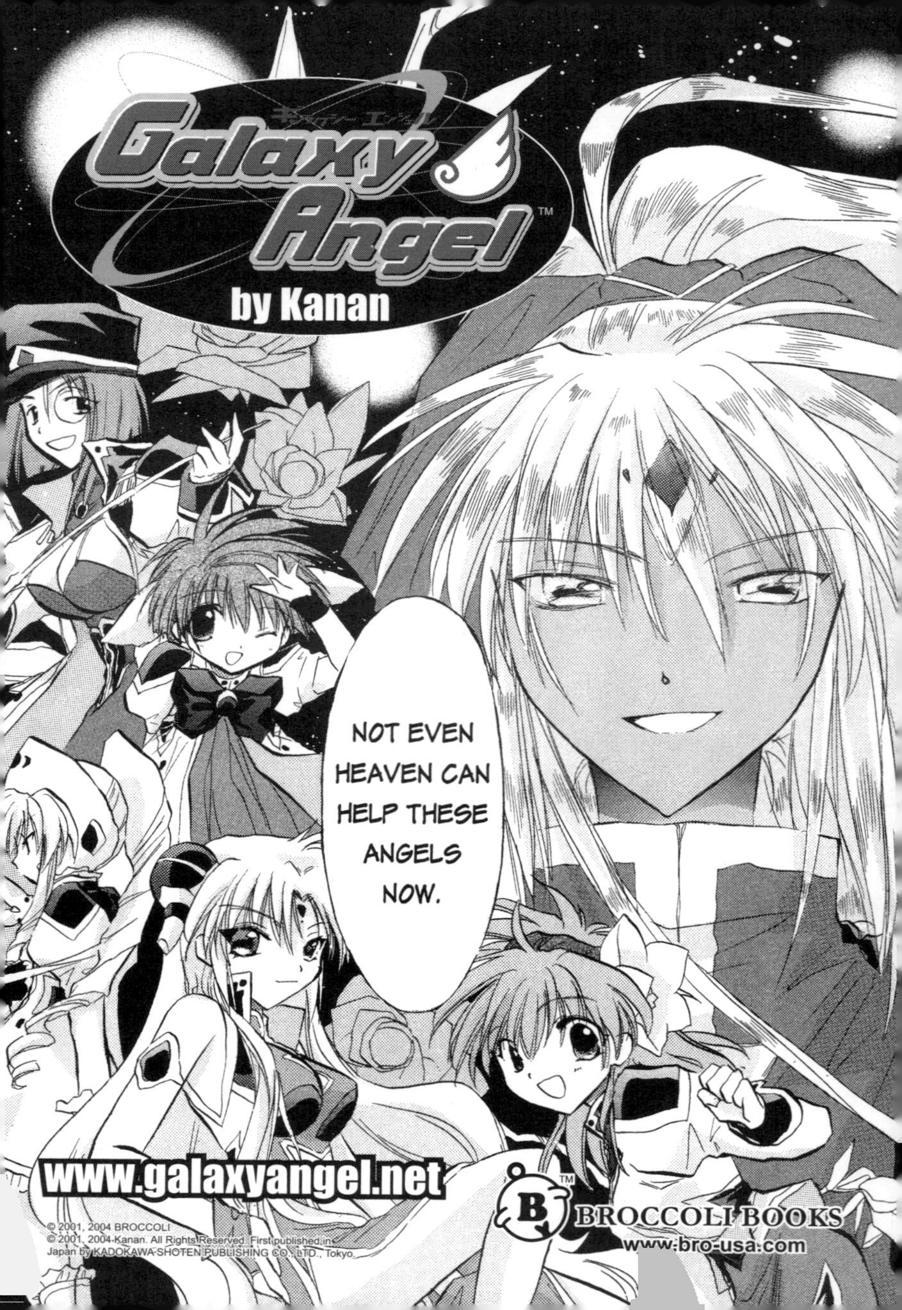
Galaxy Angel™
by Kanan
NOT EVEN HEAVEN CAN HELP THESE ANGELS NOW.
www.galaxyangel.net
BROCCOLI BOOKS
www.bro-usa.com
© 2001, 2004 BROCCOLI
© 2001, 2004 Kanan. All Rights Reserved. First published in Japan by KADOKAWA SHOTEN PUBLISHING CO., LTD., Tokyo.

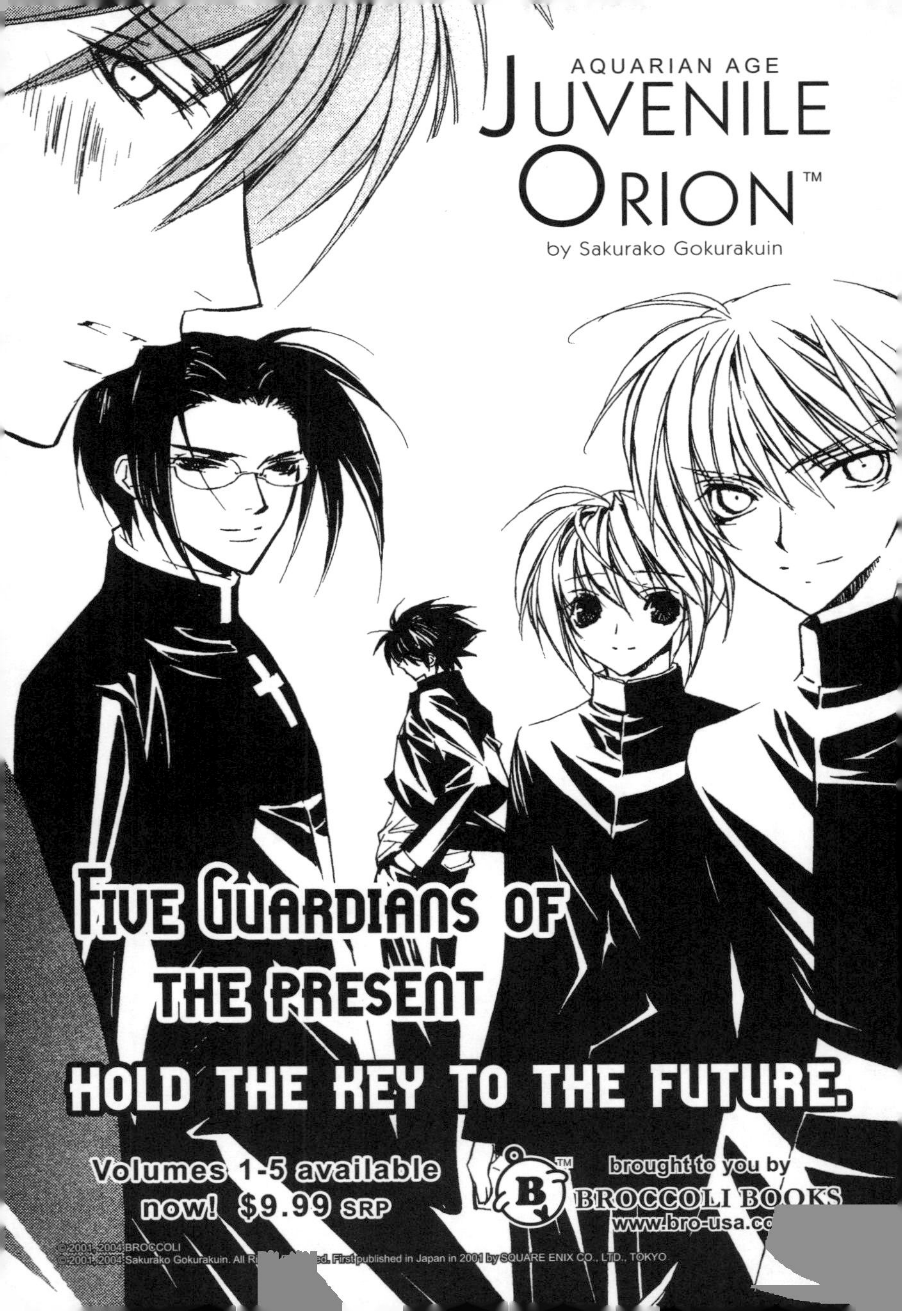
AQUARIAN AGE
JUVENILE ORION™
by Sakurako Gokurakuin
FIVE GUARDIANS OF THE PRESENT
HOLD THE KEY TO THE FUTURE.
Volumes 1-5 available now! $9.99 SRP
brought to you by
BROCCOLI BOOKS
www.bro-usa.co
© 2001, 2004 BROCCOLI
© 2001, 2004 Sakurako Gokurakuin. All Ri ed. First published in Japan in 2001 by SQUARE ENIX CO., LTD., TOKYO.

By the best selling author of FAKE!

Until the **Full Moon**

Marlo has a problem. On the night of the full moon, this half-werewolf, half-vampire undergoes a mysterious and terrifying transformation:

He turns into a girl.

Desperate for a cure, his parents call on Doctor Vincent, a long time family friend. But Marlo wants to keep his condition secret from Vincent's son, the vampire playboy David.

Unfortunately, the secret gets out, and a new problem surfaces: David is interested in Marlo's female form! If a remedy can't be found, their parents believe the next best solution is marriage – a marriage between Marlo and David!

A two volume series coming from Broccoli Books!

B™ **BROCCOLI BOOKS**
www.bro-usa.com

YOU'RE READING THE WRONG WAY!

This is the end of the book! In Japan, manga is generally read from right to left. All reading starts on the upper right corner, and ends on the lower left. American comics are generally read from left to right, starting on the upper left of each page. In order to preserve the true nature of the work, we printed this book in a right to left fashion. Those who are unfamiliar with manga may find this confusing at first, but once you start getting into the story, you will wonder how you ever read manga any other way!

THIS QUESTIONNAIRE IS REDEEMABLE FOR:

Leave it to Piyoko! Volume 1 Dust Jacket

Broccoli Books Questionnaire

Fill out and return to Broccoli Books to receive a Leave it to Piyoko dust jacket!*

PLEASE MAIL THE COMPLETE FORM, ALONG WITH UNITED STATES POSTAGE STAMPS
WORTH $1.50 ENCLOSED IN THE ENVELOPE TO:**

Broccoli International
Attn: Broccoli Books Sticker Offer
12211 W Washington Blvd #110
Los Angeles, CA 90066

(Please write legibly)

Name: _____

Address: _____

City, State, Zip: _____

E-mail: _____

Gender: ☐ Male ☐ Female **Age:** _____

(If you are under 13 years old, parental consent is required)

Parent/Guardian signature: _____

Occupation: _____

Where did you hear about this title?

☐ Magazine (Please specify): _____

☐ Flyer from: a store   convention   club   other: _____

☐ Website (Please specify): _____

☐ At a store (Please specify): _____

☐ Word of Mouth

☐ Other (Please specify): _____

Where was this title purchased? (If known)

_____

Why did you buy this title?

_____
_____
_____

How would you rate the following features of this man[...] W9-CRE-741

	Excellent	Good	Satisfactory	Poor
Translation	☐	☐	☐	☐
Art quality	☐	☐	☐	☐
Cover	☐	☐	☐	☐
Extra/Bonus Material	☐	☐	☐	☐

What would you like to see improved in Broccoli Books manga?

___

Would you recommend this manga to someone else? ☐ Yes ☐ No

What related products would you be interested in?

☐ Posters ☐ Apparel Other: ___

Which magazines do you read on a regular basis?

___

What manga titles would you like to see in English?

___

Favorite manga titles: ___

Favorite manga artists: ___

What race/ethnicity do you consider yourself? (Please check one)

☐ Asian/Pacific Islander ☐ Native American/Alaskan Native

☐ Black/African American ☐ White/Caucasian

☐ Hispanic/Latino ☐ Other: ___

Final comments about this manga:

___

___

___

Thank you!

* While supplies last.

** For residents of Canada, please send an International Reply Coupon (IRC) of $3.00 US made out to "Broccoli International."

All information provided will be used for internal purposes only. We will not sell or otherwise divulge any of the information.

Requests not in compliance with all terms of this form will not be acknowledged or returned. All submissions are subject to verification and become the property of Broccoli International USA. Fraudulent submission, including use of multiple addresses or P.O. boxes to obtain additional Broccoli International USA information or offers may result in prosecution. Broccoli International USA reserves the right to withdraw or modify any terms of this form. Void where prohibited, taxed, or restricted by law. Broccoli International USA will not be liable for lost, misdirected, mutilated, illegible, incomplete, or postage-due mail. Dust jacket offer is only available to residents of the United States and Canada. For updates to the rules and regulations, please see www.bro-usa.com.

CUT ALONG HERE